Computational Modeling: Essential Concepts and Applied Principles

Computational Modeling: Essential Concepts and Applied Principles

Edited by Tom Halt

CLANRYE
INTERNATIONAL
www.clanryeinternational.com

Clanrye International,
750 Third Avenue, 9th Floor,
New York, NY 10017, USA

ISBN: 978-1-63240-619-4

Cataloging-in-Publication Data

Computational modeling : essential concepts and applied principles / edited by Tom Halt.
p. cm.
Includes bibliographical references and index.
ISBN 978-1-63240-619-4
1. Computer simulation. 2. Model-integrated computing. 3. Materials--Computer simulation.
4. Modeling--Data processing. I. Halt, Tom.
QA76.9.C65 C66 2017
003.3--dc23

For information on all Clanrye International publications
visit our website at www.clanryeinternational.com

LANRYE
NTERNATIONAL

Printed in the United States of America.

Contents

Preface

Computational modeling is an effective method to compute, analyse and simulate theoretical and practical problems. This field is especially important for numerical modeling and mathematical calculations. This book on computational modeling delves into the essentials that are involved in the building and design of computer models. Different approaches, evaluations, methodologies and advanced studies on computational modeling have been included herein. This book is compiled in such a manner that it will provide in-depth knowledge about the theory and practice of computational modeling. It will provide comprehensive insights to students and researchers in the fields of computational science, software design and scientific modeling.

Various studies have approached the subject by analyzing it with a single perspective, but the present book provides diverse methodologies and techniques to address this field. This book contains theories and applications needed for understanding the subject from different perspectives. The aim is to keep the readers informed about the progress in the field; therefore, the contributions were carefully examined to compile novel researches by specialists from across the globe.

Indeed, the job of the editor is the most crucial and challenging in compiling all chapters into a single book. In the end, I would extend my sincere thanks to the chapter authors for their profound work. I am also thankful for the support provided by my family and colleagues during the compilation of this book.

Editor

Reduced Numerical Model for Methane Hydrate Formation under Conditions of Variable Salinity. Time-Stepping Variants and Sensitivity

Malgorzata Peszynska [1,*,†], Francis Patricia Medina [1,†], Wei-Li Hong [2,3,†] and Marta E. Torres [2,†]

Academic Editors: Qinjun Kang and Li Chen

[1] Department of Mathematics, Oregon State University, Corvallis, OR 97331, USA;
   medinaf@science.oregonstate.edu
[2] College of Earth, Ocean, and Atmospheric Sciences, Oregon State University, Corvallis, OR 97331, USA;
   wei.l.hung@uit.no (W.-L. H.); mtorres@coas.oregonstate.edu (M.E.T.)
[3] CAGE (Centre for Arctic Gas Hydrate, Environment and Climate), Department of Geology,
   UiT The Arctic University of Norway, Tromso, Norway
* Correspondence: mpesz@math.oregonstate.edu
† These authors contributed equally to this work.

Abstract: In this paper, we consider a reduced computational model of methane hydrate formation in variable salinity conditions, and give details on the discretization and phase equilibria implementation. We describe three time-stepping variants: Implicit, Semi-implicit, and Sequential, and we compare the accuracy and efficiency of these variants depending on the spatial and temporal discretization parameters. We also study the sensitivity of the model to the simulation parameters and in particular to the reduced phase equilibria model.

Keywords: methane hydrate; multiphase multicomponent flow and transport; reduced computational model; time-stepping; phase equilibria; salinity

MSC: 65M06; 76S05; 76V05; 35R35

1. Introduction

Computational simulation of complex phenomena can provide answers to problems for which no experimental data or theoretical studies are available, but it requires robust, efficient, and accurate numerical models. The problem considered in this paper is of evolution of methane hydrate, which is an ice-like substance present in large amounts in subsea sediments, and which plays an important role both as a potential energy source and environmental hazard as well as in global climate studies [1,2].

In the paper [3] we introduced a reduced model for methane hydrate formation in variable salinity conditions and provided details on the equilibrium phase behavior adapted to a case study from Ulleung Basin. One of the advantages of this reduced model in contrast to fully comprehensive models such as in, e.g., [4], is that the reduced model is easy to implement and to extend, and is amenable to various analyses.

In this paper we describe the computational aspects of the model, with the emphasis placed on the variants of time-stepping. Our reduced model accounts for three components: water, methane, and salt, and two phases: aqueous, and solid (hydrate). Thus, it places in the general framework of multiphase multicomponent models such as those in [5–7] for which accuracy and efficiency have been studied extensively in the past decades. In particular, for the oil-water or black-oil models described e.g., in [8–13] the best practice is to use mass-conservative spatial schemes combined either with an implicit treatment of pressures and explicit treatment of saturations/concentrations, or with a fully implicit treatment of all phases and components. Typically, the computational complexity of implicit models is the highest, while other variants are easier to implement. In compositional models [14] with M components the pressure solver is complemented with $M-1$ transport equations solved for concentration of the selected $M-1$ species, and followed by flash, *i.e.*, the equilibrium solver. The typical time scales of interest for reservoir simulation with these models are days to decades of production or environmental remediation. On the other hand, in [3] and here we are interested in long-term behavior and hydrate basin modeling, and it makes sense to assume that the pressures and temperatures are known and given by hydrostatic and geothermal distributions. Our models need only to resolve the interdependence between methane and water phase equilibria that depend on the presence of salt, and our time-stepping algorithms have different features than those for the oil-gas reservoir simulators.

We implement the interdependence between the components and phases as follows. The water-methane-salt equilibria are handled using the approach of nonlinear complementarity constraints, and are either tightly or loosely coupled to the salt mass conservation; their implementation is especially easy with the reduced phase behavior model adopted in [3]. We consider and compare three variants of time-stepping that realize these tight or loose couplings: the fully implicit (I), semi-implicit (SI), and sequential (SEQ) algorithms. The comparison that we carry out is intended to demonstrate the merits of these approaches, and guide the choice of a model.

In addition, in this paper we test the sensitivity of the approach to the assumed phase behavior model, as well as to various parameters defining the discretization. The latter is new and was not undertaken for the comprehensive model [4]. It is significant in that it guides the reader in the choice of optimal parameters and shows the robustness of the reduced model.

The paper is organized as follows. In Section 2 we briefly recall the model proposed in [3] including the phase behavior. In Section 3 we describe in detail the time-stepping variants and spatial discretization for that model. In Section 4 we compare the I, SI, and SEQ time-stepping variants, and in Section 5 we discuss the sensitivity of the model to the various parameters of the computational model. We conclude in Section 6.

2. Mathematical Model

In the last decade two classes of models for hydrates have been used to describe hydrate behavior in natural systems. These are the fully comprehensive equilibrium models such as [4], and the simpler conceptual models [2,15,16], in which simplified mechanisms for fluid equilibria and/or kinetics were assumed. The model presented in [3] and discussed here falls somewhere inbetween, and is a direct simplification of the comprehensive model in [4]. The simplicity of the reduced model allows for rigorous mathematical well-posedness analysis in the case of the diffusive transport in [17], and more general analysis in [18] for advective/diffusive transport.

We consider the transport of methane and salt in the sediment reservoir $\Omega \subset \mathbb{R}^d$, $d = 1, 2, 3$. The notation used throughout is provided in Table 1. Each point $x = (x_1, x_2, x_3) \in \Omega$ is at some depth $D(x)$ below the sea surface, with the origin $x = 0$ at the bottom of the Gas Hydrate Stability Zone (GHSZ). At the seafloor, *i.e.*, at the top of the reservoir Ω, we have $x = L$ where L is the thickness of the hydrate zone. Next, at the seafloor, the depth of water above seafloor is the reference depth $D_{ref} = H$, so the sea surface is at $x = L + H$. We also set the coordinate $z = D(x) - D_{ref} = D(x) - H$ measured in mbsf (meters below seafloor) which is used in other models [19]. In the general case of a 2D or 3D reservoir the bathymetry is variable, thus $D(x)$ is measured relative to the (constant) sea surface rather than to the seafloor.

Table 1. Notation and definitions (kg/kg, per kg of liquid phase).

Symbol	Definition	Units/value
\multicolumn{3}{c}{**Data about reservoir and fluids**}		
$x = (x_1, x_2, x_3)$	Spatial coordinate	[m]
t	Time variable	[yr]
G	Gravitational acceleration	9.8 m/s^2
$D(x)$	Depth of point x from sea level	[m]
$D_{ref}(x)$	Seafloor depth	[m]
	In 1D case $x = x_3$, $H = D_{ref}$	
$z = D(x_3) - H$	Depth below seafloor	[m]
(G)HSZ	(Gas) Hydrate stability zone	
P	Pressure	[Pa,MPa]
G_H	Hydrostatic gradient	$\approx 10^4 \text{ Pa/m}$
T	Temperature	[K]
G_T	Geothermal gradient	[K/m]
q	Darcy volumetric flux of liquid phase	[m/yr]
$D_M = D_S = D^0 S_l \phi_0$	Diffusivity of component C in the liquid phase	$[\text{m}^2\text{/yr}]$
	$D^0 = 10^{-9} \text{ m}^2\text{/s} = 3 \times 10^{-2} \text{ m}^2\text{/yr}$	
ρ_l	Seawater density	1030 kg/m^3
ρ_h	Hydrate density	925 kg/m^3
χ_{hM}	Mass fraction of methane in hydrate phase	0.134 kg/kg
$R = \chi_{hM}\rho_h/\rho_l$	Constant used for methane concentration	0.1203 kg/kg
$\phi_0, \phi = S_l\phi_0$	Porosity in Ω without/with hydrate present	
K_0, K	Permeability in Ω without/with hydrate present	
χ_{lS}^{sw}	Seawater salinity	0.035 [kg/kg]
f_M	Supply of methane (source/sink term)	[kg/kg/yr]
α	Parameter of the reduced model	[kg/kg]
\multicolumn{3}{c}{**Variables in the model**}		
$S_l, S_h = 1 - S_l$	Void fraction of liquid and hydrate phases	
χ_{lM}	Mass fraction of methane (solubility) in liquid phase	[kg/kg]
χ_{lS}	Mass fraction of salt (salinity) in liquid phase	[kg/kg]
N_M, N_S	Mass concentration of methane and salt	[kg/kg]

In this paper as in [3] we assume that the conditions in Ω are favorable for hydrate presence and that Ω is entirely within the GHSZ, while the methane is supplied by advection and diffusion from beneath GHSZ. We also assume that $T(x)$ is known and follows the geothermal gradient

$$T(x) = T_{ref} + (D(x) - D_{ref})G_T, \tag{1}$$

where T_{ref} is the temperature at some reference depth D_{ref} and $G_T \approx const$ is the geothermal gradient; see [3] for experimental values. The pressure $P(x)$ is assumed close to the hydrostatic

$$P(x) \approx P_l^0(x) := P_l^0|_{D_{ref}} + \rho_l G(D(x) - D_{ref}) \tag{2}$$

Here P_l^0 is known at the reference depth D_{ref}.

Finally, the actual porosity $\phi(x)$ available to the liquid phase at x is $\phi = \phi_0 S_l$, where S_l is the liquid phase saturation, *i.e.*, void fraction of the liquid phase. The actual permeability $K(x)$ in the presence of hydrate is an important property. However, it is not needed in the 1D model with a constant flux and an assumed hydrostatic pressure distribution.

2.1. Mass Conservation

In region Ω we have the following mass conservation equations for methane and salt components, respectively

$$\frac{\partial \phi_0 N_M}{\partial t} - \nabla \cdot D_M \nabla \chi_{lM} + \nabla \cdot (q\chi_{lM}) \;=\; f_M \tag{3a}$$

$$\frac{\partial \phi_0 N_S}{\partial t} - \nabla \cdot D_S \nabla \chi_{lS} + \nabla \cdot (q\chi_{lS}) \;=\; 0 \tag{3b}$$

with the definitions

$$N_M \;=\; S_l \chi_M + R(1 - S_l), \tag{3c}$$

$$N_S \;=\; \chi_{lS} S_l. \tag{3d}$$

where R is given in Table 1. The model is complemented by a pressure equation or q must be given; here we assume the latter. As we explain in [3], the Equation (3) arises as a special case of the first-principles comprehensive model in [4].

We see that in Equation (3) we have two mass conservation Equations (3a,b) with three unknowns that must be chosen from $N_M, N_S, \chi_{lS}, \chi_{lM}$ and S_l. To close the system we use the nonlinear complementarity constraint abbbreviated below as [NCC-M] phase constraint. We explain it below.

2.2. Phase Equilibria and [NCC-M] Constraint

The (maximum) amount χ_{lM}^{max} of methane that can be dissolved in the liquid phase depends on the pressure P, temperature T, and the salinity χ_{lS}. Equivalently, these variables determine the circumstances in which $S_l < 1$ and $S_h > 0$, *i.e.*, when the hydrate phase can be present. In addition, χ_{lM}^{max} determines how the total amount of methane N_M is partitioned between the liquid and hydrate phases. This phase equilibrium is expressed concisely as a nonlinear complementarity constraint [NCC-M]

$$\begin{cases} \chi_{lM} \leq \chi_{lM}^{max}, & S_l = 1 \\ \chi_{lM} = \chi_{lM}^{max}, & S_l \leq 1 \\ (\chi_{lM}^{max} - \chi_{lM})(1 - S_l) & = 0. \end{cases} \tag{3e}$$

In other words, if $N_M(x,t)$ is small enough so that $N_M < \chi_{lM}^{max}$, then only the liquid phase is present $S_l(x,t) = 1$, and $\chi_{lM} = N_M$ is the independent variable that describes how much methane is dissolved in the liquid. On the other hand, when the amount present $N_M \geq \chi_{lM}^{max}$, the excess amount of methane above χ_{lM}^{max} forms the hydrate phase with $S_h = 1 - S_l > 0$, and $S_l < 1$ becomes the independent variable while $\chi_{lM} = \chi_{lM}^{max}$. This relationship has to be satisfied at every point x,t.

2.2.1. Data for χ_{lM}^{max}

In the hydrate literature [4,20] there are tabulated data, or algebraic models, for how χ_{lM}^{max} depends on P, T, χ_{lS}. In addition, there may be dependence of Equation (3e) on the type of sediment [19,21] but this is out of scope here. In [3] we developed a particular approximation

$$\chi_{lM}^{max} \approx \chi_{lM}^{max}(x, \chi_{lS}) \approx \chi_{lM}^{max,0}(x) + \alpha(x)\chi_{lS}, \tag{4}$$

in which the data $\chi_{lM}^{max,0}(x)$ and $\alpha(x)$ must be provided. This approximation Equation (4) includes as a special case the algebraic model in [19]. In [3] we describe how to obtain $\chi_{lM}^{max,0}(x)$ and $\alpha(x)$ by a fit to the lookup tables extracted from the well known phase equilibrium software CSMGem [22], and we calibrate them for the typical depth, temperature, and salinity conditions found in Ulleung Basin; see [3] and Section 5. As is well known, $\chi_{lM}^{max,0}$ increases with depth, thus decreases with x. On the other hand, $\alpha(x)$ found with CSMGem is positive while the authors in [23] believe it should be negative; see [3] for details. In Section 5 we discuss the sensitivity of the model to the assumed profile of $\alpha(x)$.

2.2.2. Other Constraints

There are additional constraints that are not part of Equation (3) but are motivated by the physical meaning of the variables S_l, S_h, and χ_{lM}. In particular, we must have $S_h \leq 1$ or

$$S_l \geq 0, \chi_{lM} \geq 0. \tag{5}$$

With some assumptions on χ_{lM}^{max}, the boundary and initial data, and small f_M, q one can prove that Equation (5) holds as a consequence of the maximum principle and other abstract analyses. (See [17] for the diffusive case and [18] for advective and diffusive transport case).

In more general circumstances one cannot prove that Equation (5) holds. In fact, a numerical model may readily produce S_h increasing to 1 and beyond. This clearly is nonphysical, since even before the pores become plugged up and $\phi = S_l \phi_0 = 0$, all the flow and diffusion ceases, local pressures increase, and the sediment may break.

When Equation (5) is violated, a model more general than Equation (3) should be considered. In particular, such a model should include geomechanics and pore-scale effects; see, e.g., the conceptual model described in [21]. However, the analysis of such a model is presently out of scope. In the model discussed in this paper we terminate the simulation when Equation (5) does not hold.

2.3. Boundary and Initial Conditions

The model Equation (3) must be supplemented with appropriate initial conditions imposed on N_M and N_S, and the boundary conditions on the fluxes or on the values of the transport variables χ_{lM} and χ_{lS}. In this paper we set

$$N_M(x,0) = N_M^0(x), \ \ N_S(x,0) = N_S^0(x), \ \ x \in \Omega \tag{6a}$$

$$\chi_{lM}(0,t) = \chi_{lM}^0, \ \ \chi_{lM}(L,t) = \chi_{lM}^L = 0, \ \ t > 0 \tag{6b}$$

$$\chi_{lS}(0,t) = \chi_{lS}^0, \ \ \chi_{lS}(L,t) = \chi_{lS}^L \chi_{lS}^{sw}, \ \ t > 0 \tag{6c}$$

The conditions Equation (6c) assign the seawater salinity at $x = L$ and some other salinity χ_{lS}^0 at HSZ known from observations. The conditions Equation (6b) assume some methane present at HSZ $x = 0$, and that there is no methane in the ocean at $x = L$. The choice consistent with Equation (4)

$$\chi_{lM}^0 = \chi_{lM}^{max,0}(0) + \alpha(0)\chi_{lS}^0 \tag{7}$$

allows the maximum possible amount of methane to be transported by advection and diffusion from underneath the HSZ.

3. Numerical Model

Now we provide details of the numerical model for Equation (3). We use mass-conservative spatial discretization based on cell-centered finite differences (FD) with harmonic averaging and a nonuniform structured spatial grid. An alternative discretization of the case $q = 0$, with Finite Elements and mass lumping, was considered in [17], but it would not accommodate large advective fluxes and is not locally mass conservative. For time discretization we use operator splitting: we treat advection explicitly and diffusion implicitly as in [24–26]. The diffusion/equilibria handle two components and are organized in several time-stepping variants. In each variant we have to solve a linear or nonlinear system of equations; for the latter we use Newton (or semismooth Newton) iteration.

After the discretization of Equation (3), at each time step, one solves for the approximate values of the five unknowns $N_M, N_S, \chi_{lM}, \chi_{lS}, S_l$. (At this point we are not yet providing any notation specific to time steps or grid points). Note that Equation (3c) and Equation (3d) are merely the definitions of the terms used in the transport equations Equation (3a), Equation (3b) complemented by the phase equilibria Equation (3e). Thus we can eliminate and actually solve only for three variables $S_l, \chi_{lM}, \chi_{lS}$ the system of three equations which we write as

$$F_M(S_l, \chi_{lM}, \chi_{lS}) = 0 \tag{8a}$$
$$F_S(S_l, \chi_{lM}, \chi_{lS}) = 0 \tag{8b}$$
$$F_{NCC}(S_l, \chi_{lM}, \chi_{lS}) = 0 \tag{8c}$$

The details on discrete form of F_M, F_S, and F_{NCC} which correspond to Equations (3a,b,e), respectively, are developed below. We discuss first the most difficult part of implementing Equation (3e), then we provide details of discretization of the transport equations. The system Equation (8) is nonlinear, and we discuss next the particular variants of the solvers and time-stepping variants.

3.1. Implementing Phase Constraint [NCC-M] in Fully Implicit Models

While it is well known how to discretize and solve advection-diffusion equations, implementing phase equilibria constraint Equation (3e) is challenging. There are practical approaches which have been successfully implemented [4,7]. In addition, approaches known from constrained optimization [27,28] have been recently applied; see [17,29].

In the first class of approaches, the constraint Equation (3e) can be rewritten using the notion of *active/inactive sets* [27]. In this approach at each time step and/or iteration, the (grid) points are identified as either those for which the first part of the inequality Equation (3e) holds, or those where the other complementary inequality must hold. Next, the mass conservation equations are specialized depending on the state of the primary unknowns, and are grouped together and solved for the particular active set of independent unknowns. In summary, in each time step and/or iteration of the nonlinear numerical solver, the solver changes the vector of unknowns depending on which variables need to be used. In consequence, not just the values, but also the sparsity structure of the Jacobian matrix change from iteration to iteration. This approach is known as *variable switching* [4,7] where at each gridpoint one identifies the appropriate independent variable depending on which of the inequalities holds.

In another equivalent approach one takes advantage of the semismooth "min" function as proposed in [29]. We recall that the function "min(u,v)" equals u if $u \leq v$ and v otherwise. We represent Equation (3e) in an equivalent way as

$$\min(\chi_{lM}^{max} - \chi_{lM}, 1 - S_l) = 0. \tag{9}$$

In [17] we showed that the "min" representation of Equation (3e) is equivalent to variable switching discussed above. With the "min" function approach, Equation (9) is a nonlinear equation in the variables χ_{lM} and S_l, and it provides the fifth equation to complement Equations (3a)–(3d) that can be solved together for the five unknowns $N_M, N_S, \chi_{lM}, \chi_{lS}, S_l$.

Since the function "min(u,v)" is piecewise linear and non-differentiable along $u = v$, it is also *semismooth* [28]. The theory of semismooth maps developed in [28] allows us then to analyze the solvability of the resulting nonlinear system of equations.

We found that the approach using Equation (9) is easy to implement and vectorize, and is modular, *i.e.*, it does not require that we rewrite the complex logic of active/inactive sets whenever there is need to expand the logic or the physics in the model. The potential disadvantage of using Equation (9) is that the number of unknowns involved grows from two per grid point to three per grid point. In practice, however, this has minimal implications on the storage, since all the variables must be stored anyway. On the other hand, the size of the linear system that arises at each iteration when solving Equation (8) is by 50% larger than the size of that with explicit variable switching. However, the matrices in the linear systems corresponding to both approaches are sparse. An efficient implementation of the "min" approach in which sparsity is fixed, can outweigh the cost of the variable switching approach in which the pattern of sparsity varies from iteration to iteration.

3.2. Implementing Phase Constraints in Non-Implicit Models

Some of the time-stepping variants other than fully implicit require local nonlinear solvers called "flash". These are invoked at each grid point ans solve a system simpler than Equation (3e) in which the values of one or of more of the variables are assumed known.

Simple flash. The simplest situation is when N_M is known and we know χ_{lM}^{max}. To determine S_l and χ_{lM} we simply use Equations (3e), (3c) to calculate

$$S_l = \frac{N_M - R}{\chi_{lM} - R} = \begin{cases} 1, & N_M \leq \chi_{lM}^{max}(x,t), \\ \frac{N_M - R}{\chi_{lM}^{max}(x,t) - R}, & N_M > \chi_{lM}^{max}(x). \end{cases} \tag{10}$$

Simple flash only is applicable if salinity is fixed because of the dependence of χ_{lM} on χ_{lS}.

Two-variable flash. Given N_M, N_S we can solve for the three unknowns S_l, χ_{lM}, χ_{lS} using Equations (3c), (3d) and (9). The implementation is especially easy if Equation (4) is used. This flash solver typically takes 2 or 3 iterations to complete, but may fail when S_h is close to 1.

3.3. Notation in Fully Discrete Model

The notation for discretization is straightforward. We find approximations to the relevant variables at discrete time steps $t_1, t_2, \ldots t_n, \ldots$. The transport model Equation (3) advances the model variables from t_n to t_{n+1}, with the time step $\tau = t_{n+1} - t_n$ considered uniform for simplicity. Also for simplicity, we consider the 1D reservoir $\Omega = \bigcup_i \Omega_i$, where Ω_i are the cells with the centers x_i and uniform length h, and $i = 1, \ldots N_x$. We approximate $N_M(x_i, t_n) \approx N_{M,i}^n$ and set N_M^n to be a vector of $N_{M,i}^n$, with analogous notation applied to other variables.

We start by integrating each of the mass conservation equations over each Ω_i. We show the calculations for methane; the ones for salt are analogous.

Accumulation and source terms. For each i, n we calculate the approximation of accumulation and source terms as follows

$$\int_{\Omega_i} \phi_0 N_M(x, t^n) dx \approx \phi_0(x_i) N_{M,i}^n h. \quad \int_{\Omega_i} f_M(x) dx \approx h f_{M,i}. \tag{11}$$

Advection terms. It suffices to consider only methane advection, since salt advection si treated the same way. We consider first the case $q > 0$. The advective flux

$$\int_{\Omega_i} \nabla \cdot (q\chi_{lM}(x, t^n)) dx \approx q(\chi_{lM,i}^n - \chi_{lM,i-1}^n) \tag{12}$$

is handled by upwinding. Close to the inflow boundary at $i = 1$, we set $\chi_{lM,0}^n$ to the boundary value χ_{lM}^0. If $q < 0$, we replace the right hand side by $\chi_{lM,i+1}^n - q\chi_{lM,i}^n$, and use the boundary condition χ_{lM}^L on top of the reservoir.

Diffusion terms. For the spatially dependent diffusion coefficient $D_M(x)$ and the variable $\chi_{lM}(x)$ we have, in a standard way [30,31]

$$-\int_{\Omega_i} \nabla \cdot D_M \nabla \chi_{IM} dx \approx -h \left(\frac{D_{M,i+1/2}(\chi_{IM,i+1} - \chi_{IM,i}) - D_{M,i-1/2}(\chi_{IM,i} - \chi_{IM,i-1})}{h^2} \right) \tag{13}$$

where $D_{M,i+1/2}$, $D_{M,i-1/2}$ are found by harmonic averaging of the values $D_{M,i}$, $D_{M,i+1}$ and $D_{M,i}$, $D_{M,i-1}$, respectively. Close to the boundary we apply the discretization described in [32], e.g., at $i = 1$ in place of $\chi_{IM,0}$ we use the boundary value χ_{IM}^0, with $D_{M,1/2}$ set to $2D_{M,1}$.

We also define the discrete diffusion matrix A with the entries defined so that $h(A\chi_{IM})_i$ is equal to the right hand side of Equation (13). In particular, $A_{ii} = \frac{D_{M,i-1/2}+D_{M,i+1/2}}{h^2}$. With Dirichlet boundary conditions A is symmetric and positive definite, as long as $D > 0$. In 1d A is also tridiagonal. Further, since D_M depends on $\phi_0 S_l$ as in Table 1, the matrix $A = A(S_l)$ depends on the local saturation values. Finally, since $D_M = D_S$ and the type of boundary conditions on χ_{IM} matches that for χ_{IS}, the matrix for salt equation is the same as that for methane.

3.4. Advection Step

The time-stepping variants considered in this paper are explicit in the advection. This allows development of higher-order schemes as well as avoids additional numerical diffusion associated with implicit treatment of advection [24–26]. With this step, we have to consider appropriate boundary conditions which in the operator splitting come from Equations (6b,c); in the advection step we can only impose the boundary condition on the inflow boundary.

In the 1D case considered here $\nabla \cdot q = 0$ implies that q is constant, thus the inflow boundary is determined by the sign of q. If $q > 0$, the inflow bundary is at the bottom of the reservoir at $x = 0$, otherwise it is at $x = L$. In the advection step, we must know χ_{IM} and χ_{IS} on the inflow boundary, and we use here exactly two of Equations (6b,c).

The advection step is as follows. Given N_M^n from previous time step, with the corresponding χ_{IM}^n, we can easily calculate $N_M^{n+1/2}$

$$\frac{\phi_0 N_M^{n+1/2} - \phi_0 N_M^n}{\tau} + \nabla \cdot (q\chi_{IM}^n) = 0 \tag{14a}$$

where the terms $\nabla \cdot$ are approximated by Equation (12). Rearranging Equation (14a) we obtain an explicit expression for the methane amount $\phi_0 N_{M,i}^{n+1/2}$ at the intermediate auxiliary time $t^{n+1/2}$

$$\phi_0 N_{M,i}^{n+1/2} = \phi_0 N_{M,i}^n - \frac{q\tau}{h_i}(\chi_{M,i}^n - \chi_{M,i-1}^n) = 0. \tag{15}$$

As is well known, stability of this explicit advection scheme requires that

$$\frac{|q|\tau}{\phi h} \leq 1 \tag{16}$$

via the well-known Courant-Friedrichs-Lévy (CFL) condition [33] adapted to porous media.

Advection scheme for $N_S^{n+1/2}$ is defined analogously to Equation (15).

3.5. Diffusion Step

Knowing $N_M^{n+1/2}$ and $N_S^{n+1/2}$ from the advection step, we solve the coupled diffusion/phase behavior system for N_M^{n+1} and N_S^{n+1} with the boundary conditions Equations (6b,c). To distinguish between the variants and avoid additional superscripts, we reserve the notation N_M^{n+1} and N_S^{n+1} for the solutions to the fully implicit variant I.

First we recall that with Equation (13) and matrix A we have the vector equation

$$\frac{\phi_0 N_M^{n+1} - \phi_0 N_M^{n+1/2}}{\tau} + A(S_l^n)\chi_{lM}^{n+1} = f_M^{n+1} \qquad (17)$$

Note the time lagging of the dependence of matrix A on S_l.

For N_S^{n+1} we have an equation analogous to Equation (17). Additionally, we need to account for [NCC-M]. This coupled system of two component diffusion and phase equilibria is solved with one of the three variants: fully implicit (I), semi-implicit (SI), and sequential (SEQ). See Figure 1 for graphical illustration of the operator splitting and different variants.

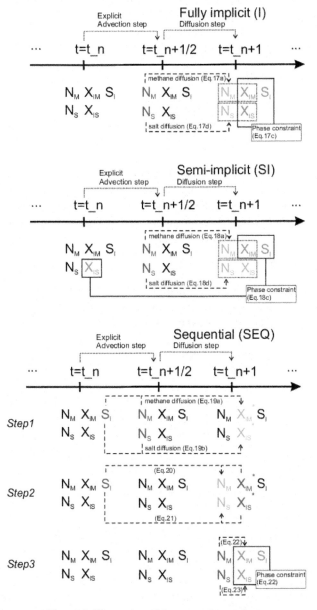

Figure 1. Illustration of time stepping variants.

3.5.1. Variant (I): Fully Implicit

The fully implicit variant solves the coupled two-component diffusion/phase behavior system for $(S_l^{n+1}, \chi_{lM}^{n+1}, \chi_{lS}^{n+1})$ as follows

$$\frac{\phi_0 N_M^{n+1} - \phi_0 N_M^{n+1/2}}{\tau} + A\chi_{lM}^{n+1} = f_M^{n+1}, \tag{18a}$$

$$N_M^{n+1} = S_l^{n+1}\chi_{lM}^{n+1} + R(1 - S_l^{n+1}). \tag{18b}$$

Here Equation (18b) provides the definition of N_M^{n+1} needed in Equation (18a), and is directly implemented in the code. The two unknowns in Equation (18a) are S_l^{n+1} and χ_{lM}^{n+1}; these are connected to each other via Equations (9) and (4)

$$\min(\chi_{lM}^{max,0}(x) + \alpha(x)\chi_{lS}^{n+1} - \chi_{lM}^{n+1}, 1 - S_l^{n+1}) = 0 \tag{18c}$$

with the dependence on χ_{lS}^{n+1} defined directly by

$$\frac{\phi_0 N_S^{n+1} - \phi_0 N_S^{n+1/2}}{\tau} + A\chi_{lS}^{n+1} = 0 \tag{18d}$$

$$N_S^{n+1} = S_l^{n+1}\chi_{lS}^{n+1} \tag{18e}$$

The Equation (18) is solved using Newton's method for $(S_l^{n+1}, \chi_{lM}^{n+1}, \chi_{lS}^{n+1})$, and the Jacobian of the system is a 3×3 sparse block matrix. Its form and particular pattern of sparsity depend on Equation (18c). Note that in Equation (18) we maintain full consistency of mass conservation between the time steps (up to the tolerance of nonlinear solver), as well as consistency of thermodynamic constraints.

3.5.2. Variant (SI): Semi-Implicit

The semi-implicit variant differs from Equation (18) in the treatment of χ_{lS} in Equation (18c). We time-lag χ_{lS} and remove the two-way coupling between the methane transport and salinity transport. Methane transport in this model is governed by

$$\frac{\phi_0 \widehat{N_M^{n+1}} - \phi_0 \widehat{N_M^{n+1/2}}}{\tau} + A\widehat{\chi_{lM}^{n+1}} = \widehat{f_M^{n+1}}, \tag{19a}$$

$$\widehat{N_M^{n+1}} = \widehat{S_l^{n+1}}\widehat{\chi_{lM}^{n+1}} + R(1 - \widehat{S_l^{n+1}}). \tag{19b}$$

$$\min(\chi_{lM}^{max,0}(x) + \alpha(x)\widehat{\chi_{lS}^{n}} - \widehat{\chi_{lM}^{n+1}}, 1 - \widehat{S_l^{n+1}}) = 0. \tag{19c}$$

so that these equations are solved for $(\widehat{S_l^{n+1}}, \widehat{\chi_{lM}^{n+1}})$ using Newton's method. The Jacobian of the system is a 2×2 sparse block matrix.

Knowing $\widehat{S_l^{n+1}}$ we can solve the system for $\widehat{\chi_{lS}^{n+1}}$ which is linear

$$\frac{\phi_0 \widehat{N_S^{n+1}} - \phi_0 \widehat{N_S^{n+1/2}}}{\tau} + A\widehat{\chi_{lS}^{n+1}} = 0, \tag{19d}$$

$$\widehat{N_S^{n+1}} = \widehat{S_l^{n+1}}\widehat{\chi_{lS}^{n+1}}. \tag{19e}$$

while the mass conservation between the time steps is enforced in this variant, there is potential inconsistency in thermodynamic constraints introduced by the time-lagging in Equation (19c). To correct this, we follow up with the two-variable local flash solver which corrects the saturations and solubilities while keeping $(\widehat{N_M^{n+1}},$ and $\widehat{N_S^{n+1}})$ fixed.

3.5.3. Variant (SEQ): Sequential

The sequential variant is the simplest to implement and one can easily adapt an existing advection-diffusion code. The advantage of this variant is that each of the global algebraic systems is linear. The disdvantage is that the phase behavior is not fully coupled to the transport dynamics, and fine time-stepping may be needed to ensure accuracy.

The SEQ variant time-lags the saturation variable in the methane and salinity transport equations

$$\frac{\phi_0 \widetilde{S_l^n} \widetilde{\chi_{lM}^{n+1,*}} - \phi_0 N_M^{n+1/2}}{\tau} + A \widetilde{\chi_{lM}^{n+1,*}} = f_M^{n+1} - \frac{\phi R(1 - \widetilde{S_l^n})}{\tau}, \tag{20a}$$

$$\frac{\phi_0 \widetilde{S_l^n} \widetilde{\chi_{lS}^{n+1,*}} - \phi_0 N_S^{n+1/2}}{\tau} + A \widetilde{\chi_{lS}^{n+1,*}} = 0 \tag{20b}$$

Note that the phase constraint is not imposed in Equation (20), and that the equations are not coupled. We solve them for the temporary unknowns $\chi_{lM}^{n+1,*}$, $\chi_{lS}^{n+1,*}$, and next we recalculate the mass concentrations corresponding to the new solubilities from Equations (19b,e)

$$\widetilde{N_M^{n+1}} = \widetilde{S_l^n} \widetilde{\chi_{lM}^{n+1,*}} + R(1 - \widetilde{S_l^n}). \tag{21}$$

$$\widetilde{N_S^{n+1}} = \widetilde{S_l^n} \widetilde{\chi_{lS}^{n+1,*}}. \tag{22}$$

To keep these consistent with Equation (9), we invoke the nonlinear two variable flash solver. Its input are the mass concentrations $\widetilde{N_M^{n+1}}, \widetilde{N_S^{n+1}}$, and its output are the final new values of solubilities $\widetilde{\chi_{lM}^{n+1}}, \widetilde{\chi_{lS}^{n+1}}$, and saturations $\widetilde{S_l^{n+1}}$ which satisfy the discrete version of Equation (9) plus the mass concentration definitions

$$\min(\chi_{lM}^{max,0}(x) + \alpha(x)\widetilde{\chi_{lS}^{n+1}} - \widetilde{\chi_{lM}^{n+1}}, 1 - \widetilde{S_l^{n+1}}) = 0 \tag{23}$$

$$\widetilde{N_M^{n+1}} = \widetilde{S_l^{n+1}} \widetilde{\chi_{lM}^{n+1}} + R(1 - \widetilde{S_l^{n+1}}) \tag{24}$$

$$\widetilde{N_S^{n+1}} = \widetilde{S_l^{n+1}} \widetilde{\chi_{lS}^{n+1}} \tag{25}$$

The flash solver for Equations 23–25 provides the consistency between the mass-related variables and thermodynamic constraints. However, the mass conservation between time steps is not strictly enforced due to time-lagging.

4. Comparison of Performance of the Time Stepping Variants

In this section we evaluate the accuracy, robustness and computational complexity of the proposed I, SI, and SEQ variants of hydrate models using realistic scenarios of methane hydrate formation in typical sediments. We also give details on what time steps appear reasonable, and how to choose discretization parameters.

In oil-gas reservoir simulation the fully implicit algorithms implement directly the backward Euler formula. The fully implicit formulations are usually the most accurate, but also most complex to implement. In turn, sequential and semi-implicit variants are typically less accurate but, at least in principle, they have smaller computational complexity per time step, and are easier to implement than the fully implicit algorithms. Typically, the results of non-implicit schemes converge to those of fully implicit models as $\tau \to 0$. In fact, non-implicit variants may require small τ in in order to resolve, e.g., complicated phase equilibria, heterogeneity, or complex well behavior; the use of small τ somewhat erases the benefits of small computational cost per time step. The non-implicit variants may still have advantages in the easiness of implementation.

The computational experiments we set up to test the variants I, SI, and SEQ are built from the following base case similar to those in [3] for the methane hydrate and salinity conditions in Ulleung Basin.

We set $\Omega = (0, L)$ with $L = 159$ m, and use uniform porosity $\phi = 0.5$. We vary q from large $q = 0.1$ m/yr for which advection dominates, to the case where diffusion is dominant and $q \leq 0.001$ m/yr. We assume that advection and diffusion provide the only transport mechanisms and that $f_M = 0 = f_S$, that is, the only sources of methane are from upward fluxes. For thermodynamics we use the reduced model Equation (4) and [NCC-M] constraint is implemented with Equation (9). Unless otherwise specified, we use the data $\chi_{max}^0(x)$ and $\alpha(x)$ calibrated for Ulleung Basin and shown in [3] and Section 5 with the same boundary and initial conditions. We use zero initial conidtions for methane, and assume that the initial distribution of salinities varies linearly between the boundary conditions χ_{IS}^0 and χ_{IS}^M. We run simulations until $T = 10^5$ yr $= 100$ Kyr, or until S_h reaches the unphysical values close to 1.

Discretization parameters are chosen as follows. We use $N_x = 100$ with $h = 1.59$ in the base case. The time step is subject to the CFL constraint Equation (16). In particular for $q = 0.01$ the largest time step $\tau_{CFL} \approx 78$ yr.

For illustration of the base case in Figure 2 we show the evolution of S_h and χ_{IS} for the case $q = 0.01$ m/yr, with small $\tau = 1$ yr. In this case of strong advective flux the hydrate forms quickly and fills up the domain. These results are similar to those in [3] and more generally to the test cases in [4]. The evolution of salinity shows that there is a boundary layer close to the outflow which forms around $T = 10 K$ and remains unchanged afterwards.

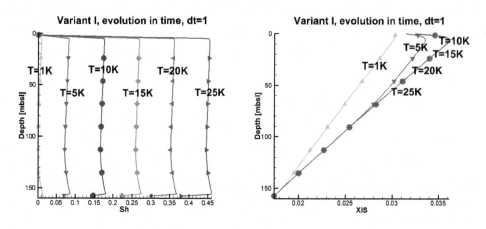

Figure 2. Evolution of hydrate saturation and of salinity for the base case. **(left)** Plot of S_h, **(right)** Plot of χ_{IS}. Variable χ_{IM} equals χ_{IM}^{max} at these times and is not shown.

4.1. Accuracy of the Time-Stepping Variants and Choice of Time Step

Here we study the sensitivity to τ which can guide its choice. In general, one wants to use small enough τ obeying the upper bound (16) and such that its further decrease does not have much influence. However, small τ means large number $\frac{T}{\tau}$ of time steps; this is significant in hydrate basin simulations since $\frac{T}{\tau}$ may be easily 10^4 or more. Further, as suggested by our experience from oil-gas reservoir simulations [10,11,13], we expect that for small τ the results of the three variants I, SI, SEQ are very similar, and that for large τ they differ.

In Figure 3 we present the plots of S_h obtained for different τ. Quantitative information supporting these observations is included in Table 2. (We do not present details concerning the evolution of χ_{IS} since the results differ by less than 0.01% in each case.) We notice that the results corresponding to $\tau = 1$ and the variants I, SI, and SEQ are essentially indistinguishable; this degree of closeness is more than expected. In addition, the results corresponding to the largest advection step $\tau = 78$ and to the variants I, SI and SEQ are close to each other as well; they tend to overpredict those for $\tau = 1$.

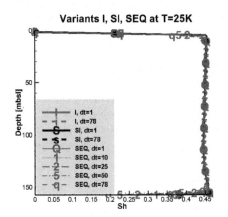
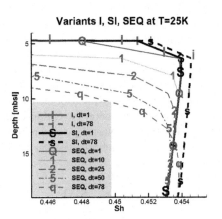

Figure 3. Plots of S_h for different time steps τ (denoted on figure by dt), and different time-stepping variants fully implicit (I), semi-implicit (SI), and sequential (SEQ). **(left)** Plots over the full range of depth and S_h are essentially indistinguishable. **(right)** The zoom of the left plot shows a small sensitivity to the choice of time step and of the model variant.

Table 2. Maximum hydrate saturation S_h obtained with different model variants and time steps at $T = 10\ K$ and $T = 25\ K$, all parameters as in base case.

τ	SEQ	SI	I
		$T = 10\ K$	
78	0.177208	0.182844	0.182844
70	0.176441	0.181803	0.181803
50	0.176834	0.181267	0.181267
25	0.177841	0.180908	0.180908
10	0.178834	0.180736	0.180736
5	0.179238	0.180688	0.180688
1	0.180183	0.180651	0.180651
		$T = 25\ K$	
78	0.456162	0.463925	0.463925
70	0.456803	0.464271	0.464271
50	0.45644	0.462797	0.462797
25	0.457708	0.462438	0.462438
10	0.458886	0.462266	0.462266
5	0.459731	0.462218	0.462218
1	0.460878	0.462181	0.462181

In addition, we see that the model SEQ is potentially the most sensitive of all three to τ close to the boundaries and in areas with larger methane gradients. (This suggests the need for adaptive gridding). In addition, as τ decreases, the results tend to converge to the value for $\tau = 1$. Further decrease of τ (not shown here) does not influence the solution much, thus $\tau = 1$ appears as the smallest sensible choice for this N_x.

4.2. Robustness and Efficiency of the Variants

Above we established that the simulated hydrate saturation values do not seem to significantly depend on the time step τ or on the variant of time stepping. Next we consider the robustness of the variants and in particular, how they handle difficult physical circumstances such as when S_h is large due to large advective fluxes.

In Table 3 we report on the performance of the nonlinear solver, tested intentionally without any fine-tuning such as line-search. We see that between $T = 25\ K$ and $T = 50\ K$ all variants I, SI, SEQ struggle when $\tau \geq 25$. The model I appears somewhat more robust than the other two and it can simulate the hydrate evolution up to higher values.

Table 3. Robustness of nonlinear solvers depending on the variant and the time step for the simulations of the base case between $T = 25\ K$ and $T = 50\ K$. The robustness is assessed by checking which solver variant is more prone or more robust to failing in the difficult modeling circumstances close to unphysical. We report the critical value S_h^{crit} obtained before the solver fails, and on the number N_{it} of iterations. When N_{it} is denoted by "-", this means the solver did not complete. For SEQ model, N_{it} denotes the number of flash iterations. For the SI and I models, N_{it} denotes the number of global Newton iterations.

τ	SEQ		SI		I	
	S_h^{crit}	N_{it}	S_h^{crit}	N_{it}	S_h^{crit}	N_{it}
78	0.75833	-	0.767473	-	0.773341	-
70	0.772449	-	0.782752	-	0.781435	-
50	0.806955	-	0.817198	-	0.817198	-
25	0.873396	-	0.880766	-	0.880766	-
10	0.925712	2	0.932267	2	0.932267	3
5	0.926744	2	0.93222	2	0.93222	3

Dependence of the results on q. Next, it is known that the advective fluxes are the hardest physically to handle for hydrate systems, since they provide the source for the fastest hydrate formation.

To test our solvers, we consider the advection-dominated case with large and moderate q, down to the purely diffusive case with $q = 0$. In Figure 4 we present the plots of hydrate saturations at $T = 31\ K$ for different fluxes q. In addition, in Table 4 we report the time T_I when the computational model I predicts that $\max_x S_h(x, T_I) \approx 0.5$. We also report the values T_{SI} and T_{SEQ} also for the variants SI and SEQ.

We see that the variants I and SI report essentially the same values. In fact, a close inspection reveals that the model results differ in less than 0.001% between I and SI for the time steps we used in our implementation. This experiment shows again the robustness of all variants with respect to q, with a slight advantage of the implicit variants.

Computational time and the choice of time step. Finally, we evaluate the computational complexity of the variants, and this is done by comparing the wall clock times for our MATLAB implementation. In order to compare the solvers on equal footing, no additional code vectorization is implemented, but the code takes advantage of the natural MATALB vector data types. In Table 5 we report the wall clock time.

In general, one expects that for the same time step τ the SEQ model is faster than SI and I, since SEQ only uses global linear solvers and local nonlinear flash routines. However, we see that all solvers require similar amounts of computational time, with a slight advantage of model SI. This may be due to the lack of vectorization applied in local flash routines, while the global linear solvers are naturally vectorized in MATLAB. In addition, the SEQ solver computes more local variables than SI and I.

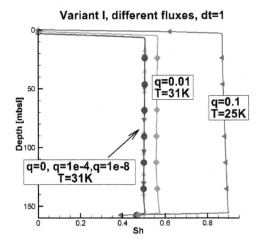

Figure 4. Hydrate saturation at $T = 31\ K$ when different advective fluxes are assumed. For $q = 0.1$ for which high saturation is attained already at $T = 25\ K$ we do not show the plot at $T = 31\ K$.

Table 4. The time T when $\max S_h \approx 0.5$ depending on q, for the base case for each time-stepping variant, respectively, T_I, T_{SI}, T_{SEQ}. Here we use $\tau = 1$.

q	T_I	T_{SI}	T_{SEQ}
0.1	13917	13917	13972
0.01	27014	27014	27091
0.005	28629	28629	28691
0.0001	30568	30568	30587
1e−08	30614	30614	30624

Since with uniform τ the total computational time scales proportionally to the number of time steps, the choice of τ balances the desired accuracy and computational time. For the case considered here it seems that the time step $\tau = 10$ may be the best practical choice.

The efficiency of the solvers may be very different in 2d or 3d simulations, and we intend to report on these in the future.

Table 5. Comparison of computational wall clock time $T^w[s]$ for the three model variants and different time steps, for the base case and $T = 25\ K$.

τ	T^w_{SEQ}	T^w_{SI}	T^w_I
1	591.801	439.806	441.394
10	60.2528	44.0688	47.6352
50	11.8322	8.81442	9.63327
78	7.55206	5.655	6.08011

5. Sensitivity to Physical and Coputational Parameters

For a computational model it is crucial to determine what discretization parameters one should use for a given model. In addition, it is important to investigate the sensitivity of the model to the data on $\alpha(x)$ in Equation (4).

Discretization parameters. As the discretization parameters $h, \tau \to 0$ and the numbers of cells $N_x = \frac{L}{h}$ and time steps increase, it is expected that the numerical solutions of a PDE model converge to the analytical ones in an appropriate sense dictated by the theoretical numerical analysis. The convergence studies for the purely diffusive one component case of Equation (3) in [17] suggest to vary τ wit h either linearly or faster, and to consider various metrics of convergence in appropriate functional spaces. For the present case with significant advection q and variable salinity, we expect the rates to be inferior of the approximate $O(h + \tau)$ rates observed in [17]. The theoretical analysis is underway and will be presented elsewhere.

Here we choose $\tau = O(h)$ and the implicit model; in Figure 5 and Table 6 we present the evidence which confirms that as h decreases, the results seem to converge. At the same time it is obvious that the convergence in saturations is quite rough, as observed earlier in [34].

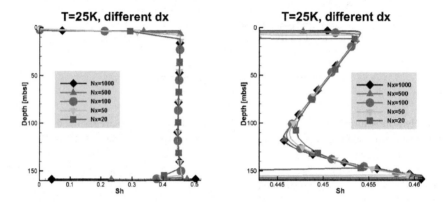

Figure 5. Hydrate saturation for different N_x and h denoted by dx. See Table 6 for the related quantitative information extracted from the simulations.

Table 6. Accuracy and complexity of the computational model depending on N_x, with the time step τ adjusted to vary linearly with h. As the quantity of interest depending on N_x we show the saturation values at $T = 25\ K$. This table complements the plots in Figure 5.

N_x	h	τ	max S_h	Wall-Clock Time
10	15.9	10	0.453079	5.6533
25	6.36	4	0.455525	32.644
50	3.18	2	0.459280	121.411
100	1.59	1	0.462181	489.101
200	0.795	0.5	0.465253	2301.53

The question then is what choice of h and τ balance the conflicting need to decrease the computational time as well as to increase the accuracy, while maintaining an adequate model resolution. From the results presented, we suggest that $N_x = 100$ or $N_x = 50$ corresponding to the discretization in space $h \approx 1$ m and in time $\tau \approx 1$ yr are a good choice, since they appear to keep the simulation results within the uncertainty envelope that might not be verifiable experimentally.

However, the sensitivity to τ and h at the boundaries needs to be addressed by a more accurate and adaptive formulation especially if nonhomogeneous sediments and/or additional physics are considered.

Sensitivity to the parameters of the reduced model Equation (4). There is large uncertainty as to what χ_{IM}^{max} one should use. In particular, there may be an error associated with the look-up table process of finding α described in [3] and due to the lack of information on salinity. More broadly, in a comprehensive model χ_{IM}^{max} depends on the unknown pressure and temperature values, and possibly rock type, thus further variability and uncertainty of $\alpha(x)$ should be expected.

We set up therefore test cases to assess this sensitivity. We dub the values of $\alpha(x)$ obtained for Ulleung Basin in [3] the "true" $\alpha_{\text{true}}(x)$. Next we simulate the hydrate formation with $\alpha(x) =$

$c\alpha_{true}(x)$ with $c = 1$, $c = 10$ and $c = -1$. Furthermore, we consider a constant value equal to the average of the true $\alpha(x) = \frac{1}{|\Omega|} \int_\Omega \alpha_{true}(x)dx$, and another $\alpha(x)$ which randomly perturbs $\alpha_{true}(x)$. The different cases of α are shown in Figure 6, with the corespnding χ_{IM}^{max} which we calculated, for illustration purposes, assuming $\chi_{lS} = \chi_{lS}^{sw}$. In Figure 7 we show the profiles of S_h at $T = 25\ K$ coresponding to the different $\alpha(x)$.

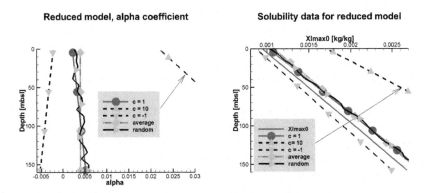

Figure 6. Parameter $\alpha(x)$ as a function of depth used in Section 5 (**left**) and the corresponding $\chi_{IM}^{max,0}(x)$ computed from Equation (4) and assuming $\chi_{LS} \approx \chi_{lS}^{sw}$ (**right**). On right the plot of $\chi_{IM}^{max,0}(x)$ is also shown. The base case from Ulleung Basin [3] in both plots is denoted with circles. The other cases correspond to $c = -1$, $c = 10$, the average of $\alpha(x)$, and to a randomly perturbed $\alpha(x)$. The plots for $c = 10$ are out of range and are not fully included.

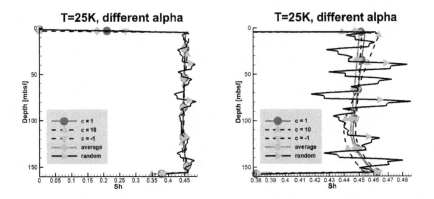

Figure 7. Hydrate saturation for different coefficients α. The figure on the (**right**) is a zoomed in version of that on the (**left**).

Comparing the hydrate saturation for $c = -1$ and $c = 10$ shown in Figure 7 to the base case with $c = 1$ we see that since χ_{IM}^{max} is significantly higher when $c = 10$, somewhat less hydrate forms. On the other hand, a randomly pertubed $\alpha(x)$ gives χ_{IM}^{max} with large local variation, and this is reflected in the corresponding hydrate saturation. This significant sensitivity appears to be of qualitative nature, and requires further studies.

6. Conclusions

In this paper we described the details of the discretization and implementation of a reduced methane hydrate model with variable salinity and significant advection proposed in [3]. We carried out several convergence and parameter studies to show that the model is robust and computationally sound. Studies of this type have not been provided for the simplified or the comprehensive implicit hydrate models from literature, but are crucial to guide the implementation and to inspire further theoretical and algorithmic developments.

In particular, we defined several time stepping variants: implicit I, semi-implicit SI, and sequential SEQ, which were tested and compared using realistic reservoir data from [3]. We found, somewhat surprisingly, that the I and SI variants give almost identical results; this may be explained by only a mild dependence of the model on the salinity variable whose treatment differs in I and SI. Furthermore, in the current implementation and 1d test cases there is no significant advantage in one variant over the others as concerns accuracy, robustness, or efficiency. Still, the I model appears as expected somewhat most robust, while SEQ is the easiest to implement by modifying standard advection-diffusion solvers. We also demonstrated the apparent convergence of the solutions when $h, \tau \to 0$, and determined practical choices of h, τ. In addition, there is apparent need for grid and model refinement near the boundaries.

Furthermore, we demonstrated the small sensitivity of the reduced thermodynamics model proposed in [3] to the particular value of the coefficient α as long as it is qualitatively close to the one from the reservoir data and is monotone. However, a randomly perturbed and nonmonotone α reveals large sensitivity, and we plan to investigate the reasons further.

Our future work includes theoretical and practical studies of the model convergence as well as its efficiency. There is further need to study additional sets of realistic data and thermodynamics models, and to consider extensions to more complex physical problems.

Acknowledgments: Malgorzata Peszynska and Francis Patricia Medina's research was partially supported by the NSF DMS-1115827 "Hybrid modeling in porous media" and by DMS-1522734 "Phase transitions in porous media across multiple scales". Marta E. Torres and Wei-Li Hong were supported by US Department of Energy grant #DE-FE00135331 and by the Research Council of Norway through its Centres of Excellence funding scheme, project 223259. The authors thank the anonymous reviewers for their comments which helped to improve the manuscript.

Author Contributions: Malgorzata Peszynska, Marta E. Torres and Wei-Li Hong adapted the reduced model to the case study from Ulleung Basin. Malgorzata Peszynska and Wei-Li Hong implemented the reduced model; Malgorzata Peszynska and Francis Patricia Medina set up and tested the numerical model.

Conflicts of Interest: The authors declare no conflict of interest.

References

1.   Dickens, G.R. Rethinking the global carbon cycle with a large, dynamic and microbially mediated gas hydrate capacitor. *Earth Planet. Sci. Lett.* **2003**, *213*, 169–183.

2.   Torres, M.; Wallmann, K.; Tréhu, A.; Bohrmann, G.; Borowski, W.; Tomaru, H. Gas hydrate growth, methane transport, and chloride enrichment at the southern summit of Hydrate Ridge, Cascadia margin off Oregon. *Earth Planet. Sci. Lett.* **2004**, *226*, 225 – 241.

3.   Peszynska, M.; Hong, W.L.; Torres, M.; Kim, J.H. Methane hydrate formation in Ulleung Basin under conditions of variable salinity. Reduced model and experiments. **2015**, submitted.

4.   Liu, X.; Flemings, P.B. Dynamic multiphase flow model of hydrate formation in marine sediments. *J. Geophys. Res.* **2007**, *112*, B03101.

5.   Lake, L.W. *Enhanced Oil Recovery*; Prentice Hall: Upper Saddle River, NJ, USA, 1989.

6.   Helmig, R. *Multiphase Flow and Transport Processes in the Subsurface*; Springer: Berlin, Germany, 1997.

7.   Class, H.; Helmig, R. Numerical simulation of non-isothermal ultiphase multicomponent processes in porous media 2. Applications for the injection of steam and air. *Adv. Water Resour.* **2002**, *25*, 533–550.

8.   Trangenstein, J.A.; Bell, J.B. Mathematical structure of the black-oil model for petroleum reservoir simulation. *SIAM J. Appl. Math.* **1989**, *49*, 749–783.

9.   Chen, Z.; Khlopina, N.L. Degenerate two-phase incompressible flow problems. I. Regularization and numerical results. *Commun. Appl. Anal.* **2001**, *5*, 319–334.

10.   Lu, Q.; Peszyńska, M.; Wheeler, M.F. A Parallel Multi-Block Black-Oil Model in Multi-Model Implementation. *SPE J.* **2002**, *7*, 278–287.

11.   Peszyńska, M.; Lu, Q.; Wheeler, M.F. Multiphysics Coupling of Codes. In *Computational Methods in Water Resources*; Balkema: Leiden, The Netherlands, 2000.

12. Wheeler, M.F.; Wheeler, J.A.; Peszyńska, M. A Distributed Computing Portal for Coupling Multi-Physics and Multiple Domains in Porous Media. In *Computational Methods in Water Resources*; Balkema: Leiden, The Netherlands, 2000.

13. Wheeler, M.F.; Peszyńska, M. Computational Engineering and Science Methodologies for Modeling and Simulation of Subsurface Applications. *Adv. Water Resour.* **2002**, *25*, 1147–1173.

14. Coats, K.H.; Thomas, L.K.; Pierson, R.G. Compositional and black oil reservoir simulator. *SPE Reserv. Eval. Eng.* **1995**, *1*, 372–379.

15. Xu, W.; Ruppel, C. Predicting the occurence, distribution, and evolution of methane hydrate in porous marine sediments. *J. Geophys. Res.* **1999**, *104*, 5081–5095.

16. Nimblett, J.; Ruppel, C. Permeability evolution during the formation of gas hydratees in marine sediments. *J. Geophys. Res.* **2003**, *108*, B9.

17. Gibson, N.L.; Medina, F.P.; Peszynska, M.; Showalter, R.E. Evolution of phase transitions in methane hydrate. *J. Math. Anal. Appl.* **2014**, *409*, 816 – 833.

18. Peszynska, M.; Showalter, R.; Webster, J. Advection of Methane in the Hydrate Zone: Model, Analysis and Examples. *Mathe. Methods Appl. Sci.* **2014**, doi:10.1002/mma.3401.

19. Rempel, A.W. Hydromechanical Processes in Freezing Soils. *Vadose Zone J.* **2012**, *11*, 4.

20. Sloan, E.; Koh, C.A. *Clathrate Hydrates of Natural Gases*, 3rd ed.; CRC Press: Leiden, The Netherlands, 2008.

21. Daigle, H.; Dugan, B. Capillary controls on methane hydrate distribution and fracturing in advective systems. *Geochem. Geophys. Geosyst.* **2011**, *12*, 1–18.

22. Center for Hydrate Research Software CSMHYD and CSMGem. Available online: http://hydrates.mines.edu/CHR/Software.html (accessed on 23 December 2015).

23. Zatsepina, O.; Buffett, B. Phase equilibrium of gas hydrate: Implications for the formation of hydrate in the deep sea floor. *Geophys. Res. Lett.* **1997**, *24*, 1567–1570.

24. Dawson, C.N. Godunov-mixed methods for advection-diffusion equations in multidimensions. *SIAM J. Numer. Anal.* **1993**, *30*, 1315–1332.

25. Dawson, C.N.; Wheeler, M.F. Time-splitting methods for advection-diffusion-reaction equations arising in contaminant transport. In Proceedings of the second International Conference on Industrial and Applied Mathematics, Washington, DC, USA, 8–12 July 1991.

26. Wheeler, M.F.; Dawson, C.N. An operator-splitting method for advection-diffusion-reaction problems. In *The Mathematics of Finite Elements and Applications VI*; Whiteman, J.R., Ed.; Academic Press: London, UK, 1987; pp. 463–482.

27. Ito, K.; Kunisch, K. Semi-smooth Newton methods for variational inequalities of the first kind. *M2AN Math. Model. Numer. Anal.* **2003**, *37*, 41–62.

28. Ulbrich, M. *Semismooth Newton Methods for Variational Inequalities and Constrained Optimization Problems in Function Spaces*; Vol. 11, MOS-SIAM Series on Optimization; Society for Industrial and Applied Mathematics (SIAM): Philadelphia, PA, USA, 2011.

29. Gharbia, I.B.; Jaffre, J. Gas phase appearance and disappearance as a problem with complementarity constraints. *Math. Comput. Simul.* **2014**, *99*, 28–36.

30. Peaceman, D.W. *Fundamentals of Numerical Reservoir Simulation*; Elsevier Scientfic Publishing Company: Amsterdam, The Netherlands, 1977.

31. Russell, T.F.; Wheeler, M.F. Finite element and finite difference methods for continuous flows in porous media. In *The Mathematics of Reservoir Simulation*; Ewing, R.E., Ed.; SIAM: Philadelphia, PA, USA, 1983.

32. Peszyńska, M.; Jenkins, E.; Wheeler, M.F. Boundary conditions for fully implicit two-phase flow model. In *Recent Advances in Numerical Methods for Partial Differential Equations and Applications*; American Mathematical Soc.: Ann Arbor, MI, USA, 2002.

33. LeVeque, R.J. *Finite Difference Methods for Ordinary and Partial Differential Equations*; Society for Industrial and Applied Mathematics (SIAM): Philadelphia, PA, USA, 2007.

34. Peszyńska, M.; Torres, M.; Tréhu, A. Adaptive modeling of methane hydrates. *Procedia Computer Sci.* **2010**, *1*, 709-717.

2

Contact Angle Effects on Pore and Corner Arc Menisci in Polygonal Capillary Tubes Studied with the Pseudopotential Multiphase Lattice Boltzmann Model

Soyoun Son [1,2,*], Li Chen [3,4], Qinjun Kang [3], Dominique Derome [1] and Jan Carmeliet [1,2]

[1] Laboratory of Multiscale Studies in Building Physics, EMPA (Swiss Federal Laboratories for Materials Science and Technology), Dübendorf 8600, Switzerland; dominique.derome@empa.ch (D.D.); carmeliet@arch.ethz.ch (J.C.)

[2] Chair of Building Physics, ETH Zürich (Swiss Federal Institute of Technology in Zürich), Zürich 8093, Switzerland

[3] Earth and Environment Sciences Division (EES-16), Los Alamos National Laboratory, Los Alamos, NM 87545, USA; lichenmt@lanl.gov (L.C.); qkang@lanl.gov (Q.K.)

[4] Key Laboratory of Thermo-Fluid Science and Engineering of MOE, School of Energy and Power Engineering, Xi'an Jiaotong University, Xi'an 710049, China

* Correspondence: soyoun.son@empa.ch

Academic Editor: Demos T. Tsahalis

Abstract: In porous media, pore geometry and wettability are determinant factors for capillary flow in drainage or imbibition. Pores are often considered as cylindrical tubes in analytical or computational studies. Such simplification prevents the capture of phenomena occurring in pore corners. Considering the corners of pores is crucial to realistically study capillary flow and to accurately estimate liquid distribution, degree of saturation and dynamic liquid behavior in pores and in porous media. In this study, capillary flow in polygonal tubes is studied with the Shan-Chen pseudopotential multiphase lattice Boltzmann model (LBM). The LB model is first validated through a contact angle test and a capillary intrusion test. Then capillary rise in square and triangular tubes is simulated and the pore meniscus height is investigated as a function of contact angle θ. Also, the occurrence of fluid in the tube corners, referred to as corner arc menisci, is studied in terms of curvature *versus* degree of saturation. In polygonal capillary tubes, the number of sides leads to a critical contact angle θ_c which is known as a key parameter for the existence of the two configurations. LBM succeeds in simulating the formation of a pore meniscus at $\theta > \theta_c$ or the occurrence of corner arc menisci at $\theta < \theta_c$. The curvature of corner arc menisci is known to decrease with increasing saturation and decreasing contact angle as described by the Mayer and Stoewe-Princen (MS-P) theory. We obtain simulation results that are in good qualitative and quantitative agreement with the analytical solutions in terms of height of pore meniscus *versus* contact angle and curvature of corner arc menisci *versus* saturation degree. LBM is a suitable and promising tool for a better understanding of the complicated phenomena of multiphase flow in porous media.

Keywords: menisci; polygonal tube; corner arc; capillary rise; wettability; saturation; curvature; single component multiphase lattice Boltzmann method

1. Introduction

Capillary flow is a common phenomenon of multiphase flow in porous media with various applications, such as in the built environment, textile dyeing industry, oil recovery and ink printing. Although capillary flow is ubiquitous and has been studied theoretically and experimentally for a long time, the determination of vapor/liquid interface configurations in complex porous media remains a challenging problem. Those configurations depend on the pore geometry and connectivity, the liquid properties and the surface wettability. Previous work often assumed simple pore geometry, modeling pores as cylindrical tubes or parallel plates. Such simplifications prevent capturing significant unsaturated phenomena such as corner flow. Therefore, to estimate liquid distributions in porous media accurately and more realistically, corner flow at the edges of pores also has to be taken into account. A common method to experimentally study capillary flow in complex pores is the use of n-sided regular polygonal tubes resulting in different cross-section geometries, such as triangle, square, hexagon, *etc.* In a n-sided, partially filled polygonal tube, the liquid surface forms a hemisphere, the configuration of which depends on the wetting or contact angle between the liquid and the solid material, as shown in Figure 1. Concus and Finn [1] identified the existence of a critical contact angle, $\theta_c = \pi/n$, in n-sided polygonal tubes based on the Rayleigh-Taylor interface instability. When the contact angle θ is between $\pi/2$ and the critical contact angle, *i.e.*, $\theta_c (= \pi/n) \leqslant \theta < \pi/2$, the liquid wets the tube walls and the liquid meniscus spans the total tube, resulting in a configuration named the pore meniscus. In contrast, if the contact angle is smaller than the critical contact angle, *i.e.*, $\theta < \theta_c (= \pi/n)$, in addition to the pore meniscus, the liquid also invades the edges or corners of the polygonal tube, forming corner arc menisci [1,2]. Corner arc menisci occur at each corner and move upward as a result of a capillary pressure gradient [3,4].

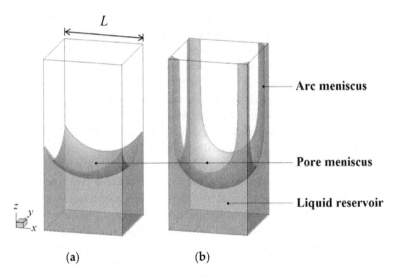

Figure 1. Schematic representation of the two liquid configurations in a square tube: (a) pore meniscus when the contact angle is larger than the critical contact angle, $\theta \geqslant \theta_c$; and (b) co-occurrence of pore and corner arc menisci when the contact angle is smaller than the critical contact angle, $\theta < \theta_c$.

Princen proposed a model for capillary rise in triangular and square tubes for a zero contact angle [5,6]. The Princen model predicts the total mass of liquid W in a square tube from the balance between capillary force and gravity considering both the liquid column under the pore meniscus and the liquid columns in the corner arc menisci of infinite height.

$$W = \rho g h L^2 + 4\rho g \int_h^\infty (1 - \pi/4)\, r_{arc}^2\,(z)\, dz \tag{1}$$

where ρ is the fluid density, g is the gravitational acceleration, h is the height of the liquid column under the pore meniscus, L is the size of the side of the rectangular polygon, z is the coordinate along the height and r_{arc} is the radius of curvature of the corner arc meniscus. In this equation, full wetting conditions with contact angle $\theta = 0°$ are assumed. The Mayer and Stowe-Princen (MS-P) model [5–8] predicts the curvature radius of the arc meniscus as a function of the effective area and perimeter of the non-wetting phase (gas), resulting in a better estimation of the interfacial area as shown by [9] using experimental data. Ma *et al.* [10] investigated capillary flow in polygonal tubes during imbibition and drainage and suggested a relationship between liquid saturation and the curvature of arc menisci in corners based on the MS-P model. In recent work, Feng and Rothstein [11] studied the pore meniscus height as a function of the contact angle for polygonal capillary tubes for contact angles higher than the critical contact angle. Furthermore, they considered different geometries with either sharped or rounded corners, showing the effect of rounded corners and contact angle on meniscus height, and compared their simulation results using Surface Evolver, which is an open-source code for surface energy minimization.

In computational fluid dynamics (CFD) studies, multiphase flow has often been studied by either the Volume of Fluid (VOF) [12] or level set [13] methods to capture or track the interface. When these methods are applied on complex geometries or small-scale problems, significant mass conservation problems arise near the interface and more complicated algorithms have been required [14,15].

The lattice Boltzmann method (LBM), which is based on microscopic models and mesoscopic equations, is a powerful technique for simulating multiphase flow involving interfacial dynamics and complex geometries, especially in porous media [16–18]. Several LB models have been developed for multiphase flow simulation including the color gradient-based LB method by Gunstensen *et al.* [19], the free-energy model by Swift *et al.* [20], the mean-field model by He *et al.* [21] and the pseudopotential model by Shan and Chen [22,23]. The pseudopotential model is the most popular LB multiphase model due to its simplicity and versatility. This model represents microscopic molecular interactions at mesoscopic scale using a pseudopotential depending on the local density [22,23]. With such interactions, a single component fluid spontaneously segregates into high and low density phases (e.g., liquid and gas), when the interaction strength (or the temperature) is below the critical point [22,23]. The automatic phase separation is an attractive characteristic of the pseudopotential model, as the phase interface is no longer a mathematical boundary and no explicit interface tracking or interface capturing technique is needed. The location of the phase interface is characterized through monitoring of the shift (jump) of the fluid density from gas to liquid. The pseudopotential model captures the essential elements of fluid behavior, namely it follows a non-ideal equation of state (EOS) and incorporates a surface tension force. Due to its remarkable computational efficiency and clear representation of the underlying microscopic physics, this model has been used as an efficient technique for simulating and investigating multiphase flow problems, particularly for these flows with complex topological changes of the interface, such as deformation, coalescence and breakup of the fluid phase, or fluid flow in complex geometries [24]. Recently, Chen *et al.* [25] thoroughly reviewed the theory and application of the pseudopential model and we refer to their publication for more details.

Capillary flow has been studied effectively using the Shan-Chen pseudopotential LB model. Sukop and Thorne [26] performed a two-dimensional capillary rise simulation using the pseudopotential LBM and compared their results with the theoretical capillary rise equation, *i.e.*, the balance between a pressure differential from the Young-Laplace equation and the gravitational force. Raiskinmaki *et al.* [26,27] investigated capillary rise in a three-dimensional cylindrical tube using multiphase LBM. The effects of contact angle, tube radius and capillary number were studied with or without taking into account gravity. Their study provided a useful benchmark for other LBM studies of capillary rise by comparing it with the Washburn solution. Although previous studies showed interesting LBM works in capillary flow, such as [28,29], only the interface of the capillary column, *i.e.*, the meniscus in cylindrical tubes or between two parallel plates, has been investigated without considering other phenomena such as corner flow.

In the present study, capillary flow in three-dimensional polygonal tubes with varying contact angle is investigated using the Shan-Chen pseudopotential LB model. The height of the pore meniscus and the radius of the corner arc meniscus are studied for different contact angles, and the latter results are compared with the theoretical values derived from the MS-P model. Given that the characteristic length used here is below capillary length, surface tension effects are more dominant and gravitational effects can be neglected. Also, contact angle hysteresis is not accounted for.

The paper is organized as follows: in Section 2, we briefly describe the pseudopotential multiphase LB model with the Carnahan-Starling (C-S) EOS and forcing scheme; in Section 3, a validation test is presented; the computational set-up and the boundary conditions used in the LB simulations are presented in Section 4; the capillary rise simulation results are compared with analytical solutions in Section 5; we draw conclusions in Section 6.

2. Numerical Model

A three-dimensional, single component, two-phase LB model is implemented for solving capillary rise phenomena. The LBM considers flow as a collective behavior of pseudoparticles residing on a mesoscopic level and solves the Boltzmann equation using a small number of velocities adapted to a regular grid in space. Fluid motion is represented by a set of particle distribution functions. The LB equation with the Bhantagar-Gross-Krock (BGK) collision operator is written as:

$$f_i\left(\mathbf{x} + c\mathbf{e}_i\Delta t, t + \Delta t\right) - f_i\left(\mathbf{x}, t\right) = -\frac{1}{\tau}\left[f_i\left(\mathbf{x}, t\right) - f_i^{eq}\left(\mathbf{x}, t\right)\right] \tag{2}$$

where $f_i(\mathbf{x},t)$ is the density distribution function and $f_i^{eq}(\mathbf{x},t)$ is the equilibrium distribution function in the ith lattice velocity direction, where $\times$ denotes the position and t is the time. A relaxation time τ is introduced, which relates to the kinematic viscosity as $v = c_s^2(\tau - 0.5)\Delta t$. The lattice sound speed c_s is equal to $c/\sqrt{3}$, where the lattice speed c is equal to $\Delta x/\Delta t$, with Δx as the grid spacing and Δt as the time step. In this study, both grid spacing and time step are set equal to 1. The equilibrium distribution function for the D3Q19 lattice model is of the form:

$$f_i^{eq} = w_i\rho\left[1 + \frac{3}{c^2}\left(\mathbf{e}_i \cdot \mathbf{u}\right) + \frac{9}{2c^4}\left(\mathbf{e}_i \cdot \mathbf{u}\right)^2 - \frac{3}{2c^2}\mathbf{u}^2\right] \tag{3}$$

For the D3Q19 lattice model [30,31], the lattice weighing factors w_i are:

$$w_i = \begin{cases} 12/36, & i = 0; \\ 2/36, & i = 1, \ldots, 6; \\ 1/36, & i = 7, \ldots, 18. \end{cases} \tag{4}$$

where the discrete velocity $\mathbf{e}_i$ is given by:

$$\mathbf{e}_i = \begin{cases} (0,0,0), & i = 0; \\ (\pm1,0,0), (0,\pm1,0), (0,0,\pm1), & i = 1, \ldots, 6; \\ (\pm1,\pm1,0), (\pm1,0,\pm1), (0,\pm1,\pm1), & i = 7, \ldots, 18. \end{cases} \tag{5}$$

The macroscopic parameters, the fluid density ρ, and the fluid velocity $\mathbf{u}$ are calculated as:

$$\rho = \sum_i f_i \tag{6}$$

$$\rho\mathbf{u} = \sum_i f_i\mathbf{e}_i. \tag{7}$$

In the Shan-Chen pseudopotential LB model, the forcing scheme, incorporating the interactive forces, greatly affects the numerical accuracy and stability of the simulation. The original Shan-Chen LB model results in an inaccurate prediction of the surface tension, dependent on the chosen density ratio and relaxation time. When combining this model with a proper forcing scheme, the model can give an accurate surface tension prediction independent of the relaxation time and density ratio. In recent studies, different forcing schemes for the Shan-Chen LB model are compared by Li *et al.* [32] and Huang *et al.* [33]. Based on these studies, the exact-difference method (EDM) developed by Kupershtokh *et al.* [34] is considered as the forcing scheme in our study. For a high density ratio with a relaxation range of $0.5 < \tau \leqslant 1$, this method shows better numerical stability [32]. In EDM, a source term Δf_i is added into the right term of the equilibrium distribution function in Equation (2) and is defined as:

$$\Delta f_i = f_i^{eq}(\rho, \mathbf{u} + \Delta\mathbf{u}) - f_i^{eq}(\rho, \mathbf{u}) \tag{8}$$

The increment of the velocity $\Delta\mathbf{u}$ is defined as:

$$\Delta\mathbf{u} = \frac{\mathbf{F}_{total}\Delta t}{\rho} \tag{9}$$

where $\mathbf{F}_{total}$ equals the sum of the total forces. By averaging the moment force before and after a collision step, the real fluid velocity is calculated as:

$$\mathbf{u}_r = \mathbf{u} + \frac{\mathbf{F}_{total}\Delta t}{2\rho} \tag{10}$$

In the single component multiphase LB model, a cohesive force $\mathbf{F}_m$ between liquid particles is needed and this force causes phase separation [26]. The force is defined as:

$$\mathbf{F}_m = -G\psi(\mathbf{x})\sum_i^N \omega\left(|\mathbf{e}_i|^2\right)\psi(\mathbf{x} + \mathbf{e}_i)\,\mathbf{e}_i \tag{11}$$

According to the interaction values, the discrete velocity is $|\mathbf{e}_i|^2 = 1$ at the four nearest neighbors or $|\mathbf{e}_i|^2 = 2$ at the next-nearest neighbors. The weight factors $\omega(|\mathbf{e}_i|^2)$ have the following values: $\omega(1) = 1/3$ and $\omega(2) = 1/12$. The parameter G reflects the interaction strength and controls the surface tension [22,23,27]. For $G < 0$, the attraction between particles increases and the force is strong. Thus, the cohesive force of the liquid phase is stronger than the force of the gas phase, leading to surface tension phenomena [26]. The adhesive force $\mathbf{F}_a$ between fluid and solid particles is obtained as follows [30]:

$$\mathbf{F}_a = -w\psi(\mathbf{x})\sum_i^N \omega\left(|\mathbf{e}_i|^2\right)s(\mathbf{x} + \mathbf{e}_i)\,\mathbf{e}_i \tag{12}$$

where w is an indicator of the wetting behavior and reflects the interactive force between fluid and solid phases, called the solid-fluid interaction parameter. The LB model does not explicitly include the contact angle [29]. By adjusting w, we can obtain different contact angles. The wall density s has a value equal to 0 and 1 for fluid nodes and solid nodes, respectively. In Equations (11) and (12), the effective mass $\psi(\mathbf{x})$ is obtained by choosing an equation of state (EOS) [35]. The EOS describes the relation between the density of the gas and liquid phases for a given pressure and temperature [35,36]. The choice of a suitable EOS is based on different criteria [35,37]. The first criterion is the choice of the maximum density ratio between liquid and gas phases. The second criterion is to avoid the appearance of spurious currents at the interface of different phases. Spurious currents are present in most multiphase models and higher density ratios promote larger spurious currents. The appearance of large spurious currents makes a numerical simulation unstable and leads to divergence. It is important in a LBM with a high density ratio to reduce the appearance of these spurious currents as much as possible. The third criterion relates to the choice of the temperature ratio T_{min}/T_c, where T_c is the critical temperature. According to the Maxwell equal area construction rule, $T < T_c$ leads to the coexistence of two phases. At a lower temperature ratio, spurious currents appear and the simulation becomes less stable. The last criterion relates to the agreement between a mechanical stability solution and thermodynamic theory. Choosing a proper EOS model reduces the appearance of spurious currents and leads to a thermodynamically consistent behavior [35]. Recently, Yuan and Schaefer [35] investigated the incorporation of various EOS models in a single component multiphase LB model and, based on their study, we apply the Carnahan-Starling (C-S) EOS. The C-S EOS generates lower spurious currents and applies to wider temperature ratio ranges. The EOS is given below:

$$p = \rho RT \frac{1 + b\rho/4 + (b\rho/4)^2 - (b\rho/4)^3}{(1 - b\rho/4)^3} - a\rho^2 \tag{13}$$

where P is the pressure, T is the temperature and R is the ideal gas constant equal to 1 in the LB model. The attraction parameter $a = 0.4963(RT_c)^2/p_c$ is chosen equal to 1 and the repulsion parameter $b = 0.1873RT_c/p_c$ is chosen equal to 4, with $T_c = 0.094$ and $p_c = 0.13044$. The effective mass ψ is calculated by:

$$\psi(\rho) = \sqrt{\frac{2(p - c_s^2 \rho)}{Gc_0}} \tag{14}$$

Substituting Equation (13) into Equation (14), we get:

$$\psi = \sqrt{\frac{2\left(\rho RT \dfrac{1 + b\rho/4 + (b\rho/4)^2 - (b\rho/4)^3}{(1 - b\rho/4)^3} - a\rho^2 - \dfrac{\rho}{3}\right)}{Gc_0}} \tag{15}$$

where c_0 equals 1 and G equals −1 to obtain a positive value inside the square root of Equations (14) and (15).

3. Validation and Parametrization

As validation, dynamic capillary rise is studied and compared with the analytical solution. Since the multiphase LB model does not provide an explicit relation for surface tension and contact angle [29], the contact angle as a function of the solid-fluid interaction parameter w is determined.

3.1. Dynamic Capillary Intrusion

A capillary intrusion test is chosen to assess the capacity of the pseudopotential model to simulate a moving contact line problem governed by capillary forces [38]. The velocity of a liquid intruding two-dimensional parallel plates, shown in Figure 2b, results from the balance between the pressure difference across the phase interface and the viscous force experienced by the intruding liquid. Neglecting the influence of the viscosity of gas, gravity and inertial forces, the force balance results in [39,40]:

$$\sigma \cos(\theta) = \frac{6}{D} \mu_L x \frac{dx}{dt} \tag{16}$$

where θ is the equilibrium contact angle between liquid and solid, D is the width between plates, μ_L is the dynamic viscosity of the liquid and x is the position of the interface. The surface tension σ in Equation (16) is determined from the Laplace law describing the pressure difference across the interface of a spherical droplet [41]. The dynamic viscosity is defined as the product of the kinematic viscosity v and the liquid density, $\mu_L = v \times \rho$, with $v = 1/6$ lattice units. Figure 2a illustrates the two-dimensional computational domain of 1600×80 lattices used for the capillary intrusion test. Periodic boundary conditions are imposed on all boundaries of the computational domain. The parallel plates of the capillary are positioned between lattices 400 to 1200 of the domain. The boundaries of the plates are treated as walls and are represented by thick black lines in Figure 2a. They have an equilibrium contact angle of 50°, equivalent to a solid-fluid interaction parameter $w = -0.06$. The density ratio equals $\rho/\rho_c = 9.4$ at $T/T_c = 0.85$. The time evolution of the interface position as obtained from the LBM shows a good agreement with Equation (16), as shown in Figure 2b. Based on this dynamic capillary intrusion test, we conclude that the Shan-Chen pseudopotential LB model is adequate to simulate capillary-driven flow.

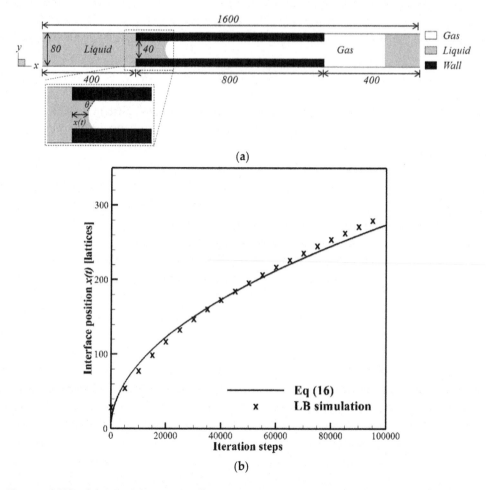

Figure 2. LBM validation of dynamic capillary intrusion test for $T/T_c= 0.85$: (**a**) computational domain; and (**b**) comparison between the LB simulation results and analytical solution of the position of phase interface as a function of time (iteration step).

3.2. Contact Angle

The equilibrium contact angle of a liquid droplet on a flat solid surface is studied by changing the solid-fluid interaction parameter w. At negative value, $w < 0$, the surface is hydrophilic with a contact angle $\theta < 90°$ and the droplet spreads on the surface. On the contrary, at $w > 0$, the solid surface is hydrophobic and a liquid droplet forms a contact angle $\theta > 90°$. A series of simulations are carried out in which an initially three-dimensional hemisphere droplet is placed on a horizontal solid surface. The simulations are performed in a 200 × 200 × 200 lattice domain with the top and bottom boundaries modeled as solid walls and the left, right, front and back boundaries as periodic boundaries. The radius of the liquid droplet is chosen to be 30 lattices at $T/T_c = 0.85$. After reaching steady state, the contact angle is measured using the method LB-ADSA in Image J [42].

The equilibrium contact angle in the function of w is illustrated by the inserted snapshots of three-dimensional iso-surfaces and cross-sections in Figure 3. With increasing values of the solid-fluid interaction parameter w, the adhesive force decreases and the surface become more and more hydrophobic. Inversely, when w is negative, the surface is hydrophilic and the droplet spreads on the surface. This relation between the solid-fluid interaction parameter and contact angle will be used in the study of pore and corner arc menisci in polygonal tubes.

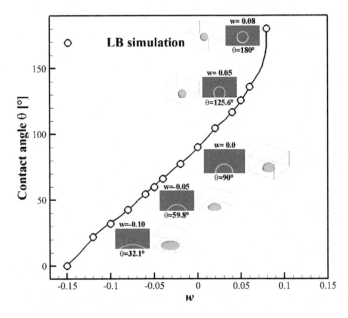

Figure 3. LBM results of contact angle test: equilibrium contact angles θ as function of solid-fluid interaction parameter w for $T/T_c = 0.85$.

4. Setup and Boundary Conditions

Two different polygonal tubes are simulated: square ($n = 4$) and triangular ($n = 3$). The cross-sections are circumscribed by a circle with a radius of $r = 100$ lattices for the square tube and a radius of $r = 200$ lattices for the triangular tube, as shown in Figure 4a,b.

Two cases are considered. The first case is when the contact angle is between $\pi/2$ and the critical contact angle $\theta_c = \pi/n$ (45° for square, 60° for triangular tube) and only a pore meniscus is built. The second case is when the contact angle is smaller than the critical contact angle and both pore and corner arc menisci are formed.

For the square tube, the domain size is $142 \times 142 \times 300$ lattices for the pore meniscus case and $142 \times 142 \times 500$ lattices for the corner arc menisci case. The spatial resolution Δx is 1 μm per lattice. This resolution has been chosen based on a mesh grid sensitivity for the corner arc menisci case, which is presented below in the result section.

For the triangular tube, the regular lattice grid results in a zigzag boundary, at least for two boundaries when the mesh is aligned to one side. This zigzag boundary introduces an artificial roughness, which in combination with the full bounce-back boundary condition produces some mesh-dependent results, as will be shown below. The bounce-back boundary condition represents a no-slip boundary condition with zero velocity at the wall. To improve the quality of the results, two measures are taken in this study. First the spatial resolution is increased: Δx equals 0.5 μm per lattice. As a result, the domain consists of $292 \times 290 \times 600$ lattices for the pore meniscus case and $292 \times 290 \times 1000$ lattices for the corner arc meniscus case. Second, the mesh is turned with an angle of 15° to decrease the side roughness (see Figure 4c). However, even when applying these measures, the corners show some roughness, especially corner 1.

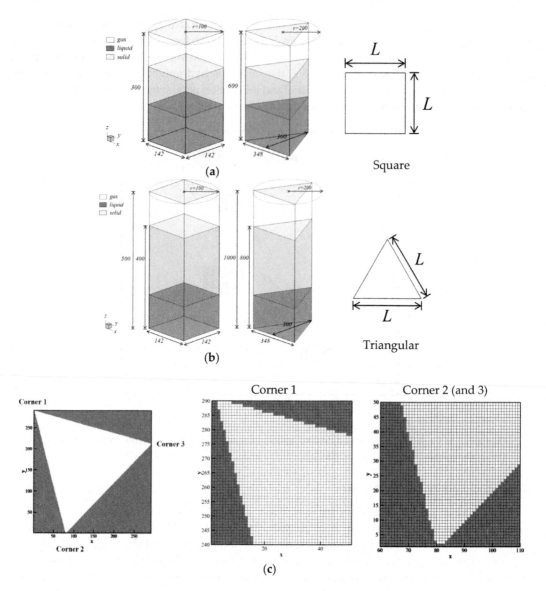

Figure 4. Schematic geometries of polygonal tubes: (**a**) computational domains for pore meniscus case, (**b**) computational domains for corner arc menisci case; and (**c**) computational mesh details for the triangular tube at different corners.

An alternative would be to apply different boundary conditions, such as the curved, the half bounce-back or the moving boundary conditions, as these three methods allow tracking the interface independently from the mesh [43,44], but such investigation was considered out of the scope of this study.

The polygonal tube is initially filled by liquid to a height of 100 lattices from the bottom, as shown in Figure 4a,b. The redistribution of the liquid is then calculated by the LB method. Liquid and gas densities are 0.28 and 0.0299 lattice units, respectively corresponding to a density ratio $\rho/\rho_c = 9.4$ at $T/T_c = 0.85$. Different contact angle ranges are applied. For the square tube, the contact angle ranges from 42.6° to 136.5° as related to a solid-fluid interaction parameter w ranging from −0.08 to 0.06. For the triangular tube, the contact angle ranges from 59.8° to 125.6° as related to a solid-fluid interaction parameter w ranging from −0.05 to 0.05. As shown in Figure 4a,b, bounce-back boundary conditions are imposed on all sides, except for the top 100 lattices on the three or four vertical sides where periodic boundary conditions are imposed to simulate an open capillary tube.

As mentioned above, gravity is neglected given the capillary length, L_{cap}, defined at standard temperature and pressure to be [11,45]

$$L_{cap} = \sqrt{\frac{\sigma}{\rho g}} \tag{17}$$

and equal to 2 mm for water. The characteristic length of our system equals the radius of the circumscribed circle shown in Figure 4a,b, thus 100 and 200 µm, which is smaller than the capillary length. Therefore, surface tension effects are dominant and the gravitational effect can be neglected.

All numerical simulations are run by parallel computing based on MPI (Message Passing Interface) at Los Alamos National Laboratory (LANL) high performance computing cluster. The cluster aggregate performance is 352 TF/s with 102.4 TB of memory for 38,400 cores. Each simulation is run on 120 or 200 processor cores for pore meniscus or corner arc meniscus simulations in square tubes and on 400 or 800 processor cores for pore meniscus or corner arc meniscus simulations in the triangular tubes, and requires 16 h to run 20,000 or 40,000 time steps, respectively.

5. Results and Discussion

5.1. Pore Meniscus

When the contact angle is larger than the critical contact angle, $\theta \geqslant \theta_c$, the liquid wets the tube walls and a pore meniscus is formed in the tube. Figure 5 shows, as an example, snapshots of pore menisci for square and triangular tubes with hydrophilic and hydrophobic surfaces after reaching steady state. For the square configuration, the meniscus is regular (Figure 5a–d), while for the triangular configuration (Figure 5e,f) the pore menisci show different heights at each corner, especially at a small contact angle (hydrophilic case). This observation is explained by the artificially introduced wall roughness for the triangular tube, as also observed by other authors such as Dos Santos et al. [28]. We found that corner 1 in Figure 4c, which has the highest roughness, shows the lowest height, while corners 2 and 3 show the same height.

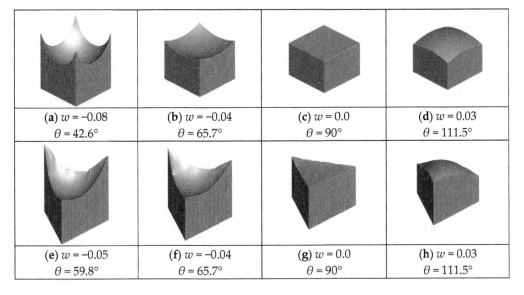

(a) $w = -0.08$	(b) $w = -0.04$	(c) $w = 0.0$	(d) $w = 0.03$
$\theta = 42.6°$	$\theta = 65.7°$	$\theta = 90°$	$\theta = 111.5°$
(e) $w = -0.05$	(f) $w = -0.04$	(g) $w = 0.0$	(h) $w = 0.03$
$\theta = 59.8°$	$\theta = 65.7°$	$\theta = 90°$	$\theta = 111.5°$

Figure 5. Liquid configurations in square and triangular tubes for different contact angles after reaching steady state.

Results are presented in terms of height of pore meniscus *versus* cosine of the contact angle after reaching equilibrium. The height is defined as the difference between the bottom and the top of the meniscus (see insets of Figure 6a,c). Since the height for the triangular tube is not equal in all corners, the average of the heights in the different corners of the tube is used. Figure 6b shows, for the square tube, diagonal profiles of the pore meniscus as a function of the solid-fluid interaction parameter w. With increasing $\cos\theta$ (more hydrophilic), the height increases. This can be explained by the fact that with increasing $\cos\theta$ or decreasing contact angle, the adhesive force $\mathbf{F}_a$ between solid and fluid in Equation (12) increases and the pressure difference to maintain hydrostatic equilibrium increases, resulting in an increase of the height. At very high (low) contact angles, the height increases (decreases) even more, resulting in an S-shape curve.

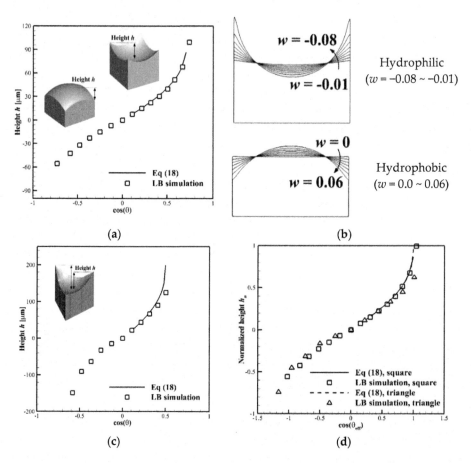

Figure 6. Height of the pore meniscus h as a function of cosine of contact angle θ. Comparison between simulation results and analytical solution: **(a)** square tube; **(b)** diagonal profiles for square tube, for different solid-fluid interaction value w; **(c)** triangular tube. **(d)** Normalized height of the pore meniscus as a function of cosine of effective contact angle θ_{eff} for square and triangular tubes and comparison with analytical solutions.

An analytical solution for the height h for a n-sided polygonal tube in the hydrophilic case ($\theta < \pi/2$) is given by [11]:

$$h = r\sin\alpha \left[1 - \sqrt{1 - (\cos\theta/\sin\alpha)^2} \right]/\cos\theta \tag{18}$$

where α is the half of the corner angle:

$$\alpha = (n-2)\,\pi/(2n) \tag{19}$$

For the square tube, the LBM heights are in good agreement with the analytical solution. For the triangular tube, the simulated average height is lower than the analytical solution for higher values of $\cos\theta$ (more hydrophilic). This difference is explained by the zigzag boundary and the artificially introduced roughness. Since the height is under-predicted in one corner, the average value is also too low. This is in agreement with the observations of Quéré [46], showing that hydrophilicity of the surface increases with roughness.

Equation (18) can be rewritten in a normalized form as:

$$\frac{h}{r} = \frac{1}{\cos\theta_{eff}}\left[1 - \sqrt{1 - \left(\cos\theta_{eff}\right)^2}\right] \tag{20}$$

with $\cos\theta_{eff} = \cos\theta/\sin\alpha$ and θ_{eff} as the equivalent contact angle. Figure 6d shows the normalized height h/r *versus* cosine of the equivalent contact angle. We observe that the analytical solutions and LB results for square and triangular tubes collapse onto a single curve. This shows that the LB results for the triangular tube, although suffering from the artificial roughness introduced, agree well over the total hydrophobic and hydrophilic range with the results of the square tube, which does not suffer from an artificial roughness.

5.2. Corner Arc Menisci

When the contact angle is smaller than the critical contact angle, $\theta < \theta_c$, the liquid invades the corners, forming corner arc menisci. We consider two contact angles of $22°$ and $32°$ ($w = -0.12$ and -0.10), both lower than the critical contact angle for the square and triangular tubes, in order to study the influence of the hydrophilic character of the surface in more detail. Figure 7a,b show snapshots of the pore and corner arc menisci as a function of time (iteration step) for the square and triangular tubes. Figure 7c shows diagonal profiles of the menisci over the height and cross-sections of the meniscus at one corner as a function of time for the square tube. For both tubes, at the early stage, the liquid invades the corners at a small thickness and reaches the top of the tube in a short time. With increasing time, the corner arc menisci thicken while their curvature decreases. At the same time, the pore menisci at the bottom evolve from a more flat shape to a concave shape. This process continues until equilibrium is reached. For the triangular tube, corner arc menisci develop only at two corners, while one corner does not show the presence of a corner arc meniscus, or it does so only at a late time. As mentioned before, this observation is attributed to the artificial roughness introduced by the zigzag surfaces, which is higher in corner 1 than in corners 2 and 3 (see Figure 4c), where the former corner is not invaded. The profiles in Figure 7c show that the thickness of the corner arc menisci is not constant over the height, since at the bottom its thickness is influenced by the pore meniscus, and at the top by the edge of the tube. We remark that the thickness of the corner arc meniscus at equilibrium depends on the initial liquid volume present in the tube. In the case of an infinite reservoir, the corner arc menisci of two adjacent corners join. The cross-sections show that the thickness and curvature for the more hydrophilic surface ($\theta = 22°$) are higher compared to the less hydrophilic case ($\theta = 32°$) at the same time step.

Figure 8a,b show the time evolution of the degree of saturation for the square and triangular tubes for the contact angles of $22°$ and $32°$ in a log-log plot. The degree of saturation is defined as the ratio of the cross-area occupied by liquid at corners to the area of the full cross-section of the tube and is calculated at the mid-height of the corner arc menisci. The curves for the two geometries and two contact angles show a similar shape. The results show that the corner filling process is faster at an early time and then slows down somewhat. As expected, the degree of saturation at a lower contact angle (more hydrophilic) is higher compared to the degree of saturation at a higher contact angle. However, this influence of contact angle is smaller when the corner angle is smaller (triangular tube).

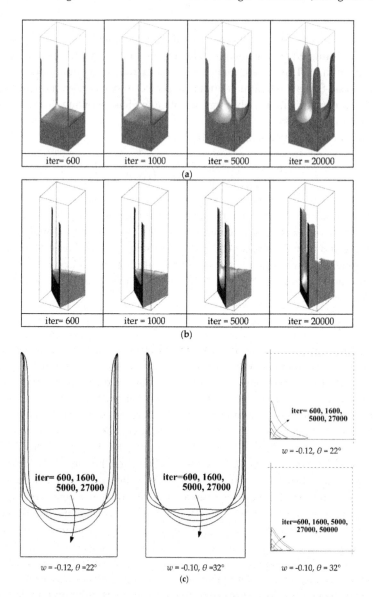

Figure 7. Liquid configuration *versus* time (iteration count) for $\theta = 22°$: (a) square tube; (b) triangular tube; and (c) diagonal profiles and cross-sections of a corner arc menisci for square tube at different iteration steps for $\theta = 22°$ and $32°$.

Further, we determined the curvature of the corner arc menisci. The normalized curvature C_n is given by [10]:

$$C_n = \frac{(L/2)\cos(\alpha + \theta)}{L_{contact}\sin\alpha} \tag{21}$$

where L is the side length of the tube, α is the half corner angle dependent on the side parameter n, θ is the contact angle and $L_{contact}$ is the side length of the corner arc meniscus wetting the side of the tube. The contact length $L_{contact}$ is determined from the LBM results at mid-height of the corner arc menisci. We note that the phase interface in LBM is not sharp but gradually decreases from liquid to gas density over three to five lattices. The position of a phase interface is evaluated at the average density between liquid and gas. Therefore, there is an uncertainty on the contact length $L_{contact}$ of around two lattices [26].

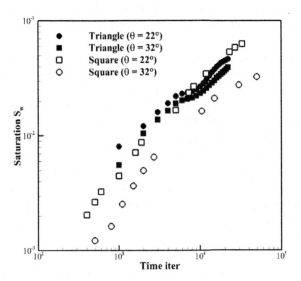

Figure 8. Log-log plot of degree of saturation S_w *versus* time for contact angles $\theta = 22°$ and $32°$ for square and triangular tubes.

Figure 9a shows the curvature *versus* degree of saturation for the two contact angles $32°$ and $22°$ for the square tube. The results for the triangular tube are not represented, since the contact length could not be determined unambiguously due to the artificial roughness problem of the wall, as mentioned above. An analytical solution for the degree of saturation S_w in the function of the curvature is given by [10]:

$$S_w = \frac{\tan\alpha}{C_n^2} \left[\frac{\cos\theta}{\sin\alpha} \cos(\alpha + \theta) - \frac{\pi}{2} \left(1 - \frac{\alpha + \theta}{90} \right) \right] \tag{22}$$

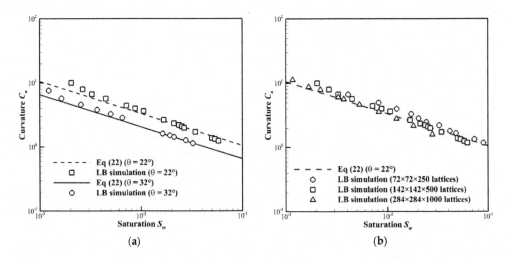

(a)   (b)

Figure 9. Log-log plot of curvature C_n *versus* degree of saturation S_w for square tube and comparison with analytical solution: **(a)** for different contact angles $\theta = 22°$ and $32°$; **(b)** Grid sensitivity analysis for coarse, reference and fine mesh.

In Figure 9a, the LB simulation results are compared with the analytical solution in a log-log plot and an overall good agreement is observed. At a low degree of saturation, the LB results over-predict the curvature slightly, which is attributed to the uncertainty (error) in determining the contact length $L_{contact}$. At a small contact length, an error of two lattices can have a non-negligible effect, as the length $L_{contact}$ appears in Equation (21) in the denominator. Based on these, we suspect that the contact length is slightly underestimated.

Finally, we report our mesh sensitivity study. Three meshes were selected for the square tube with a contact angle $\theta = 22°$ below the critical angle to study the most critical case of corner arc meniscus formation. The meshes each differ in resolution with a factor of 2: a coarser mesh of $72 \times 72 \times 250$ lattices ($\Delta x = 2$ μm/lattice), a reference mesh of $142 \times 142 \times 500$ lattices ($\Delta x = 1$ μm/lattice) and a finer mesh of $284 \times 284 \times 1000$ lattices ($\Delta x = 0.5$ μm/lattice). Figure 9b gives the curvature *versus* degree of saturation for the three meshes and compares these LBM results with the analytical solution. An overall good agreement is obtained, which convinced us that the reference mesh is fine enough to produce mesh-insensitive results for the square case. For the triangular tube, the results are more mesh-sensitive since the resolution also determines the artificial roughness introduced. This is the reason why, for the triangular tube, we chose the finest mesh, which is a compromise between calculation time and accuracy.

6. Conclusions

In this study, capillary rise in polygonal tubes is investigated, taking into account the appearance of a pore meniscus and corner arc menisci, the presence of which depends on the contact angle. Lattice Boltzmann (LB) simulations are performed using the Shan-Chen pseudopotential multiphase LB model. This multiphase LB model is validated by a dynamic capillary intrusion test. A contact angle test is performed to obtain the relation between the contact angle and the solid-fluid interaction parameter used in the LBM. The multiphase LB model is used to study capillary rise in square and triangular tubes with different contact angles and the LB results are compared with analytical solutions and an overall good agreement is obtained. This validated LB model for corner flow will be further used to analyze the effect of corner flow in more complex porous configurations.

The main conclusions of the present study are as follows:

1.   When the contact angle is larger than the critical contact angle, $\theta \geqslant \theta_c$, only a pore meniscus develops and its height increases with the decreasing contact angle for both square and triangular tubes. The LB simulation results show good agreement with the analytical solution. At a very low contact angle in the triangular tube, the height is under-predicted due to the artificial roughness introduced. The LB heights normalized with the circumscribed radius for hydrophobic and hydrophilic surfaces as a function of the effective contact angle collapse into a single S-shaped curve for square and triangular tubes.

2.   When the contact angle is smaller than the critical contact angle, $\theta < \theta_c$, LB simulations predict that the liquid invades the corners, forming corner arc menisci. The relation between the degree of saturation and the curvature of the corner arc menisci follows the Mayer and Stoewe-Princen (MS-P) model. The study of the time-dependence of the degree of saturation shows corners filling faster at an early stage and corner arc menisci thickening at a later stage.

In this study, the characteristic length is below the capillary length of water and, thus, the surface tension force is more dominant than the gravitational force. Therefore, the gravitational effect is not taken into account in our LB simulation. However, at a larger scale, gravity effects become dominant and should be considered. Furthermore, a full bounce-back boundary condition is applied, demonstrating its limitations when modeling polygonal tubes where the regular meshing is not aligned with the tube sides, leading to zigzag surfaces and the introduction of an artificial surface roughness. To describe the capillary rise in angled or curved geometries, alternative boundary conditions should be considered, such as the curved boundary condition, the half bounce-back boundary condition or the moving boundary, allowing the interface between solid and fluid to be independent of the mesh. This work illustrates that the LBM is a suitable and promising tool for further studies for a better understanding of capillary flow phenomena in angled pore geometry in porous media.

Acknowledgments: This work has been supported by Swiss National Science Foundation project no. 200021-143651. Li Chen and Qinjun Kang acknowledge the support from LANL's LDRD Program and Institutional Computing Program.

Author Contributions: Soyoun Son, Dominique Derome and Jan Carmeliet conceived and designed the research plan; Soyoun Son, Li Chen and Qinjun Kang implemented the model, Soyoun Son performed the simulations; Soyoun Son, Dominique Derome and Jan Carmeliet analyzed the data; all authors participated in writing the paper.

Conflicts of Interest: The authors declare no conflict of interest.

References

1. Concus, P.; Finn, R. On capillary free surfaces in the absence of gravity. *Acta Math.* **1974**, *132*, 177–198. [CrossRef]
2. Concus, P.; Finn, R. Dichotomous behavior of capillary surfaces in zero gravity. *Microgravity Sci. Technol.* **1990**, *3*, 87–92.
3. Wong, H.; Morris, S.; Radke, C. Three-dimensional menisci in polygonal capillaries. *J. Colloid Interface Sci.* **1992**, *148*, 317–336. [CrossRef]
4. Dong, M.; Chatzis, I. The imbibition and flow of a wetting liquid along the corners of a square capillary tube. *J. Colloid Interface Sci.* **1995**, *172*, 278–288. [CrossRef]
5. Princen, H. Capillary phenomena in assemblies of parallel cylinders: I. Capillary rise between two cylinders. *J. Colloid Interface Sci.* **1969**, *30*, 69–75. [CrossRef]
6. Princen, H. Capillary phenomena in assemblies of parallel cylinders: II. Capillary rise in systems with more than two cylinders. *J. Colloid Interface Sci.* **1969**, *30*, 359–371. [CrossRef]
7. Mayer, R.P.; Stowe, R.A. Mercury porosimetry—Breakthrough pressure for penetration between packed spheres. *J. Colloid Sci.* **1965**, *20*, 893–911. [CrossRef]
8. Princen, H. Capillary phenomena in assemblies of parallel cylinders: III. Liquid columns between horizontal parallel cylinders. *J. Colloid Interface Sci.* **1970**, *34*, 171–184. [CrossRef]
9. Bico, J.; Quéré, D. Rise of liquids and bubbles in angular capillary tubes. *J. Colloid Interface Sci.* **2002**, *247*, 162–166. [CrossRef] [PubMed]
10. Ma, S.; Mason, G.; Morrow, N.R. Effect of contact angle on drainage and imbibition in regular polygonal tubes. *Colloids Surf. A Physicochem. Eng. Asp.* **1996**, *117*, 273–291. [CrossRef]
11. Feng, J.; Rothstein, J.P. Simulations of novel nanostructures formed by capillary effects in lithography. *J. Colloid Interface Sci.* **2011**, *354*, 386–395. [CrossRef] [PubMed]
12. Hirt, C.W.; Nichols, B.D. Volume of fluid (VOF) method for the dynamics of free boundaries. *J. Comput. Phys.* **1981**, *39*, 201–225. [CrossRef]
13. Sussman, M.; Fatemi, E.; Smereka, P.; Osher, S. An improved level set method for incompressible two-phase flows. *Comput. Fluids* **1998**, *27*, 663–680. [CrossRef]
14. Tryggvason, G.; Esmaeeli, A.; Lu, J.; Biswas, S. Direct numerical simulations of gas/liquid multiphase flows. *Fluid Dyn. Res.* **2006**, *38*, 660–681. [CrossRef]
15. Owkes, M.; Desjardins, O. A computational framework for conservative, three-dimensional, unsplit, geometric transport with application to the volume-of-fluid (VOF) method. *J. Comput. Phys.* **2014**, *270*, 587–612. [CrossRef]
16. Chen, S.Y.; Doolen, G.D. Lattice Boltzmann methode for fluid flows. *Annu. Rev. Fluid Mech.* **1998**, *30*, 329–364.
17. Aidun, C.K.; Clausen, J.R. Lattice-Boltzmann method for complex flows. *Annu. Rev. Fluid Mech.* **2010**, *42*, 439–472. [CrossRef]
18. Chen, L.; Kang, Q.; Carey, B.; Tao, W.Q. Pore-scale study of diffusion-reaction processes involving dissolution and precipitation using the lattice Boltzmann method. *Int. J. Heat Mass Transf.* **2014**, *75*, 483–496. [CrossRef]
19. Gunstensen, A.K.; Rothman, D.H.; Zaleski, S.; Zanetti, G. Lattice Boltzmann model of immiscible fluids. *Phys. Rev. A* **1991**, *43*, 4320. [CrossRef] [PubMed]
20. Swift, M.R.; Orlandini, E.; Osborn, W.; Yeomans, J. Lattice Boltzmann simulations of liquid-gas and binary fluid systems. *Phys. Rev. E* **1996**, *54*, 5041. [CrossRef]

21. He, X.; Chen, S.; Zhang, R. A lattice Boltzmann scheme for incompressible multiphase flow and its application in simulation of Rayleigh-Taylor instability. *J. Comput. Phys.* **1999**, *152*, 642–663. [CrossRef]

22. Shan, X.; Chen, H. Lattice Boltzmann model for simulating flows with multiple phases and components. *Phys. Rev. E* **1993**, *47*, 1815–1819. [CrossRef]

23. Shan, X.; Chen, H. Simulation of nonideal gases and liquid-gas phase transitions by the lattice Boltzmann equation. *Phys. Rev. E* **1994**, *49*, 2941. [CrossRef]

24. Chen, L.; Luan, H.B.; He, Y.L.; Tao, W.Q. Pore-scale flow and mass transport in gas diffusion layer of proton exchange membrane fuel cell with interdigitated flow fields. *Int. J. Thermal Sci.* **2012**, *51*, 132–144. [CrossRef]

25. Chen, L.; Kang, Q.; Mu, Y.; He, Y.-L.; Tao, W.-Q. A critical review of the pseudopotential multiphase lattice Boltzmann model: Methods and applications. *Int. J. Heat Mass Transfer* **2014**, *76*, 210–236. [CrossRef]

26. Thorne, D.T.; Michael, C. *Lattice Boltzmann Modeling An Introduction for Geoscientists and Engineers*; Springer: Miami, FL, USA, 2006.

27. Raiskinmäki, P.; Shakib-Manesh, A.; Jäsberg, A.; Koponen, A.; Merikoski, J.; Timonen, J. Lattice-Boltzmann simulation of capillary rise dynamics. *J. Stat. Phys.* **2002**, *107*, 143–158. [CrossRef]

28. Dos Santos, L.O.; Wolf, F.G.; Philippi, P.C. Dynamics of interface displacement in capillary flow. *J. Stat. Phys.* **2005**, *121*, 197–207. [CrossRef]

29. Lu, G.; Wang, X.-D.; Duan, Y.-Y. Study on initial stage of capillary rise dynamics. *Colloids Surf. A Physicochem. Eng. Asp.* **2013**, *433*, 95–103. [CrossRef]

30. Martys, N.S.; Chen, H. Simulation of multicomponent fluids in complex three-dimensional geometries by the lattice Boltzmann method. *Phys. Rev. E* **1996**, *53*, 743–750. [CrossRef]

31. Hecht, M.; Harting, J. Implementation of on-site velocity boundary conditions for D3Q19 lattice Boltzmann simulations. *J. Stat. Mech.: Theory Exp.* **2010**, *2010*, P01018. [CrossRef]

32. Li, Q.; Luo, K.H.; Li, X.J. Forcing scheme in pseudopotential lattice Boltzmann model for multiphase flows. *Phys. Rev. E* **2012**, *86*, 016709. [CrossRef] [PubMed]

33. Huang, H.; Krafczyk, M.; Lu, X. Forcing term in single-phase and Shan-Chen-type multiphase lattice Boltzmann models. *Phys. Re. E* **2011**, *84*, 046710. [CrossRef] [PubMed]

34. Kupershtokh, A.; Medvedev, D.; Karpov, D. On equations of state in a lattice Boltzmann method. *Comput. Math. Appl.* **2009**, *58*, 965–974. [CrossRef]

35. Yuan, P.; Schaefer, L. Equations of state in a lattice Boltzmann model. *Phys. Fluids* **2006**, *18*, 042101. [CrossRef]

36. Azwadi, C.N.; Witrib, M.A. Simulation of multicomponent multiphase flow using lattice Boltzmann method. In Proceedings of the 4th International Meeting of Advances in Thermofluids (IMAT 2011); AIP Publishing: Melaka, Malaysia, 2012.

37. Chen, L.; Kang, Q.; Robinson, B.A.; He, Y.-L.; Tao, W.-Q. Pore-scale modeling of multiphase reactive transport with phase transitions and dissolution-precipitation processes in closed systems. *Phys. Rev. E* **2013**, *87*, 043306. [CrossRef] [PubMed]

38. Liu, H.; Valocchi, A.; Kang, Q.; Werth, C. Pore-Scale Simulations of Gas Displacing Liquid in a Homogeneous Pore Network Using the Lattice Boltzmann Method. *Transport Porous Media* **2013**, *99*, 555–580. [CrossRef]

39. Diotallevi, F.; Biferale, L.; Chibbaro, S.; Lamura, A.; Pontrelli, G.; Sbragaglia, M.; Succi, S.; Toschi, F. Capillary filling using lattice Boltzmann equations: The case of multi-phase flows. *Eur. Phys. J. Spec. Top.* **2009**, *166*, 111–116. [CrossRef]

40. Pooley, C.; Kusumaatmaja, H.; Yeomans, J. Modelling capillary filling dynamics using lattice Boltzmann simulations. *Eur. Phys. J.-Spec. Top.* **2009**, *171*, 63–71. [CrossRef]

41. Son, S.; Chen, L.; Derome, D.; Carmeliet, J. Numerical study of gravity-driven droplet displacement on a surface using the pseudopotential multiphase lattice Boltzmann model with high density ratio. *Comput. Fluids* **2015**, *117*, 42–53. [CrossRef]

42. Stalder, A.F.; Melchior, T.; Müller, M.; Sage, D.; Blu, T.; Unser, M. Low-bond axisymmetric drop shape analysis for surface tension and contact angle measurements of sessile drops. *Colloids Surf. A Physicochem. Eng. Asp.* **2010**, *364*, 72–81. [CrossRef]

43. Mei, R.; Luo, L.-S.; Shyy, W. An accurate curved boundary treatment in the lattice Boltzmann method. *J. Comput. Phys.* **1999**, *155*, 307–330. [CrossRef]

44. Mei, R.; Shyy, W.; Yu, D.; Luo, L.-S. Lattice Boltzmann method for 3-D flows with curved boundary. *J. Comput. Phys.* **2000**, *161*, 680–699. [CrossRef]
45. De Gennes, P.G. Wetting: Statics and dynamics. *Rev. Modern Phys.* **1985**, *57*, 827. [CrossRef]
46. Quéré, D. Rough ideas on wetting. *Phys. A: Stat. Mech. Appl.* **2002**, *313*, 32–46. [CrossRef]

3

A New Method to Infer Advancement of Saline Front in Coastal Groundwater Systems by 3D: The Case of Bari (Southern Italy) Fractured Aquifer

Costantino Masciopinto * and Domenico Palmiotta

Consiglio Nazionale delle Ricerche, Istituto di Ricerca Sulle Acque, Reparto di Chimica e Tecnologia delle Acque, 5 via Francesco De Blasio, 70132 Bari, Italy; domenico.palmiotta@ba.irsa.cnr.it
* Correspondence: costantino.masciopinto@ba.irsa.cnr.it

Academic Editors: Qinjun Kang and Li Chen

Abstract: A new method to study 3D saline front advancement in coastal fractured aquifers has been presented. Field groundwater salinity was measured in boreholes of the Bari (Southern Italy) coastal aquifer with depth below water table. Then, the Ghyben-Herzberg freshwater/saltwater (50%) sharp interface and saline front position were determined by model simulations of the freshwater flow in groundwater. Afterward, the best-fit procedure between groundwater salinity measurements, at assigned water depth of 1.0 m in boreholes, and distances of each borehole from the modelled freshwater/saltwater saline front was used to convert each position (x, y) in groundwater to the water salinity concentration at depth of 1.0 m. Moreover, a second best-fit procedure was applied to the salinity measurements in boreholes with depth z. These results provided a grid file (x, y, z, salinity) suitable for plotting the actual Bari aquifer salinity by 3D maps. Subsequently, in order to assess effects of pumping on the saltwater-freshwater transition zone in the coastal aquifer, the Navier-Stokes (N-S) equations were applied to study transient density-driven flow and salt mass transport into freshwater of a single fracture. The rate of seawater/freshwater interface advancement given by the N-S solution was used to define the progression of saline front in Bari groundwater, starting from the actual salinity 3D map. The impact of pumping of 335 $L \cdot s^{-1}$ during the transition period of 112.8 days was easily highlighted on 3D salinity maps of Bari aquifer.

Keywords: coastal aquifers; tracer tests; over-abstraction; modeling; salinity maps in 3D

1. Introduction

Groundwater over-abstractions typically can lower water table level and reduce freshwater fluxes, leading to severe saltwater intrusion problems in several coastal and metropolitan areas [1–3]. However, water supply is necessary for regional economic development and even for energy production. For instance, renewable sources of energy associated with the salinity gradient can be recovered in coastal areas where freshwater is mixed with saltwater. The techniques to produce electric energy from salinity gradient use the pressure-retarded reverse osmosis process [4] and associated conversion technologies. In addition, also geothermal energy production at low enthalpy should also increase at a rate of 3%–4% in Italy until 2020 [5]. Both geothermal low-enthalpy technology and the pressure-retarded reverse osmosis method require freshwater supplies (*i.e.*, pumping) from coastal aquifers.

Subsequently, the subtraction of appreciable freshwater volumes from coastal aquifers cannot be always avoided and its real impact on groundwater should be adequately investigated. The salinity maps are useful tools for coastal groundwater management and they show how inland advancements of seawater may affect coastal aquifer quality. Chongo *et al.* [6] carried out an experimental work in Africa to define groundwater salinity variation map within the sedimentary formations of the

Barotse sub-basin in the Western Province of Zambia. 39 boreholes were used to construct a database for the geological model development in this study area. The GEOSCENE 3D (I-GIS, 2016, I-GIS, Risskov, Denmark) [7] software was employed for visualizing, interpreting, editing and publishing geological data. Data derived from field measurements were analyzed using the SiTEM SEMDI (Hydrogeophysics-Group-1, 2001, University of Aarhus, Aarhus, Denmark) [8] and Res2Dinv (Geomoto, Penang, Malaysia) [9] software. In the study area the distribution of most boreholes was somewhat unidirectional and it resulted in data gaps that make geo-modeling quite difficult. For this reason, authors proposed the use of pseudo (*i.e.*, imaginary) boreholes in order to reduce the data gaps. Other researchers [10] suggest the employment of empirical models such as the Archie's law (1942) [11] to improve the best fit of experimental data (*i.e.*, water electrical conductance) collected from wells. Lesch *et al.* [12] demonstrated the efficiency of the regression-based statistical method for predicting, at field scale, soil spatial salinity conditions, starting from rapidly acquired electromagnetic induction data. This regression model incorporates multiple measurements and their trends in order to increase the prediction accuracy of soil salinity maps.

In the present work a new method is presented for a rapid 3D visualization of saltwater-freshwater transition in coastal zone under new pumping stress conditions. The method requires field salinity measurements in boreholes and simulation results from two different flow models. The first model studies the steady groundwater flow in fractures by providing the Ghyben-Herzberg seawater/freshwater sharp interface toe position along the coast. Fracture transmissivity were derived from pumping and tracer (chlorophyllin) injection tests. The second flow model studies the transient density-driven flow of seawater into freshwater of a single fracture by means of the N-S equations. The result of the latter model was used to predict the transient advancement of saline front in fractures subjected to new pumping conditions.

2. Methodology

Groundwater flow modeling was addressed in a 3D set of horizontal and parallel fractures characterized by impermeable rock walls (Figure 1). Each horizontal fracture of the 3D set has a variable aperture in the x-y plane [13] of 7240×6300 m^2. Pumping and/or injection tests carried out into Bari wells, allowed the identification of the average aperture of all fractures of the set at each well position in order to determine the experimental variogram of spatial aperture covariance. Experiments on model calibrations and validations have been extensively reported by Masciopinto [14], Masciopinto *et al.* [13,15], and Masciopinto and Palmiotta [16]. The flow solution given by the flow model yields the freshwater discharge along the top border of domain. This freshwater discharge was used to determine the Ghyben-Herzberg sharp (50%) freshwater/saltwater interface [14]. These results defined also the saline front position along the coast.

At the second step (Figure 2), the groundwater salinity into a generic borehole of the Bari aquifer was fitted as a function of the distance of the same borehole from the saline front. For this interpolation, salinity measurements in 25 boreholes of the Bari coastal aquifer (Southern Italy) at the same depth of 1.0 m below the water table were used. The resulting best-fit equation was used to convert the generic grid node position of the computational domain with respect to the saline front into the groundwater salinity concentration (at the depth of 1.0 m). Moreover, a further best-fit procedure was applied to the salinity profiles collected into 17 boreholes in order to estimate the groundwater salinity concentration with depth z below water table. These groundwater concentrations (*i.e.*, discontinuous values) were used in RockWorks15 (RockWare Inc., Golden, CO, USA) to obtain a solid model (*i.e.*, continuous values) useful to visualize groundwater salinity 3D map at Bari coastal aquifer.

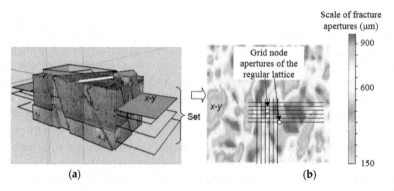

Figure 1. (a) Parallel set of horizontal (*x-y*) fractures with permeability equivalent to the real fractured medium; (b) modeled fracture apertures in each single fracture of the set: the aperture variation in the *x-y* plane is obtained by means of the experimental variogram derived from results of well pumping (or injection) tests.

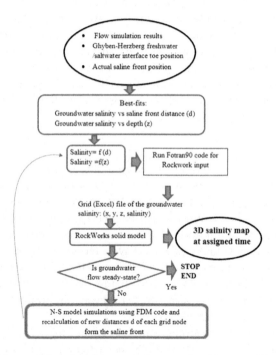

Figure 2. Flowchart of the applied methodology to produce transient 3D maps of the groundwater salinity.

Finally, the N-S solutions into a single fracture were used to define the inland progression of saline front into groundwater during saltwater-freshwater transition period due to a simulated new pumping, starting from the actual salinity data. The results produce groundwater salinity values (and 3D map), at each selected simulation time.

An alternative method to obtain the same groundwater salt concentrations on the freshwater-saltwater transition is application of specific type of software, such as HydroGeoSphere (Aquanty Inc., Waterloo, ON, Canada), or similar [17], which allows 3D simulations of density-driven flow system under transient conditions. Anyway the application of this type of models to discretely fractured media is very challenging [18] due to complexity of input data required to describe preferential flow pathways [19] and due to the unknown positions (and apertures) of actual fractures and their intersections, especially at a regional scale (>1000 m).

3. The Case Study and Field Tests

The Bari's coastal land portion (Puglia region, southern Italy) (Figure 3) has a catchment surface of around $10,000 \times 7000$ m^2 due to streams that flow into the Adriatic Sea. In this coastal area groundwater is confined within the limestone (Cretaceous) formation, and water flows in horizontal fractures in SW-NE direction, *i.e.*, towards the coast. Geologically, the Bari aquifer is located in the Murgia region. In the tested area (coastal area of the Murgia region), rock permeability is low and discontinuous both horizontally and vertically. The geological sequence of layers observed during borehole drilling, from top downward, is Pleistocene sandstone (3–5 m thick), Cretaceous limestone (26 m thick), and Jurassic dolomite (>20 m thick). Murgia shows neo-tectonic sub-vertical fractures of the Mesozoic rocks that are relatively frequent and barely open or are sealed by calcspar and terra rossa (bulk density 1.26 ± 0.1 g/cm^3). The Bari aquifer is not highly karstified. This means that calcite dissolution had taken place inside fractures of the Bari/IRSA aquifer, and an increase in hydraulic conductivity to 0.42 cm/s was found with respect to the quasi non-karstified limestone with 0.01–0.04 cm/s of hydraulic conductivity close (<1 km) to the sea coast.

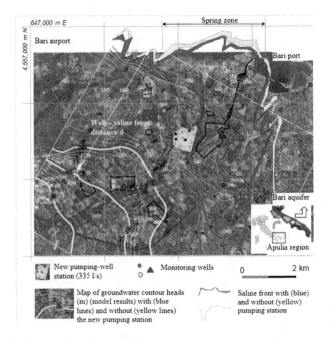

Figure 3. Spatial distribution of wells (red circles and tringles) and flow simulation results with distance d of each well from position of Ghyben-Herzberg saline front in groundwater. The yellow lines (and polygon) refer to actual groundwater flow simulation. The blue lines (and polygon) consider the flow modifications due to new pumping of 335 L·s^{-1}. The blue dashed line is the contour head at 1 m.

3.1. Field Set Up

Groundwater macroscopic parameters such as transmissivity T [$l^2 \cdot t^{-1}$] (l stand for length; t stands for time) and hydraulic conductivity K [$l \cdot t^{-1}$] were determined by inverting the semi-analytical solution of Thiem's equation. The results of 58 pumping tests and 10 tracer tests (Figure 4) carried out by IRSA on the Bari aquifer boreholes, were considered in this work. In particular, pumping (or injection) and tracer tests under undisturbed (or natural) gradient were carried out in order to estimate local values of both aquifer hydraulic transmissivity and groundwater specific discharge (see Table 1). The analytical solution of tracer (chlorophyllin) dispersion into the water was applied [13] to the breakthrough curves in Figure 4 in order to determine the horizontal water velocity in each borehole.

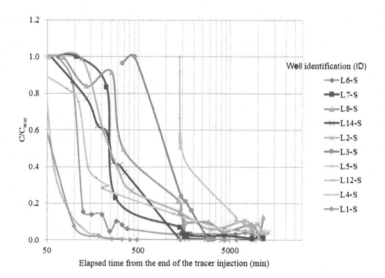

Figure 4. Breakthrough curves of relative tracer (chlorophyllin) concentrations during injection tests in ten boreholes of Bari aquifer.

Table 1. Network of monitored wells at the Bari fractured aquifer: Pumping and tracer test results.

Well ID	Coordinates (UTM) E	Coordinates (UTM) N	Tracer Test	Internal Diameter (m)	Piezometric Head (m above Sea Level) January–February 2012		Aquifer Hydraulic Transmissivity (m²/s)	Ground Water Specific Discharge (m/day)
P10	652,892.8	4,553,271.3		0.300		4.480	0.09	
L1-S	652,994.3	4,552,693.5	X	0.180	4.268	5.278	$0.6 \times 10^{-3} \pm 1.8 \times 10^{-4}$	1.3
P11	654,726.9	4,552,308.3		>1.0	1.251	1.611	0.02	
P19	654,580.1	4,552,382.9		>1.0	0.77	1.110	0.02	
P14	654,093.3	4,554,883.8		0.012	0.311	0.321	0.045	
L2-S	653,252.5	4,555,151.7	X	>1.0	0.582	0.722	0.047 ± 0.01	0.5
P4	653,053.8	4,554,841.5		0.012	0.266	0.386	0.06	
L3-S	652,431.0	4,554,429.8	X	>1.0	1.903	2.163	0.043 ± 0.02	2.6
P3	651,569.2	4,553,208.7		0.300	4.321	5.441	0.07	
P16	652,360.0	4,553,741.7		0.014	2.658	3.538	0.09	
L4-S	652,850.9	4,553,352.7	X	0.300	2.535	3.450	0.033 ± 0.03	2.2
P18	652,442.4	4,552,454.1		0.200		6.926	0.07	
L5-S	647,930.7	4,551,813.2	X	0.325		33.649	$3.0 \times 10^{-3} \pm 1.8 \times 10^{-3}$	0.2
L8-S	652,094.5	4,551,194.2	X	0.080		8.532	0.02 ± 0.01	0.4
L7-S	652,237.3	4,550,862.3	X	0.080		7.880	$0.5 \times 10^{-2} \pm 0.4 \times 10^{-2}$	0.6
L6-S	651,974.4	4,550,961.1	X	0.080		8.892	0.11 ± 0.01	1.4
P13	651,750.4	4,554,936.6		0.300		0.807	0.02	
L9	654,682.2	4,555,123.7		0.100		0.705	0.1	
L10	654,572.7	4,555,144.1		0.100		0.167	0.01	
L11	654,588.5	4,555,126.1		0.100		0.317	0.01	
L12-S	654,679.5	4,555,109.1	X	0.300		0.360	$0.01 \pm 0.7 \times 10^{-3}$	0.3
L13	654,777.0	4,555,188.8		0.100		0.418	1.2×10^{-5}	
L14-S	649,860.6	4,552,197.6	X	0.080		34.370	$1.1 \times 10^{-4} \pm 5.3 \times 10^{-5}$	0.6
L15	649,623.8	4,552,059.7		0.080		35.260	1.2×10^{-5}	
P2	651,595.4	4,551,934.3		0.300		6.760	0.025	

X means that tracer test was also performed on the borehole.

3.2. Experiment Methodology

During pumping (or injection) tests the flow rate was changed from 1 to 3 L·s⁻¹ and from 3 to 6 L·s⁻¹, on average. In addition water table depth was simultaneously monitored (and recorded) by means of the pressure probe (mini-log data logger, SIM Instrument SNC, Milan, Italy). The flow rate of each pumping (or injection) was kept constant for about 2 h; at the end of the test, pumping was stopped and the rise (or decline, after an injection) in water depth was recorded during the recovery period.

For each tracer injection, 1 m^3 of water was marked with 500 g of chlorophyll powder commercially sold as E141 hydro soluble or sodium copper chlorophyllin, which is usually used for foodstuffs such as pickles, ice creams, candies and fruit juices, and therefore it is not dangerous for human health. After mixing water and chlorophyllin powder in a tank of 1 m^3 volume, the traced mixture was injected with a constant flow rate of around 2 L·s^{-1} into a borehole, using a submersible pump and a pipeline (3 inch internal diameter). The traced water was injected at an assigned water depth (3 m) for about 8 min. The injection pipeline was then removed and groundwater was sampled at regular time intervals via a sampling pump (Grundfos BTI/MP1, Downers Grove, IL, USA) placed at the assigned water depth of 3 m into the well. Each water sample was stored in a plastic (Polyvinyl chloride or PVC) black bottle and transported in the laboratory where samples were monitored for water absorbance. Groundwater was sampled as long as the background tracer value of 10^{-3} absorbance units (AU) [20] was again achieved in the well. During injection water depth was monitored and recorded using a pressure probe and the data logger (SIM Instrument, Milano, Italy). The measurement of tracer concentration in the borehole referred to a calibration curve previously determined in the laboratory using a spectrophotometer (HACH DR/2000, Hach Lange Srl, Lainate, Italy) at a frequency of 405 nm. Test results suggest an aquifer discretization of 80 smoothed (and parallel) fractures. In fact, as n [–] defines the effective aquifer porosity, it is the uniform ratio of the void-space per unit volume of aquifer and, in each cross-section, it will be:

$$n = \frac{\sum\limits_{i=1}^{N_f} 2b_i}{B} \tag{1}$$

where $\sum 2b_i$ [l] is the sum of all horizontal fracture apertures of the aquifer column with unitary horizontal area (1 × 1 m^2) and thickness B [l], while N_f [–] is the total number of the fractures of the parallel set (see Figure 1). Assuming that all fractures of the set have the same aperture of 1.3 mm, i.e., $\sum 2b_i = N_f \times 2b = n \times B$ and for $n = 0.35\%$ and $B = 30$ m (see test results Table 1), Equation (1) suggests $N_f = 80$.

4. Groundwater Flow Simulation and Ghyben-Herzberg Interface Toe Position

At the regional scale (7200 × 6300 m^2) every fracture belonging to the 3D parallel set (Figure 1) was discretized using a grid step size of $\Delta x = \Delta y = 150$ m (i.e., 49 × 43 grid nodes). The steady and non-uniform groundwater flow was addressed in a series of parallel and horizontal fractures, with each single fracture having a spatially variable aperture and impermeable rock matrix. The model implemented the approximated analytical radial flow solution to a well in order to determine the mean conductivity of aquifer fractures at each well position by using K = $nb^2/3\, \gamma_w/\mu$, where γ_w [$M \cdot l^{-2} \cdot t^{-2}$] (M stands for mass) is the water specific weight and μ [$M \cdot l^{-1} \cdot t^{-1}$] is the dynamic water viscosity. The experimental variogram regarding the fracture apertures derived from well pumping tests was employed to perform the stochastic generation of apertures in each horizontal fracture belonging to the set. The discharge/head relationship in each fracture is defined as [15]

$$(\varphi_i - \varphi_j) = Q_{ij}^2 \left[\frac{f}{2g\Delta y} \frac{\Delta x}{\Delta y} \left(\frac{1}{(2b_i)^3} + \frac{1}{(2b_j)^3} \right) \right] \tag{2}$$

where f [–] is the friction factor derived from the Reynolds number; Q_{ij} [$l^3 \cdot t^{-1}$] is the flow rate of each fracture between two generic grid nodes i and j; Δx [l] and Δy [l] are the grid steps; and $\varphi = p/\gamma_w$ [l] is the water head, whilst g [$l \cdot t^{-2}$] is the gravity acceleration. It should be noted that Equation (2) supports flow calculations at any Reynolds number. By imposing the continuity equation, i.e., $\sum Q_{ij} = 0$, in every grid node, a system of equations was defined. The over-relaxation method was applied to solve the system of equations after that the boundary conditions were assigned. The flow simulation results enabled calculations of the seawater/freshwater 50% sharp interface positions with respect to the coastline, by applying the Ghyben-Herzberg equation. Indeed, to predict the interface toe position L [l] with respect to the coastline, the resulting groundwater outflow was managed in order to calculate the length of intrusion for every position along the coast defines as [14]

$$L - L_d = K \frac{B^2 - H_s^2}{2\delta_\gamma \times Q_0} - L_d = n \frac{b_i^2}{3} \frac{\gamma_w}{\mu} \frac{(\delta_\gamma \times \varphi_0)^2 - H_s^2}{2\delta_\gamma \times Q_0^i} - L_d \tag{3}$$

where L_d [l] is the distance of the contour head ϕ_0 (for instance 1 m) from the coastline given by flow simulation result; H_s [l] is the sharp interface depth at the outflow (usually set = 0); Q_0^i [$l^2 \cdot t^{-1}$] is the groundwater discharge along the coast predicted by model at grid node i; and $\delta_\gamma = \gamma_w / (\gamma_s - \gamma_w)$ [–] is the ratio of the specific weights.

Equation (3) shows that the extension $L - L_d$ of the sea intrusion is a function of both groundwater outflow and maximum freshwater thickness. Figure 3 saline fronts in groundwater before (in yellow) and after (in blue) a simulated new pumping of 335 L·s^{-1} (assuming that reinjections of pumped water are not allowed). Figure 3 shows how the new pumping changes the saline front position with respect to the coast. Simulation results provided a total decreases of 12% of freshwater Q_0 discharged into the sea, *i.e.*, from 10.8 to 9.5 m$^3 \cdot$ day$^{-1} \cdot$ m^{-1} in each fracture of the parallel set, due to new (or apparent) pumping wells. The maximum distance d of pumping wells from interface (see Figure 3) decreased of about 1000–1500 m, on average, due to new pumping.

Advancement of Saline Front in a Fracture Using N-S

The salt water advancement due to transient density-driven flow in a single fracture was investigated via the solution of the N-S equations. These solutions allowed the estimation of the time period required by saltwater to reach new Ghyben-Herzberg equilibrium due to simulated pumping. The governing N-S equations can be written by considering the salt mass and momentum conservation. In the Lagrangian framework can be written:

$$\frac{D\rho}{Dt} + \frac{\partial \rho u_\alpha}{\partial x_\alpha} = 0 \tag{4}$$

and

$$\frac{D\rho u_\alpha}{Dt} = -\frac{\partial \sigma_{\alpha\beta}}{\partial x_\beta} + \rho g_\alpha \text{ and } \alpha, \beta = x, y, z \tag{5}$$

where indexes α and β denoted the generic spatial component following Einstein notations, ρ [$M \cdot l^{-3}$] is water density, and u_α is the velocity [$l \cdot t^{-1}$] of the fluid particle; x_α [l] and x_β [l] are two spatial position coordinates of the fluid particle (Einstein notation); g_α [$l \cdot t^{-2}$] is the component of the gravity vector. The tensor component of the Newtonian stress component $\sigma_{\alpha\beta}$ [$M \cdot t^{-2} \cdot l^{-1}$], which was applied to each particle subject to the pressure $p\delta_{\alpha\beta}$ [$M \cdot t^{-2} \cdot l^{-1}$] can be defined:

$$\sigma_{\alpha\beta} = p\delta_{\alpha\beta} - \tau_{\alpha\beta} \tag{6}$$

where laminar and turbulent stress component τ [$M \cdot t^{-2} \cdot l^{-1}$] of the viscosity can be defined using [21,22]:

$$\tau_{\alpha\beta} = \left\{ \mu \times \left[\left(\frac{\partial u_\beta}{\partial x_\alpha} + \frac{\partial u_\alpha}{\partial x_\beta} \right) - \frac{2}{3}\delta_{\alpha\beta} \nabla \cdot u \right] \right\} + \overline{\tau}_{\alpha\beta} \tag{7}$$

where $\delta_{\alpha\beta}$ [–] is the Kroneker delta; $\overline{\tau}_{\alpha\beta}$ is the average sub-grid stress due to the fluctuating variation of velocities around the averaged values during turbulent flows. Similarly, Reynolds stress can be determined by assuming the eddy viscosity theory (Boussinesq's hypothesis), and by the Smagorinsky constant [23].

Some authors introduce also the Tait's equation [24], *i.e.*, the Equation of State, in order to complete the unknowns/equations balance.

However, when the first N-S equation is applied to a single computational cell of discretized water flow domain, water flow density remains constant by changing pressure due to water incompressibility and Equation (4) reduces to:

$$\nabla \mathbf{u} = 0 \tag{8}$$

and cannot be used to estimate velocity due to its undetermined form. By using the *projection method* the velocity $\mathbf{u}^*$ given by N-S conservation momentum Equation (5) is included in the following (Poisson) [25] equation:

$$\nabla \cdot \mathbf{u}^* = \Delta t \, \nabla \cdot (\nabla p) \tag{9}$$

in order to estimate the water pressure. In Equation (9) $\mathbf{u}^*$ is the intermediate velocity whose value is based on the viscous stress. Equation (8) is then used in a finite difference model (FDM) [16] in order to estimate the pressure of water via a separate numerical calculation. In particular, the conjugate gradient numerical method was applied to solve Equation (8) in order to calculate the water pressure by forcing the flow divergence to zero. After that the water pressure was determined, the correct velocity is obtained by Equation (9). Thus, at the next time step, the N-S momentum conservation Equation (4) is solved again to calculate the new intermediate water velocity. Moreover, in order to account for flow density variations due to the saline front advancement in the FDM code, the velocity $\mathbf{u}^*$ derived from Equation (5) was updated at each time step according to the new distribution of water densities into the cells of the fracture domain. This water density distribution due to mass salt flow advancement in the fracture was determined at every instant of the flow simulation by solving the salt advection and dispersion equation into the freshwater of the fracture, using a hydrodynamic dispersion coefficient of 10^{-9} m$^2 \cdot$ s^{-1}. In this way in every cell of the domain the divergence of the salt mass flux in the x and z directions was predicted at each simulation time.

The N-S flow equations were solved in a horizontal fracture of Bari aquifer with 5 m of extent and $2b = 3$ mm of aperture, which is the maximum fracture aperture derived from pumping-tests carried out on Bari wells. The computational domain x-z was discretized in cells of 0.3 mm × 50 mm of size, i.e., 10×100 cells. The transitory density-driven flow of seawater mixed with freshwater was performed assuming that the freshwater fracture, at the inlet section, is subjected to a constant salty water inflow at 35 g$\cdot$ L^{-1} of total concentration. Moreover, the reduction of 1.3 m$^3 \cdot$ day$^{-1} \cdot$ m^{-1} of freshwater discharge Q_0 in each fracture was also applied at the inflow section as the initial conditions during N-S simulations. Flow through the fracture cross-section ($2b \times 1$ m^2) was driven by a momentum (per unit volume) equal to 12,375 kg$\cdot$ m$^{-2} \cdot$ day^{-1}. This was defined by the product of the reduction of freshwater flowrate along the coast (from 102.9 to 90.5 m$\cdot$ day^{-1}) (due to new pumping of 335 L$\cdot$ s^{-1}) and the freshwater density (12.4 m$\cdot$ day^{-1} × 1000 kg$\cdot$ m^{-3}). Furthermore, at $t = t_0 = 0$, the salt density distribution in all cells of fracture was also imposed as initial condition.

The N-S code provided the time-dependent distribution of both water pressure and velocity in a fracture, caused by changes in water density due to salt water advancement due to the new pumping.

The FDM code results (see Figures 5 and 6) produced an almost regular flow with a maximum central value of velocity (and Reynolds number) and, subsequently, in both pressure gradient and water density. This occurs because the diffusive/convective salt mass flux divergence decreases from the centerline to the border of the fracture. By using a PC with a single Intel Pentium(R) 32 bits, the FDM code required 1 h and 12 min run-time (CPU) to simulate a period of 792 min. N-S solutions provided information regarding the freshwater/seawater sharp interface positions x_s [l] in the studied fracture at specific simulation time. Using twelve simulation run results the following linear equation was (0.99 of correlation) close-fitting in TableCurve2D:

$$x_s(t) = C_s + B_s \times t \tag{10}$$

where the position of salt water advancement in the fracture is dependent on time and two constants: $C_s = 1.08 \times 10^{-1}$ m and $B_s = 9.36 \times 10^{-3}$ m$\cdot$ min^{-1} (or 13.3 m$\cdot$ day^{-1}). The results of the N-S code simulations confirmed the strong influence of fracture aperture size on water velocity estimation.

For a fracture with 3 cm aperture, the mean water velocity (and Reynolds number) may be 100 times higher than the value determined for a fracture with 3 mm aperture. The quasi linear trend of the saline front advancement given by Equation (10) well matches the temporal trend of the progression of toe positions given by [26] during simulations. The rate of seawater advancement given by the N-S code (*i.e.*, 13.3 m· day^{-1}) is close to the expected value (12.4 m· day^{-1}), which is driven by the prescribed momentum. Using these N-S solutions, maximum elapsed time from the start of pumping to reach the new position of freshwater/saltwater sharp interface in the Bari groundwater is equal to 112.8 day (*i.e.*, 1500 m/(13.3 m· day^{-1})). Material concerning the advancement of sea movement intrusion is very useful for groundwater management practices of coastal aquifers [26–28].

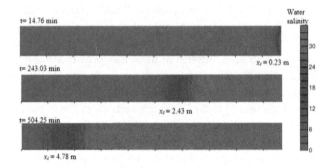

Figure 5. N-S solutions in a fracture (of aperture $2b = 3$ mm, $2b$ stands for the fracture aperture in the manuscript.) of the Bari aquifer. The rate of saline front advancement was used to determine the effects of new pumping of 335 L· s^{-1} on the freshwater/saltwater transition zone in coastal aquifers.

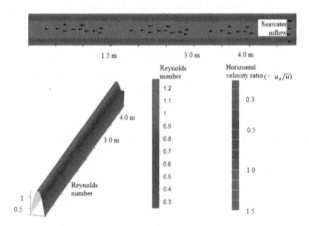

Figure 6. N-S solution at time $t = 243.03$ min from the beginning of the new pumping of 335 L· s^{-1}: horizontal flow velocity magnitude map due to freshwater/saltwater mixing in the fracture, and Reynolds number distribution.

5. Conversion of Distances from Interface into Groundwater Salinity Data

The conversion of each grid node distance from saline front into groundwater salinity concentration required two data sets, namely: (i) field salinity monitored in wells; and (ii) data from groundwater flow simulations.

5.1. Field Monitored Data

Seventeen wells of the Bari aquifer were monitored for water depth and specific water conductance. These measurements were carried out using multiparameter mini-probes (OTT Hydrolab, Kempetn,

Germany) Hydrolab-DS5 and OCEAN SEVEN 315 (IDRONAUT Srl, Brugherio, Italy). The latter one also provided dissolved the water oxygen concentration, which varied from 3.0 mg·L^{-1} (at the surface) to 0.3 mg·L^{-1} or less (at 37 m depth) in Bari's wells, and the water temperature. Each probe was previously calibrated in the laboratory in order to directly provide proper values of water salinity, temperature, pressure and dissolved oxygen *vs.* water depth. The relative monitored water specific conductance in 14 boreholes is displayed in Figure 7, where C/C_{min} is the ratio of each measurement to the minimum recorded value at each specific borehole location. Figure 7 presents anomalous salinity trends in the polluted sites that are characterized by high water temperatures.

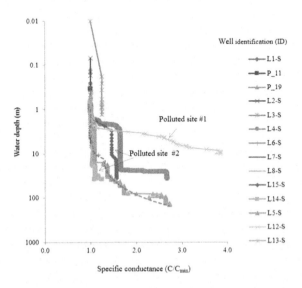

Figure 7. Relative specific conductance *vs.* water depth in 14 boreholes of the Bari aquifer positioned at different distance from Ghyben-Herzberg freshwater/sweater (50%) sharp interface position (Winter 2012) and best-fit equation (dashed line).

5.2. Ghyben-Herzberg Data

At first step, an interpolation in TableCurve2D provided the best equation (correlation coefficient of 0.92–0.9) which fits groundwater salt concentrations measured in 25 boreholes at depth of 1.0 m below water table *versus* the modeled distance d of each borehole from the saline front into groundwater provided by Ghyben-Herzberg theory (see yellow polygon in Figure 3).

$$C_{salt} = C_{s0} + A_s \left[\exp\left(-\frac{d}{D_s}\right) \right] \tag{11}$$

where, for $d \leqslant 1500$ m, the best fit constants are $C_{s0} = 1.54$ g·L^{-1}, $A_s = 12.02$ g·L^{-1} and $D_s = 592.65$ m. At distances $d > 1500$ m the following best-fit equation:

$$C_{salt} = \left[\exp\left(G_s - I_s\sqrt{d}\right) \right] \tag{11a}$$

it was preferred to Equation (11), where $G_s = 2.54$ log(g·L^{-1}) and $I_s = 0.04177$ log(g·L^{-1}·$m^{-0.5}$) are the best fit constants.

The significance of the above interpolation is that Equations (11) and (11a) enable the calculation of the salinity at depth z = 1.0 below water table at every generic position (x, y) of the computational domain, on the basis of field monitored data and distance d given by groundwater flow model solution.

Thus, a second interpolation of groundwater salinity concentrations measured in wells as a function of the water depth was performed. In particular, the use of TableCurve2D enabled the acquisition of groundwater salt concentrations with depth z at each generic location (x, y), using the best-fit curve displayed (dashed line) in Figure 7 (with correlation coefficient of 0.93).

$$C_{salt} = C_0 \times \left[\frac{E_s(z)}{F_s(z)} \right] \tag{12}$$

where E_s and F_s are two dimensionless interpolating functions with polynomial form:

$$E_s(z) = 0.99 + 2.26 \cdot 10^{-3}z - 5.32 \cdot 10^{-4}z^2 + 4.38 \cdot 10^{-6}z^3 \tag{12a}$$

$$F_s(z) = 1 - 1.80 \cdot 10^{-2}z - 1.07 \cdot 10^{-5}z^2 + 1.03 \cdot 10^{-6}z^3 \tag{12b}$$

where z [l] is water depth into borehole and C_0 is minimum salinity value at the specific borehole location. Equation (12) is valid up to a water depth of 140 m. Moreover, the following best-fit function (correlation coefficient of 0.93) could also replace Equation (12):

$$C_{salt} = C_0 \times \left\{ 1.55 \cdot \left[1 + erf \left(\frac{z - 5.6}{\sqrt{5800}} \right) \right] - 0.5 \right\} \tag{12c}$$

The significance of this interpolation is that Equation (12) or (12c) enables the calculation of the salinity with depth below water table at every generic position of the computational domain.

Once Equations (11) and (12) were determined, a FORTRAN90 (Visual FORTRAN Professional Edition 5.0.A, Microsoft Developer Studio 97, Microsoft Italia, Peschiera Borromeo (MI), Italy) code was used to perform groundwater salinity estimations. All grid-node positions of computational domain with respect to the freshwater/seawater interface were then converted to groundwater salinity data. A 3D file of 21,070 salt groundwater concentrations was obtained by using 10 grid steps of 10 m in z direction. This file was elaborated using RockWorks15 in order to determine the solid model of actual groundwater salinity, suitable for 3D map visualization. The reliability of this conversion method was quantitatively tested (Table 2) by comparing measured and predicted values at three different depths. The average uncertainty of these estimations is about 20% with respect to the mean salinity (=1.53 g· L^{-1}) (see Table 2) at depth of 1 m below water table and it may be reduced by increasing the number of boreholes for salinity measurements.

Table 2. Comparison between modelled (Mod) values of groundwater salinity (*i.e.*, Rockwork15 input data at $t = 0$) and measurements (Mea) at three water depths into boreholes of the Bari aquifer. SD stands for the standard deviation between measured and modelled values.

ID Borehole	Actual (Winter 2012) Groundwater Salinity (g· L^{-1}) at Different Water Depths								
	1 m			11 m			31 m		
	Mod	Mea	±SD	Mod	Mea	±SD	Mod	Mea	±SD
L1-S	0.9	1.54	0.46	1.06	1.65	0.41	1.31		
P11	2.76	2.99	0.16	3.14			3.9		
P19	3.75	3.71	0.03	4.27			5.29		
L2-S	3.12	2.63	0.34	3.55			4.39		
L3-S	2.11	3.40	0.91	2.4			2.97		
L4	0.98	1.05	0.05	1.1	1.72	0.44	1.38	2.77	0.98
L8-S	0.5	0.71	0.15	0.52			0.65		
L7-S	0.5	0.58	0.06	0.6			0.74		
L6-S	0.5	0.67	0.12	0.52	0.78	0.19	0.65		
L9	2.02	1.54	0.34	2.3			2.85		
L14-S	0.93	0.59	0.24	1.06	0.56	0.35	1.31	1.03	0.20
L15-S	0.93	0.86	0.05	1.06	0.95	0.08	1.31	1.75	0.31
L5-S	0.5	0.63	0.09	0.52	0.68	0.12	0.65	1.50	0.60
L12	2.02	0.56	1.03	2.3	2.26	0.03	2.85		
Mean		1.53	±0.32		1.23	±0.23		1.76	±0.52

5.3. Data from Solutions of N-S Equations

At third step, the same FORTRAN90 code previously applied was implemented applying Equation (10) to update the salinity concentrations in each grid node of computational domain at three different simulation times of 30, 75 and 112.8 days. The saline front displacement during time is given by N-S solutions, by determining the new grid node positions with respect to the salinity front. In particular, as input for this calculation, 49 distances of the top border of domain from the salinity front were provided at each simulation time. A control on the maximum distance calculated was imposed into the FORTRAN90 code in order to avoid that the advancement of the saline front may exceed the distance provided by flow model (*i.e.*, blue polygon) plotted in Figure 3. The significance of this calculation is that it enables the estimation of groundwater salinity concentrations according to the advancement of salinity front in groundwater fractures during a new pumping obtained by solutions of the Navier-Stokes equations. The results provide 3D solid models in RockWorks15. 3D maps of Figure 8 show actual salinity of Bari coastal aquifer and its progression as the consequence of the constant new simulated pumping of 335 L· s^{-1}.

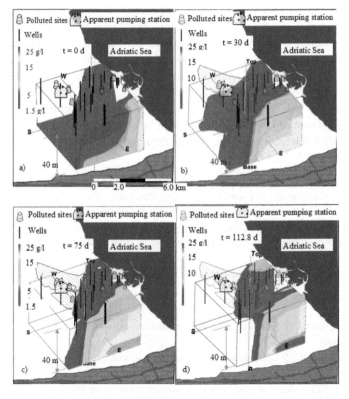

Figure 8. (a) 3D map of groundwater salinity during winter 2012 (*t* = 0 day) and its comparison with groundwater salinity maps after (b) 30; (c) 75 and (d) 112.8 days of a simulated continuous pumping of 335 L·s^{-1}.

6. Discussion and Conclusions

A new method to infer saline front advancement in a fractured coastal aquifer was applied to Bari groundwater. Results visualize the 3D maps of groundwater salinity concentrations, at different simulation times, due to the impact of an apparent pumping of 335 L· s^{-1}. The 3D maps are useful tools for coastal groundwater management and show how over-abstractions may affect groundwater salinity changes. The same method can be applied to others aquifers with discrete fractures and it requires two data sets: (i) field salinity data in boreholes (*i.e.*, logs); and (ii) results of groundwater flow model simulation to represent actual 3D maps of aquifer salinity. Moreover, solutions of the N-S equations in a fracture can provide the rate (on average) of saline front advancement in fractures during time. This result allows updates of actual salt concentrations, by defining 3D salinity maps at specific simulation times during a new pumping. Although mapping based on the sharp interface approach is not representative of real conditions of the salt mass transport in fractures, the salinity front positions at the initial and final stage of the simulated pumping stress condition in this method, take into account for the real flow conditions in the fractured aquifer. Moreover, by including approximations due to the interpolation stages (correlation coefficients >0.92–0.93) authors have estimated the 20% of uncertainty of results at the Bari aquifer. This uncertainty established an acceptable distance of results from reality.

In the present work groundwater flow modeling was based on aquifer transmissivity values derived from pumping and tracer (chlorophyllin) injection tests carried out during winter 2012. At specific sites, a minor number (<30) of monitoring wells may increase limitations of results, and the uncertainty of the presented method.

The presented method is an alternative to the application of the 3D unsteady density-driven flow models at a regional scale, which may present computational limitations in discrete fractured aquifers due to complexity of input data required to describe preferential flow pathways and the unknown position (and aperture) of the fractures and their intersections, especially at a regional scale. Moreover, conventional meshed models based on finite elements, finite differences or boundary elements, are inappropriate for flow and transport simulations in fractured aquifers, i.e., not continuous porous media. This is due to impossibility to define a representative elementary volume (REV) of appropriate size in a fractured (or very heterogeneous) aquifer.

Data regarding the seawater front advancement in the Bari aquifer are highly suitable for groundwater management of coastal aquifers. Results suggest an elapsed time of 112.8 days to achieve the new Ghyben-Herzberg interface equilibrium position, starting from the beginning of the new pumping of 335 $L \cdot s^{-1}$.

Acknowledgments: This research was supported by Regional Authority under the program for groundwater remediation of polluted sites in the industrial area of Bari. Authors are very grateful to Leonardo Castellano (MATEC, Italy) which implemented the N-S solutions into the FDM code.

Author Contributions: Costantino Masciopinto conceived and designed the experiments, wrote the software and the paper; Domenico Palmiotta performed the experiments, contributed reagents/materials/analysis tools, analyzed the data.

Conflicts of Interest: The authors declare no conflict of interest.

References

1. Barlow, P.M.; Reichard, E.G. Saltwater intrusion in coastal regions of North America. *Hydrogeol. J.* 2010, *18*, 247–260. [CrossRef]
2. Goswami, R.R.; Clement, T.P. Laboratory-scale investigation of saltwater intrusion dynamics. *Water Resour. Res.* 2007. [CrossRef]
3. Essink, G.H.P.O. Salt water intrusion in a three-dimensional groundwater system in The Netherlands: A Numerical Study. *Transp. Porous Media* 2001, *43*, 137–158. [CrossRef]
4. Panyor, L. Renewable energy from dilution of salt water with fresh water: Pressure Retarded Osmosis. *Desalination* 2006, *199*, 408–410. [CrossRef]
5. Buonasorte, G. Development of geothermal energy in Italy until 2008 and short-term prospects, Ferrara (I). In Proceedings of the Congresso Internazionale: La Geotermia in Italia e in Europa. Quale futuro?—GEO THERM EXPO2009, Ferrara, Italy, 23 September 2009.
6. Chongo, M.; Wibroe, J.; Staal-Thomsen, K.; Moses, M.; Nyambe, I.A.; Larsen, F.; Bauer-Gottwein, P. The use of Time Domain Electromagnetic method and Continuous Vertical Electrical Sounding to map groundwater salinity in the Barotse sub-basin, Zambia. *Phys. Chem. Earth* 2011, *36*, 798–805. [CrossRef]
7. I-GIS. GeoScene3D—Modelling and Visualization of Geological Data, Risskov, Denmark (DK). Available online: http://www.i-gis.dk/GeoScene3D (accessed on 3 February 2016).

8. Hydrogeophysics-Group-1. *Getting Started with SiTEM and SEMDI*; Denmark University of Aarhus: Aarhus, Denmark, 2001.

9. Geomoto Software. Res2Dinv v. 3.54 for Windows 98/Me/2000/NT/XP, Gelugor, Penang, Malaysia. Available online: http://www.geoelectrical.com (accessed on 3 February 2016).

10. Mullen, I.; Kellet, J. Groundwater salinity mapping using airborne electromagnetics and borehole data within the lower Balonne catchment, Queensland, Australia. *Int. J. Appl. Earth Obs. Geoinform.* **2007**, *9*, 116–123. [CrossRef]

11. Archie, G.E. The electrical resistivity log as an aid in determining some reservoir characteristics. *Trans. Am. Inst. Mech. Eng.* **1942**, *146*, 54–67. [CrossRef]

12. Lesch, S.M.; Strauss, D.J.; Rhoades, J.D. Spatial prediction of soil salinity using electromagnetic induction techniques 1. Statistical prediction models: A comparison of multiple linear regression and cokriging. *Water Resour. Res.* **1995**, *2*, 373–386. [CrossRef]

13. Masciopinto, C.; la Mantia, R.; Chrysikopoulos, C.V. Fate and transport of pathogens in a fractured aquifer in the Salento area, Italy. *Water Resour. Res.* **2008**. [CrossRef]

14. Masciopinto, C. Simulation of coastal groundwater remediation: The Case of Nardò Fractured Aquifer in Southern Italy. *Environ. Model. Softw.* **2006**, *21*, 85–97. [CrossRef]

15. Masciopinto, C.; Volpe, A.; Palmiotta, D.; Cherubini, C. A combined PHREEQC-2/parallel fracture model for the simulation of laminar/non-laminar flow and contaminant transport with reactions. *J. Contam. Hydrol.* **2010**, *117*, 94–108. [CrossRef]

16. Masciopinto, C.; Palmiotta, D. Relevance of solutions to the Navier-Stokes equations for explaining groundwater flow in fractured karst aquifers. *Water Resour. Res.* **2013**. [CrossRef]

17. Walther, M.; Delfs, J.O.; Grundmann, J.; Kolditz, O.; Lied, R. Saltwater intrusion modeling: Verification and Application to an Agricultural Coastal Arid Region in Oman. *J. Comput. Appl. Math.* **2012**, *236*, 4798–4809. [CrossRef]

18. Werner, A.D.; Bakker, M.; Post, V.E.A.; Vandenbohede, A.; Lu, C.; Ataie-Ashtiani, B.; Simmons, C.; Barry, D.A. Seawater intrusion processes, investigation and management: Recent Advances and Future Challenges. *Adv. Water Resour.* **2013**, *51*, 3–26. [CrossRef]

19. Masciopinto, C.; Palmiotta, D. Flow and Transport in Fractured Aquifers: New Conceptual Models Based on Field Measurements. *Transp. Porous Media* **2012**. [CrossRef]

20. Mehta, A. Ultraviolet-Visible (UV-Vis) Spectroscopy—Derivation of Beer-Lambert Law. Available online: http://pharmaxchange.info/press/2012/04/ultraviolet-visible-uv-vis-spectroscopy-%E2%80%93-derivation-of-beer-lambert-law/ (accessed on 3 February 2016).

21. Chaniotis, A.K.; Frouzakis, C.E.; Lee, J.C.; Tomboulides, A.G.; Poulikakos, D.; Boulouchos, K. Remeshed smoothed particle hydrodynamics for the simulation of laminar chemically reactive flows. *J. Comput. Phys.* **2003**, *191*, 1–17. [CrossRef]

22. Gesteira, M.G.; Rogers, B.D.; Dalrymple, R.A.; Crespo, A.J.C.; Narayanaswamy, M. SPHysics v2.0, January 2010: Open-Source Smoothed Particle Hydrodynamics Code. Available online: http://wiki.manchester.ac.uk/sphysics/index.php (accessed on 3 February 2016).

23. Meyers, J.; Geurts, B.J.; Baelmans, M. Optimality of the dynamic procedure for large-eddy simulations, American Institute of Physics. *Phys. Fluids* **2005**. [CrossRef]

24. Becker, M.; Teschner, M. Weakly Compressible SPH for Free Surface Flows. In Proceedings of the Euro graphics/ACM SIGGRAPH Symposium on Computer Animation, Aire-la-Ville, Switzerland, 3–4 August 2007.

25. Boersma, B.J. A 6th order staggered compact finite difference method for the incompressible Navier-Stokes and scalar transport equations. *J. Comput. Phys.* **2011**. [CrossRef]

26. Watson, T.A.; Werner, A.D.; Simmons, C.T. Transience of sea water intrusion in response to sea level rise. *Water Resour. Res.* **2010**. [CrossRef]

27. Yechieli, Y.; Shalev, E.; Wollman, S.; Kiro, Y.; Kafri, U. Response of the Mediterranean and Dead Sea coastal aquifers to sea level variations. *Water Resour. Res.* **2010**. [CrossRef]

28. Zlotnik, V.A.; Robinson, N.I.; Simmons, C.T. Salinity dynamics of discharge lakes in dune environments: Conceptual Model. *Water Resour. Res.* **2010**. [CrossRef]

4

Bonding Strength Effects in Hydro-Mechanical Coupling Transport in Granular Porous Media by Pore-Scale Modeling

Zhiqiang Chen, Chiyu Xie, Yu Chen and Moran Wang *

Department of Engineering Mechanics and CNMM, Tsinghua University, Beijing 100084, China; chenzhiq14@mails.tsinghua.edu.cn (Z.C.); chiyu.xie@gmail.com (C.X.); fishfrozen@gmail.com (Y.C.)
* Correspondence: mrwang@tsinghua.edu.cn

Academic Editor: Qinjun Kang

Abstract: The hydro-mechanical coupling transport process of sand production is numerically investigated with special attention paid to the bonding effect between sand grains. By coupling the lattice Boltzmann method (LBM) and the discrete element method (DEM), we are able to capture particles movements and fluid flows simultaneously. In order to account for the bonding effects on sand production, a contact bond model is introduced into the LBM-DEM framework. Our simulations first examine the experimental observation of "initial sand production is evoked by localized failure" and then show that the bonding or cement plays an important role in sand production. Lower bonding strength will lead to more sand production than higher bonding strength. It is also found that the influence of flow rate on sand production depends on the bonding strength in cemented granular media, and for low bonding strength sample, the higher the flow rate is, the more severe the erosion found in localized failure zone becomes.

Keywords: hydro-mechanical coupling transport; lattice Boltzmann method; discrete element method; bonding effects

1. Introduction

Sand production is commonly observed during the extrusion of hydrocarbons from reservoirs, which makes a great of trouble in oil or gas production [1]. It was reported that 70% of the world's gas or oil reservoir has the potential risk to produce sand during their production life [1,2]. As a result, the petroleum industry spends millions of dollars each year to find ways to solve this problem [3].

In the past few decades, some achievements on sand production have been made by experimental studies, among which two mechanisms about sand production are convincing [4,5]. Firstly, the initial sand production is evoked by localized failure near the cavity owing to concentration of external stress, which is called as mechanical instability. Secondly, this localized failure zone is eroded by flow, which is named hydro-mechanical instability. Furthermore, these two mechanisms are often coupled with each other, which leads to the complexity of sand production. However, owing to the limitation in observing and measuring the micro-information about fluid and sand grains interaction by experiment, the micro underlying physics of these mechanisms is still not clear.

Therefore, numerical studies are of great importance. For a reliable numerical model for sand production, three aspects should be considered: an efficient method to capture the elastic and plastic behavior of granular media, a good description of fluid flow, and an accurate way to consider the fluid–solid interaction. In the previous numerical studies of sand production, continuum model and discrete element method are two popular approaches [3]. For continuum method, granular media is regarded as a deformable pore-elastic or pore-elastoplastic solid described by the constitutive equation [6]. However, continuum models have difficulty completely capturing the performance of granular media due to its inherent discrete nature. Meanwhile, little micro information can be obtained in continuum method to explore the mechanism at particle scale [7]. As an alternative method, the discrete element method (DEM) [8] is an efficient way to overcome those shortcomings. Firstly, DEM can capture the discrete nature of rock by treating it as an assembly of discrete particles. Secondly, DEM is based on the particle scale and the influence of micro parameters on the macroscopic behaviors can be considered, which is important for studying mechanism of sand production. Owing to these advantages, DEM was widely used to study sand production [9–13].

In DEM simulation of sand production, the description of fluid dynamics plays an important role. In earlier works, flow in granular media was described by Darcy's law, which was coupled with DEM by some empirical formulas [9,10,13]. However, in Darcy-DEM models, flow in granular media cannot be calculated accurately, so CFD-DEM model was developed, where Navier–Stokes equations based on the local mean values over a computation cell were solved [11,12]. Zhou et al. [11] employed this approach to simulate the liquid-induced erosion in a weakly bonded granular media and captured the main features of the sand erosion. Compared with Darcy-DEM model, some progress has been made in CFD-DEM model, but empirical equations are again usually introduced to calculate hydrodynamic force on solid. In addition, due to the fact that hydrodynamic force acting on sand plays a critical role in sand production, the fluid–particle interaction must be evaluated at the particle scale or smaller [14], which means that CFD-DEM model is also not accurate enough to explore the underlying physics of sand production, especially about the fluid and sand grains interaction.

In the past three decades, the lattice Boltzmann method (LBM) has gained much popularity due to its efficiency in dealing with complex-boundary problems [15–18]. It has also been coupled with DEM to simulate particle-fluid system at pore scale [19–21]. In LBM-DEM model, the flow is calculated at pore scale, so that assumptions about the dependence between porosity and permeability are no longer needed. Therefore, the LBM-DEM model is outstanding among other numerical methods, and has been applied to study sand production process [7,14,22,23].

Boutt et al. [7] and Ghassemi et al. [22] simulated sand production in two dimensions (2D) with a coupled LBM-DEM model, and discussed the influence of the confining pressure and flow rate on sand production. In their models, the granular media is un-cemented, so there is no bonding effect between particles, and the only resistance for particle motion is friction. However, in cemented reservoir, the bonding effect is a primary property determining the macroscopic behavior of granular media, such as sandstone, and the failure of cemented granular media is generally owing to the bond breakage [24]. It was also reported that behavior of un-cemented granular media is evidently distinct from cemented granular media owing to the bonding effects between grains [25], so the conclusion obtained from un-cemented granular media may be not suitable for cemented granular media. Moreover, only limited literatures were found to simulate sand production of cemented granular media at pore scale, although some sand production experiments have been carried out for a better understanding of sand production process in cemented reservoir [2,26]. To bridge this gap, we study sand production in cemented reservoir, with special focus on the influence of bonding effect. In this paper, the LBM and DEM in a two-dimensional domain are coupled to simulate fluid–solid system, and in order to consider the effect of bonding strength, a contact bond model is incorporated in LBM-DEM framework.

The rest of this paper is organized as follows. Firstly, the numerical methods are introduced in Section 2, which includes the lattice Boltzmann method, discrete element method with contact bond model, and coupling of these two methods. In Section 3, the LBM-DEM code is validated by simulating the sedimentation of circular particles in a channel. Section 4 is the numerical results and discussion, which contains two parts: biaxial compression simulation and sand production simulation where the influence of bonding strength on sand production is discussed. Section 5 concludes the paper.

2. Numerical Methods

This section is a brief introduction of numerical methods used in our simulation: the lattice Boltzmann method for fluid phase and the discrete element method with contact bond model. The approach to couple these two methods is described at the end of this section.

2.1. Lattice Boltzmann Method (LBM)

LBM is an efficient numerical scheme to simulate fluid especially with complicated boundary condition [16,17,27–32] and multiphase interfaces [15,33–37]. Recently, LBM has been used to simulate fluid-solid coupling system [19,20,38–41] owing to its high efficiency compared with traditional methods.

The basic variable in LBM is density distribution function f_i. A widespread LBM implementation in the literature is the lattice Bhatnagar–Gross–Krook (LBGK) model, where the collision operator is simplified as a linearized version by assuming that the collision operator relaxes the local particle distribution functions at a single rate [15]. The evolution equation of "LBGK" model can be written as [15]:

$$f_i\left(x + e_i \delta_t, t + \delta_t\right) = f_i\left(x, t\right) - \frac{1}{\tau}\left(f_i\left(x, t\right) - f_i^{eq}\left(x, t\right)\right) \tag{1}$$

where f_i is the distribution function in the ith discrete velocity direction e_i, f_i^{eq} is the corresponding equilibrium distribution function, δ_t is the time step, and τ is the relaxation time related to the fluid kinematic viscosity:

$$\upsilon = \left(\tau - 0.5\right) c^2 \delta_t / 3 \tag{2}$$

where $c = \delta_x / \delta_t$ is the lattice speed with δ_x representing the lattice size, i.e., the space step. For a two-dimensional nine-speed (D2Q9) model, they are

$$\begin{cases} e_0 = (0,0), \\ e_1 = c\,(1,0), \quad e_2 = c\,(1,1), \quad\quad e_3 = c\,(0,1), \quad e_4 = c\,(-1,1), \\ e_5 = c\,(-1,0) \quad e_6 = c\,(-1,-1), \quad e_7 = c\,(0,-1), \quad e_8 = c\,(1,-1). \end{cases} \tag{3}$$

The equilibrium distribution for two-dimensional nine-speed (D2Q9) model can be given as:

$$f_i^{eq}\left(\rho, u\right) = \rho \omega_i \left[1 + \frac{3 e_i \cdot u}{c^2} + \frac{9 \left(e_i \cdot u\right)^2}{2 c^4} - \frac{3 u \cdot u}{2 c^2}\right] \tag{4}$$

where the weighting factors are:

$$\omega_i \begin{cases} \dfrac{4}{9}, & i = 0, \\ \dfrac{1}{9}, & i = 1, 3, 5, 7, \\ \dfrac{1}{36}, & i = 2, 4, 6, 8. \end{cases} \tag{5}$$

The fluid density and momentum can be obtained from the discrete distribution function,

$$\rho = \sum_i f_i \tag{6}$$

$$\rho u = \sum_i f_i e_i \tag{7}$$

and the pressure (p) is given by:

$$p = c^2 \rho / 3 \tag{8}$$

2.2. Discrete Element Method (DEM)

Discrete element method (DEM) was proposed in 1979 [8] and has been widely used in geomechanics. In our model, the classic linear spring-dashpot contact model is used [8]. The force-displacement relationship is given by:

$$F_n = -k_n \alpha - C_n v_n \tag{9}$$

$$F_s = -k_s \eta - C_s v_s \tag{10}$$

where F_n is the normal contact force, F_s the tangential contact force, k_n the normal spring stiffness, k_s the tangential spring force, C_n the normal damping, and C_s the tangential damping. The shear slider will work at the contact point, when F_n and F_s satisfy the following inequality:

$$F_s \geqslant \mu F_n \tag{11}$$

where μ is the coefficient of friction.

The motion of the particle is described by:

$$m\frac{d^2 X}{dt^2} = F \tag{12}$$

$$I\frac{d^2 \varphi}{dt^2} = M \tag{13}$$

where m is particle mass, F the total force acting on it, I the rotation inertia, and M is the total torque. In this work the explicit Verlet algorithm is applied, which is often used in DEM and MD simulation [42]. LBM-DEM coupling at each time step is realized by computing the fluid field by LBM firstly and then the hydrodynamic force and contact force between solids are calculated. Finally, different external forces are added together to update the particle position by integrating the above differential equation. The computation of LBM-DEM coupling is shown in Figure 1.

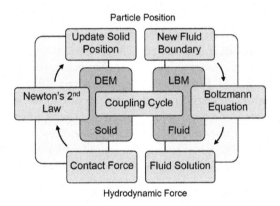

Figure 1. The computation of lattice Boltzmann method (LBM) and discrete element method (DEM) coupling.

In order to consider the bonding effect in cemented granular media, the contact bond model is incorporated into the DEM, which is simple but can efficiently capture bonding effect between particles [43]. In this model, the bond behavior is decided by the normal bonding strength R_n and the tangential bonding strength R_t, and R_t is set equal to R_n. For two contacting particles, the failure envelope can be summarized by:

$$N_s = R_n \tag{14}$$

$$T_s = \begin{cases} R_t & \text{if } -R_n < F_n \leqslant R_t/\mu, \\ \mu F_n & \text{if } F_n > R_t/\mu, \end{cases} \tag{15}$$

where N_s is the normal strength, and T_s is the tangential strength. The detail about this model can be found in [43].

2.3. Fluid and Solid Interaction

Midway bounce-back boundary condition is applied in this work, which is easy to be implemented and widely used in particle suspension model [19]. For a moving wall, an additional term is added into the classic bounce-back procedure to keep nonslip boundary condition:

$$f_{\overline{\alpha}}\left(x_f, t + \delta t\right) = \tilde{f}_{\alpha}(x_f, t) - 2w_{\alpha}\rho\frac{e_{\alpha} \cdot u_w}{c_s^2} \tag{16}$$

where u_w is the velocity on the midpoint of the boundary link, x_f is the fluid node next to the solid, e_{α} the direction from fluid node to solid node, $e_{\overline{\alpha}}$ its opposite direction, and $\tilde{f}$ is the post-collision distribution function.

The calculation of hydrodynamic force is a major topic in particle suspension simulation. Ladd proposed a shell model basing on momentum exchange, where the hydrodynamic force between fluid and solid is calculated on each boundary link [19]:

$$\delta F_w\left(x_w, e_{\alpha}\right) = -\left[f_{\overline{\alpha}}\left(x_f, t\right) e_{\overline{\alpha}} - \tilde{f}_{\alpha}(x_f, t)e_{\alpha}\right] \tag{17}$$

The total hydrodynamic force acting on the particle is the sum of $\delta F_w\left(x_w, e_{\alpha}\right)$ on each boundary link of the particle surface:

$$F_w = \sum \delta F_w\left(x_w, e_{\alpha}\right) \tag{18}$$

The corresponding total torque can be given by:

$$T_w = \sum \left(x_w - R\right) \times \delta F_w\left(x_w, e_{\alpha}\right) \tag{19}$$

where R is the mass center of the particle.

In Ladd's model [19], the fluid exists inside and outside of the particle boundary, so it is actually a shell model and the momentum exchange is calculated for both interior and exterior fluid. As a result, the interior fluid may have an influence on the particle motion [38]. Thus, Aidun *et al.* [20] proposed a non-shell model by excluding the interior fluid, and the momentum exchange is only considered for exterior fluid. As Aidun suggested, for non-shell model a named "impulse force" should be added to the conventional momentum exchange method. This "impulse force" is only calculated when the particle moves to cover or uncover a lattice node, which serves as a correction for the hydrodynamic force and the necessity of this correction for non-shell model has been confirmed by [44]. Thus in our simulation the non-shell model is applied and the "impulse force" is used as a correction. When the particle moves across a fluid node the "impulse force" is written as [20]:

$$\sum_{CN} F_c\left(x_{\text{cover}}\right) = \sum_{CN} \rho U \tag{20}$$

$$\sum_{CN} T_c\left(x_{\text{cover}}\right) = \sum_{CN} \left(x_{cover} - R\right) \times F_c\left(x_{\text{cover}}\right) \tag{21}$$

$$\sum_{UN} F_u\left(x_{uncover}\right) = -\sum_{UN} \rho U \tag{22}$$

$$\sum_{UN} T_u\left(x_{uncover}\right) = \sum_{UN} \left(x_{uncover} - R\right) \times F_u\left(x_{uncover}\right) \tag{23}$$

where CN and UN are respectively fluid nodes being covered and uncovered during a time step.

3. Benchmarks

To validate the algorithm and the code, two benchmark cases are considered: single particle sedimentation, and two-particle sedimentation. For single particle sedimentation, we replicate the results computed by Feng et al. [45] using the finite element method (FEM), which is often used to validate the fluid–solid coupling methods [20,46,47]. For two-particle sedimentation, our results capture the important phenomena named "drafting, kissing and tumbling" or DKT motion [46,47], and agree well with their results quantitatively. For the consideration of stability and accuracy, the dimensionless relaxation time (τ) in LBM is taken as 1, and a relatively high grid resolution (each particle consisting of 64 LBM grids) is applied to reduce the influence of no smoothness brought by midway bounce-back model. In a 2D system, a high grid resolution can be afforded, while it may be computationally expensive for 3D. As an alternative, some smoothing models can be used such as the immersed moving boundary method [41].

3.1. Single Particle Sedimentation

Single particle sedimentation geometry is shown in Figure 2a, where d is the particle diameter, and $l = 1.5d = 4$ cm is the width of the narrow channel. Gravity is along the X axis in the positive direction. The density and kinematic viscosity of fluid is 1000 kg/m³ and 10^{-6} m²/s, respectively. The particle with density of 1010 kg/m³ is initially placed off the centerline of channel, and then released with a zero velocity. Because the particle is heavier than the fluid, it will settle down along the direction of gravity, and oscillate around the centerline owing to the influence of channel walls as in Figure 2b. Eventually a steady state can be achieved, where the particle reaches a terminal velocity with no lateral motion, and the terminal particle Reynolds number can be calculated:

$$\text{Re} = \frac{ud}{\nu} \tag{24}$$

where u is the terminal velocity of the particle, d is the particle diameter, and ν is the kinematic viscosity. In the case of Re = 6.2, Figure 2b shows the comparison of particle settling trajectories obtained using LBM-DEM and by Feng et al. using FEM [45], and they agree well with each other.

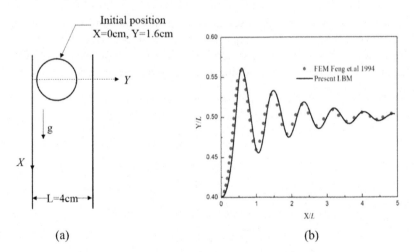

(a)   (b)

Figure 2. The benchmark case of single particle sedimentation. (**a**) The geometry of the simulation; (**b**) the comparison of particle trajectories.

3.2. Two-Particle Sedimentation

For further validating the program, two-particle sedimentation is simulated. The channel geometry is shown in Figure 3a, where the width and length of channel are 2 cm and 8 cm, respectively. The fluid has the properties of water with kinematic viscosity 10^{-6} m^2/s and density 1000 kg/m^3. The diameter of particle is 0.2 cm, and particles density is 1010 kg/m^3. The first particle is at 0.999 cm and 0.8 cm in Y and X direction, respectively. The second particle is at 1.0 cm and 1.2 cm in Y and X direction, respectively. For comparison, all these parameters are the same as those in [46,47]. Initially, the two particles are released with a zero velocity, and the upper one will settle in the wake of the other, which leads to the rearrangement mechanism called "drafting, kissing, and tumbling" or DKT motion [48]. Drafting means the particle in the wake will accelerate with an increasing acceleration owing to the low pressure in the wake. Then two particles contact with each other, which is called kissing. Due to the instability of contacting particles aligned in the direction parallel to the motion, they tend to "tumble" to another position. As a result, the center line of particles rotates an angle, and eventually the two particles depart from each other due to the unsymmetrical wake [48].

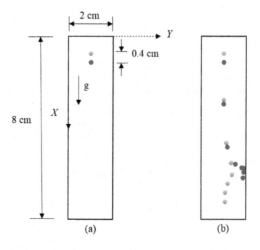

Figure 3. The benchmark case of two particles sedimentation. (**a**) The geometry of the simulation; (**b**) the settling trajectory of two-particle sedimentation.

As show in Figure 3b, our result captures the rearrangement mechanism of "drafting, kissing and tumbling". Furthermore, the quantitative comparison of particle trajectories in Y direction is presented in Figure 4, which shows that before particles collision our result agree well with that in [46,47]. After kissing stage, exact agreement may not be expected due to different discrete methods are used [47].

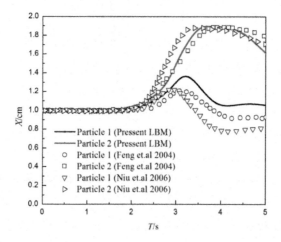

Figure 4. Transverse coordinates of the centers of the two particles.

4. Numerical Results and Discussion

This section is the main part of this paper. Firstly, the biaxial compression test is simulated to validate the contact bond model and show the influence of bonding strength on macroscopic mechanical behavior of cemented granular media. Then the sand production of cemented granular media is simulated, and the influences of bonding strength and flow rate on sand production are discussed.

The main aim of this work is to investigate the importance of often ignored bonding effect on sand production in previous work. For simplicity and clarity, we treat the porous structure as a hexagonal packing with monodisperse spheres to highlight the bonding effect between particles without the influence of packing way and particle size distribution. In future work, we will refine the porous structure with more realistic sand grains, including the effect of the particle size distribution [25] and non-spherical particles such as polyhedron [49].

4.1. Biaxial Compression Simulation

Although the bonding effect on macroscopic mechanical behavior of cemented granular media is complex, some general features can still be observed by compression test. These effects include that in cemented materials the macroscopic strength is enhanced and shear band is more likely to be observed [50]. In order to validate the contact bond model and show the influence of bonding strength on macroscopic mechanical behavior, biaxial compression is simulated to capture these effects. The main steps in biaxial compression simulation are sample generation, installing specified isotropic stress and compression.

Firstly, the rectangular DEM samples are bounded by four frictionless rigid walls as in Figure 5a. For capturing the bonding effect in cemented granular media, the contact bond model is added to the particles contacting with each other. In the simulation, three samples are considered, which have the same micro parameters except bonding strength. Due to the limitations of pressure differences that can be applied when using LBM, the samples used in the biaxial compression simulation and sand production simulation have a higher deformability and smaller strength than the real materials, which is a common consideration on simulating sand production by LBM-DEM model [23]. Based on this principal, the main DEM parameters used in biaxial compression and sand production simulation are chosen empirically and summarized in Table 1.

Table 1. The main parameters used in discrete element method (DEM).

Parameter	Value
Number of particle	600
Diameter of particle	2 mm
k_n	2.5×10^4 N/m
k_s	1.0×10^4 N/m
μ	0.2
Low bonding strength	0.0078 N
Middle bonding strength	0.039 N
High bonding strength	0.078 N

Figure 6 shows the deviatoric stress–strain responses of cemented granular media with different bonding strength. It is observed that the synthetic cemented granular media presents a brittle behavior, and the higher the bonding strength is, the more the macroscopic strength is enhanced, which is compatible with the experimental finding in [50]. In addition, the shear band is captured in the biaxial compression simulation as in Figure 7. Therefore our model successfully captures the main features of cemented granular media, and it can be used for a further study.

After sample generation, the specimen is isotropically compacted by four walls to reach the isotropic state of stress. Then the biaxial compression is carried out, where the top and bottom walls are moved inward as strain loading condition, and the left and right walls are allowed to displace to retain the confining stress as 111 Pa. In the simulation, the velocity of loading wall is set to a small enough value to ensure a quasi-static process.

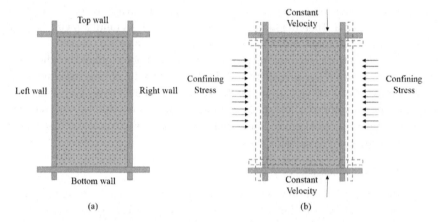

(a)   (b)

Figure 5. The DEM sample for biaxial compression simulation. (a) The hexagonal packing of the granular media; (b) the boundary condition for biaxial compression simulation.

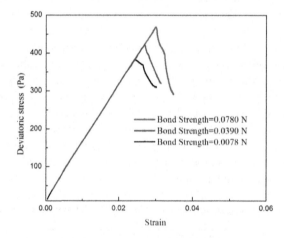

Figure 6. The deviatoric stress–strain responses of cemented granular media in biaxial compression simulation.

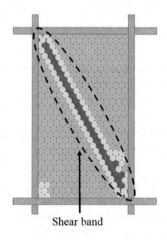

Shear band

Figure 7. Shear band after macroscopic failure of cemented granular media in the biaxial compression simulation.

In cemented granular media, bond is a primary property determining its macroscopic behavior, and the failure of granular media is generally owing to the bond breakage [24]. Thus the number of cumulative bond breakage is monitored during the biaxial compression simulation to show the relationship between bond breakage and macroscopic mechanical behavior. Figure 8 presents the number of accumulative bond during the biaxial compression simulation. It is observed that when the failure of sample occurs, the number of cumulative bond breakage increases greatly, just as in [51]. Thus, in sand production simulation, the number of accumulative bond breakage will be monitored as an indicator of the damage in the sample, and the larger the number is, the closer the sample is to macroscopic failure.

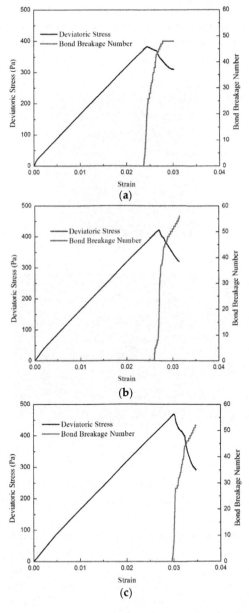

Figure 8. The deviatoric stress–strain response and number of accumulative bond breakage during biaxial compression: **(a)** bonding strength is 0.0078 N; **(b)** bonding strength is 0.039 N; and **(c)** bonding strength is 0.078 N.

4.2. Sand Production Simulation

Sand production is a phenomenon occurring during the extrusion of hydrocarbons from reservoirs, which makes a lot of trouble on the oil or gas production. Just as discussed above, the behavior of natural sands evidently is distinct from clean sands usually employed in laboratory owing to the influence of bond between sand grains [25]. Therefore, sand production of cemented granular media is simulated in this part by LBM-DEM with contact bond model, and the influences of bonding strength and flow rate on sand production are discussed.

4.2.1. Physical Model

A cross section of a single perforation through a weakly cemented reservoir is shown in Figure 9a. Owing to the high computational costs, it is difficult to consider the whole cross section. Thus the right part of the cross section is isolated to consider the flow erosion and stress loading on matrix, just as in Figure 9b.

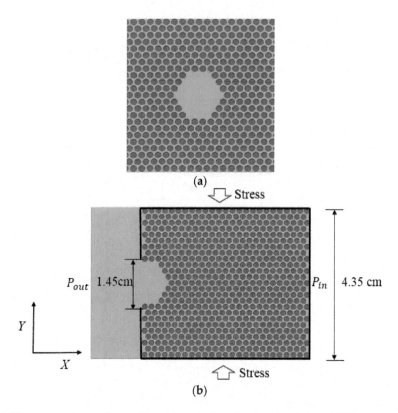

Figure 9. The cemented granular media used in sand production simulation. (a) The cross section of a single perforation in cemented reservoir; (b) the geometry of sample used in sand production simulation.

The sample is generated by hexagonal packing as in biaxial compression simulation, and for ensuring fluid connectivity in two dimensions, the hydraulic radius is used, which is a common method to deal with flow in two dimensions [7]. In three-dimensionally hexagonal packing of monodisperse sphere, the pore space is one third of the particle radius. In order to ensure the pore space in 2D close to that value, the hydraulic radius of the solid particle is take as 85% the mechanical radius. The cavity in the left part of cemented sample represents the tunnel perforation, which is 1.45 cm, and the rectangular container is created to collect the sand grains eroded by flow. In the following simulation, the dimensionless relaxation time (τ) is equal to 1, and there are 1396 lattices in Y direction leading to the grid size at 1.116×10^{-5} m. From Equation (2) the time step can be calculated ($dt = 1.6 \times 10^{-4}$ s) which is a safe value for a stable solution in DEM integration, because it is smaller than the DEM critical time step limit (9×10^{-4} s) calculated by:

$$dt_{DEM}^{cri} = \sqrt{m/K_n}$$

where m is the mass of particle, K_n is the normal spring stiffness. Moreover, under this grid system the largest Mach number in sand production simulation is $O(10^{-3})$ which is much smaller than 0.1, so the deleterious compressibility effect can be annihilated [15].

In order to couple the two mechanisms in sand production: (i) mechanical instabilities and (ii) hydro-mechanical instabilities [6], an external stress is loaded in Y direction and a fluid flow is applied in X direction. Thus the top and bottom wall are moved inwards as a stress loading in Y direction with the left and right wall fixed. During the simulation the strain in y direction is monitored to reflect loading condition. Meanwhile, the fluid with the property of water is set a pressure drop in X direction to capture the flow erosion, and in Y direction the top and bottom wall are treated as no-slip boundary condition.

4.2.2. Damage Evolution

Before quantitative discussion, the phenomenological observation of damage evolution in cemented granular media is presented firstly to understand the process of sand production, which is important to study the instability mechanism on sand production [5]. Although visualization is quite cumbersome in experiment, it can be easily achieved using simulations (Figure 10).

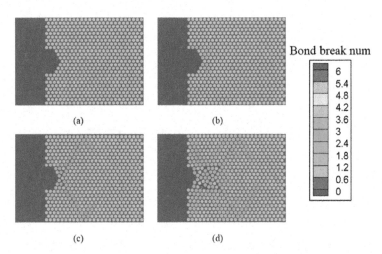

Figure 10. The process of sand production in cemented granular media. (**a**) Initially, the sample is intact with no bonding breakage; (**b**) the bond near the cavity begins to be broken; (**c**) small cracks propagate into the sample leading to the localized failure near the cavity; (**d**) the flow erodes the localized failure zone.

Figure 10 shows the damage evolution of the cemented sample with bonding strength of 0.078 N under the effective stress and flow erosion, where the color of the sand grain represents the number of bond breakage, and the warmer the color is, the more bonds on the sand grain are broken. Initially, the sample is intact with no bonding breakage (Figure 10a). With the increase of the strain, the bond near the cavity begins to be broken owing to the concentration of effective stress, and some small cracks forms in this zone (Figure 10b). Then, these small cracks propagate into the sample, which leads to the localized failure near the cavity (Figure 10c). Eventually, the flow erodes the localized failure zone and transfers the loose sand grains into the cavity (Figure 10d). It is observed that the experimental observation "initial sand production is evoked by localized failure" in [5] is examined by our simulation. What is more, although the localized failure is serious near the cavity, the zone far from the cavity is still intact, which means that sand production occurs well before macroscopic failure, just as the experimental observation by X-ray CT photographs in [5].

4.2.3. Effect of Bonding Strength

In cemented granular media, bonding strength is a primary property that influences its mechanical behavior. It is necessary to study the effect of bonding strength on sand production, so three cemented samples with different bonding strength are considered, which are 0.0078 N, 0.039 N and 0.078 N, respectively. Just as illustrated above, during sand production simulation the accumulative bond breakage is monitored as an indicator of the damage caused by effective stress and flow erosion.

Figure 11 shows the number of accumulative bond breakage in three samples under the same flow condition (dp/dx = 2.86 Pa/m). First, a staged growth of accumulative bond breakage is observed for all samples, which means a great increase of bond breakage is always followed by a very slow growth. This is owing to the fact that under effective stress and flow erosion, instability and temporary stability take place alternately in cemented sample. Before macroscopic failure, the cemented granular media is in a temporarily stable state until the effective stress increases to a value strong enough to break this temporarily stable state. Because the macroscopic failure has not occurred, another temporarily stable state can be rebuilt. As a result, on the temporarily stable state, a few bonds are broken in the sample, but when the temporarily stable state is broken, a great increase of bond breakage can be observed. These two states occurring alternately lead to the staged growth of accumulative bond breakage (Figure 11).

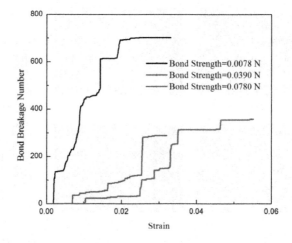

Figure 11. The number of accumulative bond breakage for three cemented samples under the pressure gradient of 2.86 Pa/m.

Although the tendencies of three curves are same, some obvious differences are still observed in Figure 11. First, the bond breakage occurs until the strain reaches a critical point, and higher bonding strength sample corresponds to a higher critical strain. This is because, for intact sample, the seepage force is too weak to break the bond, and the initial bond breakage is evoked by the concentration of effective stress near the cavity. Thus only beyond the critical strain, the effective stress is strong enough to break the bond, and the higher the bonding strength is, the higher effective stress is needed to break it. As a result, higher bonding strength leads to a higher critical strain to evoke the initial bond breakage. Another significant difference in Figure 11 is that under the same strain and flow condition, the accumulative bond breakage in low bonding strength sample is much greater than that in high bonding strength sample. Therefore, the cemented material with lower bonding strength is more likely to produce sand grains, which is confirmed in Figure 12. Figure 12 shows the states of two cemented samples with different bonding strength (0.0078 N and 0.078 N) under the same strain (0.024) and flow condition (dp/dx = 2.86 Pa/m). For higher bonding strength sample, as in Figure 12b, the cavity is stable, and no sand grains are produced. However, for lower bonding strength sample, as in Figure 12a, the stability of cavity is broken, and sand production continues up to end of the simulation. Therefore, for samples under the same condition, lower bonding strength leads to more sand production than higher bonding strength.

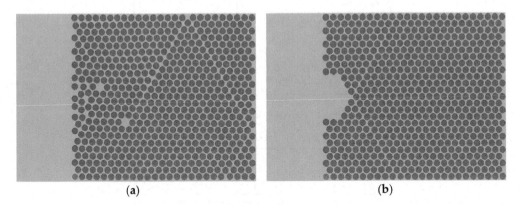

Figure 12. The state of cemented granular media with different bond strengths under the same effective stress and flow erosion: (**a**) continuous sand production for low bonding strength 0.0078 N; and (**b**) the stable cavity for high bonding strength 0.078 N.

4.2.4. The Effect of Flow Rate

Flow rate is the other important factor that influences the process of sand production in cemented reservoir, which leads to the hydro-mechanical instability. In the simulation, three kinds of pressure gradient are considered to study the influence of flow rate on sand production, which are 0.286 Pa/m, 0.572 Pa/m and 2.86 Pa/m, respectively.

Figure 13 shows the influence of flow rate on accumulative bond breakage in cemented granular media with bond strength of 0.0078 N and 0.078 N. It is observed that the influence of flow rate becomes significant until the strain reach some critical value, which confirms the conclusion that the role of flow in sand production is to erode the localized failure zone [4,5]. Before the critical strain, the cemented granular media is almost intact, and the hydrodynamic force provided by the highest flow rate cannot erode the sample. Therefore, there is little difference between various pressure gradient conditions. After the critical point, the localized failure near the cavity occurs, and the flow erosion starts to take effects, and the coupling effect of mechanical instability and hydro-mechanical instability becomes significant, so the curves of different flow rates begin to deviate from each other.

Comparing Figure 13a,b, in high bonding strength sample (0.078 N), the accumulative bond breakage under different flow conditions is almost same, but in low bonding strength sample (0.0078 N), the gap between different flow conditions is obvious and higher flow rate leads to more bond breakage. Therefore the influence of flow rate on sand production depends on the bonding strength, and it is more significant in lower bonding strength sample than in higher bonding strength sample. The same result was also obtained in [5], that the effect of flow rate on weak rock is in contrast to that on more competent rock. In competent rock, the localized failure zone is hard to be eroded by flow owing to the residual bond with high strength, so the coupling effect between mechanical instability and hydro-mechanical instability is not significant. However, in weak rock, the localized failure zone is easily eroded, which leads to a significant coupling effect between mechanical instability and hydro-chemical instability, so the influence of flow rate on sand production is more obvious in lower bonding strength sample.

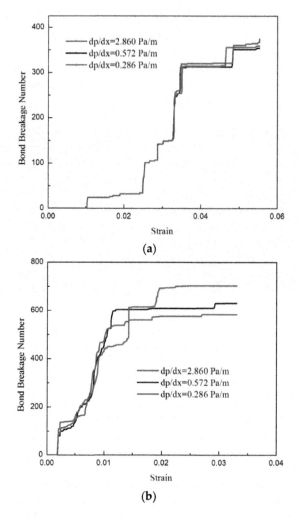

Figure 13. The number of accumulative bond breakage for synthetic cemented materials: (a) with high bonding strength 0.078 N; and (b) with low bonding strength 0.0078 N under different flow rate.

5. Conclusions

In this study, the sand production in cemented reservoir is simulated at pore scale by LBM-DEM. In order to account for the bonding effect in cemented granular media, a contact bond model is introduced into the LBM-DEM framework, which is validated by benchmark cases. By sand production simulation, the experimental observation that "initial sand production is evoked by localized failure" is confirmed, and it is also found that instability and temporary stability take place alternately in cemented granular media, until the macroscopic failure occurs. Then the influence of bonding strength on sand production is discussed. Under the same condition, the cemented granular media with low bonding strength is easier to produce sand than that with high bonding strength. Finally, the effect of flow rate is invested, and it illustrates that the influence of flow rate on sand production depends on the bonding strength. In higher bonding strength sample, the influence of flow rate on sand production is not significant. However, in low bonding strength sample, the higher the flow rate is, the more severe the erosion in localized failure zone becomes. Therefore, this simulation captures the main feature of sand production in cemented reservoir and discusses the influence of the micro parameters, which helps us understand the underlying physics of this problem at pore scale. Since only 2D simulations are performed in this paper, in the future we will consider 3D simulations and enlarge our computational scale to make it more suitable for actual situation.

Acknowledgments: This work is financially supported by the NSF grant of China (No. 51176089 and U1562217), National Science and Technology Major Project on Oil and Gas (No. 2016ZX05013001), the PetroChina Innovation Foundation (2015D-5006-0201) and the Tsinghua University Initiative Scientific Research Program (No. 2014z22074).

Author Contributions: M.W. conceived and promoted this work. Y.C. developed and tested the original code. Z.C. upgraded the code and carried out the simulation. M.W., Z.C. and C.X. analyzed the simulation results. M.W. and Z.C. wrote the paper and C.X. gave some revisions to the text.

Conflicts of Interest: The authors declare no conflict of interest.

References

1. Ranjith, P.G.; Perera, M.S.A.; Perera, W.K.G.; Wu, B.; Choi, K.S. Effective parameters for sand production in unconsolidated formations: An experimentl study. *J. Petrol. Sci. Eng.* **2013**, *105*, 34–42. [CrossRef]
2. Papamichos, E. Erosion and multiphase flow in porous media: Application to sand production. *Eur. J. Environ. Civ. Eng.* **2010**, *14*, 1129–1154. [CrossRef]
3. Ranjith, P.G.; Pereraa, M.S.A.; Pereraa, W.K.G.; Choib, S.K.; Yasarc, E. Sand production during the extrusion of hydrocarbons from geological formations: A review. *J. Petrol. Sci. Eng.* **2014**, *124*, 72–82. [CrossRef]
4. Van den Hoek, P.; Hertogh, G.M.M.; Kooijman, A.P.; de Bree, P.; Kenter, C.J.; Papamichos, E. A new concept of sand production prediction: Theory and laboratory experiments. *SPE Drill. Complet.* **2000**, *15*, 261–273. [CrossRef]
5. Tronvoll, J.; Skj, A.; Papamichos, E. Sand production: Mechanical failure or hydrodynamic erosion? *Int. J. Rock Mech. Min. Sci.* **1997**, *34*, 291. [CrossRef]
6. Vardoulakis, I.; Stavropoulou, M.; Papanastasiou, P. Hydro-mechanical aspects of the sand production problem. *Transp. Porous Med.* **1996**, *22*, 225–244. [CrossRef]
7. Boutt, D.F.; Cook, B.K.; Williams, J.R. A coupled fluid-solid model for problems in geomechanics: Application to sand production. *Int. J. Numer. Anal. Methods Geomech.* **2011**, *35*, 997–1018. [CrossRef]
8. Cundall, P.A.; Strack, O.D. A discrete numerical model for granular assemblies. *Geotechnique* **1979**, *29*, 47–65. [CrossRef]
9. O'Connor, R.M.; Torczynski, J.R.; Preece, D.S.; Klosek, J.T.; Williams, J.R. Discrete element modeling of sand production. *Int. J. Rock Mech. Min. Sci. Geomech. Abstr.* **1997**, *34*, 231. [CrossRef]
10. Jensen, R.P.; Preece, D.S. *Modeling Sand Production with Darcy-Flow Coupled with Discrete Elements*; Sandia National Labs: Albuquerque, NM, USA; Livermore, CA, USA, 2000.
11. Zhou, Z.Y.; Yu, A.B.; Choi, S.K. Numerical simulation of the liquid-induced erosion in a weakly bonded sand assembly. *Powder Technol.* **2011**, *211*, 237–249. [CrossRef]
12. Climent, N.; Arroyoa, M.; O'Sullivanb, C.; Gensa, A. Sand production simulation coupling DEM with CFD. *Eur. J. Environ. Civ. Eng.* **2014**, *18*, 983–1008. [CrossRef]
13. Li, L.; Papamichos, E.; Cerasi, P. Investigation of sand production mechanisms using DEM with fluid flow. In Proceedings of the International Symposium of the International Society for Rock Mechanics (Eurock'06), Liege, Belgium, 13–15 August 2014.
14. Han, Y.; Cundall, P.A. LBM-DEM modeling of fluid-solid interaction in porous media. *Int. J. Numer. Anal. Methods Geomech.* **2013**, *37*, 1391–1407. [CrossRef]
15. Chen, S.; Doolen, G.D. Lattice boltzmann method for fluid flows. *Annu. Rev. Fluid Mech.* **1998**, *30*, 329–364. [CrossRef]
16. Wang, M.; Chen, S. Electroosmosis in homogeneously charged micro- and nanoscale random porous media. *J. Coll. Interface Sci.* **2007**, *314*, 264–273. [CrossRef] [PubMed]
17. Wang, M.; Pan, N. Predictions of effective physical properties of complex multiphase materials. *Mater. Sci. Eng. R Rep.* **2008**, *63*, 1–30. [CrossRef]
18. Aidun, C.K.; Clausen, J.R. Lattice-Boltzmann Method for Complex Flows. *Annu. Rev. Fluid Mech.* **2010**, *42*, 439–472. [CrossRef]
19. Ladd, A.J.C. Numerical simulations of particulate suspensions via a discretized Boltzmann equation. Part 1. Theoretical foundation. *J. Fluid Mech.* **1994**, *271*, 285–309. [CrossRef]

20. Aidun, C.K.; Lu, Y.; Ding, E.J. Direct analysis of particulate suspensions with inertia using the discrete Boltzmann equation. *J. Fluid Mech.* **1998**, *373*, 287–311. [CrossRef]
21. Chen, Y.; Kanga, Q.; Caia, Q.; Wanga, M.; Zhang, D. Lattice Boltzmann Simulation of Particle Motion in Binary Immiscible Fluids. *Commun. Comput. Phys.* **2015**, *18*, 757–786. [CrossRef]
22. Ghassemi, A.; Pak, A. Numerical simulation of sand production experiment using a coupled Lattice Boltzmann-Discrete Element Method. *J. Petrol. Sci. Eng.* **2015**, *135*, 218–231. [CrossRef]
23. Velloso, R.Q.; Vargas, E.A.; Goncalves, C.J.; Prestes, A. Analysis of sand production processes at the pore scale using the discrete element method and lattice Boltzman procedures. In Proceedings of the 44th US Rock Mechanics Symposium and 5th US-Canada Rock Mechanics Symposium, Salt Lake City, UT, USA, 27–30 June 2010.
24. Tronvoll, J.; Papamichos, E.; Skjaerstein, A.; Sanfilippo, F. Sand production in ultra-weak sandstones: Is sand control absolutely necessary? In Proceedings of the Latin American and Caribbean Petroleum Engineering Conference, Rio de Janeiro, Brazil, 30 August–3 September 1997.
25. Jiang, M.; Yu, H.S.; Leroueil, S. A simple and efficient approach to capturing bonding effect in naturally microstructured sands by discrete element method. *Int. J. Numer. Methods Eng.* **2007**, *69*, 1158–1193. [CrossRef]
26. Servant, G.; Marchina, P.; Nauroy, J.F. Near Wellbore Modeling: Sand Production Issues. In Proceedings of the SPE Annual Technical Conference and Exhibition, Anaheim, CA, USA, 11–14 November 2007.
27. Wang, M.; Kang, Q.J.; Pan, N. Thermal conductivity enhancement of carbon fiber composites. *Appl. Ther. Eng.* **2009**, *29*, 418–421. [CrossRef]
28. Wang, M.; Pan, N.; Wang, J.; Chen, S. Lattice Poisson-Boltzmann simulations of electroosmotic flows in charged anisotropic porous media. *Commun. Comput. Phys.* **2007**, *2*, 1055–1070.
29. Wang, M.; Kang, Q.; Viswanathan, H.; Robinson, B. Modeling of electro-osmosis of dilute electrolyte solutions in silica microporous media. *J. Geophys. Res. Solid Earth* **2010**, *115*. [CrossRef]
30. Wang, M.R.; Kang, Q.J. Electrokinetic Transport in Microchannels with Random Roughness. *Anal. Chem.* **2009**, *81*, 2953–2961. [CrossRef] [PubMed]
31. Zhang, L.; Wang, M.R. Modeling of electrokinetic reactive transport in micropore using a coupled lattice Boltzmann method. *J. Geophys. Res. Solid Earth* **2015**, *120*, 2877–2890. [CrossRef]
32. Yang, X.; Mehmanib, Y.; Perkinsa, W.A.; Pasqualic, A.; Schönherrc, M.; Kimd, K.; Peregod, M.; Parksd, M.L.; Traske, N.; Balhoff, M.T. Intercomparison of 3D pore-scale flow and solute transport simulation methods. *Adv. Water Resour.* **2015**. [CrossRef]
33. Kang, Q.J.; Zhang, D.X.; Chen, S.Y. Displacement of a two-dimensional immiscible droplet in a channel. *Phys. Fluids* **2002**, *14*, 3203–3214. [CrossRef]
34. Huang, H.B.; Lu, X.Y. Relative permeabilities and coupling effects in steady-state gas-liquid flow in porous media: A lattice Boltzmann study. *Phys. Fluids* **2009**, *21*, 092104. [CrossRef]
35. Huang, H.B.; Wang, L.; Lu, X.Y. Evaluation of three lattice Boltzmann models for multiphase flows in porous media. *Comput. Math. Appl.* **2010**, *61*, 3606–3617. [CrossRef]
36. Huang, H.B.; Huang, J.J.; Lu, X.Y. Study of immiscible displacements in porous media using a color-gradient-based multiphase lattice Boltzmann method. *Comput. Fluids* **2014**, *93*, 164–172. [CrossRef]
37. Chen, L.; Kang, Q.; Mu, Y.; He, Y.; Tao, W. A critical review of the pseudopotential multiphase lattice Boltzmann model: Methods and applications. *Int. J. Heat Mass Transf.* **2014**, *76*, 210–236. [CrossRef]
38. Chen, Y.; Cai, Q.; Xia, Z.; Wang, M.; Chen, S. Momentum-exchange method in lattice Boltzmann simulations of particle-fluid interactions. *Phys. Rev. E Stat. Nonlinear Soft Matter Phys.* **2013**, *88*, 013303. [CrossRef] [PubMed]
39. De Rosis, A. On the dynamics of a tandem of asynchronous flapping wings: Lattice Boltzmann-immersed boundary simulations. *Phys. A Stat. Mech. Appl.* **2014**, *410*, 276–286. [CrossRef]
40. Cao, C.; Chen, S.; Li, J.; Liu, Z.; Zha, L.; Bao, S.; Zheng, C. Simulating the interactions of two freely settling spherical particles in Newtonian fluid using lattice-Boltzmann method. *Appl. Math. Comput.* **2015**, *250*, 533–551. [CrossRef]
41. Galindo-Torres, S. A coupled Discrete Element Lattice Boltzmann Method for the simulation of fluid-solid interaction with particles of general shapes. *Comput. Methods Appl. Mech. Eng.* **2013**, *265*, 107–119. [CrossRef]
42. Verlet, L. Computer "experiments" on classical fluids. I. Thermodynamical properties of Lennard-Jones molecules. *Phys. Rev.* **1967**, *159*, 98. [CrossRef]
43. Jiang, M.; Yan, H.B.; Zhu, H.H.; Utili, S. Modeling shear behavior and strain localization in cemented sands by two-dimensional distinct element method analyses. *Comput. Geotech.* **2011**, *38*, 14–29. [CrossRef]

44. Wen, B.; Li, H.; Zhang, C.; Fang, H. Lattice-type-dependent momentum-exchange method for moving boundaries. *Phys. Rev. E* **2012**, *85*, 016704. [CrossRef] [PubMed]

45. Feng, J.; Hu, H.H.; Joseph, D.D. Direct simulation of initial value problems for the motion of solid bodies in a Newtonian fluid Part 1. Sedimentation. *J. Fluid Mech.* **1994**, *261*, 95–134. [CrossRef]

46. Feng, Z.G.; Michaelides, E.E. The immersed boundary-lattice Boltzmann method for solving fluid-particles interaction problems. *J. Comput. Phys.* **2004**, *195*, 602–628. [CrossRef]

47. Niu, X.D.; Shu, C.; Chew, Y.T.; Peng, Y. A momentum exchange-based immersed boundary-lattice Boltzmann method for simulating incompressible viscous flows. *Phys. Lett. Sect. A Gen. Atom. Solid State Phys.* **2006**, *354*, 173–182. [CrossRef]

48. Fortes, A.F.; Joseph, D.D.; Lundgren, T.S. Nonlinear mechanics of fluidization of beds of spherical particles. *J. Fluid Mech.* **1987**, *177*, 467–483. [CrossRef]

49. Galindo-Torres, S.; Pedroso, D.M.; Williams, D.J.; Mühlhaus, H.B. Strength of non-spherical particles with anisotropic geometries under triaxial and shearing loading configurations. *Granul. Matter* **2013**, *15*, 531–542. [CrossRef]

50. Wang, Y.H.; Leung, S.C. A particulate-scale investigation of cemented sand behavior. *Can. Geotech. J.* **2008**, *45*, 29–44. [CrossRef]

51. Hazzard, J.F.; Young, R.P.; Maxwell, S. Micromechanical modeling of cracking and failure in brittle rocks. *J. Geophys. Res. Solid Earth* **2000**, *105*, 16683–16697. [CrossRef]

5

On the Use of Benchmarks for Multiple Properties

Bartolomeo Civalleri [1], **Roberto Dovesi** [1], **Pascal Pernot** [2,3], **Davide Presti** [4]
and Andreas Savin [5,6,*]

[1]   Department of Chemistry and Center for Nanostructured Interfaces and Surfaces, University of Torino,
      Via P. Giuria 7, Torino I-10125, Italy; bartolomeo.civalleri@unito.it (B.C.); roberto.dovesi@unito.it (R.D.)
[2]   Centre National de la Recherche Scientifique (CNRS), UMR8000, Laboratoire de Chimie Physique,
      Orsay F-91405, France; pascal.pernot@u-psud.fr
[3]   Université Paris-Sud, UMR8000, Laboratoire de Chimie Physique, Orsay F-91405, France
[4]   Department of Chemical and Geological Sciences, University of Modena and Reggio-Emilia,
      Via Campi 103, Modena I-41125, Italy; davide.presti@unimore.it
[5]   Centre National de la Recherche Scientifique (CNRS), UMR7616, Laboratoire de Chimie Théorique,
      Paris F-75005, France
[6]   Université Paris 06 (UPMC), UMR7616, Laboratoire de Chimie Théorique, F-75005 Paris, France
*   Correspondence: andreas.savin@lct.jussieu.fr
†   It is our pleasure to dedicate this paper to Prof. Evert Jan Baerends, who always insisted on not only
      producing numbers, but on deep understanding of both the theory and the experimental background.

Academic Editors: Karlheinz Schwarz and Agnes Nagy

Abstract: Benchmark calculations provide a large amount of information that can be very useful in assessing the performance of density functional approximations, and for choosing the one to use. In order to condense the information some indicators are provided. However, these indicators might be insufficient and a more careful analysis is needed, as shown by some examples from an existing data set for cubic crystals.

Keywords: benchmarks; density functional theory; method selection; uncertainty quantification

1. Introduction

An increase in computing power has allowed the replacement of personal experience with databases (see for instance [1–6]). In the realm of density functional theory, these have become a valuable tool for both tuning and tailoring new methods (see [7–10] for recent examples) and, in particular, to assess the performance of density functional approximations [5,11,12]. Ultimately, benchmarks should help computational chemists in choosing the best method to be adopted in a new study. However, the large amount of available data requires synthetic and reliable indicators [13–15] capable of providing a ranking based on the quality of the approach. Unfortunately, these indicators do not always give the necessary information, so one has to go back to the database and analyze the data according to the objectives of the study.

Some examples are given below, where indicators might lead to erroneous conclusions:

1.   choosing the method giving the best results for *two* properties, A and B;
2.   choosing the method giving the best results for property B, knowing that property A is
     well described.

Benchmark calculations for density functionals on some cubic crystals, provided in [16], will be used as a concrete example.

It is not the purpose of this paper to rank density functionals, or to advise for or against any of the density functionals cited here: the questions raised are not connected to any specific functional. Their names appear only in order to facilitate reading and enable reproducibility.

2. When Condensed Information Is Not Sufficient

2.1. Setting the Problem

Consider two methods, X and Y: method X is "better" than method Y for each of the properties A and B taken separately. Should method X be chosen

1. when good results are needed for both property A and property B?
2. when it is guaranteed (it can be checked) that A is well described, but good results for property B are also needed?

The rapid answer would be to use the method X for both (1) and (2). However, after a brief reflection, it becomes evident that the information provided by the indication that X is better for A and B separately is not sufficient.

2.2. Two Properties Simultaneously Needed

In order to formalize the problem, let us call the set of systems in the benchmark database, S. The total number of systems is $N(S)$. A subset $S_{M,P}$ gives "good" results with method $M \in (X, Y)$ for property $P \in (A, B)$. The number of elements in $S_{M,P}$ is $N(S_{M,P})$. The probability of obtaining a "good" result with method M for property P is given by $p_{M,P} = N(S_{M,P})/N(S)$. We say that method X is "better" than Y for property P when $N(S_{X,P}) > N(S_{Y,P})$, or $p_{X,P} > p_{Y,P}$.

We now consider the case where $M = X$ is better than $M = Y$ both for $P = A$, and $P = B$. This is schematically represented in Figure 1 by disks corresponding to the subsets $S_{M,P}$. The color of the disks correspond to the properties (blue for property A, orange for property B). The disks in the left panel, corresponding to $M = X$, are larger than in the right panel, corresponding to $M = Y$, indicating that $N(S_{X,P}) > N(S_{Y,P})$. However, we do not have any information about the intersection $S(M, A) \cap S(M, B)$, the number of cases when properties A and B are both well described using method M. We cannot exclude that method X gives "better" results for a larger number of systems $N(S_{X,P}) > N(S_{Y,P})$ and for A and B separately, but that the number of systems for which the results are better both for A and B is smaller for X than for Y: $N(S_{X,A} \cap S_{X,B}) < N(S_{Y,A} \cap S_{Y,B})$. A similar result is obtained for the probabilities

$$p_{X,A \cap B} = \frac{N(S_{X,A} \cap S_{X,B})}{N(S)} < \frac{N(S_{Y,A} \cap S_{Y,B})}{N(S)} = p_{Y,A \cap B}$$

This is schematically represented in Figure 1 where the overlap of the disks, corresponding to the sets $S_{X,A} \cap S_{X,B}$ (left panel) is smaller than that corresponding to $S_{Y,A} \cap S_{Y,B}$ (right panel). In such a case, when "good" results are desired for both properties, A and B, it is better choose method Y, although method X was better when analyzing each property separately.

To be more specific, let us consider data for cubic crystals given in [16], and choose as A the lattice constants (LC) , and as B the bulk moduli (BM). We consider a method to be "good", if it reproduces the lattice constants within 3 pm, and bulk moduli within 3 GPa. The probabilities of obtaining "good" results with three different density functional approximations (i.e., LDA [17,18], PBEsol [19] and HISS [20,21]) are given in Table 1.

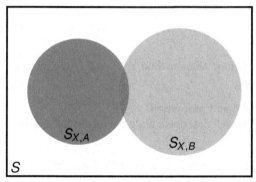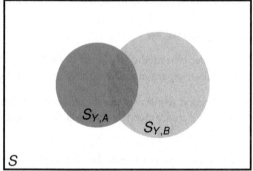

Figure 1. Diagrammatic explanation that method X can be better than method Y for property A and property B when taken separately, but method Y is better when both A and B are needed. Blue disks: cases when the method works well for property A; orange disks: cases when the method works well for property B; **(left)** method X; **(right)** method Y.

Table 1. Probability that a given method gives "good" results for the lattice constants $p_{M,LC}$, for the bulk moduli $p_{M,BM}$, and for both of them $p_{M,LC \cap BM}$. The uncertainty on all reported values, estimated by the Agresti–Coull formula [22], is about 0.1 for a data set of size 28.

Method	$p_{M,LC}$	$p_{M,BM}$	$p_{M,LC \cap BM}$	$p_{M,BM|LC}$
LDA	0.54	0.29	0.21	0.40
PBEsol	0.61	0.36	0.21	0.35
HISS	0.79	0.39	0.21	0.27

HISS gives the best results both for LC and BM. PBEsol comes next and the local density approximation is the worst. However, when we consider the performance for both LC and BM, LDA, PBEsol, and HISS perform equally. Note that the success probability is rather low.

We would like to stress that the numbers presented in the tables are only to indicate that the effects discussed here can show up. The size of the data set is too small to allow conclusions about the quality of the functionals.

The probability of obtaining a reliable result with method M is not $p_{M,A \cap B}$ as indicated above, but is the probability of obtaining a good result for B given that the result for A is good

$$p_{M,B|A} = \frac{N(S_{M,A} \cap S_{M,B})}{N(S_{M,A})}$$

Now the reference set is not the full set of data, S, but the subset of results reliable for A, $S_{M,A}$. Using the same example as above, we find now that $p_{M,BM|LC}$ increases from HISS to PBEsol, and to LDA (Table 1), in reverse order of the probability obtained for LC and BM individually.

Remark 1. *The problem presented in this paper is related to the lack of positive correlation between the errors made when computing different properties [23]. In the example given in Table 1, the rank correlation coefficients between the errors for lattice constants and bulk moduli are: -0.51 (LDA), -0.24 (PBEsol) and -0.65 (HISS).*

3. Improving the Quality of the Approximations Reduces the Risk of Unreliable Selection

The risk of such unpleasant surprises as presented above comes from the low quality of the approximations: in the limiting case when one of the method gives perfect agreement for both properties and the other does not, there is no doubt about which method to choose. In the following we will use a simple approach to improve the performance of the approximations and repeat the analysis made above.

The previous section uses the results directly provided by density functional approximations. A careful analysis of the data reveals that the parametrizations were not good enough to eliminate systematic errors. Having an exact density functional would obviously solve the problems presented above. An efficient way to correct, at least partially, errors of the actual density functionals is to apply a statistical correction, e.g., as a linear transformation [16,24,25]. This correction is a technique to eliminate the main part of the systematic errors, a necessary step to evaluate prediction uncertainty [16].

We now use *corrected* methods and evaluate their performance on the basis of prediction uncertainty, as reported in [16]. For the same methods as above, one can estimate the success probabilities reported in Table 2. One sees that the success probability has notably increased for *LC* and is slightly less for *BM*. In this group, HISS is not the best method for *LC* anymore, although it still is for *BM*.

Table 2. Probability that a given method gives "good" results for lattice constants $p_{M,LC}$, for bulk moduli $p_{M,BM}$, and for both of them $p_{M,LC \cap BM}$. The uncertainty on all reported values, estimated by the Agresti–Coull formula [22], is about 0.1 for a data set of size 28. Results are obtained using *corrected* methods.

Corrected Method	$p_{M,LC}$	$p_{M,BM}$	$p_{M,LC \cap BM}$	$p_{M,BM \mid LC}$
LDA	0.79	0.32	0.25	0.32
PBEsol	1.00	0.46	0.46	0.46
HISS	0.89	0.54	0.46	0.52

Comparing PBEsol and HISS with LDA individually we notice that the joint and conditional probabilities preserve the supremacy of both "best" methods for individual properties. With PBEsol, as *LC* is perfect the error only comes from *BM*. Joint and conditional probabilities become equal to p_{BM}. With one property perfect, the error of the other determines everything. For HISS, *LC* is not so good, but *BM* is better, so the joint probabilities are not worse than for PBEsol and the conditional probabilities are even better than for PBEsol.

4. Conclusions

The wealth of methods available, e.g., density functional approximations, require a selection to be made prior to undertaking a study. This can be made based on benchmark data sets. However, the information condensed from such data sets can be misleading and should be adapted to the study for which the method is chosen.

If a benchmark provides the information that a method X is better than a method Y for some properties $A, B, \ldots$ it does not necessarily mean that the method X is better when these properties are all needed for a given study. In other words, the probability of obtaining a "good" result for each of the properties is not the same as the probability of obtaining a "good" result for all the properties. Similarly, when a property can be tested and only systems that pass this test are considered, the statement that a given method is superior to the other methods for each of the properties is insufficient for choosing a functional for the remaining properties. Numerical results from existing benchmarks show that such situations can appear.

The solution to these problems is relatively simple, but one has to go back to the full set of data used in the benchmark and construct the measure relevant to the project. Unfortunately, this is not always possible: benchmarks are not always constructed using the same set of molecules for different properties.

A final remark: although we used "probabilities" to obtain a "good" result in this paper, confusions such as those indicated here can show up also for other measures rating the quality of an approximation.

Author Contributions: AS designed the study. AS and PP performed the calculations, analyzed the results, and drafted and finalized the paper. BC, RD and DP provided the necessary computational and reference data and contributed to the discussion and redaction. All the authors have read and approved the final manuscript.

Conflicts of Interest: The authors declare no conflict of interest.

References

1. Curtiss, L.A.; Raghavachari, K.; Redfern, P.C.; Pople, J.A. Assessment of Gaussian-3 and density functional theories for a larger experimental test set. *J. Chem. Phys.* **2000**, *112*, 7374–7383.

2. Curtiss, L.A.; Redfern, P.C.; Raghavachari, K. Assessment of Gaussian-3 and density-functional theories on the G3/05 test set of experimental energies. *J. Chem. Phys.* **2005**, *123*, doi:10.1063/1.2039080.

3. Karton, A.; Daon, S.; Martin, J.M.L. W4-11: A high-confidence benchmark dataset for computational thermochemistry derived from first-principles {W4} Data. *Chem. Phys. Lett.* **2011**, *510*, 165–178.

4. Goerigk, L.; Grimme, S. Efficient and accurate double-hybrid-meta-GGA density functionals evaluation with the extended GMTKN30 database for general main group thermochemistry, kinetics, and noncovalent interactions. *J. Chem. Theory Comput.* **2010**, *7*, 291–309.

5. Peverati, R.; Truhlar, D.G. Quest for a universal density functional: The accuracy of density functionals across a broad spectrum of databases in chemistry and physics. *Philos. Trans. R. Soc. Lond. A* **2014**, *372*, doi:10.1098/rsta.2012.0476 .

6. Lejaeghere, K.; Van Speybroeck, V.; Van Oost, G.; Cottenier, S. Error estimates for solid-state density-functional theory predictions: An overview by means of the ground-state elemental crystals. *Crit. Rev. Solid State Mater. Sci.* **2014**, *39*, 1–24.

7. Wellendorff, J.; Lundgaard, K.T.; Møgelhøj, A.; Petzold, V.; Landis, D.D.; Nørskov, J.K.; Bligaard, T.; Jacobsen, K.W. Density functionals for surface science: Exchange-correlation model development with Bayesian error estimation. *Phys. Rev. B* **2012**, *85*, doi:10.1103/PhysRevB.85.235149.

8. Wellendorff, J.; Lundgaard, K.T.; Jacobsen, K.W.; Bligaard, T. mBEEF: An accurate semi-local Bayesian error estimation density functional. *J. Chem. Phys.* **2014**, *140*, doi:10.1063/1.4870397.

9. Mardirossian, N.; Head-Gordon, M. ωB97X-V: A 10-parameter, range-separated hybrid, generalized gradient approximation density functional with nonlocal correlation, designed by a survival-of-the-fittest strategy. *Phys. Chem. Chem. Phys.* **2014**, *16*, 9904–9924.

10. Yu, H.S.; Zhang, W.; Verma, P.; Xiao Heac, X.; Truhlar, D.G. Nonseparable exchange–correlation functional for molecules, including homogeneous catalysis involving transition metals. *Phys. Chem. Chem. Phys.* **2015**, *17*, 12146–12160.

11. Goerigk, L.; Grimme, S. A thorough benchmark of density functional methods for general main group thermochemistry, kinetics, and noncovalent interactions. *Phys. Chem. Chem. Phys.* **2011**, *13*, 6670–6688.

12. Hao, P.; Sun, J.; Xiao, B.; Ruzsinszky, A.; Csonka, G.I.; Tao, J.; Glindmeyer, S.; Perdew, J.P. Performance of meta-GGA functionals on general main group thermochemistry, kinetics, and noncovalent interactions. *J. Chem. Theory Comput.* **2013**, *9*, 355–363.

13. Civalleri, B.; Presti, D.; Dovesi, R.; Savin, A. On choosing the best density functional approximation. In *Chemical Modelling: Applications and Theory*; Royal Society of Chemistry: London, UK, 2012; Volume 9, pp. 168–185.

14. Savin, A.; Johnson, E.R. Judging density functional approximations: Some pitfalls of statistics. *Top. Curr. Chem.* **2015**, *365*, 81–95.

15. Perdew, J.P.; Sun, J.; Garza, A.J.; Scuseria, G. Intensive atomization energy: Re-thinking a metric for electronic-structure-theory methods. *Z. Phys. Chem.* **2016**, in press.

16. Pernot, P.; Civalleri, B.; Presti, D.; Savin, A. Prediction uncertainty of density functional approximations for properties of crystals with cubic symmetry. *J. Phys. Chem. A* **2015**, *119*, 5288–5304.

17. Slater, J.C. A simplification of the hartree-fock method. *Phys. Rev.* **1951**, *81*, 385–390.

18. Vosko, S.H.; Wilk, L.; Nusair, M. Accurate spin-dependent electron liquid correlation energies for local spin density calculations: A critical analysis. *Can. J. Phys.* **1980**, *58*, 1200–1211.

19. Perdew, J.P.; Ruzsinszky, A.; Csonka, G.I.; Vydrov, O.A.; Scuseria, G.E.; Constantin, L.A.; Zhou, X.; Burke, K. Restoring the density-gradient expansion for exchange in solids and surfaces. *Phys. Rev. Lett.* **2008**, *100*, doi:10.1103/PhysRevLett.100.136406.

20. Henderson, T.M.; Izmaylov, A.F.; Scuseria, G.E.; Savin, A. The importance of middle-range hartree-fock-type exchange for hybrid density functionals. *J. Chem. Phys.* **2007**, *127*, doi:10.1063/1.2822021.

21. Henderson, T.M.; Izmaylov, A.F.; Scuseria, G.E.; Savin, A. Assessment of a middle-range hybrid functional. *J. Chem. Theory Comput.* **2008**, *4*, 1254–1262.

22. Brown, L.D.; Cai, T.T.; DasGupta, A. Interval estimation for a binomial proportion. *Stat. Sci.* **2001**, *16*, 101–133.

23. Lejaeghere, K.; Vanduyfhuys, L.; Verstraelen, T.; Speybroeck, V.V.; Cottenier, S. Is the error on first-principles volume predictions absolute or relative? *Comput. Mater. Sci.* **2016**, *117*, 390–396.

24. Duan, X.M.; Song, G.L.; Li, Z.H.; Wang, X.J.; Chen, G.H.; Fan, K.N. Accurate prediction of heat of formation by combining Hartree-Fock/density functional theory calculation with linear regression correction approach. *J. Chem. Phys.* **2004**, *121*, doi:10.1063/1.1786582.

25. Lejaeghere, K.; Jaeken, J.; Speybroeck, V.V.; Cottenier, S. Ab initio based thermal property predictions at a low cost: An error analysis. *Phys. Rev. B* **2014**, *89*, doi:10.1103/PhysRevB.89.014304.

6

Modeling Groundwater Flow in Heterogeneous Porous Media with YAGMod

Laura Cattaneo [1,2], **Alessandro Comunian** [1], **Giovanna de Filippis** [1,3], **Mauro Giudici** [1,2,3,*] and **Chiara Vassena** [1]

Academic Editors: Qinjun Kang and Li Chen

[1] Università degli Studi di Milano, Dipartimento di Scienze della Terra "A. Desio", via Cicognara 7, I-20129 Milano, Italy; laura.cattaneo1@unimi.it (L.C.); alessandro.comunian@unimi.it (A.C.); giovanna.defilippis@unimi.it (G.F.); chiara.vassena@guest.unimi.it (C.V.)

[2] CNR-IDPA (Consiglio Nazionale delle Ricerche, Istituto per la Dinamica dei Processi Ambientali), via Mario Bianco 9, I-20131 Milano, Italy

[3] CINFAI, Consorzio Interuniversitario Nazionale per la Fisica delle Atmosfere e delle Idrosfere, Piazza Niccolò Mauruzi 17, I-62029 Tolentino (MC), Italy

* Correspondence: mauro.giudici@unimi.it

Abstract: Modeling flow and transport in porous media requires the management of complexities related both to physical processes and to subsurface heterogeneity. A thorough approach needs a great number of spatially-distributed phenomenological parameters, which are seldom measured in the field. For instance, modeling a phreatic aquifer under high water extraction rates is very challenging, because it requires the simulation of variably-saturated flow. 3D steady groundwater flow is modeled with YAGMod (yet another groundwater flow model), a model based on a finite-difference conservative scheme and implemented in a computer code developed in Fortran90. YAGMod simulates also the presence of partially-saturated or dry cells. The proposed algorithm and other alternative methods developed to manage dry cells in the case of depleted aquifers are analyzed and compared to a simple test. Different approaches yield different solutions, among which, it is not possible to select the best one on the basis of physical arguments. A possible advantage of YAGMod is that no additional non-physical parameter is needed to overcome the numerical difficulties arising to handle drained cells. YAGMod also includes a module that allows one to identify the conductivity field for a phreatic aquifer by solving an inverse problem with the comparison model method.

Keywords: groundwater; forward problem; inverse problem

---

1. Introduction

The flow of water in porous sediments is described in mathematical terms by joining the mass conservation principle with the phenomenological Darcy's law [1,2]. This results in non-linear equations for variably-saturated media and linear equations for fully-saturated ones. Non-linearity in the forward problem, which is solved to predict the state of the system in response to some forcing (e.g., pumping rates), is introduced by source terms or boundary conditions. The forward problem can be solved analytically only for simple cases, *i.e.*, usually for homogeneous media, domains with simple geometries and for simple source terms. Therefore, analytical solutions can be useful to interpret the results of field tests, e.g., pumping and tracer tests, and of laboratory experiments, where the boundary conditions can be effectively controlled. On the other hand, their use to predict the behavior of complex natural systems is limited by the assumptions that are introduced to simplify the equations and the boundary conditions. Therefore, in practical applications, a variety of computer codes, based on the classical numerical methods of the solution of partial differential equations (finite differences, finite elements, finite volumes, *etc.*), is used to solve the forward problem.

One of the most challenging problems in hydrogeology is modeling variably-saturated groundwater flow processes. A fully-rigorous solution of this problem requires knowledge of the non-linear relationship of conductivity and matric potential with soil water content, for all the lithologies recognized in the subsoil. Therefore, approximated approaches, which introduce relatively simple modifications of the classical equations for saturated groundwater flow, are often applied. They give rise to numerical difficulties in the presence of dry cells or elements, e.g., under the influence of an extraction source term. When a cell becomes dry, *i.e.*, its calculated water level falls below the bottom of the cell, two main problems arise [3–6]. First, the dry cell cannot receive external water, if it is declared as "inactive"; neither can it contain any extraction source term, unless it is rewetted, *i.e.*, the water level rises above a prescribed threshold. Second, drying and rewetting functionality often yields difficulties for the convergence of iterative algorithms used for the solution of the algebraic equations of the discrete model. Doherty [3] proposes an asymptotically small transmissivity to avoid drained cells being deactivated, even if they actually become dry: this approach uses a function that prevents cell transmissivity from becoming negative. The innovative idea of Keating and Zyvoloski [4] is a weak scaling for vertical connectivity, from partially-saturated to dry conditions. On the other hand, Niswonger *et al.* [6] use a quadratic approximation of the function that relates horizontal conductance to hydraulic head, over small intervals close to the fully-dry and fully-saturated limits.

Within this background, the first goal of this paper is to propose a code, YAGMod (yet another groundwater flow model), developed in Fortran90, for the simulation of constant-density, groundwater flow under stationary conditions, which is the extension of the codes developed by our research team over the years [7–17]. YAGMod is based on a conservative finite difference scheme for stationary conditions and is oriented to the simulation of flow in saturated media. It takes into account the possible drying of shallow blocks of the domain with an original approach, which limits the number of additional parameters that have to be assigned by the user and that have a weak physical significance. Notice that YAGMod considers both prescribed distributed sources and variable point sources. While the former can be used to simulate aquifer recharge, the latter can be used to simulate draining systems or the effects of the water head drawdown on a water-well discharge.

The second goal of this paper is to compare the algorithm used by YAGMod to handle desaturated cells with the above-mentioned algorithms proposed by Doherty [3], Keating and Zyvoloski [4] and Niswonger *et al.* [6]. This is performed by means of a simple, but significant test case.

Moreover, YAGMod includes a module for the model calibration, namely the identification of transmissivity from the knowledge of the reference head and source fields all over the domain. The calibration is performed for 2D flow conditions implementing the comparison model method (CMM). This method was originally proposed by Scarascia and Ponzini [18], successively developed by Ponzini and Lozej [19] and cast in a more formal mathematical framework by Ponzini and Crosta [20]. The CMM has been applied and implemented with success to study 2D hydraulic flow in regional aquifers [14,16,17,21–23], and therefore, for the moment, its implementation within YAGMod covers these kinds of systems only.

The third goal of this paper is a thorough and rigorous extension of the CMM to the case of a phreatic aquifer. This is possible because YAGMod takes into account the variation of the saturated thickness of each cell for the solution of the forward problem.

Generally speaking, the "best" model should permit one to properly describe the physical processes and should run with limited computational resources. Unfortunately, these objectives are usually conflicting: physical processes in natural systems might be very complex, non-linear and dependent on a huge number of physical parameters; the computer codes that can handle such situations require supercomputers with high memory capacity and a lot of parallel processors. Simplified approaches are commonly adopted by scientists and engineers. Nevertheless, relatively simple models and tests, like those proposed in this paper, can be very useful to cope with complex natural systems with a computationally-frugal approach, which can provide first insights into the relevant natural processes, on the most sensitive parameters, *etc.*, as recently shown, e.g., by Hill *et al.* [24].

2. Forward Model

This section is dedicated to a description of YAGMod, and particular emphasis will be given to its innovative features.

2.1. Mathematical Model and Discretization

The 3D flow of groundwater, considering constant fluid density and steady-state conditions, is described by the balance equation:

$$\mathrm{div}\,\mathbf{q} = f \tag{1}$$

which, using the phenomenological Darcy's law $\mathbf{q} = -K\mathbf{grad}h$, becomes:

$$\frac{\partial}{\partial x}\left(K\frac{\partial h}{\partial x}\right) + \frac{\partial}{\partial y}\left(K\frac{\partial h}{\partial y}\right) + \frac{\partial}{\partial z}\left(K\frac{\partial h}{\partial z}\right) + f = 0 \tag{2}$$

where $\mathbf{q}$ is Darcy's velocity (LT^{-1}); h is the water or hydraulic head (L); f is the source term, *i.e.*, the volume of water injected per unit time and unit volume of the porous medium (T^{-1}); K is the hydraulic conductivity (LT^{-1}).

The numerical solution of Equation (2) is found with the finite difference method. The continuous physical system is replaced by a finite set of cells or blocks, which are identified by three integer indices (i,j,k), $1 \le i \le N_x$, $1 \le j \le N_z$ and $1 \le k \le N_z$, and could be rectangular in the horizontal plane. The side lengths of the cells along the x and y directions, Δx and Δy, are assumed to be constant for all of the grid; the cell thickness, denoted by $\Delta z_{(i,j,k)}$, can vary for each cell. The center of a cell is called a node and is denoted with the same indices as the corresponding cell. Values of the hydraulic head are referred to each node, and the spatially-varying hydraulic conductivities are considered to be effective parameters of a cell.

The saturated thickness of a cell is given by:

$$\vartheta_{(i,j,k)} = \begin{cases} \Delta z_{(i,j,k)} = z_{(i,j,k)}^{(\mathrm{top})} - z_{(i,j,k)}^{(\mathrm{bot})} & \text{if } h_{(i,j,k)} > z_{(i,j,k)}^{(\mathrm{top})}, \\ h_{(i,j,k)} - z_{(i,j,k)}^{(\mathrm{bot})} & \text{if } z_{(i,j,k)}^{(\mathrm{bot})} < h_{(i,j,k)} \le z_{(i,j,k)}^{(\mathrm{top})}, \\ 0 & \text{if } h_{(i,j,k)} \le z_{(i,j,k)}^{(\mathrm{bot})} \end{cases} \tag{3}$$

where $z_{(i,j,k)}^{(\mathrm{top})}$ and $z_{(i,j,k)}^{(\mathrm{bot})}$ represent the height of, respectively, the top and bottom surfaces of a cell.

For each cell, an integral balance equation can be written. The water discharge into or from a cell is calculated considering only the six adjacent (first-neighborhood) cells (Figure 1).

In order to handle complex aquifers' geometries, each cell is identified by a domain code (Figure 2): I identifies the internal cells, for which the hydraulic head can vary freely; D identifies the cells where Dirichlet conditions are assigned, *i.e.*, the hydraulic head is prescribed; E identifies the cells external to the domain or where no flow takes place.

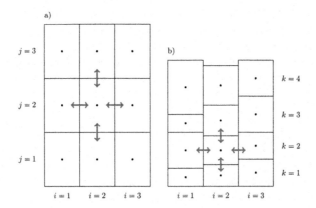

Figure 1. (a) Plan view of a domain's layer; (b) vertical section view. Red arrows are examples of groundwater fluxes through first-neighborhood cells and considered in the discrete model.

E	E	D	D	D	D	D	D	E	E
E	I	I	I	I	I	I	I	I	E
I	I	I	I	I	I	I	I	I	I
I	I	I	I	I	I	I	I	I	I
I	I	I	I	I	I	I	I	I	I
I	I	I	I	I	I	I	I	I	I
I	I	I	I	I	I	I	I	I	I
I	I	I	I	I	I	I	I	I	I
E	E	E	I	I	I	I	I	I	E
E	E	E	D	D	D	D	D	D	E

Figure 2. Domain code example in a 2D domain: I, E and D codes correspond, respectively, to internal, external and prescribed-head (Dirichlet boundary conditions) cells; the blue line denotes the border of the domain.

The integral version of Equation (2) could be discretized for each cell as:

$$K_{(i+1/2,j,k)} \frac{h_{(i+1,j,k)} - h_{(i,j,k)}}{\Delta x} \Delta y \, \vartheta_{(i+1/2,j,k)} \quad +$$

$$+ \, K_{(i-1/2,j,k)} \frac{h_{(i-1,j,k)} - h_{(i,j,k)}}{\Delta x} \Delta y \, \vartheta_{(i-1/2,j,k)} \quad +$$

$$+ \, K_{(i,j+1/2,k)} \frac{h_{(i,j+1,k)} - h_{(i,j,k)}}{\Delta y} \Delta x \, \vartheta_{(i,j+1/2,k)} \quad +$$

$$+ \, K_{(i,j-1/2,k)} \frac{h_{(i,j-1,k)} - h_{(i,j,k)}}{\Delta y} \Delta x \, \vartheta_{(i,j-1/2,k)} \quad +$$

$$+ \, K_{(i,j,k+1/2)} \frac{h_{(i,j,k+1)} - h_{(i,j,k)}}{\Delta z_{(i,j,k+1/2)}} \Delta x \, \Delta y \quad +$$

$$+ \, K_{(i,j,k-1/2)} \frac{h_{(i,j,k-1)} - h_{(i,j,k)}}{\Delta z_{(i,j,k-1/2)}} \Delta x \, \Delta y \quad + \quad F_{(i,j,k)} = 0$$

where $h_{(i,j,k)}$ is the hydraulic head at a node (L); $K_{(i-1/2,j,k)}$ and $K_{(i+1/2,j,k)}$ (LT^{-1}) are called internode (or interblock) hydraulic conductivities along the x direction (analogous definitions are used for the similar terms along the y and z directions); $\vartheta_{(i+1/2,j,k)} = \left(\vartheta_{(i,j,k)} + \vartheta_{(i+1,j,k)}\right)/2$ is the arithmetic mean of the saturated thicknesses of the cells (i,j,k) and $(i+1,j,k)$ (an analogous definition is used for cells along the y direction); $\Delta z_{(i,j,k+1/2)} = \left(\Delta z_{(i,j,k)} + \Delta z_{(i+1,j,k)}\right)/2$ is the distance between two adjacent nodes along the vertical; $F_{(i,j,k)}$ is the cell source term, *i.e.*, the volume of water injected in the cell (negative if extracted from) per unit time (L^3T^{-1}). Each of the nine terms appearing in the left-hand side of Equation (4) represents the water flux through an interface separating two cells.

A single value of hydraulic conductivity is assigned to every cell, and the internode hydraulic conductivity is calculated as the harmonic mean of the hydraulic conductivities of adjacent cells.

Equation (4) can be synthetically written for the most general case, by introducing internode transmittances as follows:

$$T_{(i+1/2,j,k)} = K_{(i+1/2,j,k)}\vartheta_{(i+1/2,j,k)}\frac{\Delta y}{\Delta x},$$

$$T_{(i,j+1/2,k)} = K_{(i,j+1/2,k)}\vartheta_{(i,j+1/2,k)}\frac{\Delta x}{\Delta y}, \tag{4}$$

$$T_{(i,j,k+1/2)} = K_{(i,j,k+1/2)}\frac{\Delta x\,\Delta y}{\Delta z_{(i,j,k+1/2)}}$$

Then, Equation (4) becomes:

$$
\begin{aligned}
& T_{(i+1/2,j,k)}\left(h_{(i+1,j,k)} - h_{(i,j,k)}\right) + T_{(i-1/2,j,k)}\left(h_{(i-1,j,k)} - h_{(i,j,k)}\right) + \\
& + T_{(i,j+1/2,k)}\left(h_{(i,j+1,k)} - h_{(i,j,k)}\right) + T_{(i,j-1/2,k)}\left(h_{(i,j-1,k)} - h_{(i,j,k)}\right) + \\
& + T_{(i,j,k+1/2)}\left(h_{(i,j,k+1)} - h_{(i,j,k)}\right) + T_{(i,j,k-1/2)}\left(h_{(i,j,k-1)} - h_{(i,j,k)}\right) = \\
& = -F_{(i,j,k)}
\end{aligned}
\tag{5}
$$

2.2. Boundary Conditions and Source Terms

Dirichlet, Neumann or Robin boundary conditions can be assigned. The cells where Dirichlet boundary conditions (prescribed head) are assigned are simply identified by using a D label for the domain code: in that case, the hydraulic head does not change during the computation of the solution. Neumann and Robin boundary conditions are implemented as specific types of source terms, as specified hereinafter.

2.2.1. Distributed Source/Sink Terms

This type of source or sink term simulates areally-distributed fixed source terms, such as rainfall recharge. For each contribution, an array of $N_x \times N_y \times N_z$ elements, $F_{(i,j,k)}^{(d)}$, represents the flow rate into each cell of the domain; it is independent from $h_{(i,j,k)}$, and its dimensions are (L^3T^{-1}). The user must consider that this type of source remains constant, even if the hydraulic head of a single cell becomes lower than the bottom of the cell during the iterative search of a solution.

2.2.2. Local Source/Sink Terms

In the YAGMod code, local sources or sinks, *i.e.*, those that are concentrated in a single cell, are modeled with the paradigmatic equation:

$$
F^{(\text{loc})} = \begin{cases} F_{(+)} - K_{(+)} \cdot (h - \mathcal{H}^{(\text{cal})}) & \text{if } h \geq \mathcal{H}^{(\text{act})}, \\ F_{(-)} - K_{(-)} \cdot (h - \mathcal{H}^{(\text{cal})}) & \text{if } h < \mathcal{H}^{(\text{act})} \end{cases}
\tag{6}
$$

where $F^{(\text{loc})}$ is the local contribution of the individual source or sink. $F^{(\text{loc})}$ depends on the hydraulic head in that cell, h, according to the difference $(h - \mathcal{H}^{(\text{cal})})$. $F_{(+)}$ and $F_{(-)}$ are fixed fluxes (L^3T^{-1}); $\mathcal{K}_{(+)}$ and $\mathcal{K}_{(-)}$ are conductances (L^2T^{-1}); $\mathcal{H}^{(\text{cal})}$ and $\mathcal{H}^{(\text{act})}$ are two reference head values (L). $\mathcal{H}^{(\text{act})}$ is a threshold, which establishes if a source or sink is active or which couple of fluxes and conductances, $(F_{(+)}, \mathcal{K}_{(+)})$ or $(F_{(-)}, \mathcal{K}_{(-)})$, should be used to compute $F^{(\text{loc})}$; $\mathcal{H}^{(\text{cal})}$, which could be equal to $\mathcal{H}^{(\text{act})}$ in many cases, is used to calculate the contribution to the source term, which linearly depends on h. All of these parameters can be separately defined for each source or sink.

Different combinations of $F_{(+)}$, $F_{(-)}$, $\mathcal{K}_{(+)}$, $\mathcal{K}_{(-)}$, $\mathcal{H}^{(\text{act})}$ and $\mathcal{H}^{(\text{cal})}$ allow the user to generate a great variety of source terms, some of which are listed and briefly described below.

- Drain:
  $F_{(+)} = F_{(-)} = 0, \mathcal{K}_{(-)} = 0; \mathcal{K}_{(+)}$ represents the drain conductance; $\mathcal{H}^{(\text{act})} = \mathcal{H}^{(\text{cal})}$ represents the drain elevation.
- Robin boundary conditions:
  These conditions can be used if the aquifer interacts with another water body and water exchange is controlled by the difference of the water head in the aquifer and in the external water body. They are introduced through Equation (6), by assigning the following parameters: $F_{(+)} = F_{(-)} = 0$; $\mathcal{H}^{(\text{act})} = \mathcal{H}^{(\text{cal})}$ are the reference hydraulic heads; $\mathcal{K}_{(+)}$ and $\mathcal{K}_{(-)}$ represent the conductances for flux out or into the cell. $\mathcal{K}_{(+)}$ and $\mathcal{K}_{(-)}$ depend on the conductivity of the materials that separate the aquifer from the water body at the reference water head and on the distance from this water body. Notice that for the simulation of limited domains of aquifers with a large extension, it is usually impossible to prescribe physically-based boundary conditions. In those cases, Robin boundary conditions are very useful to introduce fictitious boundary conditions, which are more flexible than prescribed head (Dirichlet) or flux (Neumann) boundary conditions. In these situations, $\mathcal{H}^{(\text{act})} = \mathcal{H}^{(\text{cal})}$ should be close to the estimated water head far from the aquifer system, and the conductances $\mathcal{K}_{(+)}$ and $\mathcal{K}_{(-)}$ can assume different values to take into account the geometrical, geological and hydrological characteristics of the aquifer.
- River/aquifer interaction:
  $\mathcal{H}^{(\text{act})}$ is the height of the bottom of the river: therefore, if $h \geq \mathcal{H}^{(\text{act})}$, the river and groundwater are in contact, whereas, if $h < \mathcal{H}^{(\text{act})}$, then they are separated by a vadose zone, i.e., partly-saturated sediments or rocks. In the first situation, $\mathcal{H}^{(\text{cal})}$ is the river stage; then, the river drains the aquifer if $h > \mathcal{H}^{(\text{cal})}$ and recharges the aquifer if $h < \mathcal{H}^{(\text{cal})}$. It is quite common to assume $F_{(+)} = 0$ and to consider $\mathcal{K}_{(+)}$ as a function of the conductivity of the river bed sediments, their thickness and the area of the contact surface between the river bed and the aquifer in the considered cell. In the second situation, namely if $h < \mathcal{H}^{(\text{act})}$, the river bed is assumed to be composed of fine-grained materials, which could be almost saturated, but poorly permeable, whereas the vadose zone between the river bed and the water table could be more permeable than the river bed sediments and approximated as dry. Therefore, the water flows through the river bed under a gravity-controlled, unit hydraulic gradient and freely flows through the relatively permeable vadose zone: then, $\mathcal{K}_{(-)} = 0$, whereas $F_{(-)}$ depends on the conductivity, thickness and extension of the river bed sediments in the considered cell and on the river stage.

2.2.3. Screened Wells

YAGMod considers a new kind of source term that takes into account the dependence of the wells' extraction rate on the aquifer water head. In particular, this kind of source term allows one to turn off the pumping if a cell becomes dry. Sources in this category are denoted as "screened wells", as the user has to give as input data not only the (x, y) coordinates of the well, i.e., the node indices i_W and j_W, but also the top and bottom elevation of the screened interval (top_W and bot_W) and the maximum well extraction rate, q_w.

The maximum extraction rate is subdivided among the cells intersected by screened intervals, as:

$$q^{(\text{scr})}_{(i_W,j_W,k)} = q_W \cdot \frac{K_{(i_W,j_W,k)} \, \mathcal{L}^{(\text{scr})}_{(i_W,j_W,k)}}{\sum_{k'=n^{(\min)}}^{n^{(\max)}} K_{(i_W,j_W,k')} \, \mathcal{L}^{(\text{scr})}_{(i_W,j_W,k')}} \tag{7}$$

with $k = n^{(\min)},\dots,n^{(\max)}$, where: $n^{(\min)}$ and $n^{(\max)}$ are the indices (along the vertical direction) of the cells corresponding to the top and the bottom of the screened interval of the well; $\mathcal{L}^{(\text{scr})}_{(i_W,j_W,k)}$ is the screened thickness of the well corresponding to a fully-saturated porous medium within the (i_W,j_W,k) cell and is computed as:

$$\mathcal{L}^{(\text{scr})}_{(i_W,j_W,k)} = \min\left(h_{(i_W,j_W,k)}, s^{(\text{top})}_{(i_W,j_W,k)}\right) - \min\left(h_{(i_W,j_W,k)}, s^{(\text{bot})}_{(i_W,j_W,k)}\right) \tag{8}$$

where:

$$s^{(\text{top})}_{(i_W,j_W,k)} = \begin{cases} z^{(\text{top})}_{(i_W,j_W,k)} & k = n^{(\min)},\dots,n^{(\max)}-1, \\ top_W & k = n^{(\max)} \end{cases} \tag{9}$$

and:

$$s^{(\text{bot})}_{(i_W,j_W,k)} = \begin{cases} z^{(\text{bot})}_{(i_W,j_W,k)} & k = n^{(\min)}+1,\dots,n^{(\max)}, \\ bot_W & k = n^{(\min)} \end{cases} \tag{10}$$

Notice that if $h_{(i_W,j_W,k)} < s^{(\text{bot})}_{(i_W,j_W,k)}$, then $\mathcal{L}^{(\text{scr})}_{(i_W,j_W,k)} = 0$.

If the cell (i_W,j_W,k) desaturates, the value of $q^{(\text{scr})}_{(i_W,j_W,k)}$ is corrected, so that the contribution of the well to the source term of the cell (i_W,j_W,k) is given by:

$$F^{(s)}_{(i_W,j_W,k)} = q^{(\text{scr})}_{(i_W,j_W,k)} \cdot \frac{\sqrt{\mathcal{L}^{(\text{scr})}_{(i_W,j_W,k)}}}{s^{(\text{top})}_{(i_W,j_W,k)} - s^{(\text{bot})}_{(i_W,j_W,k)}} \tag{11}$$

The latter equation implies that, at a given location, the water extracted from a cell reduces as the square root of the thickness of the screened interval that intersects a fully-saturated portion of the aquifer in that cell.

2.3. Solution of the Balance Equations

Equation (5) can be written for each internal cell, resulting in a system of possibly non-linear equations that can be written in matrix formulation as:

$$\mathbf{A}(\mathbf{x})\,\mathbf{x} = \mathbf{b}^{(\text{fix})} + \mathbf{b}^{(\text{var})}(\mathbf{x}) \tag{12}$$

where $\mathbf{x}$ includes the values of the water head in the internal nodes, $\mathbf{b}^{(\text{fix})}$ includes the fixed source/sink terms (Section 2.2.1), $\mathbf{b}^{(\text{var})}$ includes the source/sink terms that depend on the water head of the aquifer (Sections 2.2.2 and 2.2.3) and the terms appearing in the left-hand side of Equation (5) that involve the water head at D nodes. $\mathbf{A}$ is a sparse, symmetric, diagonally-dominant matrix, which is strictly diagonally dominant if at least one D node is present in the domain; its elements are built with transmittances and, therefore, depend on $\mathbf{x}$, as shown by Equations (3) and (4).

The solution to Equation (12) could be obtained with any of the methods of solution for non-linear equations that can be found in textbooks of numerical analysis. In YAGMod, a simple approach, based on a generalization of the relaxation methods for the solution of systems of algebraic linear equations, is proposed. This choice is optimal from the point of view of the memory requirement. Other approaches, e.g., Newton's or conjugate-gradient methods, could be more efficient in terms of elapsed running time, if the code is properly modified to profit from parallel computers. However, it should be noted that the specific problem addressed in this paper includes non-differentiable terms in the system of equations, like those introduced by Equation (6) and by the sequence of equations from Equations (7) to (11). Several tests showed that the generalization of relaxation methods is in general quite robust, in particular for complex physical situations.

2.4. Check of the Physical Consistency of the Solution

The proposed model does not solve equations for variably-saturated conditions, but aims at finding a solution for fully-saturated groundwater flow: the cells that become dry during the iterative algorithm of solution are not eliminated from the domain, but are used as auxiliary cells in the sense to be specified below.

If $h_{(i+1,j,k)} < z_{(i+1,j,k)}^{(bot)}$, then $\vartheta_{(i+1,j,k)} = 0$. If also the adjacent cells along the horizontal directions are dry, then the terms corresponding to horizontal fluxes in Equation (5) vanish, and therefore, the cell under examination is involved only for a balance along the vertical direction. This choice permits one to transfer the fixed source terms to deeper cells: this is necessary, e.g., to permit the aquifer recharge, which is assigned at the top active (*i.e.*, internal) cells, to reach the water table. Instead, if the adjacent cells have a non-vanishing, possibly small, thickness, then the physical situation implies that there is a horizontal transfer of water.

When the solution procedure is completed (Section 2.3), the computer code checks the physical reliability of the solution reached. First, a recursive function searches for every continuous path connecting partially- or totally-desaturated cells with the uppermost active cells. At the end of this checking step, every totally- or partially-desaturated cell needs to be connected with the surface, in order to allow air to infiltrate into the porous medium. Second, another function searches for the totally-desaturated cells for which the sum of all of the source terms is negative: such cells actually contain some outflowing source terms, but extracting water from a dry cell cannot be physically acceptable.

If one of these two physically unacceptable conditions occur (desaturated cells not connected with the surface; net outflowing source term from dry cells), YAGMod prints a warning message to the standard output and in the summary output file.

2.5. An Example

To show the relevance of these checks and the behavior of the code when dealing with screened wells, two simulations have been run using two different ways to manage an extraction source term. The domain is built up with $100 \times 100 \times 28$ cells of 2.5 m $\times$ 2.5 m $\times$ 2.5 m dimensions. A low conductivity lens ($K^{(L)} = 10^{-8}$ m/s) is included in a homogeneous, permeable medium ($K^{(H)} = 10^{-4}$ m/s). In the first simulation, a single deep well, whose extraction rate is about 0.06 m^3/s, is located beneath the lens at $x = 125$ m and $z = 20$ m; in the second one, the single deep well is replaced by a screened well, from 20 m to 45 m, whose extraction rate is the same as the other (obviously, distributed along the whole screened interval). In the latter case, the extraction rate is controlled by the hydraulic head. Results are shown in Figure 3. The simulation run with the deep fixed extraction rate yields physically inconsistent results: in fact, a group of completely desaturated cells is not connected with the surface. On the other hand, the simulation run with the screened well leads to a physically acceptable solution.

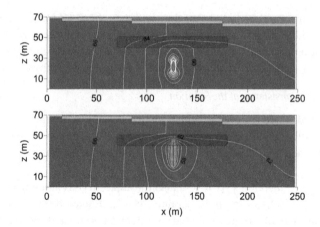

Figure 3. Contour lines of the hydraulic head (2-meter contour interval) and map of the saturation field (fully-saturated cells are drawn in blue; partially-saturated cells are drawn in green; dry cells are drawn in orange) along a vertical section for a 3D problem solved with YAGMod (yet another groundwater flow model). (**top**) A single deep well, whose fixed extraction rate is about 0.06 m^3/s, is located at $x = 125$ m and $z = 20$ m, beneath a low conductivity lens (dashed area). (**bottom**) The single deep well is replaced by a screened well, from 20 m to 45 m (yellow line).

3. A Simple Test Case to Compare Different Approaches to Handle Dry Cells

A number of different approaches to manage dry cells has been proposed [3,4,6]. Each approach calculates internode conductivities in a different way; in some cases, also effective extraction rates are calculated taking into account the saturated thickness. In this section, the algorithm implemented in YAGMod is compared to those approaches by means of a test case, which is very simple, but permits one to emphasize some significant properties of the different methods. In particular, the basic characteristics of the analyzed algorithms are briefly recalled using a simplified notation based on this example. A simple 2D domain has been constructed with a grid of $3 \times 1 \times 2$ cells whose size is 100 m $\times$ 100 m $\times$ 20 m. This 2D domain is illustrated in Figure 4, together with the cell numbering used in the following for the sake of simplicity.

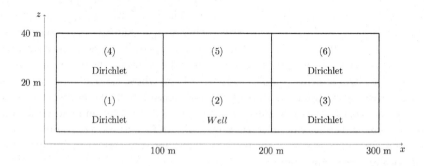

Figure 4. Scheme of the 2D domain used for the comparison test.

At cells (1), (3), (4) and (6), the hydraulic head is prescribed in such a way as to generate a hydraulic gradient along the x direction: $h_{(1)} = h_{(4)} = 40$ m, $h_{(3)} = h_{(6)} = 39$ m. At cell (2), an extraction source term is assigned.

The balance equations for the internal cells (2) and (5) can be written as:

$$K_{(1,2)}\vartheta_{(1,2)}\frac{h_{(1)} - h_{(2)}}{\Delta x}\Delta y \quad +$$

$$+ \quad K_{(3,2)}\vartheta_{(3,2)}\frac{h_{(3)} - h_{(2)}}{\Delta x}\Delta y \quad + \tag{13}$$

$$+ \quad K_{(5,2)}\frac{h_{(5)} - h_{(2)}}{\Delta z}\Delta x \Delta y \quad = \quad -F_{(2)}$$

and:

$$K_{(4,5)}\vartheta_{(4,5)}\frac{h_{(4)} - h_{(5)}}{\Delta x}\Delta y \quad +$$

$$+ \quad K_{(6,5)}\vartheta_{(6,5)}\frac{h_{(6)} - h_{(5)}}{\Delta x}\Delta y \quad + \tag{14}$$

$$+ \quad K_{(2,5)}\frac{h_{(2)} - h_{(5)}}{\Delta z}\Delta x \Delta y \quad = \quad 0$$

In the numerical experiments conducted in this work, $h_{(2)}$ and $h_{(5)}$ vary from minimum to maximum values, *i.e.*, in the interval from 0 m to 40 m. The balance errors $\epsilon_{(2)}$ and $\epsilon_{(5)}$ are calculated as:

$$\epsilon_{(2)} \quad = \quad K_{(1,2)}\vartheta_{(1,2)}\frac{h_{(1)} - h_{(2)}}{\Delta x}\Delta y \quad +$$

$$+ \quad K_{(3,2)}\vartheta_{(3,2)}\frac{h_{(3)} - h_{(2)}}{\Delta x}\Delta y \quad + \tag{15}$$

$$+ \quad K_{(5,2)}\frac{h_{(5)} - h_{(2)}}{\Delta z}\Delta x \Delta y \quad + \quad F_{(2)}$$

$$\epsilon_{(5)} \quad = \quad K_{(4,5)}\vartheta_{(4,5)}\frac{h_{(4)} - h_{(5)}}{\Delta x}\Delta y \quad +$$

$$+ \quad K_{(6,5)}\vartheta_{(6,5)}\frac{h_{(6)} - h_{(5)}}{\Delta x}\Delta y \quad + \tag{16}$$

$$+ \quad K_{(2,5)}\frac{h_{(2)} - h_{(5)}}{\Delta z}\Delta x \Delta y$$

The study of the existence and uniqueness of the solution of the problem is based on the analysis of the total quadratic balance error:

$$\epsilon_{tot}^2 = \epsilon_{(2)}^2 + \epsilon_{(5)}^2 \tag{17}$$

The method proposed by Doherty [3] uses for the horizontal interblock transmissivity an asymptotically small transmissivity function, in order to keep every cell active, even if it actually becomes dry. This approach uses a decay function that prevents the transmissivity of a dry cell from becoming non-positive:

$$T = \begin{cases} K\vartheta_r e^{-g\vartheta} + K\vartheta & \text{if } \vartheta > 0, \\ K\vartheta_r e^{f\vartheta} & \text{if } \vartheta < 0 \end{cases} \tag{18}$$

where T is the transmissivity; K is the hydraulic conductivity of a cell; ϑ is the saturated thickness, as for YAGMod; g and f, which are numerical parameters, and ϑ_r, the residual saturated thickness, are parameters supplied by the user. To ensure that the function defined in Equation (18) is continuous and continuously differentiable, the following relationship must be satisfied:

$$g = \frac{1}{\vartheta_r} - f \tag{19}$$

so that the user must specify only two parameters, f and ϑ_r. The transmissivity, calculated with Equation (18) for every cell (i, j, k) of the domain, is used to calculate interblock transmissivity with harmonic average. For the vertical water balance, Doherty [3] considers that if any cell in the domain becomes dry, then water inputs from the upper layer remain active. To improve vertical water exchange with the lower layers, *i.e.*, to permit recharge introduced at the model top to reach deeper cells, a linear reduction of vertical interblock resistance (reciprocal of conductance) is introduced using the following equations:

$$R_{(2,5)} = \begin{cases} R_{(2,5)}^{(u)} & \text{for } h_{(5)} > h_u, \\ R_{(2,5)}^{(b)} + \dfrac{h_{(5)} - z_{(5)}^{(bot)}}{h_u - z_{(5)}^{(bot)}} \left(R_{(2,5)}^{(u)} - R_{(2,5)}^{(b)} \right) & \text{for } h_u > h_{(5)} > z_{(5)}^{(bot)}, \\ R_{(2,5)}^{(b)} & \text{for } h_5 \le z_{(5)}^{(bot)} \end{cases} \tag{20}$$

where $R_{(2,5)}$ is the interblock resistance; h_u is the user-supplied water level below which the linear reduction of resistance is activated; $R_{(2,5)}^{(u)}$ is the "standard" interblock resistance given by:

$$R_{(2,5)}^{(u)} = \frac{1}{2} \left(\frac{\vartheta_{(2)}}{K_{(2)}} + \frac{\vartheta_{(5)}}{K_{(5)}} \right) \frac{1}{\Delta x \Delta y}$$

$R_{(2,5)}^{(b)}$ is the modified interblock resistance, calculated as the reciprocal of the "enhanced interblock conductance" $C_{(2,5)}^{(b)}$, given by:

$$C_{(2,5)}^{(b)} = mC_{(2,5)} = \frac{m}{R_{(2,5)}^{(u)}}$$

where m is a user-supplied multiplier. In Figure 5, the results obtained for different values of m from one to 100 and $F_{(2)} = Q = 0.1 \text{ m}^3\,\text{s}^{-1}$ are plotted: no significant difference was noticed among the simulations, so that in further tests, $m = 1$ was assigned.

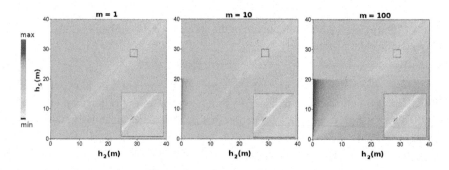

Figure 5. Map of the balance error given by Equation (17), for the approach of Doherty [3], as a function of the hydraulic heads $h_{(2)}$ (x axis) and $h_{(5)}$ (y axis), for different values of m ((**left**) $m = 1$; (**center**) $m = 10$; (**right**) $m = 100$). At the bottom right corner of each graph, the zone containing the minimum error value is enlarged.

The second investigated approach was proposed by Keating and Zyvoloski [4]. Horizontal interblock transmittance is calculated as follows:

$$T_{(1,2)} = \frac{1}{2}\left(\frac{\vartheta_{(1)}}{z_{(1)}^{(top)} - z_{(1)}^{(bot)}} + \frac{\vartheta_{(2)}}{z_{(2)}^{(top)} - z_{(2)}^{(bot)}}\right) \cdot 2\frac{K_{(1)}K_{(2)}}{K_{(1)} + K_{(2)}} \cdot$$

$$\cdot \frac{1}{2}\left(z_{(1)}^{(top)} - z_{(1)}^{(bot)} + z_{(2)}^{(top)} - z_{(2)}^{(bot)}\right)\frac{\Delta y}{\Delta x} \tag{21}$$

For vertical transmittance, the change from intrinsic vertical internode conductivity in a partially-saturated cell to zero in a dry cell would lead to a discontinuity. To improve numerical stability, Keating and Zyvoloski [4] allow a weak scaling controlled by a user-specified parameter, ξ:

$$T_{(2,5)} = \left[\min\left(1, \xi\frac{\vartheta_{(2)}}{z_{(2)}^{(top)} - z_{(2)}^{(bot)}}\right) + \min\left(1, \xi\frac{\vartheta_{(5)}}{z_{(5)}^{(top)} - z_{(5)}^{(bot)}}\right)\right] \cdot$$

$$\cdot 2\frac{K_{(2)}K_{(5)}}{K_{(2)} + K_{(5)}} \cdot 2\frac{\Delta x \Delta y}{z_{(5)}^{(top)} - z_{(2)}^{(bot)}} \tag{22}$$

Keating and Zyvoloski [4] suggest using a value of 10 for ξ, which provides both accuracy and stability for all problems.

The last approach considered for this comparison exercise is implemented in the UPW Package of the MODFLOW NTW model [6], a standalone version of MODFLOW 2005 [25]. The UPW Package smooths the horizontal conductance function during wetting and drying of a cell. Using this method, horizontal interblock conductance for our test is calculated as follows, by making reference to the example of cells (1) and (2):

$$C_{(1,2)}^{NTW} = \begin{cases} \eta & \text{if } X \leq 0, \\ \alpha K_{(1,2)}\left[\frac{0.5AX^2}{\Omega}\right] & \text{if } 0 < X \leq \Omega, \\ \alpha K_{(1,2)}\left[AX + 0.5(1 - A)\right] & \text{if } \Omega < X \leq (1 - \Omega), \\ \alpha K_{(1,2)}\left[\frac{1 - 0.5A(1 - X)^2}{\Omega}\right] & \text{if } (1 - \Omega) < X \leq 1, \\ \alpha K_{(1,2)} & \text{if } X \geq 1 \end{cases} \tag{23}$$

where $X = \left(h_{up} - z_{up}^{(bot)}\right)\left(z_{up}^{(top)} - z_{up}^{(bot)}\right)^{-1}$; h_{up} is the maximum between $h_{(1)}$ and $h_{(2)}$; $z_{up}^{(bot)}$ and $z_{up}^{(top)}$ are respectively the bottom and top level of the cell corresponding to h_{up}; η is a small value, usually taken as $\eta = 1 \times 10^{-9}$ m^{2}s^{-1}; $\alpha = \left(z_{up}^{(top)} - z_{up}^{(bot)}\right)\Delta y \Delta x^{-1}$; $K_{(1,2)}$ the internode conductivity calculated as $K_{(1,2)} = 2K_{(1)}K_{(2)}\left(K_{(1)} + K_{(2)}\right)^{-1}$; Ω is the smoothing interval length, which is suggested to be very small (10^{-5}), and $A = \Omega(1 - \Omega)^{-1}$.

In this approach, vertical conductance is calculated as in standard MODFLOW 2005 [25]:

$$C_{(2,5)} = 2\Delta x \Delta y \frac{K_{(2)}K_{(5)}}{\left(h_{(2)} - z_{(2)}^{(bot)}\right)K_{(5)} + \left(h_{(5)} - z_{(5)}^{(bot)}\right)K_{(2)}} \tag{24}$$

The pumping rate is reduced as the head in the cell drops below a user-specified percentage of the cell thickness, as:

$$Q^{NWT} = \begin{cases} 0 & \text{if } \delta \leq 0, \\ Q\left(-2\delta^3 + 3\delta^2\right) & \text{if } 0 < \delta < 1/\Phi, \\ Q & \text{if } \delta \geq 1/\Phi \end{cases} \tag{25}$$

where:

$$\delta = \frac{1}{\Phi}\frac{h - z^{(\text{bot})}}{z^{(\text{top})} - z^{(\text{bot})}}$$

and Φ is a user-specified fraction of the cell thickness, typically assigned as $\Phi = 0.25$.

The results obtained with the application of the four described approaches (*i.e.*, the three approaches described in this section and the one implemented in YAGMod), for three cases corresponding to an extraction rate Q varying from 0.1 m^3 s^{-1} to 0.2 m^3 s^{-1} and 0.3 m^3 s^{-1}, are represented in Figure 6. Notice that with the approach by Keating and Zyvoloski [4], $h_{(5)}$ cannot drop below the cell bottom; therefore, the results obtained with this method for extraction rates of 0.2 m^3 s^{-1} and 0.3 m^3 s^{-1} could not be significantly compared to those from other algorithms. Besides this remark, all of the methods give realistic results, even if the values that yield the least total balance error for alternative algorithms differ from each other.

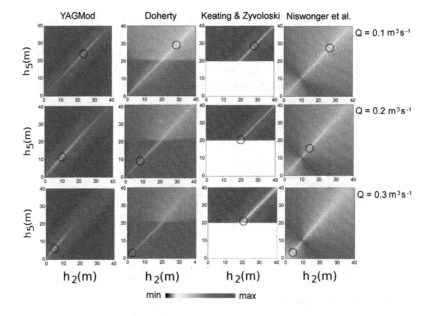

Figure 6. Map of the total quadratic balance error given by Equation (17), as a function of the hydraulic heads $h_{(2)}$ (x axis) and $h_{(5)}$ (y axis). From left to right, respectively, the results obtained with YAGMod and the approaches by Doherty [3], Keating and Zyvoloski [4] and Niswonger *et al.* [6]. From top down, the results obtained with extraction rates of 0.1 m^3 s^{-1}, 0.2 m^3 s^{-1} and 0.3 m^3 s^{-1}. The blue circles point out the zone where the least value of the total quadratic balance error is located.

The hydraulic heads computed with YAGMod for an extraction rate of 0.1 m^3 s^{-1} are smaller than those obtained with the other approaches; on the other hand, for higher extraction rates, the behavior is more complex, and no systematic difference is shown.

The color scales of the plots of Figure 6 are normalized with respect to the minimum and maximum total quadratic errors, separately for each method. Therefore, the images show that all of the methods yield a single minimum, and for YAGMod, ϵ^2_{tot} increases from the least value more rapidly than for other methods.

Finally, each of the algorithms, which are here compared to YAGMod, is based on some auxiliary parameters. Such parameters are not related to physical processes or quantities, but are necessary to apply artifices to face the numerical problems arising from the simulation of drying cells. These auxiliary parameters, which are listed in Table 1, have to be assigned by the user. On the other hand, YAGMod does not require any additional parameter. This is useful to limit the arbitrariness associated with the assignment of non-physical, auxiliary quantities.

Table 1. Parameters to be assigned by the user for the algorithms with which YAGMod is compared.

Algorithm	Parameters
Doherty [3]	θ_r, f, m
Keating and Zyvoloski [4]	ζ
Niswonger *et al.* [6]	η, Ω, Φ

4. Inverse Modeling with the Comparison Model Method

YAGMod permits the application of the comparison model method (CMM) to estimate the conductivity field for a 2D flow field by solving an inverse problem. The CMM was proposed to identify T at every node of a discretization grid [18] and successively developed to directly compute internode transmissivities [19]. Further modifications were proposed by Ponzini and Crosta [20], Ponzini *et al.* [26], Pasquier and Marcotte [27], Ponzini *et al.* [28]. The CMM was applied to alluvial aquifers in Italy [14,16,21], Switzerland [22] and Canada [23,29,30] and to a carbonatic aquifer in southern Italy [17,31].

4.1. Fundamentals of the CMM Algorithm

In this section, we summarize the working fundamentals of the CMM for the computation of the conductivity field for 2D stationary flow. Therefore, the k index is omitted in the following equations.

The CMM requires the knowledge of a reference head field, $h^{(\text{ref})}_{(i,j)}$, which is usually obtained from the interpolation of field measurements and any other relevant geological or hydrological information. Furthermore, a reference source term has to be estimated at every cell of the domain, $F^{(\text{ref})}_{(i,j)}$, and it coincides with the same term introduced in Equation (5) (for $k = 1$, as 2D flow is assumed).

Difficulties in estimating a realistic conductivity field from the application of the CMM could arise from the intrinsic instability of the inverse problem or the ill-conditioning of the discrete inverse problem [32]: these difficulties are mainly related to the behavior of the balance equation, which, when used for the forward problem, behaves as a K-to-h map, which smooths the high wavenumber (or short wavelength) components of the conductivity field. From the point of view of the inverse problem, errors on the head at high wavenumbers could be amplified, even if they have a small amplitude [33]. Therefore, it is often useful to smooth the reference head and source fields.

An initial guess of the conductivity field, $K^{(\text{CM})}_{(i,j)}$, must be assigned, for instance, by interpolating the values estimated from field tests. Then, the forward problem is solved for a comparison model (CM): the CM shares the same geometry and source terms as the model, which has to be calibrated. In particular, the forward problem aims at finding the head field, $h^{(\text{CM})}_{(i,j)}$, which solves Equation (5), for $k = 1$. For the CM, $h^{(\text{CM})}_{(i,j)} = h^{(\text{ref})}_{(i,j)}$ at the nodes where Dirichlet boundary conditions are assigned.

From the results of the forward problem for the CM, the aquifer unit discharge, *i.e.*, the water flow rate through the whole aquifer thickness per unit horizontal length, can be computed at each cell as:

$$\mathbf{Q}^{(\text{CM})}_{(i,j)} = -K^{(\text{CM})}_{(i,j)} \vartheta^{(\text{CM})}_{(i,j)} \nabla h^{(\text{CM})}_{(i,j)} \qquad (26)$$

where $\vartheta_{(i,j)}^{(CM)}$ is computed from Equation (3), with $h_{(i,j,k)} = h_{(i,j)}^{(CM)}$, and $\nabla h_{(i,j)}^{(CM)}$ is the discrete gradient obtained with a classical finite difference approximation. The real aquifer unit discharge could be estimated as:

$$\mathbf{Q}_{(i,j)} = -K_{(i,j)}\vartheta_{(i,j)}^{(ref)}\nabla h_{(i,j)}^{(ref)} \tag{27}$$

if the reference hydraulic head were a good approximation of the real head field, with the obvious meaning of the terms appearing in the right-hand side of this equation. If $K_{(i,j)}^{(CM)}$ is a good approximation of the real K field, then it is reasonable to assume that:

$$\mathbf{Q}_{(i,j)}^{(CM)} \simeq \mathbf{Q}_{(i,j)} \tag{28}$$

If we take into account only the absolute values of the previous expression, from Equations (26) and (27), the estimated conductivity can be found as:

$$K_{(i,j)}^{(est)} = K_{(i,j)}^{(CM)} \cdot \frac{\vartheta_{(i,j)}^{(CM)}}{\vartheta_{(i,j)}^{(ref)}} \cdot \frac{|\nabla h_{(i,j)}^{(CM)}|}{|\nabla h_{(i,j)}^{(ref)}|} \tag{29}$$

This is called the "integral" approach of the CMM, as opposed to the "differential" approach, which considers:

$$Q_{(i,j)} = |\mathbf{Q}_{(i,j)}| = K_{(i,j)}\vartheta_{(i,j)}|\nabla h_{(i,j)}| \tag{30}$$

as a function of $h_{(i,j)}$, both explicitly through $|\nabla h_{(i,j)}|$ and implicitly through $\vartheta_{(i,j)}$. A small variation of $K_{(i,j)}$ and $h_{(i,j)}$ should produce a small variation of $Q_{(i,j)}$; this is expressed in terms of differentials as:

$$dQ_{(i,j)} = dK_{(i,j)}\vartheta_{(i,j)}|\nabla h_{(i,j)}| + K_{(i,j)}d\vartheta_{(i,j)}|\nabla h_{(i,j)}| + K_{(i,j)}\vartheta_{(i,j)}d|\nabla h_{(i,j)}| \tag{31}$$

If the couples $\left(K_{(i,j)}^{(CM)}, h_{(i,j)}^{(CM)}\right)$ and $\left(K_{(i,j)}^{(est)}, h_{(i,j)}^{(ref)}\right)$ are considered, respectively, as the initial and final "points", so that $dK_{(i,j)} = K_{(i,j)}^{(est)} - K_{(i,j)}^{(CM)}$, $d\vartheta_{(i,j)} = \vartheta_{(i,j)}^{(ref)} - \vartheta_{(i,j)}^{(CM)}$ and $d|\nabla h_{(i,j)}| = |\nabla h_{(i,j)}^{(ref)}| - |\nabla h_{(i,j)}^{(CM)}|$, and if Equation (28) holds, then $dQ_{(i,j)} = 0$. Finally, from Equation (31), it follows:

$$K_{(i,j)}^{(est)} = K_{(i,j)}^{(CM)}\left(1 - \frac{\vartheta_{(i,j)}^{(ref)} - \vartheta_{(i,j)}^{(CM)}}{\vartheta_{(i,j)}^{(CM)}} - \frac{|\nabla h_{(i,j)}^{(ref)}| - |\nabla h_{(i,j)}^{(CM)}|}{|\nabla h_{(i,j)}^{(CM)}|}\right) \tag{32}$$

which is the expression of the estimated conductivity with the "differential" approach of the CMM.

The CMM can be modified and recast in an iterative fashion, to progressively improve the fit of the reference data. This is done by using $\ell = 0, 1, \ldots$ as the iteration index, by assuming a given initial guess $K_{(i,j)}^{(0)}$, and by substituting $K_{(i,j)}^{(est)}$ with $K_{(i,j)}^{(\ell+1)}$, $K_{(i,j)}^{(CM)}$ with $K_{(i,j)}^{(\ell)}$ and $h_{(i,j)}^{(CM)}$ with $h_{(i,j)}^{(\ell)}$ in Equations (29) and (32).

It is often useful to weight the correction introduced at each iteration with $w = \min(c|\nabla h_{(i,j)}^{(ref)}|, 1)$, where c is a positive constant, in order to avoid the excessive growth of some values where the reference hydraulic gradient is small and, therefore, the problem ill-conditioned:

$$K_{(i,j)}^{(\ell+1)} = K_{(i,j)}^{(\ell)}\left[w \cdot \left(\frac{\vartheta_{(i,j)}^{(\ell)}}{\vartheta_{(i,j)}^{(ref)}} \cdot \frac{|\nabla h_{(i,j)}^{(\ell)}|}{|\nabla h_{(i,j)}^{(ref)}|} - 1\right) + 1\right] \tag{33}$$

for the integral approach and:

$$K_{(i,j)}^{(\ell+1)} = K_{(i,j)}^{(\ell)} \left[1 - w \cdot \left(\frac{\vartheta_{(i,j)}^{(\text{ref})} - \vartheta_{(i,j)}^{(\ell)}}{\vartheta_{(i,j)}^{(\ell)}} + \frac{|\nabla h_{(i,j)}^{(\text{ref})}| - |\nabla h_{(i,j)}^{(\ell)}|}{|\nabla h_{(i,j)}^{(\ell)}|} \right) \right] \tag{34}$$

for the differential approach.

4.2. A Test

A simple test is used to show the application of the CMM. In particular, the reference K field is represented in Figure 7 (left image) for a domain with 10×10 cells and corresponds to a conductive inclusion in a less permeable domain. The reference hydraulic head is obtained by solution of the forward problem with Dirichlet boundary conditions and is represented by the image map in Figure 8. The results obtained from the CMM with a homogeneous initialization $K^{(\text{CM})} = 10^{-4}\,\text{m}\,\text{s}^{-1}$ are shown in Figure 7, both for the integral (central map) and the differential (right map) approaches.

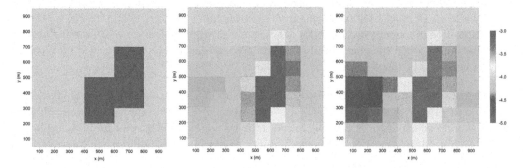

Figure 7. Simple test of the comparison model method (CMM): hydraulic conductivity field; the color scale refers to $\log_{10} K$, with K expressed in $\text{m}\,\text{s}^{-1}$. **(left)** Reference field; **(central)** field estimated from the CMM with the integral approach; **(right)** field estimated from the CMM with the differential approach.

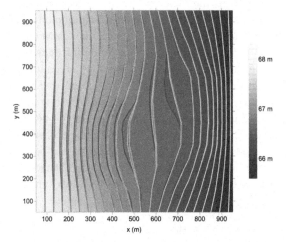

Figure 8. Simple test of the CMM: image plot of the reference hydraulic head and contour lines of the reference h field (purple) and of the h fields obtained for the K fields estimated with the CMM: yellow lines refer to the K field obtained with the integral approach (central map of Figure 7) and green lines to the K field obtained with the differential approach (right map of Figure 7).

The high conductivity region is quite well reproduced by the CMM, although it is a little bit faint, an effect that depends on the spectral response of the balance equation: this induces also some small differences between the water head computed from the K fields estimated with the CMM and the reference h field (see Figure 8), above all around the border of the high conductivity region.

5. Conclusions

Yet another groundwater flow model, YAGMod, has been described in this paper. The basic characteristics of this model are briefly summarized below.

1. When the water head in a cell is lower than the cell's top coordinate, the cell is considered as partially saturated, and its saturated thickness is used for the water balance. If the water head is lower than the cell bottom, then the cell is considered as dry, but it is not excluded from the water balance calculations. In fact, the water head in this cell is used to compute a vertical water balance that permits one to transfer source terms (namely, aquifer recharge) from the shallow layers down to the deep ones.
2. A large number of different sources or boundary conditions, which depend on the water head in the cell, are simulated with a single prototype equation.
3. If the position of the screened intervals of a water abstraction well is known, the extraction rate can be limited when the water head falls within the screened interval or turned off when the water head falls below the bottom of the screens.

The comparison of the algorithm used by YAGMod and those proposed by Doherty [3], Keating and Zyvoloski [4] and Niswonger *et al.* [6] shows that the different approaches yield different solutions, among which, it is not possible to select the best one on the basis of physical arguments. Nevertheless, the advantage of YAGMod is that it does not introduce any additional parameter whose values should be assigned by the user and which mostly have a limited physical significance. Differently, the other approaches require that the user defines one or more additional parameters. These parameters mostly have a limited physical significance, making the parameterization of the model more complex.

Moreover, YAGMod can be used also to solve the inverse problem with the CMM for a phreatic aquifer, with either an integral or a differential approach and taking into account the variability of saturation. This further strengthens the features of YAGMod, because the CMM is embedded in the source code and can be applied to estimate the hydraulic conductivity field, directly at the model scale. The present version of YAGMod is developed to apply the CMM with 2D flow fields, but it can be easily extended to 3D flows, if data with high quality and high density are available.

YAGMod is sufficiently flexible to be adapted to other situations, as was done to model groundwater flow in multi-layered coastal aquifers by De Filippis *et al.* [31], who modified YAGMod to cope with the variable thickness of the aquifer saturated with fresh water and to identify the spatial variability of a fractured and karst carbonatic aquifer with the application of the CMM to a single layer, while the parameters of other layers are fixed with estimates based on prior information.

The strategy used by YAGMod to cope with draining cells can be easily applied to integrated finite differences [34], but can be adapted also to other numerical techniques, which are based on the discretization of the integral balance equation over a given subdomain.

Acknowledgments: This work was partially supported by the Flagship Project RITMARE (La Ricerca Italiana per il Mare) coordinated by the National Research Council and funded by the Ministry for Education, University and Research within the National Research Program 2011 to 2013.

Author Contributions: MG promoted and coordinated the work. CV developed and tested the original code. LC, AC and GDF tested and upgraded the code. LC performed the comparison study for drying cells and the test for the CMM.

Conflicts of Interest: The authors declare no conflict of interest.

References

1. Bear, J. *Hydraulics of Groundwater*; Springer-Verlag: New York, NY, USA, 1979; p. 567.
2. De Marsily, G. *Quantitative Hydrogeology—Groundwater Hydrology for Engineers*; Academic Press: New York, NY, USA, 1986.
3. Doherty, J. Improved calculations for dewatered cells in MODFLOW. *Groundwater* **2001**, *39*, 863–869.
4. Keating, E.; Zyvoloski, G. A stable and efficient numerical algorithm for unconfined aquifer analysis. *Groundwater* **2009**, *47*, 569–579.
5. Bedekar, V.; Niswonger, R.G.; Kipp, K.; Panday, S.; Tonkin, M. Approaches to the simulation of unconfined flow and perched groundwater flow in MODFLOW. *Groundwater* **2012**, *50*, 187–198.
6. Niswonger, R.G.; Panday, S.; Ibaraki, M. *MODFLOW-NWT, a Newton Formulation for MODFLOW-2005*; US Geological Survey Techniques and Methods; USGS: Reston, VA, USA, 2011;Volume 6, p. A37.
7. Ponzini, G.; Crosta, G.; Giudici, M. The hydrogeological role of an aquitard in preventing drinkable water well contamination: A case study. *Environ. Health Perspect.* **1989**, *83*, 77–95.
8. Bersezio, R.; Bini, A.; Giudici, M. Effects of sedimentary heterogeneity on groundwater flow in a quaternary pro-glacial delta environment: Joining facies analysis and numerical modelling. *Sediment. Geol.* **1999**, *129*, 327–344.
9. Giudici, M.; Foglia, L.; Parravicini, G.; Ponzini, G.; Sincich, B. A quasi three dimensional model of water flow in the subsurface of Milano (Italy): The stationary flow. *Hydrol. Earth Syst. Sci.* **2000**, *4*, 113–124.
10. Valota, G.; Giudici, M.; Parravicini, G.; Ponzini, G.; Romano, E. Is the forward problem of ground water hydrology always well posed? *Ground Water* **2002**, *40*, 500–508.
11. Zappa, G.; Bersezio, R.; Felletti, F.; Giudici, M. Modeling heterogeneity of gravel-sand, braided stream, alluvial aquifers at the facies scale. *J. Hydrol.* **2006**, *325*, 134–153.
12. Felletti, F.; Bersezio, R.; Giudici, M. Geostatistical simulation and numerical upscaling, to model ground water flow in a sandy-gravel, braided river, aquifer analogue. *J. Sediment. Res.* **2006**, *76*, 1215–1229.
13. Giudici, M.; Ponzini, G.; Romano, E.; Vassena, C. Some lessons from modelling ground water flow in the metropolitan area of Milano (Italy) at different scales. *Mem. Descr. Della Carta Geol. d'Italia* **2007**, *76*, 207–218.
14. Vassena, C.; Durante, C.; Giudici, M.; Ponzini, G. The importance of observations on fluxes to constrain ground water model calibration. *Phys. Chem. Earth A B C* **2008**, *33*, 1105–1110.
15. Vassena, C.; Cattaneo, L.; Giudici, M. Assessment of the role of facies heterogeneity at the fine scale by numerical transport experiments and connectivity indicators. *Hydrogeol. J.* **2010**, *18*, 651–668.
16. Vassena, C.; Rienzner, M.; Ponzini, G.; Giudici, M.; Gandolfi, C.; Durante, C.; Agostani, D. Modeling water resources of an highly irrigated alluvial plain: Coupling and calibrating soil and ground water models. *Hydrogeol. J.* **2011**, *20*, 449–467.
17. Giudici, M.; Margiotta, S.; Mazzone, F.; Negri, S.; Vassena, C. Modeling hydrostratigraphy and groundwater flow of a fractured and karst aquifer in a Mediterranean basin (Salento peninsula, southeastern Italy). *Environ. Earth Sci.* **2012**, *67*, 1891–1907.
18. Scarascia, S.; Ponzini, G. An approximate solution for the inverse problem in hydraulics. *L'Energia Elettr.* **1972**, *49*, 518–531.
19. Ponzini, G.; Lozej, A. Identification of aquifer transmissivities: The comparison model method. *Water Resour. Res.* **1982**, *18*, 597–622.
20. Ponzini, G.; Crosta, G. The comparison model method: A new arithmetic approach to the discrete inverse problem of groundwater hydrology, 1, One-dimensional flow. *Transp. Porous Media* **1988**, *3*, 415–436.
21. Associazione Irrigazione Est Sesia. *Le Acque Sotterranee Della Pianura Irrigua Novarese-Lomellina. Studi e Ricerche Per La Realizzazione di un Modello Gestionale (Subsurface Water of Irrigated Novara-Lomellina Plain. Study and Research for a Managing Model Realization.)*; Report; Associazione Irrigazione Est Sesia: Novara, Italy, 1979. (In Italian)
22. Beatrizotti, G.; Hansen, W.J.; Spocci, R. Optimierung der Benötigten daten für ein numerisches Modell der Grundwasserbewirtschaftung im Lockergestein (Optimization of the required data for a numerical model of groundwater management in soil). *Gas Wasser Abwasser* **1983**, *63*, 469–476. (In German)
23. Benoit, N.; Pasquier, P.; Marcotte, D.; Nastev, M. Conditional stochastic inverse modelling of the Châteauguay river aquifers. In Proceedings of the ModelCARE 2005, The Hague (Scheveningen), The Netherlands, 6–9 June 2005; pp. 515–521.

24. Hill, M.C.; Kavetski, D.; Clark, M.; Ye, M.; Arabi, M.; Lu, D.; Foglia, L.; Mehl, S.   Practical Use of Computationally Frugal Model Analysis Methods. *Groundwater* **2015**, doi:10.1111/gwat.12330.

25. Harbaugh, A.W. *MODFLOW-2005, the US Geological Survey Modular Ground-Water Model: The Ground-Water Flow Process*; US Department of the Interior, US Geological Survey: Reston, VA, USA, 2005.

26. Ponzini, G.; Crosta, G.; Giudici, M.   Identification of thermal conductivities by temperature gradient profiles: One-dimensional steady state flow. *Geophysics* **1989**, *54*, 643–653.

27. Pasquier, P.; Marcotte, D.   Steady- and transient-state inversion in hydrogeology by successive flux estimation. *Adv. Water Resour.* **2006**, *29*, 1934–1952.

28. Ponzini, G.; Giudici, M.; Vassena, C. Comment to "Steady- and transient-state inversion in hydrogeology by successive flux estimation" by P. Pasquier and D. Marcotte. *Adv. Water Resour.* **2007**, *30*, 2051–2053.

29. Pasquier, P.   Résolution du probléme inverse en hydrogéologie par une estimation successive des flux (Solving hydrogeological inverse problem by successive flux estimation).   Ph.D. Thesis, École Polytechnique de Montréal, Montréal, QC, Canada, 2005.

30. Pasquier, P.; Marcotte, D.   Solving the Groundwater Inverse Problem by Successive Flux Estimation. In *Proceedings of the Fifth European Conference on Geostatistics for Environmental Applications*; Renard, P., Demougeot-Renard, H.F.R., Eds.; Springer Verlag: Berlin, Germany, 2005.

31. De Filippis, G.; Giudici, M.; Negri, S.; Margiotta, S. Conceptualization and preliminary characterization of a karst, coastal aquifer in the Mediterranean area of the Taranto gulf (southern Italy). *Environ. Earth Sci.* **2015**, submitted.

32. Giudici, M.; Ginn, T.; Vassena, C.; Haeri, H.; Foglia, L. A critical review of the properties of forward and inverse problems in groundwater hydrology. In *Calibration and Reliability in Groundwater Modelling: Credibility of Modelling*; Refsgaard, J., Kovar, K., Haarder, E., Nygaard, E., Eds.; IAHS: Wallingford, UK, 2008; Volume 320, pp. 240–244.

33. Giudici, M.; Vassena, C. Spectral analysis of the balance equation of ground water hydrology. *Transp. Porous Media* **2008**, *72*, 171–178.

34. Narasimhan, T.N.; Witherspoon, P.A. An integrated finite difference method for analyzing fluid flow in porous media. *Water Resour. Res.* **1976**, *12*, 57–64.

7

Extracting Conformational Ensembles of Small Molecules from Molecular Dynamics Simulations: Ampicillin as a Test Case

Giuliano Malloci *, Giovanni Serra, Andrea Bosin and Attilio Vittorio Vargiu *

Dipartimento di Fisica, Università di Cagliari, Cittadella Universitaria, I-09042 Monserrato (CA), Italy; giovanni.serra@dsf.unica.it (G.S.); andrea.bosin@dsf.unica.it (A.B.)
* Correspondence: giuliano.malloci@dsf.unica.it (G.M.); attilio.vargiu@dsf.unica.it (A.V.V.);

Academic Editor: Karlheinz Schwarz

Abstract: The accurate and exhaustive description of the conformational ensemble sampled by small molecules in solution, possibly at different physiological conditions, is of primary interest in many fields of medicinal chemistry and computational biology. Recently, we have built an on-line database of compounds with antimicrobial properties, where we provide all-atom force-field parameters and a set of molecular properties, including representative structures extracted from cluster analysis over μs-long molecular dynamics (MD) trajectories. In the present work, we used a medium-sized antibiotic from our sample, namely ampicillin, to assess the quality of the conformational ensemble. To this aim, we compared the conformational landscape extracted from previous unbiased MD simulations to those obtained by means of Replica Exchange MD (REMD) and those originating from three freely-available conformer generation tools widely adopted in computer-aided drug-design. In addition, for different charge/protonation states of ampicillin, we made available force-field parameters and static/dynamic properties derived from both Density Functional Theory and MD calculations. For the specific system investigated here, we found that: (i) the conformational statistics extracted from plain MD simulations is consistent with that obtained from REMD simulations; (ii) overall, our MD-based approach performs slightly better than any of the conformer generator tools if one takes into account both the diversity of the generated conformational set and the ability to reproduce experimentally-determined structures.

Keywords: ampicillin; molecular databases; molecular descriptors; all-atom force fields; molecular dynamics simulations; computer-aided drug design; conformer generation tools

1. Introduction

The accurate and exhaustive description of the conformational ensemble sampled by small molecules in solution, possibly at different physiological conditions, is of primary interest in many fields of medicinal chemistry and computational biology (e.g., [1–3]). Among other tools, numerical calculations, including molecular dynamics (MD) simulations, have gained an ever increasing role in addressing key structural, dynamical, thermodynamic and kinetic features at the molecular level of detail [4–15]. In particular, MD simulations based on all-atom empirical force-fields (FF) are nowadays routinely carried out in the μs timescale and over, reaching a very good level of description of the structural and dynamical properties of biological systems, such as membranes [16], proteins [17] and nucleic acids [18]. However, the parametrization of generic molecules (drugs, dyes, *etc.*) remains often a non-trivial task [19], despite the efforts in developing (semi-)automatic parametrization tools (see, e.g., [20–25]).

Recently, in the framework of the TRANSLOCATION consortium [26], we have started building a large database of antimicrobial compounds containing all-atom FF parameters, as well as physico-chemical descriptors derived from both quantum-mechanics and µs-long MD simulations [27]. Our database, freely accessible online, is to our knowledge the first extensive one including dynamical properties for a large set of compounds. Besides the specific application to the translocation of antibiotics through bacterial porins [28,29] and to their extrusion by efflux pumps [30,31], this piece of information can be useful for protein-ligand molecular docking [32], whose success rate is known to be strongly dependent on the generation of accurate input geometries and on the description of the flexibility of both partners involved in the binding process [33]. While receptor flexibility is nowadays routinely considered using different techniques [34–36], in the vast majority of docking campaigns, ligand flexibility is generally taken into account by considering the rotatable bonds of one given input structure, sometimes generating the 3D structure from 2D drawings or directly from SMILES strings [33]. In addition, stable protomers of ligands are usually generated only at physiological pH 7.4. However, catalytic sites might feature micro-conditions that differ from those found at physiological pH, thus affecting the most likely charge/protonation state of the ligand [33]. An alternative and less exploited way of generating ligand conformations is by means of MD simulations in explicit solvent. Though this methodology is computationally demanding, it has theoretically the advantage of propagating all of the conformational degrees of freedom (not only dihedrals) included in the FF function in the presence of explicit solvent and ions. Furthermore, a plethora of methods exist to accelerate the conformational sampling (e.g., metadynamics [37], accelerated MD [38] and Replica Exchange MD [39]). Therefore, MD-based methods can be useful to improve the reliability and predictive power of molecular docking.

Following the considerations above, the aim of the present work is two-fold: (i) to assess the conformational ensemble extracted from our µs-long MD simulations in terms of both the diversity of the generated conformational set and the ability to reproduce experimentally-determined structures; (ii) to provide parameters of ligands at different pHs, thus making available static and dynamic properties of a given compound as a function of different charge/protonation states. To these aims, we selected a medium-sized molecule in our sample, namely ampicillin (43 atoms, molecular formula $C_{16}H_{19}N_3O_4S$, molecular weight 349.40476 Da; see Figure 1), a broad-spectrum β-lactam penicillin antibiotic used extensively to treat bacterial infections for more than 50 years [40]. In the following, we will simply refer to the molecule using the corresponding Protein Data Bank chemical component identifier AMP. Thus, considering the AMP neutral zwitterionic form, the most populated one at physiological pH 7.4, we first compared our conformational landscape extracted from plain MD simulations [27] with those obtained by means of: (i) Replica Exchange MD (REMD) [39]; and (ii) some freely-available conformer generation tools widely used in computer-aided drug-design [41]. We additionally generated the General AMBER Force Field (GAFF) parameters [42] for each major tautomer in the pH range 2–14 and performed µs-long MD simulations for the species bearing net charges −2, −1 and +1. The parameters and the molecular descriptors extracted from both quantum-mechanics and MD simulations are available online [27]. Our results indicate that the conformational statistics extracted from plain MD simulations is: (i) consistent with that obtained from REMD simulations; and (ii) performs slightly better than some widely-used conformer generation tools when considering both the abilities to generate high-diversity conformational ensembles and to reproduce experimentally the available structures.

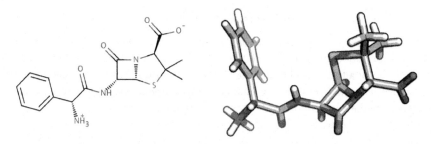

Figure 1. 2D and 3D structures of zwitterionic ampicillin (oxygen, nitrogen, carbon, sulfur and hydrogens atoms are marked in red, blue, gray, yellow and white, respectively).

2. Computational Methods

2.1. Molecular Characterization and Quantum-Chemistry Calculations

Starting from the structure data file (CID_6249.sdf) downloaded from PubChem [43], we used the package MARVIN [44] to compute the net charge dependence on pH, the isoelectric point pI and the microspecies distribution in the pH range 2–14. In particular, the microspecies distribution curves as a function of pH have been obtained using the pKa plugin [45] implemented in MARVIN [44]. This plugin calculates the pKa values of all proton gaining/loosing atoms on the basis of the partial charge distribution computed empirically using the MARVIN charge plugin [44,45]. We thus focused on the species bearing net charges −2, −1, 0 and +1, which are the major tautomers in the pH range 2–14. The same program has been used to obtain molecular formula, molecular weight, number of H-bond donors/acceptors, number of rotatable bonds and van der Waals volume. The 3D structure of each microspecies has been subsequently used to perform density functional theory (DFT) calculations [46] with the GAUSSIAN09 package [47]. As already done in our systematic investigation [27], we employed the hybrid B3LYP functional [48,49] and the 6-31G** basis-set [50]. The combination B3LYP/6-31G** is a good compromise between accuracy and computational cost [51,52]. All GAUSSIAN09 calculations were performed using the same settings adopted in our previous study [27]. For each major tautomer in the pH range 2–14, we used the DFT optimized geometry to compute logP values with XLOGP3 [53] and polar/non-polar molecular surfaces through the PLATINUM web interface [54]. We then generated three sets of atomic partial charges using the RESP method [55] implemented in the ANTECHAMBER package [56]: the standard Hartree-FockF/6-31G*, and the B3LYP/6-31G** charges fitting the molecular electrostatic potential using both CHELPG [57] and Merz–Kollman (MK) [58] schemes. We report in Appendix A a comparison between some of the molecular descriptors extracted from MD trajectories obtained with CHELPG-B3LYP/6-31G** and MK-Hartree–Fock/6-31G*.

2.2. MD Simulations and Post-Processing of the MD Trajectories

For each major microspecies of AMP with total charge −2, −1 and +1, we performed all-atom MD simulations in the presence of explicit water solution (0.1M KCl) using the AMBER14 package [59]. Model systems were prepared with the program TLEAP of AMBERTOOLS14 [59] adopting GAFF parameters [42] for the molecule and the TIP3P model of water [60]. For all microspecies, we used the same protocol adopted in our previous systematic investigation [27]. After production runs, we obtained structural and dynamical properties of the molecules by using the CPPTRAJ program [61]. During the MD runs, we monitored minimum and maximum projection areas using the MARVIN geometry plugin [44,45] and three morphologic descriptors related to the gyration tensor, *i.e.*, asphericity, acylindricity and kappa2, as implemented in the PLUMED plugin [62]. Asphericity and acylindricity give a measure of the deviation of the mass distribution from spherical and cylindrical symmetry, respectively; the relative shape anisotropy kappa2 is limited between zero and one and reflects both symmetry and dimensionality [63]. Again, the full list of molecular descriptors extracted from MD simulations and the numerical settings adopted can be found in [27].

2.3. REMD Calculations and Conformer Generation Methods Adopted

REMD simulations were performed for the zwitterionic form of AMP using the AMBER14 package [59]. We adopt a set of 72 replicas in the temperature range from 275–600 K. Each replica was simulated for 50 ns, for a total simulation time of 3.6 μs. The number of exchange attempts between replica pairs was 50,000, and temperature exchanges between replicas were attempted with a frequency of 1 ps^{-1}. We achieved a very uniform rate of exchanges among replicas of 0.33%.

Following the recent extensive comparison between different conformer generation tools [41], we selected three methods having the option of generating a fixed user-specified number of conformers: FROG2 [64], OPENBABEL [65] and RDKIT [66]. More precisely,

- FROG2: We loaded the 3D structure data file CID_6249.sdf taken from PubChem [43] in the web portal and adopted default settings. The server returned an ensemble of diverse conformers generated using a two-stage Monte-Carlo approach in the dihedral space.
- OPENBABEL: We used the same structure CID_6249.sdf as an input to the genetic algorithm code implemented in the program. This is a stochastic conformer generator producing a population of conformers that arrive iteratively at an optimal solution in terms of root-mean-squared diversity (we used a cutoff of 2.0 Å), after a series of generations.
- RDKIT: We used the python script provided in the user manual by loading the CID_6249 structure in .mol2format. The script generates the desired number of conformers and, for each of them, performs energy minimizations with the Universal Force Field [67].

For the purpose of comparing the features of the conformational ensemble extracted from our MD simulations (plain and replica-exchange) to the structures generated by conformer generators (*vide infra*), we performed a symmetric root mean square displacement-based cluster analysis using the hierarchical agglomerative algorithm [68] with a fixed number (30) of representatives. All figures have been produced by using PYMOL [69], VMD [70] and GNUPLOT [71] graphics programs.

3. Results and Discussion

3.1. Comparison among Different Conformational Ensembles

We first assessed the ability of MD simulations: (i) to generate high-diversity conformational ensembles; and (ii) to reproduce the experimentally-available structure of zwitterionic AMP, the one in the co-crystal with OmpF, one of the main general diffusion porins of *Escherichia coli* [72]. First, we compared the structural clusters representatives of the whole μs-long trajectory with those obtained from a 50 ns-long REMD simulation with 72 replicas in the temperature range 275–600 K. Figure 2 compares the pair-wise root mean square displacement (RMSD) matrix for 30 configurations (all generated *vs.* all generated) extracted with the two simulations; the picture reports also the corresponding histogram distributions, whose maximum values (mean ± SD) are found to be 5.8 Å (3.2 ± 1.1) and 5.4 Å (3.1 ± 1.0), respectively. As demonstrated by these numbers and clearly seen from a visual inspection of Figure 2, the conformational statistics extracted from the plain μs-long MD simulation at T = 310 K is consistent with the 50 ns-long REMD simulations spanning 72 temperatures in the range 275–600 K. Note that we arrive at the same conclusion by comparing the pair-wise RMSD matrix for 50 and 100 conformers generated with both plain MD and REMD simulations.

As an additional test, we compared the variability of the conformational ensemble extracted from the plain μs-long MD simulation with that obtained using some freely-available conformer generation tools widely used in protein-ligand docking and, more in general, in computer-aided drug-design studies. Following the recent extensive comparison between different conformer generation tools [41], we selected FROG2 [64], OPENBABEL [65] and RDKIT [66]. Similar to Figure 2, Figure 3 displays the pair-wise RMSD matrices and the corresponding histogram distributions for 30 AMP configurations generated with the three methods. While the RMSDs between the FROG2 conformations appear to follow a bi-modal distribution peaking at ~1.5 and ~3.0 Å, OPENBABEL and RDKIT values follow unimodal distributions centered at 3.7 ± 1.2 and 3.9 ± 1.3 Å, respectively. By comparing Figures 2 and 3, it is clear that our data for AMP, in terms of the diversity of the generated conformers: (i) appear to perform better than FROG2; (ii) are of similar quality as those of OPENBABEL; and (iii) cover a smaller conformational space with respect to RDKIT. Again, please note that similar conclusions can be draw by repeating the same comparison for 50 and 100 conformers generated with the three methods.

In order to quantify the ability to generate conformers that are structurally similar to the experimentally-determined structure of AMP [72], we compared the RMSD between the experimental configuration and each of the 30 conformers extracted from our plain MD simulation or generated with the different conformer generator tools considered. The resulting comparison is reported in Figure 4. We found that RDKIT yields structures differing, on average, by about 4–5 Å in terms of RMSD from the experimental structure. By looking in detail at the generated structures, we found that 17 over 30 conformers generated with RDKIT present a flipped conformation with respect to the experimental structure. In particular, the dihedral angle between the planes of the four-membered β-lactam ring and the five-membered ring is found to be ~240°, while the experimental value is about ~120°. This can be seen in the green box of Figure 4 and partly explains the larger scatter observed on average in the case of RDKIT. On the contrary, FROG2, OPENBABEL and our own MD results appear to oscillate around a lower mean value of about 3.0 Å, and interestingly, one of the clusters in these three ensembles is found to be very close to the experimental structure with a minimum RMSD of 0.9 Å, 1.7 Å, and 1.0 Å, respectively. For the four cases considered, the visual comparison between the lowest RMSD structure and the experimental one is reported in the same Figure 4.

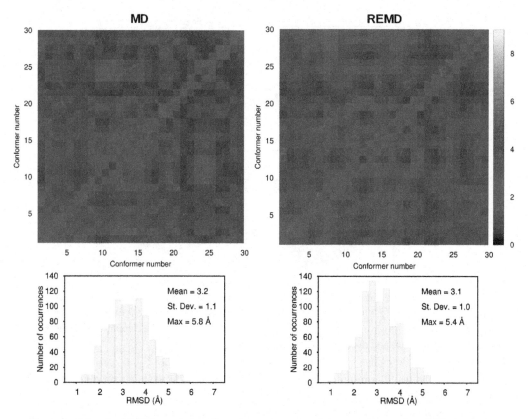

Figure 2. Pair-wise RMSD matrix for 30 conformers extracted from a plain μs-long MD simulation (**left**) and a 50 ns-long REMD simulation with 72 replicas in the range 275–600 K (**right**; see Section 2). The color scale reflects the RMSD values expressed in Å, as shown in the right box. For each case, the bottom panel shows the corresponding histogram distribution.

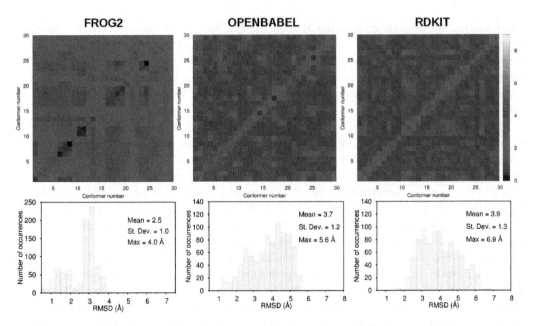

Figure 3. Same as Figure 2 for 30 AMP conformers generated using three different conformer generation tools: FROG2 (**left**), OPENBABEL (**center**) and RDKIT (**right**).

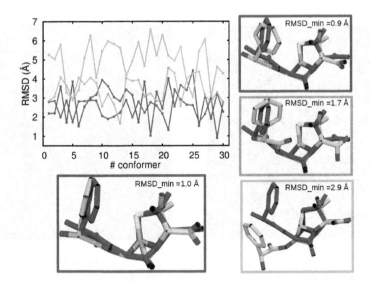

Figure 4. RMSD between the experimental configuration of AMP [72] and each of the 30 conformers extracted from a μs-long MD simulation (red) or generated with FROG2 (blue), OPENBABEL (orange), and RDKIT (green). The boxes, with the same color-codes, show the comparison between the lowest-RMSD structure and the experimental one (blue).

In summary, the results presented in Figures 2–4 for the specific system investigated here show that: (i) the conformational statistics extracted from plain MD simulations is consistent with that obtained from REMD simulations and comparable to those generated by the conformer generator tools considered; (ii) our MD-based approach performs slightly better than any of the conformer generator tools if one takes into account both the diversity of the generated conformational set and the ability to reproduce experimentally-determined structures. Clearly, we are aware that the μs-long MD simulations are not computationally inexpensive, even for small compounds. However, the main reason why we performed here 1 μs-long MD simulations is the consistency with our previous work concerning the creation of an online database of antimicrobial compounds differing in size and flexibility [27]. Thus, such long simulations could not be needed in all cases, at least for compounds with a limited number of rotatable bonds. To show that this is the case for AMP, we addressed the convergence of the conformational diversity and of a few molecular properties as a function of the total simulation time. As shown in Appendix B, for the specific case of AMP, we could have reduced the computational cost grossly by one order of magnitude.

3.2. Force-Field Parameters and Molecular Properties of Different Microspecies

As shown in Figure 5A, in the pH range 2–14 considered in this work, AMP has two proton-donating atoms, one oxygen of the external carboxylic group (pKa = 3.24) and one internal nitrogen (pKa = 11.97), and one proton accepting atom, namely the nitrogen atom (pKa = 7.44) opposite the β-lactam group. As a result, the molecule can exist in four different charge/protonation states, as shown in the pH-dependent net charge distribution (Figure 5B) and the fractional microspecies distribution (Figure 2C): cationic at pH $\leq$ 3.0, zwitterionic between $\simeq$3.0 and $\simeq$7.5, anionic between $\simeq$7.5 and $\simeq$12.0 and dianionic for pH $\geq$12.0. For each of the above microspecies, we followed the same general protocol adopted to build the on-line database [27], not taking into account possible chemical changes induced by pH, such as opening of the β-lactam ring [73]. In this work, we added the individual pages of each AMP microspecies displayed in Figure 5 in our online database [27].

In particular, the DFT optimized geometry (in both .xyz and .sdf formats) and the GAFF parameters files (.prep and .frcmod formats [42]) can be freely downloaded for each charge/protonation state. As previously done for the full set of compounds, we provide three sets of atomic partial charges as detailed in Section 2. The availability of the FF parameters for the major microspecies of the same compound makes it possible to perform straightforwardly MD simulations with ready-to-use input files. In the above web page, for each microspecies, separate tables report general-purpose properties and molecular descriptors derived from both DFT and MD simulations. The comparison for some of the different properties listed for the different microspecies is reported in Figures 6–8, displaying polar/non-polar molecular surfaces [54], the magnitude and spatial orientation of electric dipoles and the dynamical behavior of the spherical shape anisotropy kappa2 [62], respectively.

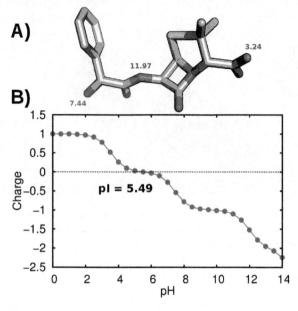

Figure 5. *Cont.*

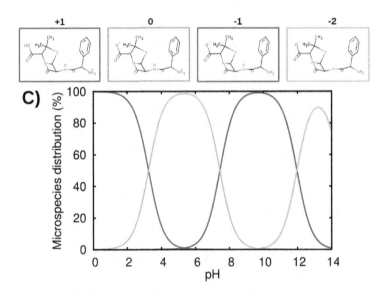

Figure 5. AMP protonation-related properties in the pH range 2–14: (**A**) pKa values of the proton receiving (7.44) and proton-donating (3.24 and 11.97) atoms; (**B**) pH-dependent net charge distribution (isoelectric point pI = 5.49); (**C**) fractional distribution of each microspecies: cationic (blue), neutral (orange), anionic (red) and dianionic (green).

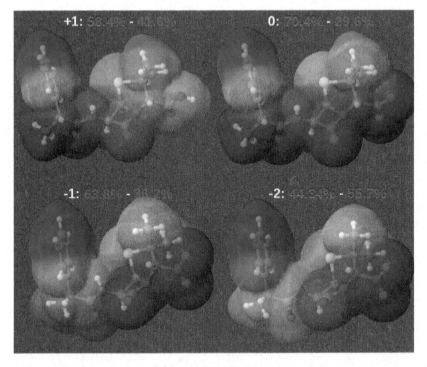

Figure 6. Comparison between the polar/non-polar molecular surfaces (red-white-blue color scale) as evaluated with the PLATINUM web server [54] for the AMP microspecies considered (see Figure 5). The polar (non-polar) fractions are reported in red (blue).

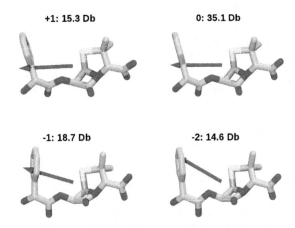

Figure 7. Comparison between the electric dipoles of the AMP microspecies considered. For each charge/protonation state, we report the absolute values (expressed in debyes); to ease visual comparison, the dipole's moduli have been arbitrarily normalized to the same quantity. Hydrogen atoms have been omitted for clarity.

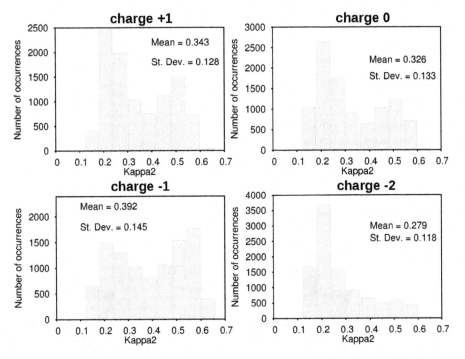

Figure 8. Comparison between the relative shape anisotropy kappa2 of the four AMP microspecies considered. This quantity, related to the gyration tensor, has been monitored during the MD runs using PLUMED [62].

4. Conclusions

In this work, we presented a follow-up of our long-term project of building a multi-purpose database of force-field parameters, dynamics and molecular descriptors of compounds with antimicrobial activity. We selected a medium-sized antibiotic, ampicillin, and assessed the quality of the conformational ensemble extracted from μs-long MD simulations. For the different charge/protonation states of ampicillin in the pH range 2–14, we additionally made available the GAFF parameters, as well as some general properties and molecular descriptors derived from both DFT and MD simulations. For the specific case considered in this work, we found that the finite ensemble best reproducing the whole MD trajectory is fully consistent with REMD simulations performed with 72 replicas distributed in the range 275–600 K and comparable to those generated by some widely-used conformer generation methods. In addition, by taking into account both the diversity of the generated conformational set and ability to reproduce available experimental structures, our MD-based approach is found to perform slightly better than any of the conformer generator tools considered.

Acknowledgments: The research leading to these results was conducted as part of the TRANSLOCATION consortium (www.translocation.eu) and has received support from the Innovative Medicines Initiatives Joint Undertaking under Grant Agreement n115525, resources that are composed of a financial contribution from the European Union Seventh Framework Programme (FP7/2007–2013) and the European Federation of Pharmaceutical Industries and Associations companies in kind contribution. The authors thank Matteo Ceccarelli and Paolo Ruggerone for useful discussions.

Author Contributions: Giuliano Malloci and Attilio Vittorio Vargiu designed the research. Giuliano Malloci and Attilio Vittorio Vargiu performed the research. Giovanni Serra and Andrea Bosin provided technical support. All authors wrote, read and approved the final manuscript.

Conflicts of Interest: The authors declare no conflict of interest.

Abbreviations

AMP: chemical component identifier of ampicillin
CHELPG: charges from electrostatic potentials using a grid-based method
DFT: density functional theory
GAFF: General Amber Force Field
MD: molecular dynamics
MK: Merz-Kollman
PDB: Protein Data Bank
REMD: Replica Exchange Molecular Dynamics
RMSD: root mean square displacement
RESP: restrained electrostatic potential

Appendix

A. Impact of Atomic Partial Charges

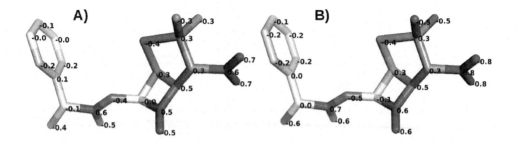

Figure A1. Atomic partial charges (in units of the elementary charge e) of zwitterionic AMP as computed at: (**A**) the B3LYP/6-31G** level using the CHELPG scheme (chgs-1); (**B**) the HF/6-31G* level using the Merz–Kollman scheme (chgs-2). Heavy atoms are colored in a blue-white-red scale according to their charge; hydrogens are omitted for clarity.

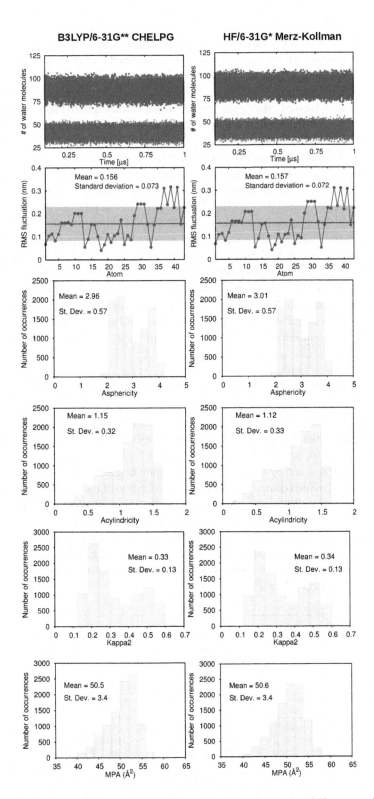

Figure A2. Comparison between dynamical properties of zwitterionic AMP extracted from MD trajectories obtained using chgs-1 (**left**) and chgs-2 (**right**) partial charges. From top to bottom: number of water molecules in the first (red) and second (blue) shell, root mean square fluctuations, asphericity, acylindricity, kappa2 and minimal projection area.

Atomic partial charges are among the primary FF parameters determining the dynamical behavior of a small organic molecule. All-atom MD simulations performed for the compounds included in our online database used GAFF parameters [42] for the major tautomer at physiological pH = 7.4, with CHELPG atomic charges computed at the B3LYP/6-31G** level (see Section 2). To assess this specific choice, here, we compared some of the dynamical properties extracted from MD trajectories obtained to the above charges (in the following denoted as chgs-1), with the same descriptors extracted from MD simulations using the standard MK partial charges derived from Hartree–Fock/6-31G* calculations (labeled as chgs-2). Figure 6 compares the RESP point charges computed with the two schemes for zwitterionic ampicillin, the most populated microspecies at physiological pH = 7.4 (see Figure 2).

We found some quantitative differences among the values of the two sets of charges. Overall, the MK-Hartree-Fock/6-31G* point charges turn out to be larger than the corresponding CHELPG-B3LYP/6-31G**, something that is well known from previous investigations [55]. Nonetheless, the charges are qualitatively similar, as seen by comparing the corresponding color patterns (see Figure A1). Moreover, there is a negligible impact of these differences on zwitterionic AMP dynamics as sampled along μs-long MD simulations using both sets of charges. In particular, as shown in Figure A2, we found coincident within statistical deviations all of the molecular descriptors extracted from the MD trajectories, namely the number of solvent molecules within the first and second shells, the molecular flexibility expressed in terms of root mean square fluctuations and some morphological descriptors as a function of time: asphericity, acylindricity, kappa2 and minimal projection area.

B. Assessment of the Convergence of Structural Properties *vs.* Simulation Time

To validate the importance of an extensive sampling, we addressed the convergence of the conformational diversity as a function of the total simulation time. Figure B1 displays the comparison between the histogram distribution of the pair-wise RMSD for the 30 conformers extracted from plain MD simulations at 10, 100, 500 and 1000 ns. We found convergent trends, as shown by a visual inspection of the histograms and by comparing the corresponding statistical parameters. This is further confirmed by Figure B2, which compares the spatial distribution of the 30 conformers corresponding to 10, 100 and 1000 ns-long MD runs. As shown by the figure, clusters corresponding to longer simulations are able to cover a larger portion of the configurational space.

We performed a similar convergence check by looking at the evolution of some molecular properties extracted from MD runs at increasing simulation times. Similar to Figure B1, Figures B3 and B4 compare the distributions of minimal and maximal projection areas, respectively, showing again a convergent trend in both cases.

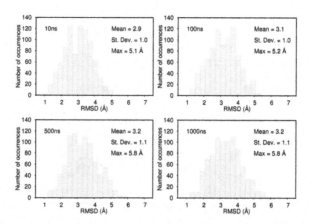

Figure B1. Comparison between the histogram distribution of the pair-wise RMSD for the 30 conformers extracted from plain MD simulations at 10, 100, 500 and 1000 ns.

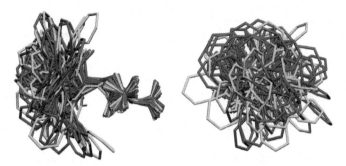

Figure B2. Side (**left**) and front (**right**) views of the spatial distribution of the 30 conformers corresponding to 10, 100 and 1000 ns-long MD runs (blue, red, green, respectively). All of the structures have been aligned with respect to the penam group (formed by the four-membered β-lactam ring fused to the five-membered ring).

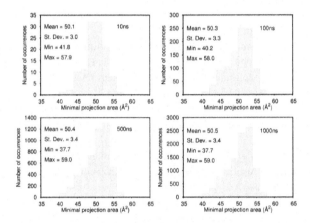

Figure B3. Same as Figure B1 for the minimal projection area.

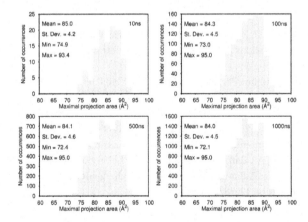

Figure B4. Same as Figure B1 for the maximal projection area.

References

1. Csermely, P.; Palotai, R.; Nussinov, R. Induced fit, conformational selection and independent dynamic segments: an extended view of binding events. *Trends Biochem. Sci.* **2010**, *35*, 539–546.

2. Baron, R.; McCammon, J.A. Molecular Recognition and Ligand Association. *Ann. Rev. Phys. Chem.* **2013**, *64*, 151–175.

3.   Pisani, P.; Piro, P.; Decherchi, S.; Bottegoni, G.; Sona, D.; Murino, V.; Rocchia, W.; Cavalli, A. Describing the Conformational Landscape of Small Organic Molecules through Gaussian Mixtures in Dihedral Space. *J. Chem. Theory Comput.* **2014**, *10*, 2557–2568.

4.   Jorgensen, W.L. The many roles of computation in drug discovery. *Science* **2004**, *303*, 1813–1818.

5.   Van Gunsteren, W.F.; Bakowies, D.; Baron, R.; Chandrasekhar, I.; Christen, M.; Daura, X.; Gee, P.; Geerke, D.P.; Glaettli, A.; Huenenberger, P.H.; *et al.* Biomolecular modeling: Goals, problems, perspectives. *Angew. Chem. Int. Ed.* **2006**, *45*, 4064–4092.

6.   Gilson, M.K.; Zhou, H.X. Calculation of Protein-Ligand Binding Affinities. *Ann. Rev. Biophys. Biomol. Struct.* **2007**, *36*, 21–42.

7.   Sherwood, P.; Brooks, B.R.; Sansom, M.S.P. Multiscale methods for macromolecular simulations. *Curr. Opin. Struc. Biol.* **2008**, *18*, 630–640.

8.   Dodson, G.G.; Lane, D.P.; Verma, C.S. Molecular simulations of protein dynamics: New windows on mechanisms in biology. *EMBO Rep.* **2008**, *9*, 144–150.

9.   Lee, E.H.; Hsin, J.; Sotomayor, M.; Comellas, G.; Schulten, K. Discovery Through the Computational Microscope. *Structure* **2009**, *17*, 1295–1306.

10.   Boehr, D.D.; Nussinov, R.; Wright, P.E. The role of dynamic conformational ensembles in biomolecular recognition. *Nat. Chem. Biol.* **2009**, *5*, 789–796.

11.   Dror, R.O.; Dirks, R.M.; Grossman, J.P.; Xu, H.; Shaw, D.E. Biomolecular Simulation: A Computational Microscope for Molecular Biology. *Ann. Rev. Biophys.* **2012**, *41*, 429–452.

12.   Baron, R.; McCammon, J.A. Molecular Recognition and Ligand Association. *Ann. Rev. Phys. Chem.* **2013**, *64*, 151–175.

13.   Cheatham, T.E.; Case, D.A. Twenty-Five Years of Nucleic Acid Simulations. *Biopolymers* **2013**, *99*, 969–977.

14.   Karplus, M.; Lavery, R. Significance of Molecular Dynamics Simulations for Life Sciences. *Isr. J. Chem.* **2014**, *54*, 1042–1051.

15.   Mortier, J.; Rakers, C.; Bermudez, M.; Murgueitio, M.S.; Riniker, S.; Wolber, G. The impact of molecular dynamics on drug design: Applications for the characterization of ligand-macromolecule complexes. *Drug Discov. Today* **2015**, *20*, 686–702.

16.   Schmidt, T.H.; Kandt, C. LAMBADA and InflateGRO2: Efficient Membrane Alignment and Insertion of Membrane Proteins for Molecular Dynamics Simulations. *J. Chem. Inf. Mod.* **2012**, *52*, 2657–2669.

17.   Piana, S.; Klepeis, J.L.; Shaw, D.E. Assessing the accuracy of physical models used in protein-folding simulations: quantitative evidence from long molecular dynamics simulations. *Curr. Opin. Struc. Biol.* **2014**, *24*, 98–105.

18.   Šponer, J.; Banáš, P.; Jurečka, P.; Zgarbová, M.; Kührová, P.; Havrila, M.; Krepl, M.; Stadlbauer, P.; Otyepka, M. Molecular Dynamics Simulations of Nucleic Acids. From Tetranucleotides to the Ribosome. *J. Phys. Chem. Lett.* **2014**, *5*, 1771–1782.

19.   Graen, T.; Hoefling, M.; Grubmueller, H. AMBER-DYES: Characterization of Charge Fluctuations and Force Field Parameterization of Fluorescent Dyes for Molecular Dynamics Simulations. *J. Chem. Theory Comput.* **2014**, *10*, 5505–5512.

20.   Dupradeau, F.Y.; Cézard, C.; Lelong, R.; Stanislawiak, É.; Pêcher, J.; Delepine, J.C.; Cieplak, P. R.E. DD. B.: A database for RESP and ESP atomic charges, and force field libraries. *Nucleic Acids Res.* **2008**, *36*, D360–D367.

21.   Dupradeau, F.Y.; Pigache, A.; Zaffran, T.; Savineau, C.; Lelong, R.; Grivel, N.; Lelong, D.; Rosanski, W.; Cieplak, P. The R.E.D. tools: Advances in RESP and ESP charge derivation and force field library building. *Phys. Chem. Chem. Phys.* **2010**, *12*, 7821–7839.

22.   AMBER Parameter Database. Available online: http://www.pharmacy.manchester.ac.uk/bryce/amber/ (accessed on 22 January 2016).

23.   Vanommeslaeghe, K.; MacKerell, A.D., Jr. Automation of the CHARMM General Force Field (CGenFF) I: Bond Perception and Atom Typing. *J. Chem. Inf. Mod.* **2012**, *52*, 3144–3154.

24.   Vanommeslaeghe, K.; Raman, E.P.; MacKerell, A.D., Jr. Automation of the CHARMM General Force Field (CGenFF) II: Assignment of Bonded Parameters and Partial Atomic Charges. *J. Chem. Inf. Mod.* **2012**, *52*, 3155–3168.

25.   Malde, A.K.; Zuo, L.; Breeze, M.; Stroet, M.; Poger, D.; Nair, P.C.; Oostenbrink, C.; Mark, A.E. An Automated Force Field Topology Builder (ATB) and Repository: Version 1.0. *J. Chem. Theory Comput.* **2011**, *7*, 4026–4037.

26. Stavenger, R.A.; Winterhalter, M. TRANSLOCATION Project: How to Get Good Drugs into Bad Bugs. *Sci. Transl. Med.* **2014**, *6*, 228ed7.

27. Malloci, G.; Vargiu, A.V.; Serra, G.; Bosin, A.; Ruggerone, P.; Ceccarelli, M. A Database of Force-Field Parameters, Dynamics, and Properties of Antimicrobial Compounds. *Molecules* **2015**, *20*, 13997–14021.

28. Kumar, A.; Hajjar, E.; Ruggerone, P.; Ceccarelli, M. Molecular simulations reveal the mechanism and the determinants for ampicillin translocation through OmpF. *J. Phys. Chem. B* **2010**, *114*, 9608–9616.

29. Hajjar, E.; Bessonov, A.; Molitor, A.; Kumar, A.; Mahendran, K.R.; Winterhalter, M.; Pagès, J.M.; Ruggerone, P.; Ceccarelli, M. Toward screening for antibiotics with enhanced permeation properties through bacterial porins. *Biochemistry* **2010**, *49*, 6928–6935.

30. Collu, F.; Vargiu, A.V.; Dreier, J.; Cascella, M.; Ruggerone, P. Recognition of Imipenem and Meropenem by the RND-Transporter MexB Studied by Computer Simulations. *J. Am. Chem. Soc.* **2012**, *134*, 19146–19158.

31. Vargiu, A.V.; Nikaido, H. Multidrug binding properties of the AcrB efflux pump characterized by molecular dynamics simulations. *Proc. Natl. Acad. Sci. USA* **2012**, *109*, 20637–20642.

32. Ferreira, L.G.; dos Santos, R.N.; Oliva, G.; Andricopulo, A.D. Molecular Docking and Structure-Based Drug Design Strategies. *Molecules* **2015**, *20*, 13384–13421.

33. Forli, S. Charting a Path to Success in Virtual Screening. *Molecules* **2015**, *20*, 18732–18758.

34. Sinko, W.; Lindert, S.; McCammon, J.A. Accounting for Receptor Flexibility and Enhanced Sampling Methods in Computer-Aided Drug Design. *Chem. Biol. Drug Des.* **2013**, *81*, 41–49.

35. Amaro, R.E.; Baron, R.; McCammon, J.A. An improved relaxed complex scheme for receptor flexibility in computer-aided drug design. *J. Comput.-Aided Mol. Des.* **2008**, *22*, 693–705.

36. Zacharias, M. Protein-protein docking with a reduced protein model accounting for side-chain flexibility. *Protein Sci.* **2003**, *12*, 1271–1282.

37. Laio, A.; Parrinello, M. Escaping free-energy minima. *Proc. Natl. Acad. Sci. USA* **2002**, *99*, 12562–12566.

38. Hamelberg, D.; Mongan, J.; McCammon, J.A. Accelerated molecular dynamics: A promising and efficient simulation method for biomolecules. *J. Chem. Phys.* **2004**, *120*, 11919–11929.

39. Sugita, Y.; Okamoto, Y. Replica-exchange molecular dynamics method for protein folding. *Chem. Phys. Lett.* **1999**, *314*, 141–151.

40. Acred, P.; Brown, D.M.; Turner, D.H.; Wilson, M.J. Pharmacology and Chemotherapy of Ampicillin. A New Broad-Spectrum Penicillin. *Brit. J. Pharm. Chemother.* **1962**, *18*, 356–369.

41. Ebejer, J.P.; Morris, G.M.; Deane, C.M. Freely Available Conformer Generation Methods: How Good Are They? *J. Chem. Inf. Mod.* **2012**, *52*, 1146–1158.

42. Wang, J.; Wolf, R.M.; Caldwell, J.W.; Kollman, P.A.; Case, D.A. Development and testing of a general amber force field. *J. Comput. Chem.* **2004**, *25*, 1157–1174.

43. Bolton, E.E.; Wangand, Y.; Thiessenand, P.A.; Bryant, S.H. PubChem: Integrated Platform of Small Molecules and Biological Activities. *Annu. Rep. Comput. Chem.* **2008**, *4*, 217–241.

44. Marvin 14.8.25.0. ChemAxon 2014. Available online: http://www.chemaxon.com (accessed on 22 January 2016).

45. Calculator Plugins. ChemAxon 2014. Available online: https://www.chemaxon.com/products/calculator-plugins/ (accessed on 22 January 2016).

46. Kohn, W. Nobel Lecture: Electronic structure of matter-wave functions and density functionals. *Rev. Mod. Phys.* **1999**, *71*, 1253–1266.

47. Frisch, M.J.; Trucks, G.W.; Schlegel, H.B.; Scuseria, G.E.; Robb, M.A.; Cheeseman, J.R.; Scalmani, G.; Barone, V.; Mennucci, B.; Petersson, G.A.; *et al. Gaussian09 Revision A.02*; Gaussian Inc.: Wallingford, CT, USA, 2009.

48. Becke, A.D. Density-functional thermochemistry. III. The role of exact exchange. *J. Chem. Phys.* **1993**, *98*, 5648–5652.

49. Kim, K.; Jordan, K.D. Comparison of Density Functional and MP2 Calculations on the Water Monomer and Dimer. *J. Phys. Chem.* **1994**, *98*, 10089–10094.

50. Pople, J.A. Quantum Chemical Models (Nobel Lecture). *Angew. Chem. Int. Ed.* **1999**, *38*, 1894–1902.

51. Malloci, G.; Joblin, C.; Mulas, G. On-line database of the spectral properties of polycyclic aromatic hydrocarbons. *Chem. Phys.* **2007**, *332*, 353–359.

52. Malloci, G.; Cappellini, G.; Mulas, G.; Mattoni, A. Electronic and optical properties of families of polycyclic aromatic hydrocarbons: A systematic (time-dependent) density functional theory study. *Chem. Phys.* **2011**, *384*, 19–27.

53. Cheng, T.; Zhao, Y.; Li, X.; Lin, F.; Xu, Y.; Zhang, X.; Li, Y.; Wang, R.; Lai, L. Computation of Octanol-Water Partition Coefficients by Guiding an Additive Model with Knowledge. *J. Chem. Inf. Model.* **2007**, *47*, 2140–2148.

54. Pyrkov, T.V.; Chugunov, A.O.; Krylov, N.A.; Nolde, D.E.; Efremov, R.G. PLATINUM: a web tool for analysis of hydrophobic/hydrophilic organization of biomolecular complexes. *Bioinformatics* **2009**, *25*, 1201–1202.

55. Bayly, C.I.; Cieplak, P.; Cornell, W.; Kollman, P.A. A well-behaved electrostatic potential based method using charge restraints for deriving atomic charges: the RESP model. *J. Phys. Chem.* **1993**, *97*, 10269–10280.

56. Wang, J.; Wang, W.; Kollman, P.A.; Case, D.A. Automatic atom type and bond type perception in molecular mechanical calculations. *J. Mol. Graphics Modell.* **2006**, *25*, 247–260.

57. Breneman, C.M.; Wiberg, K.B. Determining atom-centered monopoles from molecular electrostatic potentials. The need for high sampling density in formamide conformational analysis. *J. Comput. Chem.* **1990**, *11*, 361–373.

58. Singh, U.C.; Kollman, P.A. An approach to computing electrostatic charges for molecules. *J. Comput. Chem.* **1984**, *5*, 129–145.

59. Case, D.; Babin, V.; Berryman, J.; Betz, R.; Cai, Q.; Cerutti, D.; Cheatham, T.; Darden, T.; Duke, R.; Gohlke, H.; *et al. Amber 14*; University of California: San Francisco, CA, USA, 2014.

60. Jorgensen, W.L.; Chandrasekhar, J.; Madura, J.D.; Impey, R.W.; Klein, M.L. Comparison of simple potential functions for simulating liquid water. *J. Chem. Phys.* **1983**, *79*, 926–935.

61. Roe, D.R.; Cheatham, T.E. PTRAJ and CPPTRAJ: Software for Processing and Analysis of Molecular Dynamics Trajectory Data. *J. Chem. Theory Comput.* **2013**, *9*, 3084–3095.

62. Bonomi, M.; Branduardi, D.; Bussi, G.; Camilloni, C.; Provasi, D.; Raiteri, P.; Donadio, D.; Marinelli, F.; Pietrucci, F.; Broglia, R.A.; *et al.* PLUMED: A portable plugin for free-energy calculations with molecular dynamics. *Comput. Phys. Commun.* **2009**, *180*, 1961–1972.

63. Theodorou, D.N.; Suter, U.W. Shape of unperturbed linear polymers: polypropylene. *Macromolecules* **1985**, *18*, 1206–1214.

64. Miteva, M.A.; Guyon, F.; Tufféry, P. Frog2: Efficient 3D conformation ensemble generator for small compounds. *Nucleic Acids Res.* **2010**, *38*, W622–W627.

65. O'Boyle, N.; Banck, M.; James, C.; Morley, C.; Vandermeersch, T.; Hutchison, G. Open Babel: An open chemical toolbox. *J. Cheminf.* **2011**, *3*, 33.

66. RDKit: Open-Source Cheminformatics Software. Available online: http://www.rdkit.org (accessed on 22 January 2015).

67. Rappe, A.K.; Casewit, C.J.; Colwell, K.S.; Goddard, W.A.G.; Skiff, W.M. UFF, a full periodic table force field for molecular mechanics and molecular dynamics simulations. *J. Am. Chem. Soc.* **1992**, *114*, 10024–10035.

68. Shao, J.; Tanner, S.W.; Thompson, N.; Cheatham, T.E. Clustering Molecular Dynamics Trajectories: 1. Characterizing the Performance of Different Clustering Algorithms. *J. Chem. Theory Comput.* **2007**, *3*, 2312–2334.

69. DeLano, W.L. Schrodinger LLC (2010) The PyMOL Molecular Graphics System, version 1.3r1. Available online: http://www.pymol.org (accessed on 25 January 2016).

70. Humphrey, W.; Dalke, A.; Schulten, K. VMD—Visual Molecular Dynamics. *J. Mol. Graph.* **1996**, *14*, 33–38.

71. Gnuplot. Available online: http://www.gnuplot.info (accessed on 22 January 2016).

72. Ziervogel, B.; Roux, B. The Binding of Antibiotics in OmpF Porin. *Structure* **2013**, *21*, 76–87.

73. Mitchell, S.M.; Ullman, J.L.; Teel, A.L.; Watts, R.J. pH and temperature effects on the hydrolysis of three β-lactam antibiotics: Ampicillin, cefalotin and cefoxitin. *Sci. Total Environ.* **2014**, *466–467*, 547–555.

Current Issues in Finite-T Density-Functional Theory and Warm-Correlated Matter

M. W. C. Dharma-wardana [1,2]

[1] National Research Council of Canada, 1200, Montreal Rd, Ottawa, ON K1A 0R6, Canada;
chandre.dharma-wardana@nrc-cnrc.gc.ca

[2] Département de Physique, Université de Montreal, Montreal, QC H3C 3J7, Canada

† This paper is an extended version of our paper published in "Current Issues in Finite-T Density-Functional Theory and Warm-Correlated Matter". In Proceedings of the 16th International Conference on Density Functional Theory and Its Applications, Celebrating the 50th Anniversary of the Kohn-Sham Theory, Debrecen, Hungary, 31 August–4 September 2015.

Academic Editors: Karlheinz Schwarz and Agnes Nagy

Abstract: Finite-temperature density functional theory (DFT) has become of topical interest, partly due to the increasing ability to create novel states of warm-correlated matter (WCM). Warm-dense matter (WDM), ultra-fast matter (UFM), and high-energy density matter (HEDM) may all be regarded as subclasses of WCM. Strong electron-electron, ion-ion and electron-ion correlation effects and partial degeneracies are found in these systems where the electron temperature T_e is comparable to the electron Fermi energy E_F. Thus, many electrons are in continuum states which are partially occupied. The ion subsystem may be solid, liquid or plasma, with many states of ionization with ionic charge Z_j. Quasi-equilibria with the ion temperature $T_i \neq T_e$ are common. The ion subsystem in WCM can no longer be treated as a passive "external potential", as is customary in $T = 0$ DFT dominated by solid-state theory or quantum chemistry. Many basic questions arise in trying to implement DFT for WCM. Hohenberg-Kohn-Mermin theory can be adapted for treating these systems if suitable finite-T exchange-correlation (XC) functionals can be constructed. They are functionals of both the one-body electron density n_e and the one-body ion densities ρ_j. Here, j counts many species of nuclei or charge states. A method of approximately but accurately mapping the quantum electrons to a classical Coulomb gas enables one to treat electron-ion systems entirely classically at any temperature and arbitrary spin polarization, using exchange-correlation effects calculated *in situ*, directly from the pair-distribution functions. This eliminates the need for any XC-functionals. This classical map has been used to calculate the equation of state of WDM systems, and construct a finite-T XC functional that is found to be in close agreement with recent quantum path-integral simulation data. In this review, current developments and concerns in finite-T DFT, especially in the context of non-relativistic warm-dense matter and ultra-fast matter will be presented.

Keywords: exchange and correlation; warm dense matter; density functional theory; ultra-fast matter; high-energy density matter; finite-temperature effects

PACS: 52.25.Os, 52.35.Fp, 52.50.Jm, 78.70.Ck

1. Introduction

Although there are no systems at zero temperature available to us, it is the quantum mechanics of the simpler $T = 0$ systems that has engaged the attention of theorists. Thermal ensembles usually require the study of extended systems attached to a "heat bath", and within some statistical ensemble.

Even perturbation-theory approaches to model systems like the electron gas at finite-T were full of surprises [1,2].

Condensed matter physics and chemistry could get by with $T = 0$ quantum mechanics as the input to some sort of thermal theory which is not integrated into the many-body problem. Much of plasma physics and astrophysics could manage with simple extensions of hydrogenic models, Thomas-Fermi theory, extended-Debye theory, and classical "one-component-plasma" models as long as the accuracy of observations, experiments and theoretical models did not demand anything more from quantum mechanics. On the other hand, at the level of foundations of quantum mechanics, the whole issue of quantized thermo-field dynamics has been an open problem [3]. Similarly, the theory of "mixed" systems with classical and quantum components is also a topic of discussion [4]. It is in this context that we need to look at the advent of density-functional theory (DFT) as a great step forward in the quantum many-body problem. The Hohenberg-Kohn theorem published in 1964 was soon followed by its finite-T generalization by Mermin, providing a "thermal" density-functional theory (th-DFT) in 1965 [5–7], which also saw the advent of Kohn-Sham theory. Hence, in 2015, we are celebrating the fiftieth anniversary of both Kohn-Sham theory, and Mermin's extension of Hohenberg-Kohn theory to finite-T [8].

While DFT provided chemistry and condensed-matter physics, an escape from the intractable "n-electron" problem, in addition to its computational implications, DFT has deep epistemological implications in regard to the foundational ideas of physics. DFT claims that the many-body wavefunction can be dispensed with, and that the physics of a given system can be discussed as a functional of the one-body density. Thus, even entanglement can be discussed in terms of density functionals [9,10]. However, it is the computational power of DFT that has been universally exploited in many fields of physics.

The interest in thermonuclear fusion via laser compression and related techniques, and the advent of ultra-fast lasers, have created novel states of matter where the electron temperature T_e is usually of the order of the Fermi energy E_F, under conditions where they are identified as warm dense matter (WDM) [11]. When WDM is created using a fast laser within femto-second time-scales, the photons couple strongly to the electrons which are heated very rapidly to many thousands of degrees, while the ions remain essentially at the initial "ambient" temperature [12,13]. In addition to highly non-equilibrium systems, this often leads to two-temperature systems with the ion temperature $T_i \neq T_e$, with $T_e \gg T_i$. Alternatively, if shock waves are used to generate a WDM, we may have $T_i > T_e$. Such ultra-fast matter (UFM) systems can be studied using a fs-probe laser within timescales t such that $t \ll \tau_{ei}$, where τ_{ei} is the electron-ion temperature relaxation time [14,15] of the UFM system. These WCM systems are of interest in astrophysics and planetary science [16], inertial fusion [11], materials ablation [17,18], machining, and in the hot-carrier physics of field-effect transistors, nano-devices *etc.* [19,20].

Early attempts to apply thermal-DFT (also called finite-T DFT, th-DFT) to WDM-like systems were undertaken by the present author and François Perrot in the early 1980s as reviewed in Reference [21]. This involved a reformulation of the neutral-pseudoatom (NPA) model that had been formulated by Dagens [22] for zero-T problems, as it has the versatility to treat solids, liquids and plasmas.

Originally it was Ziman [23] (and possibly others, see [24]) who had proposed the NPA model as an intuitive physical idea in the context of solid-state physics. The electronic structure of matter is regarded as a superposition of charge densities $n_j(\vec{r} - \vec{R}_j)$ located on each nuclear centre at $\vec{R}_j$. In other words, if the total charge density in momentum space was $n_T(\vec{k})$, then this is considered as being made up of the individual charge distributions $n_j(\vec{k})$ put together using the ionic structure factor $S(\vec{k})$. This was more explicitly implemented in muffin-tin models of solids, or "atoms-in molecules" models of chemical bonds that were actively pursued in the 1960s, with the increasing availability of fast computers. The NPA model was formulated rigorously within $T = 0$ DFT by Dagens who showed that it was capable of the same level of accuracy, at least for "simple metals", as the Linear Muffin-Tin Orbital (LMTO) method, Augmented Plane-Wave (APW) method or the Korringa-Kohn-Rostoker codes that were becoming available in the 1970s [22]. Wigner's $T = 0$ exchange-correlation (XC) "functional" in the local-density approximation (LDA) was used by Dagens.

In the finite-T NPA that we have used as our "work-horse", we solve the Kohn-Sham Mermin equation for a single nucleus placed at the centre of a large "correlation sphere" of radius R_c which is of the order of $10r_{ws}$, where r_{ws} is the Wigner-Seitz radius per ion. Here, $r_{ws} = \{3/(4\pi\bar{\rho})\}^{1/3}$, where $\bar{\rho}$ is the ion density given as the number of ions per unit atomic volume. For WDM aluminium at normal compression, $r_{ws} \simeq 3$ a.u. All types of particle correlations induced by the nucleus at the centre of the "correlation sphere" would have died down to bulk-values when $r \to R_c$. The ion distribution $\rho(r) = \bar{\rho}g_{ii}(r)$ is approximated as a spherical cavity of radius r_{ws} surrounding the nucleus, and then becoming a uniform positive background [25,26]. This is simpler to implement than the full method implemented in Reference [27]. The latter involved a self-consistent iteration of the ion density $\rho(r)$ and the electron density $n(r)$ obtained from the Kohn-Sham procedure coupled to a classical integral equation or even molecular dynamics; the simpler NPA procedure is sufficient in most cases.

There have also been several practical formulations of NPA-like models in more recent times. Some of these [28] are extensions of the INFERNO cell-model of Lieberman [29], while others [30] use a mixture of NPA ideas as well as elements of Chihara's "quantal-hyper-netted-chain (QHNC)" models [31]. We have discussed Chihara's model to some extent in Reference [32]. In true DFT models, the electrons are mapped to a non-interacting Kohn-Sham electron gas having the same interacting density but at the non-interacting chemical potential. This feature is absent in INFERNO-like cell-models where the chemical potential is determined via an integration within the ion-sphere or by some such consideration. Thus, different physical results may arise (e.g., for the conductivity) depending on how the chemical potential is fixed. Chihara's models use an ion subsystem and an electron subsystem coupled via a "quantal Ornstein-Zernike" equation. However, if a one-component electron-gas calculation was attempted via the "quantal HNC", the known $g_{ee}(r)$ are not recovered. In the two component case, as far as we can ascertain, the ion-$S(k \to 0)$ limit is not correctly related to the electron compressibility.

Thus, the Kohn-Sham NPA calculation provides the free-electron charge density pile-up $n_f(r)$ around the nucleus. This is sufficient to calculate an electron-ion pseudopotential U_{ei}, and hence an on-ion pair potential $V_{ii}(r)$ as discussed in, say, Reference [26]. Once the pair-potential is available, the Hyper-Netted Chain equation (and its modified form incorporating a bridge function) can be used to calculate an accurate $g_{ii}(r)$ if desired, rather than via the direct iterative procedure used in Reference [27]. This finite-T NPA approach is capable of accurate prediction of phonons (*i.e.*, milli-volt energies) in WDM systems, as shown explicitly by Harbour *et al.* [33] using comparisons with results reported by Recoules *et al.* [34] who used the Vienna *Ab Initio* Simulation Package (VASP).

Since the XC-functional of DFT is directly connected with the pair-distribution function (PDF), or equivalently with the two-particle density matrix [35], we sought to formulate the many-body problem of ion-electron systems directly in terms of the pair distribution functions $g_{\alpha,\beta}$ of the system, where α and β count over types of particles (ions and electrons, with two types of electrons with spin up, or down) [25-27]. The ionic species may be regarded as classical particles without spin as their thermal de Broglie length is in the femto-meter regime at WDM temperatures. This approach led to the formulation of the Classical-map Hyper-Netted-Chain (CHNC) method that will be briefly described in Section 3.1.

The attempt to use thermal DFT for actual calculations naturally required an effort towards the development of finite-T XC-functionals [36–42]. Meanwhile, large-scale codes implementing $T = 0$ DFT (e.g., CASTEP [43], VASP [44], ABINIT [45], Amsterdam density-functional (ADF) code [46], Gaussian [47] *etc.*) became available, where well-tested $T = 0$ XC-functionals (e.g., the PBE functional [48]) as well as $T = 0$ DFT-based pseudopotentials are implemented. Currently, these codes also included versions where the single-particle states could be chosen as a Fermi distribution [49] at a given temperature, while they do not include the finite-T XC functionals that are needed for a proper implementation of thermal DFT. These codes are meant to be used at $T = 0$ or small T since finite-T

calculations require a very rapid increase in the basis sets needed for such calculations. It should also be mentioned that Karasiev *et al.* [50] have recently implemented finite-T XC within the "Quantum Espresso" code, as well as given an "orbital-free" implementation, although, as far as we can see, the non-locality problem in the kinetic-energy functional has not been resolved.

However, the availability of DFT-electronic structure codes have opened up the possibility of using them even in the WDM regime. We give several references to such work that contain additional citations to other calculations [34,51–55]. This renewed interest has re-kindled an interest in the theory of thermal DFT in the context of current concerns [56]. In the following, we discuss some of the typical issues that arise in applying thermal-DFT to current problems, as these may range from basic issues to the simple question of "if one can get away with" just using the $T = 0$ XC functional.

The use of a functional, augmented with gradient approximations *etc.* is satisfactory as long as the "external potential" can be considered fixed, as is the usual case in quantum chemistry and solid-state physics. In situations where the external potential arises from a dynamic ion distribution $\rho(r)$, since $\rho(r)$ as well as the electron distribution $n(r)$ depend self-consistently on each other, it is clear that the XC-contribution is a functional of both ρ and n, *i.e.*, the XC-functional is of the form $F[n(r), \rho(r)]$. Under such circumstances, a direct *in situ* calculation of the electron $g(r)$ in the presence of the ion distribution has to be carried out, and an "on-the-fly" coupling constant integration is needed for each self-consistent loop determining $n(r)$ and $\rho(r)$. We presented examples of such calculations for a system of electrons and protons at finite temperatures, in [57,58], using the classical-map Hyper-Netted Chain technique (CHNC) that enables an easy *in situ* calculation of the $g_{ee}(r), g_{ei}(r)$ and $g_{ii}(r)$. This approach is at once non-local and hence avoids the need for gradient approximations. Furthermore, the ion-ion correlations are highly non-local and the LDA or its extensions are totally inadequate since they are described by the HNC approximation.

2. Exchange-Correlation at Finite-T

It may be useful to present this section as an "FAQ" (Frequently Asked Questions) rather than a formal discussion on thermal-XC functionals.

2.1. Do We Have Reliable Thermal-XC Functionals?

The finite-T XC-functional in the random-phase approximation (RPA) [37–39] has been available since 1982, while formulations and parametrizations that go beyond RPA have been available since the late 1980s [40–42]. Finite-T XC-data from quantum simulations for the uniform finite-T electron fluid were provided in 2013 by Brown *et al.* [59], while an analytical fit to their data is found in Karasiev *et al.* [60]. The XC-parametrization of Perrot and Dharma-wardana given in 2000, Reference [42], was based on a coupling-constant evaluation of the finite-T electron-fluid PDF calculated via the Classical-map Hyper-Netted-Chain (CHNC) [61] method. It closely agrees with the recent quantum-simulation results (Figure 1). Finite-T CHNC-based results are available for the 2D- [62] and 3D-[61] electron gas, as well as other electron-layer systems [63–65]. They are in good agreement with path-integral and other Monte Carlo (PIMC) calculations where available.

We consider the data for the 3D system that have been conveniently parametrized by Karasiev *et al.* (labeled KSDT in Figure 1). The CHNC $f_{xc}(T)$ at high temperatures (beyond what is displayed in the figure) show somewhat less correlation than given by PIMC, but correctly approaches the Debye-Hückel limit at high temperatures. In the high-density regime ($r_s < 1$), the RPA-functionals become increasingly accurate as $r_s \to 0$. The small-r_s regime has also been recently treated by Schoof *et al.* [66]. It should be stated that when the CHNC mapping was constructed, Franҫis Perrot and the present author did not attempt to map the $r_s < 1$ regime in detail as it is fairly well treated by RPA methods. Recent simulations by Malone *et al.* [67] find some differences between their work, and that of Brown *et al.* [59] for r_s in the neighbourhood of unity. Similarly, the CHNC data show differences for the $r_s = 1$ curve, as shown in Figure 1. However, it is too early to re-examine the small r_s

regime and review the data of Reference [67] which are given as the internal energy and not converted to a free energy.

However, it is clear that there is no shortage of reliable finite-T XC-functionals for those who wish to use them.

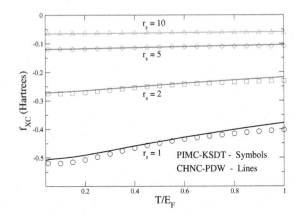

Figure 1. (Color online) Finite-T exchange and correlation free energy $f_{xc}(r_s, T)$ per electron (Hartrees) *versus* the reduced temperature T/E_F in units of the Fermi energy. The symbols, labeled PIMC-KSDT are the fit given by Karasiev *et al.* (Reference [60] to the path-integral Monte Carlo (PIMC) data of Brown *et al.* [59]). The continuous lines, labeled CHNC-PDW are from the classical-map HNC procedure of Perrot and Dharma-wardana [42]. The temperature range $0 < T/E_F \leq 1$ is the region of interest for WDM studies.

2.2. Can We Ignore Thermal Corrections and Use the $T = 0$ Implementations?

While finite-T XC functionals can be easily incorporated into the NPA model or average-atom cell models *etc.* [29], this is much more difficult in the context of large DFT codes like VASP or ABINIT. Hence, the already installed $T = 0$ XC-functionals have been used as a part of the "package" for a significant number of calculations for WDM materials, ranging from equation of state (EOS), X-ray Thomson scattering, conductivity *etc.* Hence, the question has been raised as to whether the thermal corrections to the $T = 0$ XC-functional may be conveniently disregarded.

The push for accurate XC-functionals in quantum chemistry came from the need for "chemical accuracy" in predicting molecular interactions in the milli-Rydberg range. The current level of accuracy in WDM experiments is nowhere near that. Furthermore, many properties (e.g., the EOS and the total energy) are insensitive to details since total energies are usually very large compared to XC-energies, even at $T = 0$, unless one is dealing with unusually contrived few-particle systems. However, one can give a number of counter examples which are designed to show that there are many situations where the thermal modification of the $T = 0$ XC-energy and XC-potential are important.

As a model system, we may consider the uniform electron fluid with a density of n electrons per atomic volume, and thus having an electron-sphere radius $r_s = \{3/(4\pi n)\}^{1/3}$. Since the Fermi momentum $k_F = 1/(\alpha r_s)$, where $\alpha = (4/9\pi)^{1/3}$, the kinetic energy at $T = 0$ scales as $1/r_s^2$, while the Coulomb energy scales as $1/r_s$. Hence, the ratio of the Coulomb-interaction energy to the kinetic energy scales as r_s. Thus, the electron-sphere radius r_s is also the "coupling constant" that indicates the deviation of the system from the non-interacting independent particle model. The RPA is valid when $r_s < 1$ for $T = 0$ systems, for Coulomb fluids. On the other hand, at very high temperatures, the kinetic energy becomes T (or $k_B T$ where $k_B = 1$ in our units), while the Coulomb energy is Z^2/r_s, where $Z = e = -1$ for the electron fluid. Hence the ratio of the Coulomb energy to the kinetic energy, *viz.*, $\Gamma = Z^2/(r_s T)$ for Classical Coulomb systems. Here, the role of r_s is reversed to that at $T = 0$, and the system behaves as an "ideal gas" for large r_s in systems where $T \gg E_F$. The equivalent of the

RPA-theory in the high-T limit is the Debye-Hückel theory which is valid for $\Gamma < 1$. A generalized coupling constant that "switches over" correctly from its $T = 0$ behavior to the classical-fluid behavior at high T can be given as in Equations (1) and (2):

$$\Gamma(r_s, T) = P \cdot E / K \cdot E = Z^2 / (r_s T_{kin}), \tag{1}$$

$$\Gamma(r_s, T \to 0) = r_s, \quad \Gamma(r_s, T \to \infty) = Z^2 / (r_s T). \tag{2}$$

The equivalent kinetic temperature T_{kin} referred to in the above equation can be constructed from the mean kinetic energy as in Equation (A2) given in the appendix to [42]. However, the main point here is that there are *two non-interacting limits* for studying Coulomb fluids. We can start from the $T = 0$ non-interacting limit and carry out perturbation theory, or coupling-constant integrations to include the effect of the Coulomb interaction $\lambda Z^2 / r$, with λ moving from 0 to unity (e.g., see Equation (71) of Reference [56] for a discussion and references). Alternatively, we can start from the $T \to \infty$ non-interacting limit. This high temperature limit is the "classical limit" where the system is a non-interacting Boltzmann gas. One can do perturbation theory as well as coupling constant integrations over Γ' going from 0 to its required value Γ. The latter approach is well known in the theory of classical fluids. Such results provide standard "benchmarks" in the context of the classical one-component plasma [68,69], just as the electron gas does for the quantum many-electron problem. However, there is no clear way of evolving from a classical Boltzmann gas at $\Gamma = 0$ into a quantum fluid by increasing the Coulomb coupling to its full value, as the anti-symmetry of the underlying wavefunction needs to be included. This problem does not arise if we start from a non-interacting Fermi gas at $T = 0$. How this problem is solved within a classical scheme is discussed below, in the context of the CHNC method. The "temperature connection formula" referred to recently by Burke *et al.* [70] in a thermal-DFT context may be closely related to this discussion.

Although XC effects are important, it is a small fraction of the total energy. They become negligible as T becomes very large, when the total energy itself becomes very large. Thus, it is easy to understand that finite-T XC effects are most important, for any given r_s, in the WDM range, where $0 \leq T/E_F \leq 1$, with $E_F = 0.5/(\alpha r_s)^2$. Furthermore, in any electron-ion system containing *even one* bound state, the electron density $n(r)$ becomes large as one approaches the atomic core, and hence there are spatial regions r where $T/E_F(r) \leq 1$, when finite-T XC comes into play. Since the "free-electron" states are orthogonal to the core states, the free-electron density pile-up $n_f(r)$ near a nucleus immersed in a hot-electron fluid is also equally affected, directly and via the core. Furthermore, $n_f(r)$ is a property that directly enters into the calculation of the X-Ray Thomson scattering signal as well as the electron-ion pseudopotential $U_{ei}(r)$. Hence, the effect of finite-T XC, and the need to include thermal-XC functionals in such calculations can be experimentally ascertained.

In Figure 2, we present the $n_f(r)$ near an Aluminium nucleus in an electron fluid of density 1.81×10^{23} electrons/cm^3, *i.e.*, at $r_s = 2.07$ and at $T = 10$ eV, calculated using the neutral-pseudo-atom method. This temperature corresponds to $T/E_F \simeq 0.84$. Calculations using VASP code for an actual experiment covering this regime has also been given by Plageman *et al.* [52]. Although the difference in charge densities that arises from the difference between the $T = 0$ XC and the finite-T XC shown in Figure 2 may seem small, such charge-density differences translate into significant energy differences as well as into significant X-ray scattering features.

Although Kohn-Sham energies are not to be interpreted as the one-particle excitation energies of the system, they can be regarded as the one-particle energies of the non-interacting electron fluid (at the interacting density) that appears in Kohn-Sham theory. These eigen-energies are also sensitive to whether we use the $T = 0$ XC-functional, or even to different finite-T functionals. For instance, in Section 6 of Reference [42] we give the Kohn-Sham energy spectrum of warm-dense Aluminium at 15 eV calculated using the PDW-finite-T XC-functional [42], as well as the finite-T Iyatomi-Ichimaru (YI) functional. In summary, the Kohn-Sham (KS)-bound states obtained by the two methods (with YI given second) are: at energies (in Rydbergs) of 2115.044 and 2110.199 for the *1s* level, 27.86214 and

27.53968 for the 2s level. The outermost level, the 2p-state, has an energy of 25.05646 and 24.81116 from Perrot and Dharma-wardana (PWD) and YI, respectively. Similar proportionate changes are seen in the phase shifts of the continuum states. Thus, it is clear that the XC-potentials should have a significant impact, especially in determining the regimes of plasma phase transitions [26,71], finite-T magnetic transitions, as well as in the theory of ionization processes [54] and transport properties.

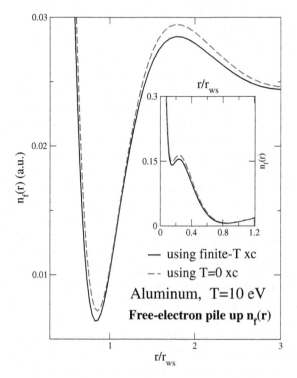

Figure 2. (Color online) The NPA free-electron density $n_f(r)$ using PDW finite-T XC and with the $T = 0$ XC. Inset: $n_f(r)$ inside the Wigner-Seitz sphere, with $r_{ws} \simeq 3.0$ Bohr.

Another example of the need for finite-T XC functionals is given by Sjostrom and Daligault [72] in their discussion of gradient-corrected thermal functionals. They conclude that "finite-temperature functionals show improvement over zero-temperature functionals, as compared to path-integral Monte Carlo calculations for deuterium equations of state, and perform without computational cost increase compared to zero-temperature functionals and so should be used for finite-temperature calculations".

Karasiev et al. [50] have recently implemented the PDW-finite-T XC functional as well as their new fit to the PIMC data in the "Quantum Espresso" code. They have made calculations of the bandstructure and electrical conductivity of WDM Aluminium. They find that the use of finite-T XC is necessary if significant errors (up to 15% at $T/Ef \simeq 0.11$ in the case of Al) are to be avoided [73].

2.3. Can We Define Free and Bound Electrons in an "Unambiguous" Manner?

In a "fully-ionized" plasma, all the electrons are in delocalized states. Thus, in stark contrast to quantum chemistry, most plasma physics deals with continuum processes. WDM systems usually contain some partially occupied bound states as well as continuum states. Thus, if the Hamiltonian is bounded, and if there is no frequency dependent external field acting on the system, there is no difficulty in identifying the bound states and continuum states of the non-interacting electron system used in Kohn-Sham theory. If a strong frequency-dependent external field is acting on the system, the concept of "bound" electrons as distinct from "free" electrons becomes much more hazy and will not be discussed here.

Depending on the nature of the "external potential", a system at $T = 0$ may be such that all electrons are in "bound states". The latter are usually eigenstates ψ_j whose square $\psi_j(r)$ becomes rapidly negligible as r goes beyond a region of localization. The spectrum contains occupied and unoccupied "bound states" as well as positive-energy states which are not localized within a given region. All states become partially occupied in finite-T systems, and treatments that restrict themselves to a small basis set of functions localized over a finite region of space become too restrictive. Most DFT codes use a simulation cell of linear dimension L with periodic boundary conditions. In such a model, the smallest value of k in momentum space is $\sim \pi/L$, and this prevents the direct evaluation of various properties (e.g., $S(k)$) as $k \to 0$. In the NPA model, a large sphere of radius R such that all particle correlations have died out is used, and phase shifts of continuum states, taken as plane waves, are calculated. This procedure allows an essentially direct access to $k \to 0$ properties as well as the bound and continuum spectrum of the ion in the plasma. However, the difficulty arises when the electronic bound-states spread beyond the Wigner-Seitz radius of the ion.

The question of determining the number of free electrons per ion, $viz.$, $\bar{Z}$ is usually posed in the context of the mean-ionic charge $\bar{Z}$ used in metal physics and plasma theory. If the nuclear charge is Z_n, and if the total number of bound electrons attributed to that nucleus is n_b, then clearly $\bar{Z} = Z_n - n_b$ if the charge distribution $n_b(r)$ is fully contained within the Wigner-Seitz sphere of the ion. While n_b is well-defined in that sense for many elements under standard conditions, giving, for example $\bar{Z} = 3$ for Al at normal compression and up to about $T = 20$ eV, this simple picture breaks down for many elements even under normal conditions. If the electronic charge density cannot be accurately represented as a superposition of individual atomic charge densities, the definition of n_b becomes more complicated since a bound electron may be shared between two or more neighbouring atoms that form bonds. Transition-metal solids and WDMs have d-electron states, which extend outside the atomic Wigner-Seitz sphere. Hence, assigning them to a particular nuclear centre becomes a delicate exercise. However, even in such situations, there are meaningful ways to define n_b and $\bar{Z}$ that lead to consistence with experiments. In such situations, the proper value of $\bar{Z}$ may differ from one physical property to another as the averaging involved in constructing the mean value $\bar{Z}$ may change. A similar situation applies to the effective electron mass m_e^* which deviates from the ideal value of unity (in atomic units), and takes on different values according to whether we are discussing a thermal mass, an optical effective mass, or a band mass that we may use in a Luttinger-Kohn $k \cdot p$ calculation.

Experimentally, $\bar{Z}$ is a measure of the number of free electrons released per atom. This can be measured from the $\omega \to 0$ limit of the optical conductivity $\sigma(\omega)$. Thus, although transition metals like gold have delocalized d-electrons, the static conductivity up to about 2 eV is found to indicate that $\bar{Z} = 1$, with the optical mass $m_e^* = 1$. Another property which measures $\bar{Z}$ is the electronic specific heat. Here again, the specific heat evaluated from DFT calculations that use a $\bar{Z} = 1$ pseudopotential for Au agrees with experimental data up to 2 eV, while those that use the density of states from *all 11 electrons* as free-electron states will obtain significantly different answers [74,75] that need to be used with circumspection. That is, such a calculation will be valid only if the d-electrons are fully delocalized and partake in the heating process by being coupled with the pump laser creating the WDM.

The argument that $\bar{Z}$ is not a valid concept or a quantum property because there is no "operator" corresponding to it has no merit. The temperature also does not correspond to the mean value of a quantum operator. In fact, T is a Lagrange multiplier ensuring the constancy of the Hamiltonian within the relevant times scales, while $\bar{Z}$ is the Lagrange multiplier that sets the charge neutrality condition $\bar{n} = \bar{Z}\bar{\rho}$ relating the average electron density to the average ion density [27].

Additional discussions regarding $\bar{Z}$ may be found in References [21,58] and in Reference [26] where the case of a WDM mixture of ions with different ionization, $viz.$, Al^{Z_j+} is treated within a first-principles DFT scheme.

3. Future Challenges in Formulating Finite-T XC Functionals

In considering a system of ions with a distribution $\rho(\vec{r}) = \sum_j \delta(\vec{r} - \vec{R}_j)$, and an electron distribution interacting with it, the free energy F has to be regarded as a functional of both $\rho(r)$ and $n(r)$. Hence, the ground state has to be determined by a coupled variational problem involving a constrained-search minimization with respect to all physically possible electron charge distributions $n(r)$, and ion distributions $\rho(r)$, subject to the usual formal constraints of n-representability *etc.* The Euler-Lagrange variational equation from the derivative of F with respect to $n(r)$, for a fixed $\rho(r)$ would yield the usual Kohn-Sham procedure with the rigid electrostatic potential of $\rho(r)$ providing the external potential. However, if no static approximation or Born-Oppenheimer approximation is made, we can obtain another Euler-Lagrange variational equation from the derivative of F with respect to ρ. This coupled pair of equations treated via density-functional theory involves not only the f_{xc}^{ee}, but also f_{xc}^{ei} and f_c^{ii}, the latter involving correlations (but no exchange) as it arises from ion-ion interactions beyond the self-consistent-field approximation. In effect, just as the electron many-body problem can be reduced to an effective one-body problem in the Kohn-Sham sense, we can thus reduce the many-ion problem into a "single-ion problem". Such an analysis was given by us long ago [27].

The ion-ion correlations cannot be approximated by any type of local-density approximation, or even with a sophisticated gradient approximation. However, Perrot and the present author were able to show that a fully non-local approximation where an ion-ion pair-distribution can be constructed *in situ* using the HNC equation provides a very satisfactory solution. This is equivalent to positing that the ion-ion correlation functional is made up of the hyper-netted-chain diagrams. However, significant insights are needed in regard to the electron-ion correlation functionals which involve the coupling between a quantum subsystem and a classical subsystem [4]. This is largely an open problem that we have attempted to deal with via the classical-map HNC approach, to be discussed below.

The advent of WDM and ultra-fast matter has thrown out a number of new challenges to the implementation of thermal DFT. A simple but at the moment unsolved problem in UFM may be briefly described as follows. A metallic solid like Al at room temperature (T_r) is subject to a short-pulse laser which heats the conduction electrons to a temperature T_e that may be 6 eV. The core electrons (which occupy energy bands deep down in energy and hence not excitable by the laser) remain essentially unperturbed in the core region and at the core temperature, *i.e.*, at $T_r \simeq 0.026$ eV. The temperature relaxation by electron-ion processes is "slow", *i.e.*, it occurs in pico-second times scales. On the other hand, electron-electron processes are "fast", and hence one would expect that the conduction-band electrons at T_e to undergo exchange as well as Coulomb scattering within femto-second time scales, consistent with electron-electron interactions timescales. Thus, while we have a quasi-equilibrium of a two-temperature system holding for up to pico-second timescales, the question arises if one can meaningfully calculate an exchange and correlation potential between the bound electrons in the core at the temperature T_r, and the conduction-band electrons at T_e, with $T_e \gg T_i$. While we believe on physical grounds that a thermal DFT is applicable at least in an approximate sense, an unambiguous method for calculating the two-temperature XC-energies and potentials is as yet unavailable.

3.1. Classical-Map Hyper-Netted Chain Method

Once the pair-distribution function of a classical or quantum Coulomb system is known, all the thermodynamic functions of the system can be calculated from $g(r)$. The XC-information is also in the $g(r)$. Only the ground-state correlations are needed in calculating the linear transport properties of the system. Hence, most properties of the system become available. It is well known that correlations among classical charges (*i.e.*, ions) can be treated with good accuracy via the the hyper-netted-chain equation, but dealing with the quantum equivalent of hyper-netted-chain diagrams for quantum systems is difficult, even at $T = 0$ [76].

When we have an electron subsystem interacting with the ion subsystem, obtaining the PDFs becomes a difficult quantum problem even via more standard methods. We need to solve for a many-particle wavefunction which rapidly becomes intractable as the number of electrons is increased beyond a small number. The message of DFT is that the many-body wavefunction is not needed, and that the one-particle charge distribution $n(r)$ is sufficient. While the charge distribution at $T = 0$ involves a sum over the squares of the occupied Kohn-Sham wavefunctions, at very high T, the classical charge distribution is given by a Boltzmann distribution containing an effective potential felt by a single "field" particle and characterized by the temperature which is directly proportional to the classical kinetic energy.

In CHNC, we attempt to replace the quantum-electron problem by a classical Coulomb problem where we can use a simple method like the ordinary HNC equation to directly obtain the needed PDFs, at some effective "classical fluid" temperature T_{cf} having the same density distribution as the quantum fluid. The electron PDF $g^0(r)$ of the non-interacting quantum electron fluid is known at any temperature and embodies the effect of quantum statistics (Pauli principle). Hence, we can ask for the effective potential $\beta V_{Pau}(r)$ which, when used in the HNC, gives us the $g^0(r)$, an idea dating back to a publication by Lado [77]. This ensures that the non-interacting density has the required "n-representable" form of a Slater determinant. Of course, only the product $P(r) = \beta V_{Pau}(r)$ can be determined by this method, and it exists even at $T = 0$. Then the total pair potential to be used in the equivalent classical fluid is taken as $\beta \phi(r) = P(r) + \beta V_{Cou}(r)$. How does one choose $\beta = 1/T_{cf}$ since the Pauli term is independent of it?

To a very good approximation, if T_{cf} is chosen such that the classical fluid has the same Coulomb correlation energy E_c as the quantum electron fluid, then it is found that the PDF of the classical Coulomb fluid is a very close approximation to the PDF of the quantum electron fluid at $T = 0$. There is of course no mathematical proof of this. However, from DFT, we know that only the "correct" ground state distribution will give us the correct energy, and perhaps it is not surprising that this choice is found to work. The T_{cf} that works for the $T = 0$ quantum electron gas is called the "quantum temperature" T_q. More details of the method are given in Reference [42]. There it is argued that, to a good approximation, for a finite-T electron gas at the physical temperature T, the effective classical fluid temperature $T_{cf} = \sqrt{T_q^2 + T^2}$. This has been confirmed independently by Datta and Dufty [78] in their study of classical approximations to the quantum electron fluid. Thus, CHNC provides all the tools necessary for implementing a classical HNC calculation of the PDFs of the quantum electron gas at finite-T.

We display in Figure 3 pair-distribution functions calculated using CHNC, and those available in the literature from quantum simulations at $T = 0$, as finite-T PDFs from quantum simulations are hard to find. In any case, the classical map is expected to be better as T increases and the $T = 0$ comparison is important. In the figure, diffusion Monte Carlo (DMC) and variational Monte Carlo (VMC) data [79] are compared with CHNC results. In Figure 3, the parallel-spin PDF is marked $g_{11}(r)$, while the anti-parallel spin PDF is marked $g_{12}(r)$. The latter has a finite value as $r \to 0$ as there is no Pauli exclusion principle operating on them. Furthermore, the the mean value of the operator of the Coulomb potential, i.e., e^2/r, is of the form $\{1 - \exp(-k_{dB}r)\}/r$, where k_{dB} is the thermal de Broglie wavelength of the electron pair, as discussed in [61]. This "quantum-diffraction" correction ensures that $g_{12}(r \to 0)$ has a finite value, as seen in the figure. It is in good agreement with Quantum Monte Carlo results. Thus, the CHNC is capable of providing a good interpretation of the physics underlying the results of quantum simulations. Needless to say, unlike Quantum Monte Carlo or Path-Integral simulation methods, the CHNC integral equations can be implemented on a laptop and the computational times are imperceptible.

Using the PDFs $g(r, T, \lambda)$ calculated with a scaled Coulomb potential $\lambda V_{Cou}(r)$, a coupling constant integration over λ can be carried out to obtain the XC-free energy $F_{xc}(r_s, T)$ as described in detail in Reference [42]. As seen from Figure 1, this procedure leads to good agreement with the thermal-XC results from the PIMC method, while only the $T = 0$ spin-polarized E_c data were used in constructing T_q. Furthermore, since T_{cf} tends to the physical temperature at high T, and since the HNC provides an excellent approximation to the PDFs of the high-T electron system, the method naturally recovers the high-T limit of the classical one-component plasma. Note that we could NOT have started from the high-T limit of an ideal classical gas and used the well-known classical coupling constant (*i.e.*, Γ integration method, e.g., see Baus and Hansen or Ichimaru [68,69]) to determine f_{xc} from an integration that ranges from $\Gamma = 0, T = \infty$ to the needed temperature (*i.e.*, the needed Γ). This is because there is no clear method of capturing the physics contained in T_q, and ensuring that Fermi statistics are obeyed (e.g., via the introduction of a $\beta V_{Pau}(r)$), as there is only Boltzmann statistics at $\Gamma = 0$.

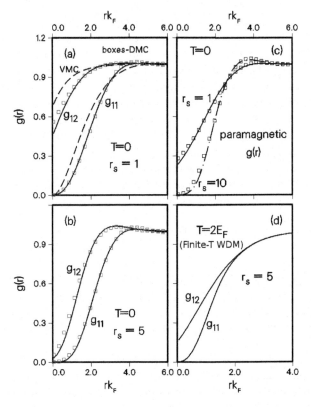

Figure 3. (a) Here, the CHNC g(r) are compared with VMC and DMC simulation results: the interacting PDFs $g_{11}(r)$ and $g_{12}(r)$ at $r_s = 1$ are shown. Solid lines: CHNC, boxes: DMC, dashed line: VMC [79]; Panel (b) $r_s = 5$, DMC [79] and HNC; In (c), the paramagnetic g(r) at $r_s = 1$ and $r_s = 10$, $T = 0$ are compared with DMC; (d) Finite temperature PDFs (CHNC) for $T/E_F = 2$, $r_s = 5$ would correspond to a WDM at $\simeq 3.6$ eV ($\sim 42{,}000$ K).

The ability of the CHNC to correctly capture the thermal-DFT properties of the finite-T quantum fluid suggests its use for electron-ion systems like compressed hydrogen (electron-proton gas), or complex plasmas with many different classical ions interacting with electrons [57], *without having to solve the Kohn-Sham equations*, as demonstrated in Bredow *et al.* [80]. The extensive calculations of Bredow *et al.* establish the ease and rapidity provided by CHNC, without sacrificing accuracy. CHNC has potential applications for electron-positron systems or electron-hole systems where both quantum components can be treated via the classical map. It also provides a partial solution to the still unresolved problem of formulating a fully-nonlocal "orbital-free" approach that directly exploits the Hohenberg-Kohn-Mermin theory, without the need to go via the Kohn-Sham orbital formulation.

4. Conclusions

We have argued that our current knowledge of the thermal XC-functionals is satisfactory and the stage is set for their implementation in practical DFT codes. Noting the complexity of warm-dense matter, we have emphasized simplifications as well as extensions which do not sacrifice accuracy. In this respect, the neutral-pseudo atom model can, in most cases, do the work of the *ab initio* codes like VASP, and handle high-temperature problems that are beyond their scope. Orbital-free approaches [50] will also become increasingly useful, especially at intermediate and high T/E_F. Nevertheless, the *ab initio* codes are needed at low-temperature low-density situations involving molecular formation, where the NPA breaks down as it is a "single-centre" approach. However, in many WDM cases, we need to go beyond the picture where the ion subsystem is held static, and the electrons only feel them as an "external potential". Hence, we have emphasized the need for calculating not just the XC-functionals for electrons, but also the classical correlation functionals for ions, as well as the ion-electron correlations directly, *in situ*, via direct coupling-constant integrations of all the pair-distribution functions of the system, ensuring a fully non-local formulation where gradient expansions are not needed. In fact, there is no need for any XC-functionals in such a scheme. To do this efficiently and accurately, we have proposed a classical map of the quantum electrons and implemented it in the CHNC scheme that depends on DFT ideas. This capacity is not found in any of the currently available methods. CHNC has been used to construct a finite-T XC functional for electrons more than a decade before PIMC results became available, and it turns out that the CHNC results are accurate. The CHNC scheme has been successfully used for calculating the equation of state and other properties of warm dense matter as well as multi-component $T = 0$ electron-layer systems, thick layers *etc.*, that are expensive to treat by quantum simulation methods, but relevant for nanostructure physics.

Conflicts of Interest: The author declares no conflict of interest.

References

1. Luttinger, J.M.; Ward, J.C. Ground-State Energy of a Many-Fermion System—II. *Phys. Rev.* **1960**, *118*, 1417.
2. Kohn, W.; Luttinger, J.M. Ground-State Energy of a Many-Fermion System. *Phys. Rev.* **1960**, *118*, 41.
3. Takahashi, Y.; Umezawa, H. Thermofield Dynamics. In *Collective Phenomena*; Gordon and Beach: New York, NY, USA, 1975; Volume 2, pp. 55–80; Reprinted in *Int. J. Mod. Phys. B* **1996**, *10*, 1755, doi:10.1142/S0217979296000817.
4. Heslot, A. Quantum mechanics as a classical theory. *Phys. Rev. D* **1985**, *31*, 1341.
5. Hohenberg, P.; Kohn, W. Inhomogeneous Electron Gas. *Phys. Rev.* **1964** *136*, B864.
6. Kohn, W.; Sham, L.J. Self-Consistent Equations Including Exchange and Correlation Effects. *Phys. Rev.* **1965**, *140*, A1133.
7. Mermin, N.D. Thermal Properties of the Inhomogeneous Electron Gas. *Phys. Rev.* **1965**, *137*, A1441.
8. Dharma-wardana, M.W.C. Current Issues in Finite-T Density-Functional Theory and Warm-Correlated Matter. In Proceedings of the 16th International Conference on Density Functional Theory and Its Applications, Celebrating the 50th Anniversary of the Kohn-Sham Theory, Debrecen, Hungary, 31 August–4 September 2015.
9. Dharma-wardana, M.W.C. *A Physicists's View of Matter and Mind*; World Scientific: Singapore, 2014.
10. Dharma-wardana, M.W.C. Density-Functional Theory, finite-temperature classical maps, and their implications for foundational studies of quantum systems. *ArXiv E-Prints* **2013**, arXiv:1307.4369.
11. Graziani, F.; Desjarlais, M.P.; Redmer, R.; Trickey, S.B. (Eds.) *Frontiers and Challenges in Warm Dense Matter*; Lecture Notes in Computational Science and Engineering; Springer International Publishing: Heidelberg, Germany, 2014; Volume 96.
12. Milchberg, H.M.; Freeman, R.R.; Davy, S.C.; More, R.M. Resistivity of a Simple Metal from Room Temperature to 10^6 K. *Phys. Rev. Lett.* **1988**, *61*, 2364.
13. Ng, A. Outstanding questions in electron-ion energy relaxation, lattice stability, and dielectric function of warm dense matter. *Int. J. Quant. Chem.* **2012**, *112*, 150–160.
14. Dharma-wardana, M.W.C. Results on the energy-relaxation rates of dense two-temperature aluminum, carbon, and silicon plasmas close to liquid-metal conditions. *Phys. Rev. E* **2001**, *64*, 035401(R).
15. Benedict, L.X.; Surh, M.P.; Castor, J.; Khairallah, S.A.; Whitley, H.D.; Richards, D.F.; Glosli, D.N.; Murillo, M.S.; Scullard, C.R.; Grabowski, P.E.; *et al.* Molecular dynamics simulations and generalized Lenard-Balescu calculations of electron-ion temperature equilibration in plasmas. *Phys. Rev. E* **2012**, *86*, 046406.

16. Driver, K.P.; Militzer, B. All-Electron Path Integral Monte Carlo Simulations of Warm Dense Matter: Application to Water and Carbon Plasmas. *Phys. Rev. Lett.* **2012**, *108*, 115502.

17. Lorazo, P.; Lewis, L.J.; Meunier, M. Short-Pulse Laser Ablation of Solids: From Phase Explosion to Fragmentation. *Phys. Rev. Lett.* **2003** *91*, 225502

18. Lorazo, P.; Lewis, L.J.; Meunier, M. Thermodynamic pathways to melting, ablation, and solidification in absorbing solids under pulsed laser irradiation. *Phys. Rev. B* **2006**, *73*, 134108.

19. Shah, J. *Ultrafast Spectroscopy of Semiconductor Nanostructures*; Springer: Heidleberg, Germany, 1999.

20. Dharma-wardana, M.W.C. Coupled-mode hot electron relaxation and the hot-phonon effect in polar semiconductors. *Solid State Commun.* **1993**, *86*, 83–86.

21. Dharma-wardana, M.W.C. A Review of Studies on Strongly-Coupled Coulomb Systems Since the Rise of DFT and SCCS-1977. *Contr. Plasma Phys.* **2015**, *55*, 85–101.

22. Dagens, L. A selfconsistent calculation of the rigid neutral atom density according to the auxiliary neutral atom model. *J. Phys. C Solid State Phys.* **1972**, *5*, 2333.

23. Ziman, J.H. The method of neutral pseudo-atoms in the theory of metals. *Adv. Phys.* **1964**, *13*, 89–138.

24. Dagens, L. Densité de valence et énergie de liaison d'un métal simple par la méthode de l'atome neutre : Le potentiel ionique Hartree-Fock. *J. Phys. France* **1975**, *36*, 521–529. (In French)

25. Perrot, F. Ion-ion interaction and equation of state of a dense plasma: Application to beryllium. *Phys. Rev. E* **1993**, *47*, doi:10.1103/PhysRevE.47.570.

26. Perrot, F.; Dharma-wardana, M.W.C. Equation of state and transport properties of an interacting multispecies plasma: Application to a multiply ionized Al plasma. *Phys. Rev. E.* **1995**, *52*, 5352.

27. Dharma-wardana, M.W.C.; Perrot, F. Density-functional theory of hydrogen plasmas. *Phys. Rev. A* **1982**, *26*, 2096.

28. Wilson, B.; Sonnad, V.; Sterne, P.; Isaacs, W. Purgatorio—A new implementation of the Inferno algorithm. *J. Quant. Spectrosc. Radiat. Transfer.* **2006**, *99*, 658–679.

29. Liberman, D.A. Inferno: A better model of atoms in dense plasmas. *J. Quant. Spectrosc. Radiat. Transf.* **1982**, *27*, 335–339.

30. Starrett, C.E.; Saumon, D. Models of the elastic x-ray scattering feature for warm dense aluminum. *Phys. Rev. E* **2015**, *92*, 033101.

31. Chihara, J.; Kambayashi, S. Ionic and electronic structures of liquid aluminium from the quantal hypernetted-chain equations combined with the molecular dynamics method. *J. Phys. Condens. Matter.* **1994**, *6*, 10221.

32. Dharma-wardana, M.W.C. The classical-map hyper-netted-chain (CHNC) method and associated novel density-functional techniques for warm dense matter. *Int. J. Quant. Chem.* **2012**, *112*, 53–64.

33. Harbour, L.; Dharma-wardana, M.W.C.; Klug, D.D.; Lewis, L.J. Two-Temperature Pair Potentials and Phonon Spectra for Simple Metals in the Warm Dense Matter Regime. *Contrib. Plasma Phys.* **2015**, *55*, 144–151.

34. Recoules, V.; Clérouin, J.; Zérah, G.; Anglade, P.M.; Mazevet, S. Effect of Intense Laser Irradiation on the Lattice Stability of Semiconductors and Metals. *Phys. Rev. Lett.* **2006**, *96*, 055503.

35. Gilbert, T. L. Hohenberg-Kohn theorem for nonlocal external potentials. *Phys. Rev. B* **1975**, *12*, 2111.

36. Dharma-wardana, M.W.C.; Taylor, T. Exchange and correlation potentials for finite temperature quantum calculations at intermediate degeneracies. *J. Phys. C Solid State Phys.* **1981**, *14*, 629–646.

37. Gupta, U.; Rajagopal, A.K. Density functional formalism at finite temperatures with some applications. *Phys. Rep.* **1982**, *87*, 259–311.

38. Perrot, F.; Dharma-wardana, M.W.C. Exchange and correlation potentials for electron-ion systems at finite temperatures. *Phys. Rev. A* **1984**, *30*, 2619.

39. Kanhere, D.C.; Panat, P.V.; Rajagopal, A.K.; Callaway, J. Exchange-correlation potentials for spin-polarized systems at finite temperatures. *Phys. Rev. A* **1986**, *33*, 490.

40. Dandrea, R.G.; Ashcroft, N.W.; Carlsson, A.E. Electron liquid at any degeneracy. *Phys. Rev. B* **1986**, *34*, 2097.

41. Ichimaru, S.; Iyetomi, H.; Tanaka, S. Statistical physics of dense plasmas: Thermodynamics, transport coefficients and dynamic correlations. *Phys. Rep.* **1987**, *149*, 91–205.

42. Perrot, F.; Dharma-wardana, M.W.C. Spin-polarized electron liquid at arbitrary temperatures: Exchange-correlation energies, electron-distribution functions, and the static response functions. *Phys. Rev. B* **2000**, *62*, 16536; Erratum in **2003**, *67*, 79901.

43. About CASTEP. Available online: http://www.castep.org/CASTEP/CASTEP (accessed on 21 March 2016).

44. VASP. Available online: https://www.vasp.at/ (accessed on 21 March 2016).
45. ABINIT. Available online: http://www.abinit.org/ (accessed on 21 March 2016).
46. ADF: Powerful DFT Software. Available online: https://www.scm.com/(accessed on 21 March 2016).
47. The Official Gaussian Website. Available online: http://www.gaussian.com/ (accessed on 21 March 2016).
48. Perdew, J.P.; Burke, K.; Ernzerhof, M. Generalized Gradient Approximation Made Simple. *Phys. Rev. Lett.* **1996**, *77*, 3865; Erratum in **1997**, *78*, 1396.
49. Gonze, X. First-principles responses of solids to atomic displacements and homogeneous electric fields: Implementation of a conjugate-gradient algorithm. *Phys. Rev. B* **1997**, *55*, 10337.
50. Karasiev, V.V.; Sjostrom, T.; Trickey, S.B. Finite-temperature orbital-free DFT molecular dynamics: Coupling Profess and Quantum Espresso. *Comput. Phys. Commun.* **2014**, *185*, 3240–3249.
51. Silvestrelli, P.L.; Alavi, A.; Parrinello, M. Electrical-conductivity calculation in *ab initio* simulations of metals:Application to liquid sodium. *Phys. Rev. B* **1997**, *55*, 15515.
52. Plagemann, K.U.; Rüter, H.R.; Bornath, T.; Shihab, M.; Desjarlais, M.P.; Fortmann, C.; Glenzer, S.H.; Redmer, R. *Ab initio* calculation of the ion feature in x-ray Thomson scattering. *Phys. Rev. E* **2015**, *92*, 013103.
53. Sperling, P.; Gamboa, E.J.; Lee, H.J.; Chung, H.K.; Galtier, E.; Omarbakiyeva, Y.; Reinholz, H.; Röpke, G.; Zastrau, U.; Hastings, J.; *et al.* Free-Electron X-Ray Laser Measurements of Collisional-Damped Plasmons in Isochorically Heated Warm Dense Matter. *Phys. Rev. Lett.* **2015**, *115*, 115001.
54. Vinko, S.M.; Ciricosta, O.; Preston, T.R.; Rackstraw, D.S.; Brown, C.R.; Burian, T.; Chalupský, J.; Cho, B.I.; Chung, H.K.; Engelhorn, K.; *et al.* Investigation of femtosecond collisional ionization rates in a solid-density aluminium plasma. *Nat. Commun.* **2015**, *6*, 6397.
55. Dharma-wardana, M.W.C. The dynamic conductivity and the plasmon profile of Aluminium in the ultra-fast-matter regime; an analysis of recent X-ray scattering data from the LCLS. *ArXiv E-Prints* **2015**, arXiv:1601.07566.
56. Pribram-Jones, A.; Pittalis, S.; Gross, E.K.U.; Burke, K. Thermal Density Functional Theory in Context. In *Frontiers and Challenges in Warm Dense Matter*; Lecture Notes in Computational Science and Engineering; Springer International Publishing: Cham, Switzerland, 2014; Volume 96.
57. Dharma-wardana, M.W.C.; Perrot, F. Equation of state and the Hugoniot of laser shock-compressed deuterium: Demonstration of a basis-function-free method for quantum calculations. *Phys. Rev. B* **2002**, *66*, 014110.
58. Dharma-wardana, M.W.C. Electron-ion and ion-ion potentials for modeling warm dense matter: Applications to laser-heated or shock-compressed Al and Si. *Phys. Rev. E* **2012**, *86*, 036407.
59. Brown, E.W.; DuBois, J.L.; Holzman, M.; Ceperley, D.M. Exchange-correlation energy for the three-dimensional homogeneous electron gas at arbitrary temperature. *Phys. Rev. B* **2013**, *88*, 081102(R); Erratum in **2013**, *88*, 199901.
60. Karasiev, V.V.; Sjostrom, T.; Dufty, J.; Trickey, S.B. Accurate Homogeneous Electron Gas Exchange-Correlation Free Energy for Local Spin-Density Calculations. *Phys. Rev. Lett.* **2014**, *112*, 076403.
61. Dharma-wardana, M.W.C.; Perrot, F. A simple classical mapping of the spin-polarized quantum electron gas distribution functions and local field corrections. *Phys. Rev. Lett.* **2000**, *84*, 959.
62. Perrot, F.; Dharma-wardana, M.W.C. 2D-Electron Gas at Arbitrary Spin Polarizations and Coupling Strengths: Exchange-Correlation Energies, Distribution Functions, and the Spin-Polarized Phase. *Phys. Rev. Lett.* **2001**, *87*, 206404.
63. Dharma-wardana, M.W.C.; Perrot, F. Spin-polarized stable phases of the 2DES at finite temperatures. *Phys. Rev. Lett.* **2003** *90*, 136601.
64. Dharma-wardana, M.W.C.; Perrot, F. Spin- and valley-dependent analysis of the two-dimensional low-density electron system in Si MOSFETs. *Phys. Rev. B* **2004**, *70*, 035308.
65. Dharma-wardana, M.W.C. Spin and temperature dependent study of exchange and correlation in thick two-dimensional electron layers. *Phys. Rev. B* **2005**, *72*, 125339.
66. Schoof, T.; Groth, S.; Vorberger, J.; Bonitz, M. *Ab Initio* Thermodynamic Results for the Degenerate Electron Gas at Finite Temperature. *Phys. Rev. Lett.* **2015**, *115*, 130402.
67. Malone, F.D.; Blunt, N.S.; Brown, E.W.; Lee, D.K.K.; Spencer, J.S.; Foulkes, W.M.C.; Shepherd. J.J. Accurate exchange-correlation energies for the warm dense electron gas. Available online: http://arxiv.org/pdf/1602.05104v2.pdf (accessed on 21 March 2016).
68. Baus, M.; Hansen, J.-P. Statistical Mechanics of Simple Coulomb Systems. *Phys. Rep.* **1980**, *59*, 2.

69. Ichimaru, S. Strongly coupled plasmas: High-density classical plasmas and degenerate electron liquids. *Rev. Mod. Phys.* **1982**, *54*, 1017.

70. Smith, J.C.; Pribram-Jones, A.; Burke, K. Thermal Corrections to Density Functional Simulations of Warm Dense Matter. *ArXiv E-Prints* **2015**, arXiv:1509.03097.

71. Norman, G.E.; Starostin, A.N. Failure of the classical description of nondegenerate dense plasma. *High Temp.* **1968**, *6*, 394.

72. Sjostrom, T.; Daligault, J. Gradient corrections to the exchange-correlation free energy. *Phys. Rev. B* **2014**, *90*, 155109.

73. Karasiev, V.V.; Calderin, L.; Trickey, S.B. The importance of finite-temperature exchange-correlation for warm dense matter calculations. *ArXiv E-Prints* **2016**, arXiv:1601.04543.

74. Lin, Z.; Zhigilei, L.V.; Celli, V. Electron-phonon coupling and electron heat capacity of metals under conditions of strong electron-phonon nonequilibrium. *Phys. Rev. B* **2008**, *77*, 075133.

75. Chen, Z.; Holst, B.; Kirkwood, S.E.; Sametoglu, V.; Reid, M.; Tsui, Y.Y.; Recoules, V.; Ng, A. Evolution of ac Conductivity in Nonequilibrium Warm Dense Gold. *Phys. Rev. Lett.* **2013**, *110*, 135001.

76. Zabolitsky, J.G. *Advances in Nuclear Physics*; Negale, W., Vogt, E., Eds.; Springer US: New York, NY, USA, 1981; pp. 1–58.

77. Lado, F. Effective Potential Description of the Quantum Ideal Gases. *J. Chem. Phys.* **1967**, *47*, 5369.

78. Dufty, J.; Dutta, S. Classical representation of a quantum system at equilibrium: Theory. *Phys. Rev. E* **2013**, *87*, 032101.

79. Ortiz, G.; Ballone, P. Correlation energy, structure factor, radial distribution function, and momentum distribution of the spin-polarized uniform electron gas. *Phys. Rev. B* **1994**, *50*, 1391; Erratum in **1997**, *56*, 9970.

80. Bredow, R.; Bornath, T.; Kraeft, W.-D.; Dharma-wardana, C.; Redmer, R. Classical-Map Hypernetted Chain Calculations for Dense Plasmas. *Contrib. Plasma Phys.* **2015**, *55*, 222–229.

9

Computation of the Likelihood of Joint Site Frequency Spectra Using Orthogonal Polynomials

Claus Vogl [1,*] and Juraj Bergman [2,3]

[1]   Institute of Animal Breedings and Genetics, Veterinärmedizinische Universität Wien, Veterinärplatz 1, A-1210 Vienna, Austria

[2]   Institut für Populationsgenetik, Veterinärmedizinische Universität Wien, Veterinärplatz 1, A-1210 Vienna, Austria; juraj.bergman@vetmeduni.ac.at

[3]   Vienna Graduate School of Population Genetics, Veterinärmedizinische Universität Wien, Veterinärplatz 1, A-1210 Vienna, Austria

*   Correspondence: claus.vogl@vetmeduni.ac.at

Academic Editor: Rainer Breitling

Abstract: In population genetics, information about evolutionary forces, e.g., mutation, selection and genetic drift, is often inferred from DNA sequence information. Generally, DNA consists of two long strands of nucleotides or sites that pair via the complementary bases cytosine and guanine (C and G), on the one hand, and adenine and thymine (A and T), on the other. With whole genome sequencing, most genomic information stored in the DNA has become available for multiple individuals of one or more populations, at least in humans and model species, such as fruit flies of the genus *Drosophila*. In a genome-wide sample of L sites for M (haploid) individuals, the state of each site may be made binary, by binning the complementary bases, e.g., C with G to C/G, and contrasting C/G to A/T, to obtain a "site frequency spectrum" (SFS). Two such samples of either a single population from different time-points or two related populations from a single time-point are called joint site frequency spectra (joint SFS). While mathematical models describing the interplay of mutation, drift and selection have been available for more than 80 years, calculation of exact likelihoods from joint SFS is difficult. Sufficient statistics for inference of, e.g., mutation or selection parameters that would make use of all the information in the genomic data are rarely available. Hence, often suites of crude summary statistics are combined in simulation-based computational approaches. In this article, we use a bi-allelic boundary-mutation and drift population genetic model to compute the transition probabilities of joint SFS using orthogonal polynomials. This allows inference of population genetic parameters, such as the mutation rate (scaled by the population size) and the time separating the two samples. We apply this inference method to a population dataset of neutrally-evolving short intronic sites from six DNA sequences of the fruit fly *Drosophila melanogaster* and the reference sequence of the related species *Drosophila sechellia*.

Keywords: bi-allelic mutation-drift model; small-scaled mutation rate; orthogonal polynomials; transition probability

1. Introduction

Evolutionary forces, e.g., mutation, selection and genetic drift, shape DNA sequence information. Typically, the evolutionary processes that have influenced the data reach back millions of generations or years. Mathematical theory that describes these processes has been available for more than 80 years (e.g., [1,2]), yet inference of population genetic parameters using probabilistic models is difficult, and only few analytical maximum-likelihood estimators are available; those based on diffusion theory, so far, assume independence among sites and are briefly reviewed in Vogl [3], Vogl and Bergman [4] and in the theory section below.

A DNA molecule is a string (or strand) of nucleotides (or sites) that usually pairs with a complementary strand to form a double-stranded chromosome. Pairing of sites is accomplished by hydrogen bonds between the complementary base pairs adenine (A) and thymine (T), on the one hand, and cytosine (C) and guanine (G), on the other. An assortment of chromosomes forms a genome, which is specific for a species. The main functional units of genomes are genes that often code for proteins. Proteins provide structure, catalyze metabolism or mediate physiological pathways in all living organisms. While the single-celled Bacteria and Archaea generally have compact genomes, genes of the more complex eukaryotic organisms are often interrupted by non-coding introns. Introns are spliced out, *i.e.*, eliminated, during maturation of the messenger RNA, which is then translated into the chain of amino acids that makes up proteins.

A point mutation at a certain nucleotide or site creates a new genetic variant, *i.e.*, an allele. Mutation is not strand-specific, but may be biased towards A or T (A/T) over C or G (C/G) or *vice versa*, because mutation rates between these two allelic classes may vary. Genome-wide sequence data may be made bi-allelic (binary), by considering A/T nucleotides as Allele 0 and C/G nucleotides as Allele 1. This simplifies mathematical analysis, such that maximum-likelihood inference becomes possible. Mutations introduce new variants into the genome and, thus, increase genomic variation. Conversely, stochastic fluctuations of the allelic proportion due to finite population sizes, *i.e.*, random genetic drift, eventually cause fixation of an allelic type, thus eliminating variation. An equilibrium between mutation and drift may establish with time.

Recently, relatively inexpensive, high throughput DNA sequencing methods have made available population data from whole genomes (in multicellular organisms typically comprising $10^7 - 10^{11}$ sites), at least for humans and model species, such as fruit flies of the genus *Drosophila*. These data provide the basis for inference of population genetic forces, such as random genetic drift, the mutation rate scaled by the population size, directional selection and the time of the split between two populations.

In this article, we focus on inferring population genetic parameters using a mutation-drift model of the allelic proportion x. For mathematical convenience, genomic sites are classified as binary with respect to their nucleotide (C/G *vs.* A/T). A total of L sites are classified into categories, depending on the count y of Allele 1 (C/G) among M aligned genomic sequences. Together, these counts form a site frequency spectrum (SFS) of size $(M + 1)$ with $0 \leq y \leq M$. Joint SFS may be constructed considering the allelic states of sites within a single population at two different time points or two related populations at a single time point.

The solution of the diffusion equation describing the evolution of x conditional on mutation and drift parameters has previously been represented as a series expansion of orthogonal polynomials (e.g., [5–9]). In this article, we extend the mathematical theory to a boundary-mutation model [4], which describes the evolution of x when the scaled mutation rate θ is small, *i.e.*, on the order 0.1 or smaller [10]. Using this model, a method for the inference of θ and the time of split t is derived and applied to both simulated and empirical *Drosophila* population data. The empirical data are joint SFS of short introns, as the nucleotide composition of this site class is considered to not be affected by selection, but only by the joint forces of mutation and drift [11–13]. Therefore, the study of these sites likely provides an accurate estimate of the population demography and the genome-wide scaled mutation rate. The joint SFS from a sample of six individuals from the Malawian *D. melanogaster* population [14] and the *D. sechellia* reference sequence (Release 1.0; [15]) is used to infer mutation and drift parameters.

1.1. Inference with a Single Site Frequency Spectrum Assuming Equilibrium

Assume that a sample of L genomic loci or sites is available for M haploid individuals. The sample space of the allelic count for each locus l is then $y_l = (0, \ldots, M)$ copies of Allele 1, with $1 \leq l \leq L$. In regions of high recombination rates relative to mutation rates, sites may be assumed to be independently and identically distributed, such that the probabilities given the model parameters of all L sites can be multiplied. In this case, the theory developed below can be considered maximum likelihood. In regions of relatively low recombination rates, estimators are still consistent and may be considered a composite likelihood. For notational convenience, the index l is often dropped in the following.

1.2. Inference Based on the Beta Equilibrium Distribution

In a classical study, Wright [2] proposed a model for the evolution of a bi-allelic locus under the influence of the population genetic forces: mutation, directional selection and drift. He also derived the equilibrium distribution of the allelic proportion, conditional on the scaled mutation rate, the mutation bias and the scaled strength of directional selection. In the absence of selection, the equilibrium distribution of the population allelic proportion x of Allele 1 is a beta:

$$p(x|\alpha,\theta) = \frac{\Gamma(\theta)}{\Gamma(\alpha\theta)\Gamma(\beta\theta)} \, x^{\alpha\theta-1}(1-x)^{\beta\theta-1}, \tag{1}$$

where α is the mutation bias towards Allele 1 and $\beta = (1-\alpha)$ and θ the overall scaled mutation rate, i.e., the product of the per-generation mutation rate μ and the effective population number or size N.

Conditional on x, the distribution of the allelic count y is assumed to be binomial. Especially with genome-wide samples, the allelic proportions at particular sites are not interesting and "integrated out", which leads to the beta-binomial distribution of the allelic count:

$$p(y\,|\,\alpha,\theta) = \binom{M}{y} \frac{\Gamma(\theta)}{\Gamma(\alpha\theta)\Gamma(\beta\theta)} \frac{\Gamma(\alpha\theta+y)\Gamma(\beta\theta+M-y)}{\Gamma(\theta+M)}. \tag{2}$$

Given a sample of L independent loci for M individuals for each locus and a common α and θ, let L_y represent the counts of sites with y alleles of Type 1. Set $q_y = p(y\,|\,\alpha,\theta)$. The likelihood is then:

$$\ell(L_0,\dots,L_M\,|\,\alpha,\theta,L) = \frac{L!}{L_0!\cdots L_M!} \, q_0^{L_0}\cdots q_M^{L_M}. \tag{3}$$

For arbitrarily large values of θ, only iterative algorithms have been derived to obtain maximum likelihood estimates of α and θ [3], even in the simple case without selection. Note that this model corresponds to the canonical model of the empirical Bayes method, and maximizing this marginal likelihood corresponds to a parametric empirical Bayes approach [16].

In the limit of small θ, the beta-binomial compound distribution (2) can be expanded into a Taylor series in θ at $\theta = 0$, up to first order. The "folded" site frequency spectrum (folded SFS) is derived from the general site frequency spectrum by lumping the samples L_y with L_{M-y}, such that the state space becomes $0 \leq y \leq [M/2]$ per locus. For a polymorphic sample of such a folded SFS, the Taylor series expansion in θ of the beta-binomial compound distribution has been derived by RoyChoudhury and Wakeley [17]. In the general situation with $0 \leq y \leq M$, the series expansion of the beta-binomial compound distribution leads to the general "RoyChoudhury–Wakeley" distribution [3]:

$$p(y\,|\,\alpha,\theta) = \begin{cases} \beta - \alpha\beta\theta \sum_{y=1}^{M-1} \frac{1}{y} & \text{for } y = 0, \\ \alpha\beta\theta\frac{M}{y(M-y)} = \alpha\beta\theta\left(\frac{1}{y}+\frac{1}{M-y}\right) & \text{for } 1 \leq y \leq M, \\ \alpha - \alpha\beta\theta \sum_{y=1}^{M-1} \frac{1}{y} & \text{for } y = M. \end{cases} \tag{4}$$

With this first order expansion of the beta-binomial in θ, approximate maximum likelihood (ML) estimators of α and θ and their posterior distributions can be obtained easily [3]. In particular, the approximate ML estimator for the scaled mutation rate is:

$$\hat{\vartheta} = \frac{L_p}{2L \sum_{y=1}^{M-1} 1/y}, \tag{5}$$

where $\hat{\vartheta} = \hat{\alpha}\hat{\beta}\hat{\theta}$ and $L_p = \sum_{y=1}^{M-1} L_y$, i.e., the sum over all polymorphic sites in the sample, while the approximate ML estimator for α is:

$$\hat{\alpha} = \frac{L_M + L_p/2}{L}. \tag{6}$$

If the boundary mutation model is assumed, these estimators are maximum likelihood, rather than approximations in the limit of small-scaled mutation rates θ [4].

1.3. Inference Based on the Assumptions of Equilibrium and Rare Mutations

The estimator $\hat{\vartheta}$ of Formula (5) is a variant of the well-known Ewens–Watterson estimator of the scaled mutation rate [18,19], $\hat{\theta}_w = L_p/(L \sum_{y=1}^{M-1} 1/y)$. The latter was originally derived assuming the infinite sites model [20,21], which in turn was based on a model with irreversible mutation [2]. With the infinite sites model, infinitely many sites may be hit by mutation at a finite rate, such that each site is hit only once [19,21]. Furthermore, it is usually assumed that the ancestral and derived allelic states can be inferred with outgroup information, i.e., with information from closely-related species or populations (e.g., [12,13,22–24]). Then, segregating mutations are assumed to only arise once from the ancestral background. Alleles at a site are thus not defined as having bases A/T *versus* C/G, but as being ancestral *versus* derived. Note that the factor of two difference between $\hat{\vartheta}$ of Formula (5) and the Ewens–Watterson estimator reflects that mutations arise from both boundaries in the former and only one boundary in the latter. Obviously, the mutation bias cannot be inferred with polarization. Yet, irrespective of whether or not data are polarized, a polymorphic site is scored as polymorphic.

The Ewens–Watterson estimator is generally unbiased. If sites are unlinked, it can be shown that it is also the maximum likelihood estimator of θ and, thus, a sufficient statistic (e.g., [3]). Ewens [18] neglected to show this explicitly, while he earlier showed that the estimator for the corresponding infinite alleles model is maximum likelihood [25]. Furthermore, it can been shown that the estimators are unbiased (e.g., [3,18]). Note that if assumptions are met, $\hat{\theta}_w$ corresponds to the "expected heterozygosity", i.e., the expected proportion of polymorphism in a sample of size $M = 2$.

Similar to the infinite sites model, applications of the Poisson random field (PRF) model to population genetics generally assume small mutation rates. The PRF theory is often based on irreversible mutation models and, like the infinite sites model of Kimura [21], usually assumes the presence of directional selection. For an equilibrium distribution to exist, an inexhaustible and unvarying supply of sites must be assumed. Furthermore, the ancestral state of all sites must be known without errors and conditioned on. This is because, as discussed above, the rates of mutation from A/T to C/G generally differ, and the force of directional selection is reversed if an A/T mutates to a C/G or *vice versa*. The above assumptions are not met with real datasets: genomes are finite, and inference of the ancestral state is error-prone. Nevertheless, if appropriate outgroup information is available and quasi-equilibrium is assumed, the approach is sensible [26–29].

While RoyChoudhury and Wakeley [17] also use the PRF approach, they do not assume outgroup information, but rather start from a Taylor series expansion in θ of the equilibrium beta distribution (1). As shown above (Equation (5)), the estimator RoyChoudhury and Wakeley [17] derived is essentially identical to the Ewens–Watterson estimator of θ. Starting from a Moran model that only allows for mutations from the boundaries, Vogl and Clemente [10] derive a generalization of the estimator also for the case with directional selection, without assuming outgroup information. Vogl and Bergman [4] derive ML estimators for all three parameters: mutation bias α, scaled mutation rate θ and scaled selection strength γ, with the same assumptions, but base the analysis on a diffusion model.

2. Mathematical Theory and Algorithms

The Ewens–Watterson estimator $\hat{\theta}_w$ [18,19] or its varieties are sufficient statistics for the analysis of site frequency spectra assuming the infinite sites model, equilibrium and unlinked sites. With real datasets, however, changes in demography or mutation parameters usually invalidate the equilibrium assumption. Moreover, the approach to equilibrium is dominated by the scaled mutation rate θ. Since θ is often on the order of 10^{-2} per unit of diffusion time, which is scaled in N generations, it takes on the order of $100 \cdot N$ generations to reach equilibrium. This is on the order of $10^7 - 10^9$ generations. Even with the short-lived fruit flies, equilibrium is thus usually not reached before a change in population demography, the selection regime or the mutation bias. For probabilistic analysis of datasets that have not yet reached equilibrium, calculation of transition probabilities or densities is necessary. This is also necessary for joint site frequency spectra, where samples are drawn from a single population at two different time points or two closely-related populations at a single time point, which we will present in this article.

Consider a population of haploid population size $N(t)$, where t is time. The dynamics are governed by only two population genetic forces: mutation and drift. Generally, the diffusion limit, i.e., $N \to \infty$, is considered such that, at each time point only two quantities matter: the scaled mutation rate $\theta(t) = \mu(t)N(t)$ and the mutation bias $\alpha(t) = (1 - \beta(t)) = \mu_1(t)/(\mu_0(t) + \mu_1(t))$. Let $x(t)$ denote the proportion of the first allelic type, which in our case may be identified with the proportion of C/G at this site in the population at time t. Assume now that the parameters $N(t)$, $\mu(t)$ and $\alpha(t)$ are piecewise constant and consider only a single such epoch of constant parameters. Usually, the following forward operator is obtained [3,30]:

$$\mathcal{L}_f = \frac{\partial^2}{\partial x^2}x(1-x) - \frac{\partial}{\partial x}\theta(\alpha - x).\tag{7}$$

The corresponding forward diffusion or Kolmogorov equation is:

$$\frac{\partial}{\partial t}\phi(x,t) = \frac{\partial^2}{\partial x^2}\left(x(1-x)\phi(x,t)\right) - \frac{\partial}{\partial x}\left(\theta(\alpha - x)\phi(x,t)\right),\tag{8}$$

where $\phi(x,t)$ is the transition density of the allelic proportion x at any time t. To solve this equation, Song and Steinrücken [7] employ a series expansion with the modified Jacobi polynomials:

$$R_i^{(\theta,\alpha)}(x) = P_i^{(\beta\theta-1,\alpha\theta-1)}(2x - 1),\tag{9}$$

where $P_i^{(a,b)}(z)$ are the classical Jacobi polynomials [31]. Note that Song and Steinrücken [7] primarily analyze the backward diffusion equation (but also use the forward diffusion equation in the section: "Empirical Transition Densities and Stationary Distributions"). However, the relationship between the adjoint backward and forward diffusion equations is such that adaption of the theory concerning the backward equation to the forward equation is minimal (compare [9]).

2.1. The Boundary-Mutation Model

Further in the text, we will follow Vogl and Bergman [4] and model mutations as only affecting the boundaries. Then, $\phi(x,t)$ must be interpreted as a generalized probability measure that integrates to one over the unit interval, but may contain point masses at the boundaries (compare [32]). Within the polymorphic region, $1/N \le x \le (N-1)/N$, the dynamics are purely governed by drift, such that the diffusion generator is:

$$\mathcal{L}_f = \frac{\partial^2}{\partial x^2}x(1-x),\tag{10}$$

and the corresponding Kolmogorov forward (or forward diffusion) equation is:

$$\frac{\partial}{\partial t}\phi(x,t) = \frac{\partial^2}{\partial x^2}\left(x(1-x)\phi(x,t)\right). \tag{11}$$

Mutations are assumed to arise at the boundaries and correspond to a transition from $x = 0$ to $x = 1/N$, for a mutation from A/T to C/G, or from $x = 1$ to $x = (N-1)/N$, for a mutation from C/G to A/T.

The Wright–Fisher model is most familiar to population geneticists. With this model, the transition between subsequent generations due to drift is modeled via binomial sampling, such that transitions between distant states are possible. The slightly less familiar Moran model only allows transitions between neighboring states, which simplifies the math. This simplification pertains also to the boundaries [4]. With the boundary-mutation model, mutations are assumed to arise only at the boundaries; a transition from $x = 0$ to $x = 1/N$ corresponds to a mutation from a monomorphic state with only A/T to a polymorphic state with a single C/G in the population; conversely, a transition from $x = 1$ to $x = (N-1)/N$ corresponds to a mutation from C/G to A/T. The reverse transitions from the polymorphic region to the boundaries at $x = 0$ and $x = 1$ are caused by drift. In particular, the flow from $x = 1/N$ towards zero is proportional to drift times the probability mass at $x = 1/N$, and similarly at the other boundary.

With a change from the Moran to the diffusion model, the formulas for the flow towards the boundaries due to drift are:

$$\frac{d\,F(\alpha,\theta)}{dt} = \begin{cases} -\frac{N-1}{N}\phi(x=\frac{1}{N},t\,|\,\alpha,\theta) & \text{for } x = 1/N \text{ to } x = 0, \\ \frac{N-1}{N}\phi(x=\frac{N-1}{N},t\,|\,\alpha,\theta) & \text{for } x = (N-1)/N \text{ to } x = 1, \end{cases} \tag{12}$$

where the sign of the flow represents the direction. Conversely, the mutational flow from the boundaries to the interior is given by:

$$\frac{d\,F(\alpha,\theta)}{dt} = \begin{cases} N\alpha\theta \int_0^1 (1-x)\phi(1-x,t\,|\,\alpha,\theta)\,dx & \text{for } x = 0 \text{ to } x = 1/N, \\ N\beta\theta \int_0^1 x\phi(x,t\,|\,\alpha,\theta)\,dx & \text{for } x = 1 \text{ to } x = (N-1)/N. \end{cases} \tag{13}$$

2.2. Modified Gegenbauer Polynomials

We will first analyze the situation without mutations, *i.e.*, $\theta = 0$. With pure drift, the transition density $\phi(x,t)$ can be expanded into a series of Gegenbauer polynomials (e.g., [5,7–9,33]). Define:

$$U_{i+2}(x) = x^{-1}(1-x)^{-1}G_i(x) = -\frac{2}{i+2}C_i^{(3/2)}(2x-1), \tag{14}$$

where the $G_i(x)$ are the modified Gegenbauer polynomials of Song and Steinrücken [7], and the $C_i^{(\alpha)}(z)$ correspond to the classical ultraspherical or Gegenbauer polynomials with $\alpha = 3/2$ ([31], Chapter 22), also used by Kimura [5] and Tran *et al.* [8]. The forward and backward diffusion generators are adjoint, such that the modified Gegenbauer polynomials from Song and Steinrücken [7] can also be used to solve the forward diffusion equation. Multiplication of the weight function $x^{-1}(1-x)^{-1}$ and $G_i(x)$ in (14) transforms a solution of the backward equation into that of the forward equation (compare [9]).

The first two polynomials are $U_2(x) = -1$ and $U_3(x) = (2-4x)$; the recurrence relation to calculate all other polynomials is [7]:

$$U_{i+1}(x)\frac{(i+1)(i-1)}{2i(2i-1)} = U_i(x)\left(x-\frac{1}{2}\right) - U_{i-1}(x)\frac{(i-1)}{2(2i-1)}. \tag{15}$$

The $U_i(x)$ solve the differential equation:

$$-\lambda_i U_i(x) = \frac{d^2}{dx^2}\left(x(1-x)U_i(x)\right),\qquad(16)$$

with:

$$\lambda_i = i(i-1).\qquad(17)$$

The $U_i(x)$ are orthogonal with the weight function:

$$w(x) = x(1-x),\qquad(18)$$

and the proportionality constant:

$$\Delta_i = \frac{i-1}{(2i-1)i}.\qquad(19)$$

A function $f(x)$ defined within $]0,1[$ can be represented by an expansion of the $U_i(x)$. The coefficients c_i can be calculated using:

$$c_i = \frac{1}{\Delta_i}\int_0^1 x(1-x)U_i(x)f(x)\,dx.\qquad(20)$$

2.2.1. Solution of the Pure Drift Forward Equation with Gegenbauer Polynomials

Substituting $\phi(x,t) = \sum_{i=2}^{\infty}\tau_i(t)U_i(x)$, where $\tau_i(t)$ is a function pertaining to the temporal part of the transition density, into the diffusion Equation (11) leads to:

$$\frac{\partial}{\partial t}\left(\sum_{i=2}^{\infty}\tau_i(t)U_i(x)\right) = \frac{\partial^2}{\partial x^2}\left(x(1-x)\sum_{i=2}^{\infty}\tau_i(t)U_i(x)\right).\qquad(21)$$

For each i, we have:

$$\frac{\partial}{\partial t}\left(\tau_i(t)U_i(x)\right) = \frac{\partial^2}{\partial x^2}\left(x(1-x)\tau_i(t)U_i(x)\right),\qquad(22)$$

which can be rearranged to:

$$\frac{\frac{\partial}{\partial t}\tau_i(t)}{\tau_i(t)} = \frac{\frac{\partial^2}{\partial x^2}\left(x(1-x)U_i(x)\right)}{U_i(x)},\qquad(23)$$

Observing Equation (16), we obtain the eigenvalue equations:

$$\begin{cases} -\lambda_i &= \frac{\frac{d^2}{dx^2}\left(x(1-x)U_i(x)\right)}{U_i(x)}, \\ -\lambda_i &= \frac{\frac{d}{dt}\tau_i(t)}{\tau_i(t)}. \end{cases}\qquad(24)$$

As stated above, the $U_i(x)$ solve the spatial differential Equation in (24) for each i, while $\tau_i(t) = c_i e^{-\lambda_i t}$ solves the temporally homogeneous, linear differential Equation in (24). The c_i depend on the starting conditions and can be obtained from Formula (20). Since any function in $]0,1[$ can be represented by $\sum_{i=2}^{\infty}c_i U_i(x)$,

$$\phi(x,t) = \sum_{i=2}^{\infty}\tau_i(t)U_i(x) = \sum_{i=2}^{\infty}c_i e^{-\lambda_i t}U_i(x)\qquad(25)$$

solves the diffusion Equation (11) for any starting condition.

Integrating (16) from zero to one for the symmetric eigenvectors with even i, we obtain:

$$-\lambda_i \int_0^1 U_i(x)\,dx = \int_0^1 \frac{d^2}{dx^2}\left(x(1-x)U_i(x)\right)dx$$
$$= \int_0^1 \frac{d}{dx}\left(x(1-x)\frac{d}{dx}U_i(x) + (1-2x)U_i(x)\right)dx \qquad (26)$$
$$= \left(x(1-x)\frac{d}{dx}U_i(x) + (1-2x)U_i(x)\right)\Big|_0^1$$
$$= -U_i(1) - U_i(0)\,.$$

Note that, for odd i, we have $U_i(x) = -U_i(1-x)$, such that $U_i(0) = -U_i(1)$, $U_i(1/2) = 0$, and $\int_0^1 U_i(x)\,dx = 0$. Equation (26) is therefore trivially true for odd i.

Following Kimura [5], we substitute $\phi(x,t) = \sum_{i=2}^\infty \tau_i(t)U_i(x)$ into the differential Equation (11) and integrate from zero to one observing Equation (26):

$$\frac{\partial}{\partial t}\left(\lim_{N\to\infty}\int_{1/N}^{(N-1)/N}\phi(x,t)\,dx\right) = \lim_{N\to\infty}\int_{1/N}^{(N-1)/N}\frac{\partial^2}{\partial x^2}\left(x(1-x)\phi(x,t)\right)dx$$
$$\frac{\partial}{\partial t}\left(\sum_{i=2}^\infty \tau_i(t)\int_0^1 U_i(x)\,dx\right) = \sum_{i=2}^\infty \tau_i(t)\int_0^1 \frac{\partial^2}{\partial x^2}\left(x(1-x)U_i(x)\right)dx \qquad (27)$$
$$\frac{\partial}{\partial t}\left(\sum_{i=2}^\infty \frac{\tau_i(t)}{\lambda_i}\left(U_i(0) + U_i(1)\right)\right) = -\sum_{i=2}^\infty \tau_i(t)\left(U_i(0) + U_i(1)\right)\,.$$

As in the temporal part of Formula (24), substituting $\tau_i(t) = c_i e^{-\lambda_i t}$ solves the system of differential equations:

$$\frac{d}{dt}\tau_i(t) = -\lambda_i \tau_i(t)\,. \qquad (28)$$

For even i, the flow out at the boundaries zero and one per unit time is symmetric and corresponds to what is present just inside the boundaries, i.e., $U_i(0)$ and $U_i(1)$. The rate of loss is the eigenvalue λ_i.

Now, multiply $\phi(x,t)$ with x and integrate again from zero to one:

$$\frac{\partial}{\partial t}\left(\lim_{N\to\infty}\int_{1/N}^{(N-1)/N}x\phi(x,t)\,dx\right) = \lim_{N\to\infty}\int_{1/N}^{(N-1)/N}\frac{\partial^2}{\partial x^2}\left(x(1-x)x\phi(x,t)\right)dx$$
$$\frac{\partial}{\partial t}\left(\sum_{i=2}^\infty \tau_i(t)\int_0^1 xU_i(x)\,dx\right) = \sum_{i=2}^\infty \tau_i(t)\int_0^1 \frac{\partial^2}{\partial x^2}\left(x^2(1-x)U_i(x)\right)dx \qquad (29)$$
$$\frac{\partial}{\partial t}\left(\sum_{i=2}^\infty \frac{\tau_i(t)}{\lambda_i}U_i(1)\right) = -\sum_{i=2}^\infty \tau_i(t)U_i(1)\,.$$

Thus, $x\phi(x,t)$ will eventually drift to Boundary 1, and conversely $(1-x)\phi(x,t)$ to Boundary 0. This is expected, since drift is symmetric, such that the probability of eventual fixation is equal to the proportion x, for the boundary at one, and $(1-x)$, for the boundary at zero (see also [30], Chapter 4.3). As in the temporal part of Formula (24), substituting $\tau_i(t) = c_i e^{-\lambda_i t}$ solves the system of differential Equations (28).

The solution of the diagonal system of differential Equations (28) thus fulfills Equation (11) for all t, as well as the boundary conditions at both zero and one (12).

Note that:

$$\begin{cases} U_i(0)/\lambda_i = \int_0^1 (1-x)U_i(x)\,dx \\ U_i(1)/\lambda_i = \int_0^1 xU_i(x)\,dx\,. \end{cases} \qquad (30)$$

The above results suggest augmenting the $U_i(x)$ with the boundary terms:

$$
\begin{cases}
-U_i(0)/\lambda_i = (-1)^i/i \\
-U_i(1)/\lambda_i = 1/i.
\end{cases}
\tag{31}
$$

Furthermore, the result (30) shows that the boundary terms derived above correspond to those defined by Tran *et al.* [8].

We therefore define the following set of orthogonal polynomials augmented with boundary terms:

$$
H_i(x) = \frac{(-1)^i \delta(x) + \delta(x-1)}{i} + U_i(x),
\tag{32}
$$

where $\delta(x)$ is the Dirac delta function (compare Tran *et al.* [8], who arrive at the corresponding set of augmented eigenfunctions). With this definition of eigenfunctions, the probability mass that leaves the polymorphic region for each i at $1/N$ and $(N-1)/N$ is added to the monomorphic boundaries at $x = 0$ and $x = 1$. The integral over the closed interval between zero and one thus remains unity for all times. In Appendix A.1, we show that these augmented orthogonal polynomials can also be obtained by a Taylor series expansion of the general eigensystem solving the diffusion Equation (11) using the modified Jacobi polynomials $R^{(\alpha,\theta)}(x)$.

2.2.2. Starting and Prior Distributions

We base the following description on the theory of hierarchical Bayesian models and the empirical Bayes method [16] that we also employed earlier [3,4]. In a frequentist context, one would rather use the context of marginal likelihoods.

Traditionally, a Dirac delta function at a certain position p has been used as a starting condition [33]. With a site frequency spectrum, however, the joint density of the population allelic proportion x and the observed allelic count y in a sample of size M_0 must be used as starting density. Most naturally, the conditional distribution of the data y given the allelic proportion x is modeled as a binomial:

$$
p(y \mid x, M_0) = \binom{M_0}{y} x^y (1-x)^{M_0-y}.
\tag{33}
$$

With the pure drift model, we are generally interested in the polymorphic region, since probability mass at a boundary remains there due to the absence of mutations.

For "integrating out" the population allelic proportions x, a prior distribution for x must be assumed. With small-scaled mutation rates, an "improper prior" proportional to $x^{-1}(1-x)^{-1}$ within $1/N$ and $(N-1)/N$ is appropriate, as this is proportional to the equilibrium distribution (see also Subsections 2.3.4 and 2.3.5 below). Note that this prior corresponds to the inverse of the weight function. Thus, the inner product (20) to calculate the initial coefficients becomes:

$$
\begin{aligned}
c_i &= \frac{1}{\Delta_i} \lim_{N \to \infty} \int_{1/N}^{(N-1)/N} x(1-x) U_i(x) \, p(y \mid x, M_0) x^{-1}(1-x)^{-1} \, dx \\
&= \frac{1}{\Delta_i} \lim_{N \to \infty} \int_{1/N}^{(N-1)/N} U_i(x) \, p(y \mid x, M_0) \, dx,
\end{aligned}
\tag{34}
$$

where the limit notation indicates that the integration includes only the polymorphic region, *i.e.*, no point masses at the boundaries.

We can thus specify a general algorithm that also includes the boundaries.

2.2.3. Algorithm 1: Allelic Proportions x with Pure Drift for All Times t, Conditional on Initial Values

- A measure $f(x)$ between zero and one, which may have point masses m_0 and m_1 at Boundaries 0 and 1, is represented by an expansion of the $H_i(x)$ up to $i = n$. The coefficients c_i are calculated according to Equation (34). The expansion of $g(x)$ times the prior, up to the order n, is then:

$$g(x) = \left(m_0 - \sum_{i=2}^{n} c_i \frac{(-1)^i}{i}\right) \delta(x) + \left(m_1 - \sum_{i=2}^{n} \frac{c_i}{i}\right) \delta(x-1) + \sum_{i=2}^{n} (c_i H_i(x)) + O(n+1). \quad (35)$$

- The solution of Equation (28) for all t conditional on the initial distribution can be represented by a series expansion up to n:

$$g(x,t) = \left(m_0 - \sum_{i=2}^{n} c_i \frac{(-1)^i}{i}\right) \delta(x) + \left(m_1 - \sum_{i=2}^{n} \frac{c_i}{i}\right) \delta(x-1) + \sum_{i=2}^{n} \left(c_i H_i(x) e^{-\lambda_i t}\right) + O(n+1),$$
$$(36)$$

with $\lambda_i = i(i-1)$.

Note that the $H_i(x)$ contain the boundary terms that balance the probability masses at zero and one. This is obvious if the initial probability measure $f(x)$ does not contain point masses at the boundaries, i.e., if $m_0 = m_1 = 0$.

2.3. Modified Gegenbauer Polynomials and the Boundary-Mutation Model

In this subsection, we will use the expansion in orthogonal polynomials with boundary terms to model both mutation and drift.

2.3.1. Mutation and Drift: Slowly Evolving Dynamics

For the slowly evolving dynamics at the boundaries, we augment the system with two eigenfunctions. Starting from the system for general θ, which can be expanded in a series of modified Jacobi polynomials (see Equation (9) in Song and Steinrücken [7]), we note that the eigenfunction for $i = 0$ does not change with time, i.e., $\lambda_0 = 0$. The eigenfunction for $i = 1$ has the eigenvalue $\lambda_1 = \theta$ (compare: [7]) and reflects the slow change in allele frequencies through mutation. Expressing the Jacobi polynomials as beta distributions and taking the limit $\theta \to 0$, such that only probability masses at the boundaries remain, the first two eigenvectors become:

$$\begin{cases} H_0^{(\alpha)}(x) = \beta\delta(x) + \alpha\delta(x-1), \\ H_1(x) = -\delta(x) + \delta(x-1). \end{cases} \quad (37)$$

(see Appendix A.1). Obviously, these two eigenfunctions are unaffected by the dynamics in the polymorphic region inside $[1/N, (N-1)/N]$.

These two eigenvectors have no probability mass within the polymorphic region, such that only eigenvectors with $i \geq 2$ have nonzero probability masses in the polymorphic region. Hence, the model separates two spatial regions: the monomorphic boundaries and the polymorphic interior. As $\lambda_1 = \theta \ll 1$ while the $\lambda_i > 1$ for all eigenvalues with $i > 2$, two different temporal regions can also be distinguished, in addition to the two spatial regions. Thus, evolution is modeled as a two-time process, where the slow dynamics captured by the eigenfunctions $i = 0$ and $i = 1$ are evolving independently from the polymorphic region, while the fast dynamics in the polymorphic region are in quasi-equilibrium with the slow dynamics at the boundaries. Generally, we are thus looking at a system of differential equations that for the slowly evolving part of the system is:

$$\begin{cases} \tau_0(t) = 1, \\ \frac{d}{dt}\tau_1(t) = -\theta\tau_1(t). \end{cases} \quad (38)$$

Initially at $t = 0$, the boundary values are $b_0(0) = \int_0^1 xf(1 - x\,|\,t = 0)\,dx$ and $b_1(0) = \int_0^1 xf(x\,|\,t = 0)\,dx = (1 - b_0(0))$. The solution over time is $\tau_1(t) = (b_1(t) - \alpha)e^{-\theta t}$, such that the boundary values will slowly, at a rate of θ, approach the equilibrium values:

$$b_1(t) = \alpha + (b_1(0) - \alpha)e^{-\theta t} = 1 - b_0(t) \tag{39}$$

If $f(x)$ does not integrate to one, i.e., $b_0(t) + b_1(t) \neq 1$, modifications are trivial. Note that $b_0(t = 0)$ and $b_1(t = 0)$ correspond to the probability mass currently at the boundaries plus the part of the probability mass within the polymorphic region that is expected to be fixed by drift (i.e., without any further mutations) at the respective boundaries. They would only be identical to the probability mass currently at the boundaries if there were no probability mass in the polymorphic region.

2.3.2. Mutation and Drift: Quickly Evolving Dynamics

The slowly evolving part of the system is given in (39). For the quickly evolving part, note that, from Equation (13), mutation moves probability mass from the boundary at zero $x = 0$ to $x = 1/N$ and from $x = 1$ to $x = (N - 1)/N$, respectively. We can model this with a Dirac delta function at $x = 1/N$ and $x = (N - 1)/N$:

$$\begin{cases} N\alpha\theta\delta(x - 1/N)b_0(t) & \text{for } x = 0 \text{ to } x = 1/N, \\ N\beta\theta\delta(x - (N - 1)/N)b_1(t) & \text{for } x = 1 \text{ to } x = (N - 1)/N, \end{cases} \tag{40}$$

with $b_0(t)$ and $b_1(t)$ as above. Combined with the pure drift diffusion Equation (11), we thus obtain the following diffusion equation within the interval between $1/N$ and $(N - 1)/N$:

$$\frac{\partial}{\partial t}\phi(x, t) = \frac{\partial^2}{\partial x^2}\left(x(1 - x)\phi(x, t)\right) + N\alpha\theta\delta(x - 1/N)b_0(t) + N\beta\theta\delta(x - (N - 1)/N)b_1(t), \tag{41}$$

Equation (41) is an extension of Equation (21) to mutations from the boundaries.

2.3.3. Mutation and Drift: Slowly and Quickly Evolving Dynamics

Theorem 1. *Starting from a generalized probability measure $f(x)$ within the unit interval (Equation (11)), with the boundary Conditions (12) and (13), and letting $N \to \infty$, the following function provides the general solution for all times of the Kolmogorov forward equation of boundary-mutation drift diffusion:*

$$\phi(x, t) = H_0^{(\alpha)}(x) + \sum_{i=1}^{\infty} \tau_i(t)\,H_i(x), \tag{42}$$

with the previously-defined eigenfunctions (Equations (37) and (32)); the $\tau_i(t)$ are given by a system of linear inhomogenous first order differential equations:

$$\begin{cases} \frac{d}{dt}\tau_1(t) = -\theta\tau_1(t) \\ \frac{d}{dt}\tau_i(t) = -\lambda_i\tau_i(t) + \theta(2i - 1)i\left((-1)^i\alpha b_0(t) + \beta b_1(t)\right), \text{ for } i \geq 2. \end{cases} \tag{43}$$

The starting values, $\tau_i(t = 0)$ for $i \geq 1$, are given by the initial probability masses at the boundaries and by the expansion of the initial density $f(x)$ in the interior into the eigenvectors.

Proof. The slowly evolving part of the system is given in (39). The coefficients for expanding the delta function in (40) are (compare Equation (20)) for the boundary at zero:

$$\frac{1}{\Delta_i} \lim_{N \to \infty} \int_{1/N}^{(N-1)/N} Nx(1-x)U_i(1/N)\delta(x-1/N)\,dx = \frac{U_i(0)}{\Delta_i} = \frac{(2i-1)iU_i(0)}{(i-1)}$$

$$= -\frac{(2i-1)i(-1)^i(i-1)}{i-1} \tag{44}$$

$$= -(-1)^i(2i-1)i,$$

and similarly for the boundary at one. Substituting the Gegenbauer expansion into Equation (41), we obtain:

$$\frac{\partial}{\partial t}\left(\sum_{i=2}^{\infty} \tau_i(t)U_i(x)\right) = \frac{\partial^2}{\partial x^2}\left(x(1-x)\sum_{i=2}^{\infty} \tau_i(t)U_i(x)\right) - \theta(2i-1)i\left((-1)^i\alpha b_0(t) + \beta b_1(t)\right)U_i(x). \tag{45}$$

For each i, we have:

$$\frac{\partial}{\partial t}\left(\tau_i(t)U_i(x)\right) = \frac{\partial^2}{\partial x^2}\left(x(1-x)\tau_i(t)U_i(x)\right) - \theta(2i-1)i\left((-1)^i\alpha b_0(t) + \beta b_1(t)\right)U_i(x), \tag{46}$$

which can be rearranged to:

$$\frac{\frac{\partial}{\partial t}\tau_i(t) + \theta(2i-1)i\left((-1)^i\alpha b_0(t) + \beta b_1(t)\right)}{\tau_i(t)} = \frac{\frac{\partial^2}{\partial x^2}\left(x(1-x)U_i(x)\right)}{U_i(x)}, \tag{47}$$

Observing Equation (16), we obtain eigenvalue equations corresponding to those in (24):

$$\begin{cases} -\lambda_i &= \frac{\frac{d^2}{dx^2}\left(x(1-x)U_i(x)\right)}{U_i(x)}, \\ -\lambda_i &= \frac{\frac{d}{dt}\tau_i(t) + \theta(2i-1)i\left(\alpha(-1)^i b_0(t) + \beta b_1(t)\right)}{\tau_i(t)}. \end{cases} \tag{48}$$

Compared to the case without mutation, the spatial part is unchanged, while the temporal part becomes a system of linear inhomogenous first order differential equations:

$$\frac{d}{dt}\tau_i(t) = -\lambda_i\tau_i(t) - \theta(2i-1)i\left((-1)^i\alpha b_0(t) + \beta b_1(t)\right). \tag{49}$$

All other considerations correspond to the case without mutation. □

Note that, substituting $b_0(t)$ and $b_1(t)$, Equation (49) can also be written as:

$$\frac{d}{dt}\tau_i(t) = -\lambda_i\tau_i(t) + A_i + B_i e^{-\theta t}, \tag{50}$$

with constants:

$$A_i = -\alpha\beta\theta(2i-1)i\left((-1)^i + 1\right),$$
$$B_i = -\theta(2i-1)i(b_0(0) - \beta)\left((-1)^i\alpha - \beta\right). \tag{51}$$

Furthermore, note that we assumed that the probability measure $f(x)$ integrates to one over the closed interval between zero and one, i.e., $\int_0^1 f(x)\,dx = 1$. If this is not the case, the constants A_i and B_i must be multiplied by $\int_0^1 f(x)\,dx$.

2.3.4. Boundary-Mutation-Drift Equilibrium Distribution

In earlier work [4], we show that the equilibrium solution of the boundary-mutation model is the measure:

$$BME(x\,|\,\alpha,\theta,N) = \begin{cases} \beta - \alpha\beta\theta \int_{1/N}^{(N-1)/N} \frac{1}{x}\,dx & \text{for } x = 0, \\ \alpha\beta\theta \frac{1}{x(1-x)} & \text{for } 1/N \le x \le (N-1)/N, \\ \alpha - \alpha\beta\theta \int_{1/N}^{(N-1)/N} \frac{1}{1-x}\,dx & \text{for } x = 1, \end{cases} \tag{52}$$

where the interior region is bounded by $1/N$ and $(N-1)/N$ and BME stands for boundary-mutation equilibrium. $BME(x\,|\,\alpha,\theta,N)$ integrates to one over the unit interval, irrespective of N. However, note that for large N, it integrates to more than one inside the interval $[1/N, (N-1)/N]$, while assuming negative values at the boundaries. In this limit, it therefore must be considered an "improper distribution" [4,34].

In Appendix A.2, we show that, with time, Solution (43) converges to the BME (Equation (52)).

2.3.5. Prior Distribution

With the BME as prior and a binomial likelihood $p(y\,|\,x, M_0)$ with $0 \le y \le M_0$, the coefficients of the joint distribution $p(x, y\,|\,M_0, \alpha, \theta) = p(y\,|\,x, M_0)x^{-1}(1-x)^{-1}$ become:

$$c_i = \alpha\beta\theta \frac{1}{\Delta_i} \lim_{N\to\infty} \int_{1/N}^{(N-1)/N} x(1-x)U_i(x)\,p(y\,|\,x, M_0)x^{-1}(1-x)^{-1}\,dx. \tag{53}$$

where the limit notation indicates that the integration includes only the polymorphic region. Note that already Ewens used the same limit for inference [18,25]. For polymorphic data, i.e., $1 \le y \le (M_0 - 1)$, this function is a polynomial and, thus, can be represented accurately as a series of Gegenbauer polynomials as long as $n > M_0$. The boundary terms can also be derived easily because the probability of drifting to boundary one corresponds to the current proportion x (and to $(1 - x)$ to the boundary zero), such that:

$$\begin{cases} b_1(1 \le y \le M_0, t = 0) = \alpha\beta\theta \int_0^1 p(y\,|\,x, M_0)(1-x)^{-1}\,dx = \alpha\beta\theta\frac{1}{y} \\ b_0(1 \le y \le M_0, t = 0) = \alpha\beta\theta \int_0^1 p(y\,|\,x, M_0)x^{-1}\,dx = \alpha\beta\theta\frac{1}{M_0-y}, \end{cases} \tag{54}$$

where the limit notation is not used for brevity.

For monomorphic y, i.e., $y = 0$ or $y = M_0$, the c_i for the probability mass in the interior are also given by Equation (53) with $i \le n$. The corresponding boundary terms are:

$$\begin{cases} b_1(y = M_0, t = 0) = \alpha - \alpha\beta\theta \sum_{y=1}^{M_0} \frac{1}{y} \\ b_0(y = M_0, t = 0) = \alpha\beta\theta\frac{1}{M_0} \end{cases} \tag{55}$$

and analogously for $y = 0$.

2.3.6. Algorithm 2: Allelic Proportions x with Boundary-Mutations and Drift for All Times t, Conditional on Initial Values

- The interior of a joint distribution $p(x, y \mid M_0, \alpha, \theta)$ is represented as a Gegenbauer series (53).
- The slowly evolving part of the system consists of the dynamics at the boundaries. Set the boundary terms at $t = 0$ to $b_0(t = 0)$ and $b_1(t = 0)$ as in Equations (54) and (55). With time, the boundary terms $b_0(t)$ and $b_1(t)$ then change slowly at the rate of θ according to the exponential function in Equation (39).
- Set $\omega = \int_0^1 p(x, y \mid M_0, \alpha, \theta)\, dx = b_0(t) + b_1(t)$. The solution of Equation (41) for all t conditional on $f(x)$ can be represented by a series expansion up to n:

$$f(x, t) = b_0(t)\delta(x) + b_1(t)\delta(x - 1) + \sum_{i=2}^{n} \left(\tau_i(t) H_i(x) \right) + O(n + 1), \tag{56}$$

with:

$$\tau_i(t) = \frac{A'_i}{\lambda_i} + \left(c_i - \frac{A'_i}{\lambda_i} - \frac{B'_i}{\lambda_i - \theta} \right) e^{-\lambda_i t} + \frac{B'_i}{\lambda_i - \theta} e^{-\theta t}, \tag{57}$$

and constants analogous to (51):

$$\begin{aligned} A'_i &= -\omega \alpha \beta \theta (2i - 1) i \left((-1)^i + 1 \right), \\ B'_i &= -\theta (2i - 1) i (b_0(0) - \omega \beta) \left((-1)^i \alpha - \beta \right). \end{aligned} \tag{58}$$

Equation (57) is a solution to (50), as can be shown by substitution.

3. Applications

In this section, we illustrate the calculation of the marginal likelihoods of a mock dataset and an empirical fruit fly dataset using the expansion of Gegenbauer polynomials up to degree $n = 52$.

3.1. A Joint Site Frequency Spectrum under Pure Drift

With the pure drift model, the time between two time points $t_0 = 0$ and $t_1 > 0$ is assumed to be so small that newly arising mutations can be neglected. Moreover, sites where the samples from both time points are monomorphic for the same allele are usually ignored with such data analysis. For simplicity, assume that the sample size of the initial sample at time t_0 is $M_0 = 3$ and that of time t_1 also $M_1 = 3$. Four different cases need to be considered: (i) a site is polymorphic in both samples; (ii) a site is polymorphic in the first sample and monomorphic in the second; (iii) a site is monomorphic in the first sample and polymorphic in the second; and (iv) a site is monomorphic in the first sample for one allelic type and polymorphic in the second sample for the other allelic type. For Cases (i) and (ii), assume, e.g., a sample with two alleles of a certain type (zero or one), i.e., $y_0 = 2$. Thus, the joint density of the sample y_0 and the allelic proportions x become:

$$p(y_0 = 2, x \mid M_0 = 3, t = 0) \propto \binom{3}{2} x^2 (1 - x) x^{-1} (1 - x)^{-1} = 3x. \tag{59}$$

This is represented by a sum of the modified Gegenbauer polynomials of degree up to three with $c_3 = -\frac{3}{4}$ and $c_2 = -\frac{3}{2}$. At time t_1, before considering the second sample, the probability mass of the joint interior distribution has diminished:

$$p(y_0 = 2, 0 < x < 1 \mid M_0 = 3, t = t_1) \propto -\frac{3}{2} e^{-2t_1}(-1) - \frac{3}{4} e^{-6t_1}(2 - 4x), \tag{60}$$

while it has grown at the boundaries:

$$p(y_0 = 2, x = 0 \mid M_0 = 3, t = t_1) \propto \frac{3}{2} \cdot \frac{1}{2} (1 - e^{-2t_1}) - \frac{3}{4} \cdot \frac{1}{3} (1 - e^{-6t_1}) \qquad (61)$$

and:

$$p(y_0 = 2, x = 1 \mid M_0 = 3, t = t_1) \propto \frac{3}{4} (1 - e^{-2t_1}) + \frac{1}{4} (1 - e^{-6t_1}). \qquad (62)$$

For Case (i), the likelihood of a second sample of size $M_1 = 3$ with $y_1 = 1$ alleles of the first type is binomial: $3x(1 - x)^2$. The joint distribution consists only of an interior part, from which x can be integrated out to obtain the marginal likelihood:

$$\ell(y_0 = 2, y_1 = 1 \mid M_0 = 3, M_1 = 3, t = t_1) \propto \int_0^1 3x(1 - x)^2 \left(\frac{3}{2} e^{-2t_1} - \frac{3}{4} e^{-6t_1} (2 - 4x) \right) dx$$
$$= \frac{3}{8} e^{-2t_1} - \frac{3}{40} e^{-6t_1}. \qquad (63)$$

For Case (ii), the likelihood of a second sample of, e.g., size $M_1 = 3$ with $y_1 = 3$ alleles of the first type, is binomial: x^3. The joint distribution consists of an interior part, from which x can be integrated out:

$$p(y_0 = 2, y_1 = 3 \mid M_0 = 3, M_1 = 3, t = t_1, 0 < x < 1) \propto \int_0^1 x^3 \left(\frac{3}{2} e^{-2t_1} + \frac{3}{4} e^{-6t_1} (-2 + 4x) \right) dx$$
$$= \frac{3}{8} e^{-2t_1} + \frac{9}{40} e^{-6t_1}. \qquad (64)$$

Summing the interior and the boundary part, the marginal likelihood of the two samples is obtained:

$$\ell(y_0 = 2, y_1 = 3 \mid M_0 = 3, M_1 = 3, t = t_1) \propto \frac{3}{8} e^{-2t_1} + \frac{9}{40} e^{-6t_1} + \frac{3}{4} (1 - e^{-2t_1}) + \frac{1}{4} (1 - e^{-6t_1}). \qquad (65)$$

For Cases (i) and (ii), thus, a finite expansion of the Gegenbauer polynomials was sufficient.

For Cases (iii) and (iv), the product of the likelihood and prior at time $t = 0$ results in an infinite series of Gegenbauer polynomials. Note that the monomorphic term at $t = 0$ does not need to be included since, without new mutation, a polymorphism or a monomorphic alternative allele at $t = t_1$ implies that the population allelic proportion x must have been in the polymorphic region already at $t = 0$. Take, e.g., $M_0 = 3$ and $y_0 = 3$, which results in:

$$p(y_0 = 3, x \mid M_0 = 3, t = 0) \propto x^3 x^{-1} (1 - x)^{-1} = x^2 (1 - x)^{-1}. \qquad (66)$$

While Equation (20) can be used in this case, it results in a rather "wiggly" function of x (Figure 1). With the expansion $(1 - x)^{-1} = \sum_{i=0}^{n-2} x^i$ a much smoother polynomial of degree n will be obtained, which can be expressed without loss as a sum of Gegenbauer polynomials up to that degree. Even with only moderate n, the two expansions will produce nearly indistinguishable likelihoods. In either case, the algebra cannot easily be reproduced here, but likelihoods corresponding to transitions between all possible allelic states with arbitrary (but moderate) M_0, M_1 and t_1 can be easily calculated using computers. We implemented such an algorithm and tested inference using simulated datasets of $L = 10^5$ and $M_0 = M_1 = 3$, while varying the parameter t_1. As expected, the modes of the likelihood curves closely coincide with the true values of t_1 (Figure 2).

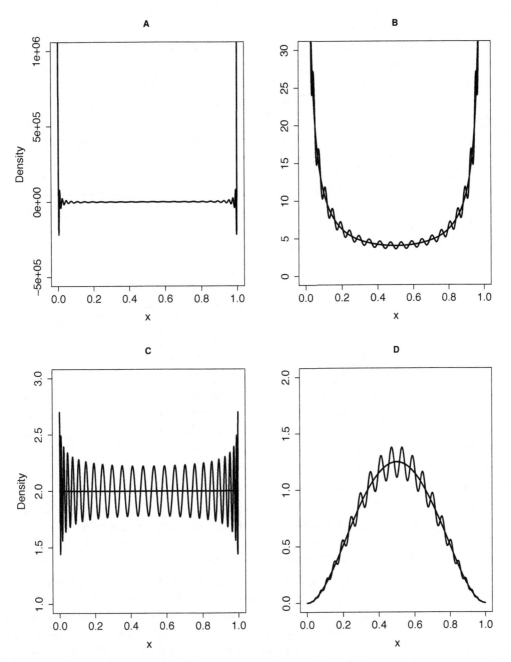

Figure 1. Approximate densities using the Gegenbauer polynomial expansion with terms up to $n = 52$. (**A**) Approximation to point masses at both boundaries, but without mass in the interior region; (**B**) approximation to the equilibrium improper density overlying the function $x^{-1}(1-x)^{-1}$; (**C**) approximation to the joint posterior distribution for a sample with $y = 1$, $M = 1$ overlying the joint distribution $2\,x^{1-1}(1-x)^{1-1}$; (**D**) approximation to the joint posterior distribution for a sample with $y = 3$, $M = 6$ overlying the joint distribution $\binom{6}{3}\,x^{3-1}(1-x)^{3-1}$.

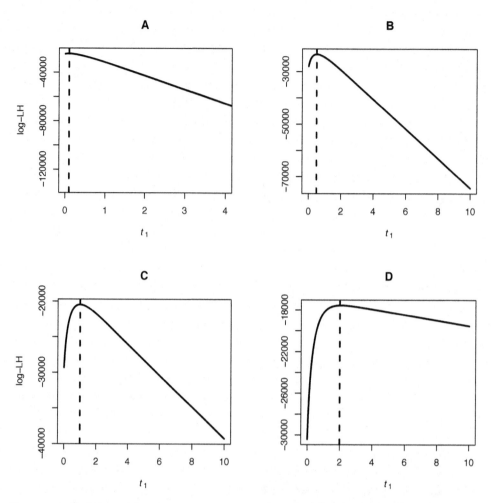

Figure 2. Pure drift model. Likelihood curves of the parameter t_1 given a sample of $L = 10,000$, $M_0 = M_1 = 3$ and true t_1 (dashed vertical lines) equal to 0.1 (**A**), 0.5 (**B**), 1 (**C**) and 2 (**D**).

3.2. Application to Drosophila Population Data

The joint site frequency spectrum of putatively neutral short intronic sites (positions 8–30 of introns less than 66 bp in length [11]) was used for inference (Table 1). The interior part of short introns is unlikely to contain selectively-constrained sequences. Short introns also show the highest intra- and inter-species diversity of any sequence class within the *Drosophila* genome [11]. Furthermore, short introns are the most abundant intron type within the *Drosophila* genome. It is therefore assumed that mutation-drift dynamics shape the nucleotide composition of short intronic sites, and since polymorphism within a single intron is rare and linkage disequilibria decrease quickly, free recombination among sites may be assumed. Sites were classified as binary by lumping A and T nucleotides together as Allele 0 and C and G nucleotides as Allele 1. The reference sequence from *D. sechellia* (Release 1.0; [15]) was taken as ancestral, *i.e.*, the initial sample of size $M_0 = 1$ at time $t_0 = 0$. While the states of closely related species are routinely taken as ancestral (e.g., [12,13,22–24]), this practice violates the model assumptions that data are from a single populations and two time points. A *D. melanogaster* Malawian population sample [14] of size $M_1 = 6$ was considered as a sample from a later time point t_1. The sequences were annotated by aligning the *D. sechellia* reference and the *D. melanogaster* population sample to the *D. melanogaster* reference sequence (Release 5.9; [15]).

Table 1. A joint site frequency spectrum of *Drosophila* short intronic sites with $M_0 = 1$ and $M_1 = 6$. The left-most column and the upper row of the table represent the possible allelic states of sites for the sample M_0 and M_1, respectively. The interior entries of the table are the counts of sites with a specific allelic state with respect to Allele 1.

	0	1	2	3	4	5	6
0	84,294	862	369	59	233	293	5121
1	5637	259	276	310	475	1168	41,531

Interest is centered on inferring the time point t_1, *i.e.*, the time in N generations since the split of the two *Drosophila* species and the scaled mutation rate θ_1, corresponding to the current mutation rate of the *D. melanogaster* population sample. Firstly, a prior distribution of allelic counts needed to be determined by setting initial parameters, α_0 and θ_0. The ancestral mutation bias α_0 was inferred from the *D. sechellia* data to be $\hat{\alpha}_0 = 0.35$ and is assumed to not change, *i.e.*, $\alpha_1 = \alpha_0$. We estimate the ancestral scaled mutation rate to be about $\hat{\theta}_0 = 0.079$ [4] from *D. simulans* data, as this closely related species most likely reflects the ancestral state of both *D. sechellia* and *D. melanogaster* species due to its relatively constant (over the evolutionary times considered) and large effective population size [35].

We implemented a direct grid search algorithm, with the likelihood calculated as in Subsection 2.3.6, to obtain maximum likelihood estimates of parameters t_1 and θ_1 (Figure 3). The maximum likelihood estimates $\hat{t}_1 = 4.5$ and $\hat{\theta}_1 = 0.03$ correspond closely to previously published estimates [36,37].

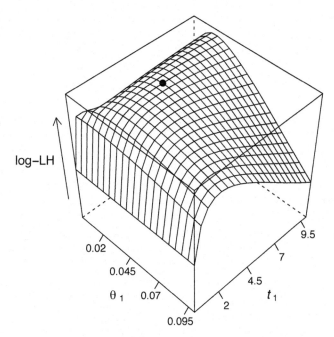

Figure 3. Likelihood surface with respect to parameters θ_1 and t_1 estimated from the joint site frequency spectrum in Table 1. The point on the likelihood surface corresponds to ML estimates: $\hat{\theta}_1 = 0.03$ and $\hat{t}_1 = 4.5$.

4. Discussion

Most population genetic models, e.g., the Wright–Fisher and Moran models and the corresponding (forward) Wright–Fisher or Moran diffusion models, do not restrict the number of mutations segregating in a population at a given site and time. By contrast, most population genetic methods that allow for analytical maximum likelihood estimators assume that variation at a specific site originates from only a single mutation, such that no more than two alleles can be present at any given site and time. This assumption is made for the Ewens–Watterson estimators of the scaled mutation rate [18,19] and the Poisson random field (PRF) models [26–29]. These approaches thus implicitly assume low scaled mutation rates. Usually, it is also assumed that the ancestral state of a site is known. Both of these assumptions are made explicit with the infinite sites model. When introducing the infinite sites model, Kimura [20,21] assumed selection against the mutant allelic variant, such that only the favored ancestral allele would exist in the monomorphic state, while a mutant allele is eventually lost from the population by the joint action of adverse selection and drift. Kimura based the mathematics on a model of irreversible mutation [2].

In later developments of the infinite sites model [18,19], the assumption of selection was dropped. Without selection, sites may become monomorphic for all possible allelic states (usually two states are assumed, such that the model is bi-allelic). In practical applications, the ancestral state has to be inferred via "outgroup" information. For this inference, which is also called "polarization", data from an extant closely related population or species, *i.e.*, an "outgroup", are used (e.g., [12,13,22–24]). Polarization can only be successful if the outgroup is related closely enough to the focal population, such that double mutations are improbable, but distantly enough, such that allelic polymorphism is not shared with the focal population. These biological assumptions are rather restrictive.

With unrestricted mutations, *i.e.*, with the assumptions of the Wright–Fisher diffusion or the Moran models, allelic proportions in a population converge to a beta equilibrium distribution. For a sample of moderate size, a beta-binomial equilibrium distribution is obtained. It seems that RoyChoudhury and Wakeley [17] were the first to expand the beta-binomial equilibrium distribution into a Taylor series up to first order in the scaled mutation rate θ to derive the sample distribution of a bi-allelic locus. With this approach, polarization is not necessary. Rather, DNA sequence data can be made binary by grouping together sites with the bases adenine (A) and thymine (T) to A/T and cytosine (C) and guanine (G) to C/G. In spite of this difference of the original infinite sites model, the sample distribution of polymorphic sites is a variant of the infinite sites model [18], and the maximum likelihood estimator of the scaled mutation rate derived from this distribution is a variant of the Ewens–Watterson estimator. Based on the Moran model, Vogl and Clemente [10] arrived at the same distribution of polymorphic sites if mutations only occur at the monomorphic boundaries. A Moran model with mutations only at the boundaries approximates a Moran model with mutations at any allelic state sufficiently well if the scaled mutation rate θ is below 0.1 [10]. Obviously, the critical assumption that allows for analytical derivation of the maximum likelihood estimator is not that the ancestral state is known, but rather that only a single mutation segregates. Indeed, without selection equivalence of the estimators derived from the Taylor series expansion in θ of the general mutation model, estimators assuming the boundary mutation model can be shown [4]. In the latter case, the ML estimators can be considered exact. Note that mutation bias has generally been ignored when analyzing DNA sequence data. In contrast to the usual infinite sites model, which assumes that ancestral and derived states can be inferred, a mutation bias α creating an imbalance between A/T and C/G sites can be modeled naturally with our approach. As deviations in the A/T:C/G ratio from 1:1 are generally observed and as inference of ancestral states is difficult, such theory is practically useful. Vogl [3] derived a maximum likelihood estimator for not only the scaled mutation rate θ, but also the mutation bias α.

Computation-intensive, probabilistic methods for estimating population genetic parameters, such as the ones implemented in the LAMARC software package [38], are suitable for the analysis of populations governed by non-equilibrium dynamics. Our method also considers non-equilibrium population dynamics, such as changes in the effective size of the population, the mutation rate and mutation bias between different time points, but poses less computational burden. This is achieved by extending the boundary mutation model [4] to joint site frequency spectra and using modified Gegenbauer polynomials to solve the transition density $\phi(x, t)$ of the allelic proportion x at any time t. If these model assumptions hold, the method also provides maximum likelihood estimates.

Gutenkunst *et al.* [39] estimate migration rates, selection coefficients and split times from joint site frequency spectra in their program $\partial a \partial i$ by approximating the diffusion process using a numerical grid of population proportions x. Influx of mutations is modeled by "injecting ϕ density at low frequency in each population (at a rate proportional to the total mutation flux θ)". This presumably corresponds to the boundary mutation model, but seems to assume influx in equal proportions from the boundaries. Furthermore, this method is directed towards evaluating population sizes, growth rates and migration rates from joint site frequency spectra, rather than scaled mutation rates. The difference in mutation rates of the different allelic classes, *i.e.*, mutation bias, is not taken into account.

With mutations arising only at the boundaries, evolution of the allelic proportion x separates into a slowly evolving part, where the proportions of alleles at the boundaries change at a rate of θ, while the interior dynamics adjust relatively quickly to the slowly evolving boundary proportions. This process leads to a system of inhomogeneous linear differential equations. With this theory, changes in the parameters, *i.e.*, the scaled mutation rate θ or the mutation bias α, do not necessitate a recalculation of the eigensystem, unlike the approach described in Song and Steinrücken [7]. Thus, our approach speeds up computation, such that more complicated population genetic scenarios may be modeled, e.g., growing or shrinking population sizes that are commonly observed in nature. Since the equilibrium is reached at the rate of the scaled mutation rate θ, natural populations are rarely in equilibrium, and non-equilibrium dynamics need to be considered when inferring population genetic parameters.

We note that Evans *et al.* [40] also arrived at a system of inhomogeneous linear differential equations assuming the infinite sites model as defined above. Furthermore, they assume directional selection. Their analysis is based on iteration of moments, rather than on orthogonal polynomials, which leads to a recursive inhomogeneous system of differential equations. Nevertheless, the similarities between their and our approaches are readily apparent. In a follow-up study, Zivkovic *et al.* [41] apply their algorithm to human and fruit fly data.

So far, we have only discussed approaches based on the Kolmogorov (or diffusion) forward or backward equations. Another approach successfully employed for analyzing joint site frequency spectra is based on Kingman's coalescence [42,43]. With the coalescence, the starting point is the sample. Inference proceeds by summing and integrating over the sample's genealogical history. It is also possible to derive the beta-binomial equilibrium distribution with the coalescent. In more complicated cases, one or the other of the two approaches may be more suited. Generally, the coalescence seems preferable if the sample distribution can be derived fairly easily compared to the population distribution. This is the case for the infinite sites model without recombination, where only the coalescence approach has been used to derive joint site frequency spectra, as far as we are aware. Recently, Chen [44,45] and Kamm *et al.* [46] improved the computational efficiency of the coalescence approach to joint site frequency spectra. We note that changes in the mutation bias, as incorporated into our approach, have not yet been incorporated into the coalescence approach.

Our algorithm allows for inference of the mutation bias α, the scaled mutation rate θ and the time separating the samples of joint site frequency spectra. A fruit fly dataset consisting of a joint site frequency spectrum of two *Drosophila* species is analyzed to illustrate the method.

5. Conclusions

In this article, we present a method for inferring population genetic parameters from joint site frequency spectra, *i.e.*, from allelic frequencies at two (or more) time points. The parameters inferred are the time between the samples t and the mutation rate θ, scaled by the (effective) population size N. In contrast to earlier approaches [7,47,48], we assume a small mutation rate θ, such that only a mutation of single origin may segregate per site at any given time point in a sample. This assumption simplifies the mathematical treatment because, unlike with earlier approaches, changes in the parameters do not lead to a change in the eigensystem. Rather, the spatial expansion in orthogonal polynomials, specifically in Gegenbauer polynomials, remains unaffected. Compared to the case without mutations, *i.e.*, to the pure drift model, the temporal part changes from a system of homogeneous to one of inhomogenous linear differential equations. In effect, the system separates into the slowly evolving boundaries, which change at a rate of the scaled mutation rate θ, and a fast evolving interior polymorphic region, which changes at the rate of drift, conditional on the dynamics at the boundaries. We show that the eigenvectors can be derived from the general Jacobi polynomials by a Taylor series expansion. Furthermore, the equilibrium distribution corresponds to the Taylor series expansion of the equilibrium distribution for general θ. Due to the underlying boundary mutation model, parameter estimation is computationally efficient, and the method can be expanded to accommodate analysis of more complex population genetic scenarios.

Acknowledgments: The authors thank all members of the Institute of Population Genetics for support, especially Andrea Betancourt and Dominik Schrempf for discussions and suggestions. We also thank two anonymous reviewers whose suggestions helped to improve the article. The study was funded by the Austrian Science Fund (FWF): DK W1225-B20.

Author Contributions: CV conceived of the project, provided the mathematical derivations and wrote a first draft of the manuscript. JB improved the mathematical notation, downloaded, prepared and analyzed the *Drosophila* data. JB and CV jointly implemented the algorithms and wrote the final version of the manuscript.

Conflicts of Interest: The authors declare no conflict of interest.

Appendices

A.1. Appendix: Modified Gegenbauer Polynomials as the Limit of Modified Jacobi Polynomials

Lemma 1. *The set of eigenvectors $H_i(x)$, for $i \geq 2$, can be derived from the modified Jacobi polynomials in Equation (9) [7] multiplied by the weight function, $w^{(\theta,\alpha)}(x)R_i^{(\theta,\alpha)}(x)$ if: (i) only terms in a Taylor expansion in θ up to zeroth order are kept in the polymorphic region $]0,1[$, while (ii) terms that, for $\theta \to 0$, vanish in the interior and converge to point masses at the boundaries are set to point masses at the boundaries; compactly,*

$$w^{(\theta,\alpha)}(x)R_i^{(\theta,\alpha)}(x) = H_i(x) + O(\theta).\tag{A1}$$

Proof. The modified Jacobi polynomials times the weight functions can be expressed as a sum of polynomials, which in turn can be expressed as a sum of beta distributions:

$$w^{(\theta,\alpha)}(x)R_i^{(\theta,\alpha)}(x) = \sum_{m=0}^{i} \frac{(-1)^{i-m}\Gamma(i+\alpha\theta)\Gamma(i+\beta\theta)}{\Gamma(m+1)\Gamma(i-m+1)\Gamma(m+\alpha\theta)\Gamma(i-m+\beta\theta)}$$
$$\cdot x^{m+\alpha\theta-1}(1-x)^{i-m+\beta\theta-1}\tag{A2}$$
$$= \sum_{m=0}^{i} \frac{(-1)^{i-m}\Gamma(i+\alpha\theta)\Gamma(i+\beta\theta)}{\Gamma(m+1)\Gamma(i-m+1)\Gamma(i+\theta)} \, beta(x \mid m+\alpha\theta, i-m+\beta\theta).$$

For $m = 0$, the beta distribution converges to a delta function for small θ and $i \geq 1$:

$$\frac{(-1)^i\Gamma(i+\alpha\theta)\Gamma(i+\beta\theta)}{\Gamma(1)\Gamma(i+1)\Gamma(i+\theta)} \, beta(x \mid \alpha\theta, i+\beta\theta) = \frac{(-1)^i\Gamma(i)\Gamma(i)}{\Gamma(1)\Gamma(i+1)\Gamma(i)}\delta(x) + O(\theta)$$
$$= \frac{(-1)^i}{i}\delta(x) + O(\theta),\tag{A3}$$

and analogously for $m = i$.

For $i = 1$, we therefore have:

$$w^{(\theta,\alpha)}(x)R_1^{(\theta,\alpha)}(x) = -\delta(x) + \delta(x-1) + O(\theta).\tag{A4}$$

For $i \geq 2$, we have:

$$
\begin{aligned}
w^{(\theta,\alpha)}(x)R_i^{(\theta,\alpha)}(x) &= \sum_{m=0}^{i} \frac{(-1)^{i-m}\Gamma(i+\alpha\theta)\Gamma(i+\beta\theta)}{\Gamma(m+1)\Gamma(i-m+1)\Gamma(m+\alpha\theta)\Gamma(i-m+\beta\theta)} \\
&\quad \cdot x^{m+\alpha\theta-1}(1-x)^{i-m+\beta\theta-1} \\
&= \sum_{m=1}^{i-1} \frac{(-1)^{i-m}\Gamma(i)\Gamma(i)}{\Gamma(m+1)\Gamma(i-m)\Gamma(i-m+1)\Gamma(m)} \\
&\quad \cdot x^{m-1}(1-x)^{i-m-1} + (-1)^i\delta(x)/i + \delta(x-1)/i + O(\theta) \qquad \text{(A5)} \\
&= \sum_{m=0}^{i-2} \frac{(-1)^{i-m-1}\Gamma(i)\Gamma(i)}{\Gamma(m+2)\Gamma(i-m-1)\Gamma(i-m)\Gamma(m+1)} \\
&\quad \cdot x^{m}(1-x)^{i-m-2} + (-1)^i\delta(x)/i + \delta(x-1)/i + O(\theta) \\
&= U_i(x) + (-1)^i\delta(x)/i + \delta(x-1)/i + O(\theta) \\
&= H_i(x) + O(\theta).
\end{aligned}
$$

□

Remark 1. The $H_i(x)$ are obviously independent of θ and α for $i \geq 1$.

Note that the integrals over the whole region, including the boundary terms, are:

$$
\begin{cases}
-\int_0^1 xH_i(x)\,dx = 0 \\
-\int_0^1 (1-x)H_i(x)\,dx = 0;
\end{cases} \qquad \text{(A6)}
$$

such that the probability masses at the boundaries exactly offset that in the interior.

A.2. Appendix: Mutation-Drift Equilibrium

Theorem 2. *The equilibrium solution of the dynamic system with the slowly evolving part given by Equation (39) and the boundary Conditions (12) and (13) is given by (52) in the limit of $N \to \infty$.*

Proof. For any starting value, $b_0(t)$ will converge to $b_0(\infty) = \beta$ and similarly $b_1(\infty) = \alpha$. Substituting these values into Equation (50) and setting the derivatives to zero, we obtain:

$$
\tau_i(\infty) = \frac{A_i}{\lambda_i} \qquad \text{(A7)}
$$

It follows that, for all odd i, $\tau_i(\infty) = 0$, and, for all even i,

$$
\tau_i(\infty) = -\alpha\beta\theta(4i-2)/(i-1). \qquad \text{(A8)}
$$

The function:

$$
\phi(x,\infty) = \beta\delta(x) + \alpha\delta(x-1) + \alpha\beta\theta\sum_{i=1}^{\infty} c_{2i}\,H_{2i}(x) \qquad \text{(A9)}
$$

corresponds to the modified Gegenbauer expansion of the equilibrium solution for $N \to \infty$ where:

$$
c_{2i} = \frac{1}{\Delta_{2i}}\int_0^1 x(1-x)U_{2i}(x)x^{-1}(1-x)^{-1}\,dx = -\frac{(4i-1)2i}{2i-1}\frac{2}{2i} = -\frac{4(2i)-2}{2i-1}. \qquad \text{(A10)}
$$

□

References

1. Fisher, R. *The Genetical Theory of Natural Selection*; Clarendon Press: Oxford, UK, 1930.
2. Wright, S. Evolution in Mendelian populations. *Genetics* **1931**, *16*, 97–159.
3. Vogl, C. Estimating the scaled mutation rate and mutation bias with site frequency data. *Theor. Popul. Biol.* **2014**, *98*, 19–27.
4. Vogl, C.; Bergman, J. Inference of directional selection and mutation parameters assuming equilibrium. *Theor. Popul. Biol.* **2015**, *106*, 71–82.
5. Kimura, M. Solution of a process of random genetic drift with a continuous model. *Proc. Natl. Acad. Sci. USA* **1955**, *41*, 144–150.
6. Griffiths, R.; Spanò, D. Diffusion processes and coalescent trees. In *Probability and Mathematical Genetics: Papers in Honour of Sir John Kingman*; Cambridge University Press: Cambridge, UK, 2010; pp. 358–375.
7. Song, Y.; Steinrücken, M. A simple method for finding explicit analytic transition densities of diffusion processes with general diploid selection. *Genetics* **2012**, *190*, 1117–1129.
8. Tran, T.; Hofrichter, J.; Jost, J. An introduction to the mathematical structure of the Wright-Fisher model of population genetics. *Theory Biosci.* **2013**, *132*, 73–82.
9. Vogl, C. Computation of the likelihood in biallelic diffusion models using orthogonal polynomials. *Computation* **2014**, *2*, 199–220.
10. Vogl, C.; Clemente, F. The allele-frequency spectrum in a decoupled Moran model with mutation, drift, and directional selection, assuming small mutation rates. *Theor. Popul. Genet.* **2012**, *81*, 197–209.
11. Parsch, J.; Novozhilov, S.; Saminadin-Peter, S.; Wong, K.; Andolfatto, P. On the utility of short intron sequences as a reference for the detection of positive and negative selection in *Drosophila*. *Mol. Biol. Evol.* **2010**, *27*, 1226–1234.
12. Clemente, F.; Vogl, C. Unconstrained evolution in short introns?—An analysis of genome-wide polymorphism and divergence data from *Drosophila*. *J. Evol. Biol.* **2012**, *25*, 1975–1990.
13. Clemente, F.; Vogl, C. Evidence for complex selection on four-fold degenerate sites in *Drosophila melanogaster*. *J. Evol. Biol.* **2012**, *25*, 2582–2595.
14. Lack, J.; Cardeno, C.; Crepeau, M.; Taylor, W.; Corbett-Detig, R.B.; Stevens, K.; Langley, C.; Pool, J. The *Drosophila* Genome Nexus: A population genomic resource of 623 *Drosophila melanogaster* genomes, including 197 from a single ancestral range population. *Genetics* **2015**, *199*, 1229–1241.
15. NCBI Updates of Drosophila Annotations. Available online: http://www.flybase.org/ (accessed on 21 October 2015).
16. Carlin, B.; Louis, T., Eds. *Bayes and Empirical Bayes Methods for Data Analysis*, 2nd ed.; Chapman and Hall: Boca Raton, FL, USA, 2000.
17. RoyChoudhury, A.; Wakeley, J. Sufficiency of the number of segregating sites in the limit under finite-sites mutation. *Theor. Popul. Biol.* **2010**, *78*, 118–122.
18. Ewens, W. A note on the sampling theory for infinite alleles and infinite sites models. *Theor. Popul. Biol.* **1974**, *6*, 143–148.
19. Watterson, G. On the number of segregating sites in genetical models without recombination. *Theor. Popul. Biol.* **1975**, *7*, 256–276.
20. Kimura, M. Diffusion models in population genetics. *J. Appl. Probab.* **1964**, *1*, 177–232.
21. Kimura, M. The number of heterozygous nucleotide sites maintained in a finite population due to steady flux of mutations. *Genetics* **1969**, *61*, 893–903.
22. Chan, A.; Jenkins, P.; Song, Y. Genome-Wide Fine-Scale Recombination Rate Variation in *Drosophila melanogaster*. *PLoS Genet.* **2012**, *8*, e1003090.
23. Campos, J.L.; Zeng, K.; Parker, D.; Charlesworth, B.; Haddrill, P. Codon usage bias and effective population sizes on the X chromosome versus the autosomes in *Drosophila melanogaster*. *Mol. Biol. Evol.* **2013**, *30*, 811–823.
24. Campos, J.L.; Halligan, D.L.; Haddrill, P.R.; Charlesworth, B. The relation between recombination rate and patterns of molecular evolution and variation in Drosophila melanogaster. *Mol. Biol. Evol.* **2014**, *31*, 1010–1028.
25. Ewens, W. The sampling theory of selectively neutral alleles. *Theor. Popul. Biol.* **1972**, *3*, 87–112.
26. Sawyer, S.; Hartl, D. Population genetics of polymorphism and divergence. *Genetics* **1992**, *132*, 1161–1176.

27. Bustamante, C.; Wakeley, J.; Sawyer, S.; Hartl, D. Directional selection and the site-frequency spectrum. *Genetics* **2001**, *159*, 1779–1788.

28. Bustamante, C.; Nielsen, R.; Hartl, D. Maximum likelihood and Bayesian methods for estimating the distribution of selective effects among classes of mutations using DNA polymorphism data. *Theor. Popul. Biol.* **2003**, *63*, 91–103.

29. Williamson, S.; Fledel-Alon, A.; Bustamante, C. Population genetics of polymorphism and divergence for diploid selection models with arbitrary dominance. *Genetics* **2004**, *168*, 463–475.

30. Ewens, W. *Mathematical Population Genetics*; Springer: New York, NY, USA, 1979.

31. Abramowitz, M.; Stegun, I. (Eds.) *Handbook of Mathematical Functions*, 9th ed.; Dover: Mineola, NY, USA, 1970.

32. Zhao, L.; Yue, X.; Waxman, D. Complete numerical solution of the diffusion equation of random genetic drift. *Genetics* **2013**, *194*, 973–985.

33. Ewens, W. *Mathematical Population Genetics*, 2nd ed.; Springer: New York, NY, USA, 2004.

34. Gelman, A.; Carlin, J.; Stern, H.; Rubin, D. *Bayesian Data Analysis*; Chapman & Hall: London, UK, 1995.

35. Lachaise, D.; Cariou, M.; David, J.; Lemeunier, F.; Tsacas, L.; Ashburner, M. Historical biogeography of the *Drosophila melanogaster* species subgroup. *Evol. Biol.* **1988**, *22*, 159–225.

36. Russo, C.; Takezaki, N.; Nei, M. Molecular phylogeny and divergence times of *Drosophilid* species. *Mol. Biol. Evol.* **1995**, *12*, 391–404.

37. Cutter, A. Divergence times in *Caenorhabditis* and *Drosophila* inferred from direct estimates of the neutral mutation rate. *Mol. Biol. Evol.* **2008**, *25*, 778–786.

38. Kuhner, M. LAMARC 2.0: Maximum likelihood and Bayesian estimation of population parameters. *Bioinformatics* **2006**, *15*, 768–770.

39. Gutenkunst, R.; Hernandez, R.; Williamson, S.; Bustamante, C. Inferring the Joint Demographic History of Multiple Populations from Multidimensional SNP Frequency Data. *PLoS Genet.* **2009**, *5*, e1000695.

40. Evans, S.; Shvets, Y.; Slatkin, M. Non-equilibrium theory of the allele frequency spectrum. *Theor. Popul. Biol.* **2007**, *71*, 109–119.

41. Zivkovic, D.; Steinrücken, M.; Song, Y.; Stephan, W. Transition densities and sample frequency spectra of diffusion processes with selection and variable population size. *Genetics* **2015**, *200*, 601–617.

42. Hein, J.; Schierup, M.; Wiuf, C. *Gene Genealogies, Variation, and Evolution: A Primer in Coalescent Theory*; Oxford University Press: Oxford, UK, 2005.

43. Wakeley, J. *Coalescent Theory: An Introduction*; Roberts and Co.: Greenwood Village, CO, USA, 2009.

44. Chen, H. The joint allele frequency spectrum of multiple populations: A coalescent theory approach. *Theor. Popul. Biol.* **2012**, *81*, 179–195.

45. Chen, H. Intercoalescence time distribution of incomplete gene genealogies in temporally varying populations and applications in population genetic inference. *Ann. Hum. Genet.* **2013**, *77*, 158–173.

46. Kamm, J.; Terhorst, J.; Song, Y. Efficient computation of the joint sample frequency spectra for multiple populations. 2015, arXiv: 1503.01133. Available online: http://arxiv.org/abs/1503.01133 (accessed on 3 March 2015).

47. Steinrücken, M.; Wang, R.; Song, Y. An explicit transition density expansion for a multi-allelic Wright-Fisher diffusion with general diploid selection. *Theor. Popul. Biol.* **2013**, *83*, 1–14.

48. Steinrücken, M.; Bhaskar, A.; Song, Y. A novel method for inferring general diploid selection from time series genetic data. *Ann. Appl. Stat.* **2014**, *8*, 2203–2222.

10

Localized Polycentric Orbital Basis Set for Quantum Monte Carlo Calculations Derived from the Decomposition of Kohn-Sham Optimized Orbitals

Claudio Amovilli *, Franca Maria Floris [†] and Andrea Grisafi [†]

Dipartimento di Chimica e Chimica Industriale, University of Pisa, Via Giuseppe Moruzzi 13, Pisa 56124, Italy; floris@dcci.unipi.it (F.M.F.); andreagrisafi@hotmail.it (A.G.)
* Correspondence: claudio.amovilli@unipi.it
† These authors contributed equally to this work.

Academic Editor: Karlheinz Schwarz

Abstract: In this work, we present a simple decomposition scheme of the Kohn-Sham optimized orbitals which is able to provide a reduced basis set, made of localized polycentric orbitals, specifically designed for Quantum Monte Carlo. The decomposition follows a standard Density functional theory (DFT) calculation and is based on atomic connectivity and shell structure. The new orbitals are used to construct a compact correlated wave function of the Slater–Jastrow form which is optimized at the Variational Monte Carlo level and then used as the trial wave function for a final Diffusion Monte Carlo accurate energy calculation. We are able, in this way, to capture the basic information on the real system brought by the Kohn-Sham orbitals and use it for the calculation of the ground state energy within a strictly variational method. Here, we show test calculations performed on some small selected systems to assess the validity of the proposed approach in a molecular fragmentation, in the calculation of a barrier height of a chemical reaction and in the determination of intermolecular potentials. The final Diffusion Monte Carlo energies are in very good agreement with the best literature data within chemical accuracy.

Keywords: Kohn-Sham orbitals; quantum Monte Carlo; electronic structure of molecules

PACS: 31.15.E-

---

1. Introduction

Density functional theory (DFT) is a quantum-mechanical approach mainly developed for the study of the electronic structure of many body systems like atoms, molecules and solids. The Thomas-Fermi [1,2] statistical method laid the foundations of DFT but only with the Hohenberg-Kohn [3] theorems was this new method put on a firm theoretical footing. This approach is completely different from standard quantum-mechanical methodologies based on the calculation of an N particle wave function. In DFT, the basic quantity is the electron density, namely a much simpler function of only the position of a point in a three-dimensional space. For this reason, DFT was initially the most popular for the treatment of solids where, in principle, one has to deal with an infinite number of electrons. After important work on N-representability of density functions (see Levy [4]) and the generation of a plethora of valuable approximated energy density functionals, DFT is nowadays one of the most used techniques also for the study of molecules and molecular aggregates. Following DFT, the total electronic density is thus the fundamental variable on which any ground-state n-body property depends. In order to better understand this relation, which is also extremely important to improve the existing energy density functionals, a deep analysis of the density itself as well as of the related functions and derivatives is requested. In this context, we should mention the study of Bader and co-workers [5], mainly based on gradient and Laplacian of the density, and the electron localization function introduced by Becke and Edgecombe [6].

In this work, we focus on how one can get useful information on a real molecular system by starting from the electronic density. Although we use the basic knowledge of working with N-electron wave functions, we seek to define a route capable of bringing directly from the density to the construction of the wave function and then to the computation of an accurate energy. By decomposing the Kohn–Sham orbitals, which are the building blocks of the density, we use the concept of pairs together with the information on shell structure and connectivity to build an accurate correlated wave function whose nodal (Fermionic) structure is able to provide a very good energy through a diffusion Quantum Monte Carlo (QMC) calculation.

The outline of the paper is then as follows. In Section 2, we show the theoretical detail of our decomposition scheme. Application of the present approach to some illustrative examples is presented in Section 3. Finally, concluding remarks are given in Section 4.

2. Theory

The first theorem of Hohenberg-Kohn [3] shows that there is a one-to-one correspondence between the electron density $\rho(\mathbf{r})$ and the external potential $v(\mathbf{r})$ for a non-degenerate ground state of a system of electrons. The immediate consequence of this statement is that the corresponding energy is a functional of the electron density and that the N-electron wave function itself depends only on such a density. However, despite the enormous progress done in the last twenty years, the exact form of the energy functional is still unknown. In the practical implementation of DFT, the Kohn-Sham (KS) approach [7] takes a role of primary importance. In the Kohn-Sham theory, such a density is constructed from the orbitals of an independent particle model. Provided the so-called exchange-correlation energy functional is known, a set of one-particle equations can be derived and solved within a standard Self-Consistent-Field (SCF) framework. These building blocks, namely the KS orbitals, thus bring information from the real system. In the spirit of building the N-electron wave function from the exact density, we start from KS orbitals and define a route which leads to an accurate variational energy through the construction of a correlated well-defined wave function. To this end, we use the QMC method in both variational (VMC) and diffusional (DMC) versions.

The QMC is a robust method and is one of the most accurate to compute the electronic energy of the ground state of a molecular system [8,9]. In the last two decades, the interest in QMC has grown considerably [10,11]. In QMC, a common way to build a many-body wave function to describe a system of electrons is by employing a spin-free Slater-Jastrow (SJ) form of the type.

$$\Psi_{VMC}(\mathbf{r}_1, \mathbf{r}_2, ...) = \Phi(\mathbf{r}_1, \mathbf{r}_2, ...)\mathcal{J}(r_1, r_2, ..., r_{12}, ...), \tag{1}$$

where Φ is given by

$$\Phi = \sum_K D_K^{\uparrow} D_K^{\downarrow} d_K \tag{2}$$

in which $D_K^{\uparrow}$ and $D_K^{\downarrow}$ are the Slater determinants written in terms of occupied orbitals of spin-up and spin-down electrons, respectively, and d_K are the mixing coefficients. The Jastrow factor $\mathcal{J}$ is, instead, a function which depends explicitly on interparticle distances and is capable of treating the short range Coulomb correlation. This type of wave function is, in general, compact and is able to introduce a very large fraction of dynamical correlation through the Jastrow factor.

It is well known that KS orbitals are better than the Hartree-Fock ones in QMC calculations with a single determinant Slater–Jastrow wave function [12]. This is already evidence that KS orbitals bring information on electron correlation. To get more information, we go here beyond the single determinant form in QMC. A very compact and many determinant SJ wave function can be obtained in a Jastrow-Linear Generalized Valence Bond of order n (J-LGVBn) framework [13]. These wave functions are inspired by the generalized valence bond (GVB) approach and are constructed with localized orbitals (bonding, anti-bonding, lone-pair, and diffuse lone-pair functions with nodes). The use of localized orbitals allows the definition of a coupling scheme between electron pairs, which progressively includes new classes of excitations in the determinantal component. The resulting forms are rather compact and have a number of determinants that grows linearly with respect to the size of the molecule. The highest class of excitations included is indicated by n. In order to get localized bonding or pair functions and corresponding anti-bonding orbitals, KS orbitals must undergo a decomposition scheme, which involves a localization followed by a further generation of partner orbitals by taking account of connectivity and atomic shell structure.

Let us start from the density written in terms of KS orbitals in a more general spin unrestricted form, namely

$$\rho(\mathbf{r}) = \sum_{\sigma} \sum_{j=1}^{N_\sigma} |\psi_{j\sigma}^{(KS)}|^2(\mathbf{r}) \tag{3}$$

where σ is the one electron spin state. We can separately transform the $\{\psi_{j\alpha}^{(KS)}\}$ and $\{\psi_{j\beta}^{(KS)}\}$ sets to derive localized orbitals for α and β spins. This operation can be performed with any suitable localization technique through a unitary transformation within each of the two sets. By writing

$$\psi_{i\sigma}^{(loc)}(\mathbf{r}) = \sum_{j=1}^{N_\sigma} \psi_{j\sigma}^{(KS)}(\mathbf{r}) T_{ji}^{(\sigma)} \qquad (\mathbf{T}^{(\sigma)\dagger} \mathbf{T}^{(\sigma)} = \mathbf{1}) \tag{4}$$

We still have

$$\rho(\mathbf{r}) = \sum_{\sigma} \sum_{j=1}^{N_\sigma} |\psi_{j\sigma}^{(loc)}|^2(\mathbf{r}) \tag{5}$$

The localized orbitals $\psi_{j\sigma}^{(loc)}(\mathbf{r})$, depending on the nature of the electronic system, can be localized on one center (lone pair), two centers (bond) or, in some particular case, on three or more centers. If we consider the more frequent case of a bond function between two atoms, A and B say, we can identify in the corresponding localized orbital a contribution coming from each atom. Thus, we can write, regardless of normalization,

$$\psi_i^{(loc)}(AB|\mathbf{r}) = \phi_i^A(\mathbf{r}) + \phi_i^B(\mathbf{r}) \tag{6}$$

which allows us to define a new linearly independent orbital of anti-bonding type in the form

$$\psi_i^{(antibonding)}(AB|\mathbf{r}) = \phi_i^A(\mathbf{r}) - \phi_i^B(\mathbf{r}) \tag{7}$$

that can be used as the starting partner orbital of $\psi_i^{(loc)}(AB|\mathbf{r})$ in the J-LGVBn wave function. This part of the decomposition is dictated by connectivity. For a three-center (A-B-C) localized function recognized as

$$\psi_i^{(loc)}(ABC|\mathbf{r}) = \phi_i^A(\mathbf{r}) + \phi_i^B(\mathbf{r}) + \phi_i^C(\mathbf{r}) \tag{8}$$

a possible, but not unique, definition of appropriate partner orbitals can be the following

$$\psi_i^{(non-bonding)}(ABC|\mathbf{r}) = \phi_i^A(\mathbf{r}) - \phi_i^C(\mathbf{r}) \tag{9}$$

and

$$\psi_i^{(antibonding)}(ABC|\mathbf{r}) = \phi_i^A(\mathbf{r}) - 2\phi_i^B(\mathbf{r}) + \phi_i^C(\mathbf{r}) \tag{10}$$

A further decomposition can be invoked resorting to shell structure. Atomic-like $\phi_i^A(\mathbf{r})$ functions so far derived are essentially generalized hybrid orbitals with a well defined orientation in space depending on chemical sorrounding. These orbitals have atomic basis set components of s-, p-, d-, f-type and so on. We can split these generalized hybrids in several oriented atomic hybrids by acting on the separate shell components without changing the orientation. For instance, a typical sp^3 orbital will generate two hybrids of the same type, namely $s_1 p_1^3$ and $s_2 p_2^3$, if there are two $\{sp\}$ shells in the atomic basis set. Thus, if we can write

$$\phi_i^A(\mathbf{r}) = \sum_k^{shells} \chi_{ki}^A(\mathbf{r}) \tag{11}$$

We can use the components $\chi_{ki}^A(\mathbf{r})$ to define directly partner orbitals for lone pair $\phi_i^A(\mathbf{r})$, if this is already obtained from the localization of KS orbitals, or external orbitals of the type

$$\psi_{i'}^{(ext)}(AB|\mathbf{r}) = \chi_{ki}^A(\mathbf{r}) \pm \chi_{ki}^B(\mathbf{r}) \tag{12}$$

to improve the J-LGVBn orbitals at the VMC optimization of the QMC wave function. In order to avoid linear dependencies, localized KS orbitals, partner and external orbitals, to be used at VMC level and coming from the double decomposition scheme above, are orthogonalized. This orthogonalization is performed in two steps, (i) the first step is a hierarchical orthogonalization of partner and external orbitals with respect to KS localized orbitals, namely

$$\varphi_i^{(X)}(\mathbf{r}) = \psi_i^{(X)}(\mathbf{r}) - \sum_j \psi_j^{(loc)}(\mathbf{r}) < \psi_j^{(loc)}|\psi_i^{(X)} > \tag{13}$$

and (ii) the second step by a symmetric (Löwdin) orthogonalization, namely

$$\bar{\varphi}_i(\mathbf{r}) = \sum_j \varphi_j(\mathbf{r})(S^{-1/2})_{ji} \tag{14}$$

where $\mathbf{S}$ is the overlap matrix after the step (i). Step (ii) allows the cancellation of all linear dependencies from the set of new orbitals. In this process, the localized KS orbitals are not modified in order to start from a J-LGVB0 wave function of good quality. Finally, once the aforementioned polycentric basis set has been prepared, we pass to the VMC calculation and perform the optimization at J-LGVB0, J-LGVB1 and J-LGVB2 levels. All the orbitals of the complementary space spanned by the starting atomic orbital basis set have been removed. The number of variational parameters is then greatly reduced. The determinantal functions of the SJ form of the three cases considered here are defined as follows

$$\Phi_{LGVB1} = c_0 \Phi_0 + \sum_{j=1}^{N/2} c_j \Phi_0 (b_j^2 \to a_j^2) \tag{15}$$

and

$$\Phi_{LGVB2} = c_0 \Phi_0 + \sum_{j=1}^{N/2} c_j \Phi_0 (b_j^2 \to a_j^2) + \sum_{i-j} c_{ij} \Phi_0 (b_i \to a_i, b_j \to a_j) \tag{16}$$

where Φ_0 is the LGVB0 form, namely a determinant made by assigning all electrons to the localized KS orbitals. Here, N is the number of valence electrons, b_j are, more generally, bond orbitals and a_j antibonding orbitals and where the arrow indicates a single or double substitution of a bonding orbital with the corresponding antibonding. In the computing of excited functions, all the electrons are coupled to give the same spin state of Φ_0. Excited functions are, in fact, configuration state functions (CSF). More details for the construction of J-LGVBn wave functions can be found in the source paper [13]. During the VMC step, orbitals, determinant coefficients and Jastrow factor parameters are optimized. More precisely, following Fracchia *et al.* [13], we optimize orbitals and Jastrow factor of J-LGVB0 wave function, orbitals, determinant coefficients and Jastrow factor of the J-LGVB1 one, while we keep the J-LGVB1 orbitals in the optimization of determinant coefficients and Jastrow factor at the J-LGVB2 level of calculation. The resulting wave functions are used as trial wave function in the last DMC energy calculations. It is important to remark that a single determinant SJ wave function involves for the energy evaluation a scaling with the number of electrons similar to that of DFT, namely between N^3 and N^4 even if with a proportionality constant approximately a few thousand times larger. The use of multi determinant wave functions normally worsens this behavior but the J-LGVBn functions involve a number of determinants which grows linearly with the size of the molecules. Moreover, although not attempted in this work, the use of the present decomposition scheme should lead to a number of orbital parameters linearly dependent with the number of electrons if the mixing of the orbitals is allowed only between orbitals localized in the same region. This latter approximation is well founded and finds a logical application in calculations performed on large molecules.

In the next section, we show test results following this approach on a molecular fragmentation, in a hydrogen transfer reaction and in the calculation of a weak intermolecular potential.

3. Results and Discussion

By way of example, we tested the KS decomposition scheme proposed here in some prototypical process for which the accurate calculation of the potential energy surface (PES) must be performed through high quality quantum chemistry methods. We chose the fragmentation of hydrazine as an example of a homolytic bond breaking, a hydrogen transfer reaction and the formation of a weak van der Waals complex such as the methane dimer.

3.1. Computational Details

The KS orbitals have been optimized using the GAMESS-US package [14] with the hybrid Perdew-Burke-Ernzerhof functional PBE0 [15,16]. We have chosen the PBE0 functional because it derives from an improvement of the original PBE functional which has been classified as possibly variationally valid [17]. For the localization, we adopted the Edmiston-Ruedenberg method [18] implemented in GAMESS. The QMC calculations, instead, were performed with the CHAMP program [19]. In all calculations, we employed the Burkatzki-Filippi-Dolg (BFD) pseudopotentials [20,21] and the VTZ basis set specifically developed for these pseudopotentials. For the hydrogen transfer and the methane dimer formation, we added a set of diffuse functions taken from all-electron standard aug-cc-pVDZ basis set [22]. The pseudopotentials are treated beyond the locality approximation using the T-move approach [23]. The Jastrow factors contain electron-nuclear, electron-electron, and electron-electron-nuclear terms [24]. For the optimization of all parameters in our SJ wave functions, we used the iterative linear method developed by Umrigar *et al.* [25]. Here, we used a time step of 0.05 a.u. in all the DMC fixed-node calculations and also of 0.01 a.u. for the methane dimer. Finally, we used Gaussian 09 package [26] for standard quantum chemistry calculations on the methane dimer.

3.2. Fragmentation of Hydrazine

The fragmentation of hydrazine,

$$N_2H_4 \rightarrow 2NH_2 \tag{17}$$

is a homolytic bond breaking in which the number of electronic pairs is not conserved. For this reason, the computational method must be capable of providing a good estimate of the correlation energy and must be size extensive. The J-LGVBn wave functions, already with $n = 2$, are able to provide a good estimate of the corresponding reaction energy [13]. Fracchia *et al.* used the full variational space spanned by the VTZ basis set in the global optimization of the J-LGVB2 wave function. This means to use all the 128 atomic orbitals of the hydrazine basis set. In this work, the KS decomposition scheme described in the previous section leads to a basis set made of 36 polycentric orbitals with a significant reduction of the number of parameters for the VMC optimization. In Table 1, we show the comparison between the VMC and DMC electronic energies of hydrazine calculated in this work and the corresponding values calculated by Fracchia *et al.* [13] with the full atomic basis set. The variational energy loss ranges from 0.0029 to 0.0031 Hartree at VMC level and from 0.0003 to 0.0007 Hartree with DMC. Resulting fragmentation energies are shown, instead, in Table 2. In this Table, we report also, for comparison purposes, Fracchia *et al.* theoretical results [13] and the experimental value [27,28]. As shown by Fracchia *et al.* [13], the level 2 of J-LGVBn theory is enough to approach the limiting value corresponding to the maximum level, namely 10. Moreover, DMC is needed to achieve chemical accuracy. Results obtained with the present approach are in close agreement with those of the previous QMC calculation showing that our decomposition scheme of KS orbitals is a valid alternative to standard J-LGVBn approach. We remind readers that standard J-LGVBn theory subsumes the use of the full atomic basis set and a Multi-Configuration SCF (MCSCF) preliminary calculation for the VMC setup. Finally, we note that our J-LGVB2 DMC fragmentation energy differs only by 0.5 kcal/mol from the experimental value. For a comparison with DFT calculations, we remind readers that Fracchia *et al.* [13] found that, for some of the most used functionals, the discrepancies with the experiment range from 1.5 to more than 4 kcal/mol.

Table 1. Comparison between variational Monte Carlo (VMC) and diffusion Monte Carlo (DMC) electronic energies (Hartree) of hydrazine computed with the full atomic basis set [13] and with the reduced basis set obtained from KS orbital decomposition presented in this work. The wave function form is indicated by the level n of the Jastrow-Linear Generalized Valence Bond (J-LGVBn) theory [13]. Statistical error is about 0.0001 Hartree.

J-LGVBn	VMC [13]	VMC (This Work)	DMC [13]	DMC (This Work)
0	−22.2438	−22.2406	−22.2724	−22.2721
1	−22.2538	−22.2509	−22.2762	−22.2755
2	−22.2565	−22.2534	−22.2777	−22.2771

Table 2. Fragmentation energy (kcal/mol) of hydrazine computed at various level of calculation and comparison with experimental data. Statistical error is about 0.1 kcal/mol. The experimental (exp) reference is active thermochemical tables (ATcT) [27] data corrected for zero-point energy, spin-orbit interaction, and Born–Oppenheimer approximation [28].

J-LGVBn	VMC [13]	DMC [13]	VMC (This Work)	DMC (This Work)	Exp [27]
0	67.3	70.8	65.4	71.6	–
1	69.5	71.8	69.3	72.3	–
2	70.8	72.4	70.3	72.9	–
10	71.1	72.8	–	–	–
exp	–	–	–	–	73.39

3.3. Barrier Height in a Prototypical Hydrogen Transfer Reaction

The hydrogen transfer reaction

$$NH_2 + H_2O \rightarrow NH_3 + OH \qquad (18)$$

plays an important role in atmospheric chemistry and is included in the HTB38/04 database [29], a reference database for computed reaction and activation energies. This reference is based on a semi-experimental recipe in which kinetic and thermodynamic data are combined with results from dynamical simulations and quantum mechanical calculations.

For this reaction, DFT gives poor results on barrier heights apart for the hybrid meta-functional MPWB1K [30] which is able to provide forward and reverse barrier heights within a deviation of 2 kcal/mol. In Table 3, we report our calculations and we compare our results with the previous work of Fracchia *et al.* [31] and with literature reference data. Fracchia *et al.* used 148 atomic orbitals for the basis set while, here, we have 39 basis functions from KS orbital decomposition. The two sets of J-LGVBn data are in agreement with each other with small differences between 0 and 0.5 kcal/mol. In addition, in this case, J-LGVB2 is the level of calculation closest to reference values. Our J-LGVB2 calculation is in good agreement (within chemical accuracy) with the Coupled Cluster method with the Single Double and the perturbative Triple (CCSD(T))/aug-cc-pvTZ results while showing a discrepancy with the best reference of 1.6 and 1.5 kcal/mol with forward and reverse barrier heights, respectively. For the reaction energy, the agreement is instead very good. This fact suggests that there could be a small inaccuracy in the description of three electrons localized on a molecular subunit made of three nuclei, as it happens here when the hydrogen is in the middle between the two molecules. This will be investigated in future work.

Table 3. Barrier heights and reaction energies (kcal/mol) for the hydrogen transfer $NH_2 + H_2O \rightarrow NH_3 + OH$ at various level of calculation and comparison with literature data. Statistical error is about 0.1 kcal/mol.

Method	DMC [31]	DMC (This Work)	Literature
Forward Reaction Barrier Height			
J-LGVB0	15.3	14.8	–
J-LGVB1	14.9	14.5	–
J-LGVB2	14.6	14.3	–
CCSD(T)/aug-cc-pvQZ [31]	–	–	14.19
DFT(MPWB1K) [30,32]	–	–	13.15
best reference [29,33]	–	–	12.7
Reverse Reaction Barrier Height			
J-LGVB0	5.2	4.9	–
J-LGVB1	4.7	4.7	–
J-LGVB2	4.6	4.7	–
CCSD(T)/aug-cc-pvQZ [31]	–	–	3.86
DFT(MPWB1K) [30,32]	–	–	5.04
reference [29,33]	–	–	3.2
Reaction Energy			
J-LGVB0	10.1	9.9	–
J-LGVB1	10.2	9.8	–
J-LGVB2	10.0	9.6	–
CCSD(T)/aug-cc-pvQZ [31]	–	–	10.33
DFT(MPWB1K) [30,32]	–	–	8.12
reference [29,33]	–	–	9.5

3.4. Methane Dimer Intermolecular Potential

The accurate calculation of interaction energies of weakly bound van der Waals complexes is a challenge for both QMC and DFT for different reasons. The "gold standard" for these type of calculations is the CCSD(T) excitations extrapolated in the limit of the Complete Basis Set (CBS). Such an approach can be used to establish a benchmark for relatively small systems, but it has an unfavorable scaling with the size of the intermolecular complex. Both QMC and DFT have a better scaling but present some difficulties to be overcome. QMC, provided a trial wave function with the right nodes is given, should give, at the DMC level, the exact total energy within the statistical error. The two main points are, in fact, the form of the wave function and the length of the simulation. While the form of the wave function with standard quantum chemistry methods must account for the dynamical correlation energy to provide good interaction potentials, it is not yet clear which more compact and simplified functional forms should account for the correct nodes. The second point is related to the statistical error. For weak interaction energies, it is mandatory to have an error on the total energy of the order of 0.00001 Hartree (sub chemical accuracy). Such a precision in a standard QMC calculation can be achieved only by very long simulations or by highly parallelized calculations. In this regard, it is important to remind readers that, in order to reduce an error by a factor of 10, one has to perform a simulation 100 times longer. DFT presents, instead, the well known problem of the evaluation of the dispersion energy. Dispersion energy is a contribution to non local intermolecular correlation energy. Although many proposed functionals afford some possible solutions to this problem, an exact treatment of the dispersion energy in the framework of DFT has not yet been provided.

The computation of the intermolecular potential of methane dimer is a good test case to check the reliability of the present approach in this context. In this case, the size of the system is small enough to guarantee a good analysis of the wave function for the DMC step and to compute energies with relatively small statistical errors. We have analyzed eight structures whose geometries are displayed in Figure 1. By starting from the 228 atomic orbitals of the aug-VTZ basis set, we have generated, through the PBE0 KS orbital decomposition described in this work, a basis set made of 48 two center orbitals, namely six along each C-H bond. A schematic representation of these orbitals is given in Figure 2. Finally, we have performed DMC energy calculations as done for the two examples above. In these QMC computations, we have not included the e-e-n three-body Jastrow term. We have checked the importance of this term on a selected structure, and we noticed that the corresponding effect on the interaction energy is negligible. A summary of all VMC and DMC calculations performed on the methane dimer is given in the Supplementary Information (Tables S1–S11). Here, we report the more significant results of this study.

For the DMC calculation, we have produced two sets of results for different values of time step, namely 0.05 and 0.01 a.u. In this way, we can have an estimate of the finite time step error on the intermolecular potential. In the previous two cases, Fracchia et al. [13] made a similar test and concluded that the value of 0.05 a.u. was accurate enough for the evaluation of energy differences like reaction energy and barrier height. Here, instead, the interaction potential is a much smaller quantity and consequently a smaller time step could be necessary. The resulting DMC interaction energies are displayed in Figure 3 for the eight structures and for two levels of calculation J-LGVB0 and J-LGVB1. The J-LGVB2 case gives results comparable with the J-LGVB1 level with the higher time step (see Tables S9–S11 of Supplementary Information). This is in line with what was expected considering that, for the methane dimer, the interaction energy is very small and the convergence, with the level of the J-LGVBn theory, should be very fast. In this Figure, the points are connected by lines in order to help the reader in the assignment of the corresponding level of computation. Although the differences between different geometries are, in some cases, of the same order of magnitude of the statistical error, the difference in the relative stability is quite evident. In this plot, we have added the patterns of analogous calculations performed at the second order Möller-Plessett (MP2) perturbation theory with a standard aug-cc-pvTZ basis set with and without countepoise correction [34]. In this model system and with such a basis set, MP2 overestimates the attraction while the so-called basis set superposition error (BSSE) coming from the use of counterpoise method tends to overestimate the necessary correction to the potential. This suggests that, in our plot, the best estimate of interaction energy should give a broken line between the two of the corrected and uncorrected MP2 calculations. For the smaller time step values, this happens only for the J-LGVB1 case. From the comparison of the two time step sets of data, it is evident that, in order to achieve the subchemical accuracy, one has to resort to a time step of 0.01 a.u. or smaller.

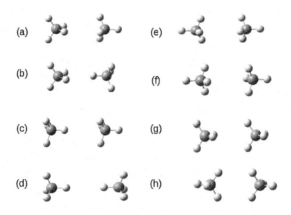

Figure 1. Methane dimer structures considered in this work.

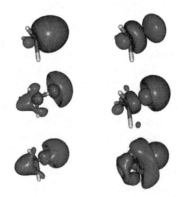

Figure 2. Two center (C–H) localized basis set orbitals of methane.

The literature benchmark data from a CCSD(T)/CBS [35] estimate of the methane dimer PES predicts the (f) structure as the most stable with a value of −0.53 kcal/mol as interaction energy, corresponding to −0.00084 Hartree. Here, at DMC/J-LGVB1 level, we find −0.58 ± 0.04 kcal/mol with the highest time step and −0.51 ± 0.04 kcal/mol in the other case. The agreement is very good in both cases. In a recent work, Dubecký *et al.* [36] proposed a simplified protocol for the evaluation of intermolecular potential energies following a DMC calculation. Their protocol is based on a single-determinant SJ wave function made with B3LYP orbitals computed with an aug-VTZ basis set and with an optimized elaborated Jastrow factor. They analyzed several complexes with an average error on the binding energies of about 0.1–0.2 kcal/mol. For the methane dimer in the minimal energy configuration, they computed an interaction energy of −0.44 ± 0.05 kcal/mol. Here, we go beyond the single-determinant SJ wave function allowing a larger flexibility in the description of the position of nodes and, moreover, we optimize the orbitals at VMC level. Our J-LGVB1 wave function seems to be the more accurate in determining the interaction energy, the J-LVB0 being slightly more attractive. Some explanation for the bahavior of all these DMC calculations can be given by considering that the Pauli repulsion is related to antisymmetry, so the change of the nodal structure could affect the intermolecular potential. Moreover, dispersion energy also depends on isolated molecule polarizabilities and such response properties depend strongly on correlation energy as well. At present, it is very difficult to quantify these effects, but we think that our results on the methane dimer can offer some interesting ideas for future developments.

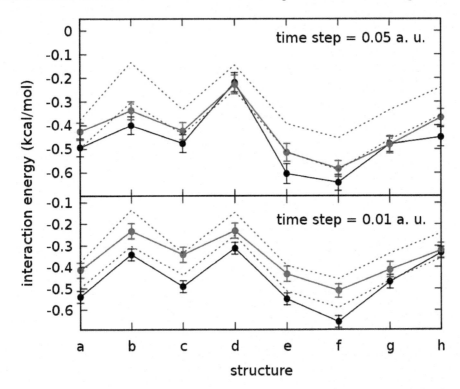

Figure 3.   DMC interaction energies for the methane dimer structures considered in this work calculated at J-LGVB0 (**black**) and J-LGVB1 (**red**) levels of the theory.   Dashed lines correspond to counterpoise corrected (**upper**) and uncorrected (**lower**) MP2/aug-cc-pvTZ data plotted for comparison.

Finally, in Figure 4 we show results from some DFT calculations. More precisely, we report PBE0 interaction energies obtained with the same basis set and pseudopotential used for QMC and with the ωB97XD functional [37] with the standard aug-cc-pvTZ basis set. As we can see, PBE0, which is a good hybrid functional for many purposes, here clearly suffers of the lack of a good description of dispersion energy. ωB97XD, instead, is a range-separated hybrid functional with the inclusion of empirical dispersion. Results with this functional for the methane dimer seem to be good, at least for these eight structures. For comparison purposes, we have included in this Figure also the minimal energy from CCSD(T)/CBS literature reference [35] and from QMC calculation of Dubecký *et al.* [36].

At this point, because the quality of a PES cannot be checked on a single geometry, we have attempted the calculation of the second virial coefficient from the computed interaction energies of the eight dimer configurations. In order to build a PES with these few data, we have fitted the DMC interaction energies with scaled Hartree-Fock (HF) and second order Möller-Plessett (MP) corresponding values, namely we have written

$$\Delta E_{DMC} \approx \alpha \Delta E_{HF} + \beta \Delta E_{MP}^{(2)}, \tag{19}$$

where α and β are linear fitting parameters. The HF interaction energy is dominated by Pauli repulsion, the quadrupole-quadrupole electrostatic interaction being much smaller in magnitude at the most stable geometries. The second order MP intermolecular energy is instead always attractive, being the main contribution to the dispersion energy. By performing an MP2/aug-cc-pvTZ all electron calculation, our fit leads to $\alpha = 0.865$ and $\beta = 0.857$. This is an interesting result which tells us that electron correlation affects both Pauli repulsion and London interaction (dispersion energy) with a resulting modulation of the MP2 PES. With the purpose of computing the second virial coefficient, we have fitted the modified PES with the following analytical form

$$\Delta E_{int} = \sum_i \sum_j \left[\frac{q_i q_j}{r_{ij}} f_1(ar_{ij}) + \frac{C_{ij}^{(4)}}{r_{ij}^4} f_4(ar_{ij}) + \frac{C_{ij}^{(6)}}{r_{ij}^6} f_6(ar_{ij}) + \frac{C_{ij}^{(8)}}{r_{ij}^8} f_8(ar_{ij}) \right.$$
$$\left. + \frac{C_{ij}^{(10)}}{r_{ij}^{10}} f_{10}(ar_{ij}) + \frac{C_{ij}^{(12)}}{r_{ij}^{12}} f_{12}(ar_{ij}) \right]$$
(20)

where $f_n(x)$ is the damping function

$$f_n(x) = 1 - \left(\sum_{i=1}^{n} \frac{x^i}{i!} \right) e^{-x}$$
(21)

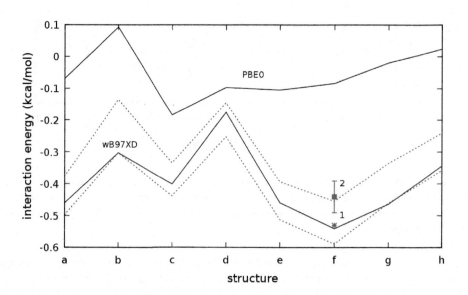

Figure 4. PBE0 and ωB97XD KS DFT interaction energies for the methane dimer structures considered in this work. Dashed lines correspond to counterpoise corrected (**upper**) and uncorrected (**lower**) MP2/aug-cc-pvTZ data plotted for comparison. Isolated points refer to the minimum energy configuration literature benchmark CCSD(T)/CBS (1) [35] and of the QMC calculation of Dubecký *et al.* [36] (2).

The second virial coefficient $B_2(T)$ measures the first correction from the ideality of a real gas in the equation of state

$$\frac{P}{RT} \approx \rho + B_2(T)\rho^2$$
(22)

where here ρ is the molar density of the gas. $B_2(T)$ depends on the intermolecular potential and has the following expression [35]

$$B_2(T) = -\frac{N_A}{16\pi^2} \int_0^{2\pi} d\phi \int_0^\pi \sin\theta d\theta \int_0^{2\pi} d\alpha \int_0^\pi \sin\beta d\beta \int_0^{2\pi} d\gamma$$
$$\int_0^\infty r^2 dr \left(\exp\left[-\frac{U(r,\phi,\theta,\alpha,\beta,\gamma)}{k_B T} \right] - 1 \right) \tag{23}$$

where U is the intermolecular potential written in terms of the relative coordinates of the two methane molecules and corresponding to ΔE_{int} above and N_A is the Avogadro's number. The expression above does not include the quantum correction which is always positive and decreases very rapidly with the temperature; it is about 20 cm^3/mol at 100 K and about 2 cm^3/mol at 200 K [35]. $B_2(T)$ can be accurately measured at room temperature and, hence, it provides a reliable reference to test a computed intermolecular potential. In this work, we have computed the integral of Equation (23) by a one-dimensional grid along the C-C distance and by a Monte Carlo integration over all the other variables related to the relative orientations. In Figure 5, we compare our computed value from J-LGVB1 DMC calculation with the time step 0.01 a.u. at different temperatures with some experimental data and with the corresponding value computed from unmodified MP2 PES. From this comparison, we can see that the modified PES has a better agreement with experimental data [38–43] than that obtained directly from MP2 calculation. We believe that this result is promising for future development of this approach, although we must recognize that our extrapolated PES is based on only very few points computed at the highest level of calculation. On the other hand, the full calculation of a DMC PES is still not practicable, and our approach could be a suggestion for, at least, a preliminary study of a complex system like that made of interacting molecules.

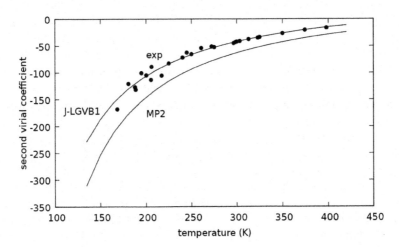

Figure 5.   Second virial coefficient (cm^3/mol) of methane as a function of temperature. Comparison between calculated (this work, solid line, and experimental values (circle, [38–43]).

4. Conclusions

A procedure to decompose the KS optimized orbitals with the aim of generating a new basis set specifically designed for QMC calculations is given. The proposed scheme preserves the initial KS orbitals in a localized form and adds new partner and external orbitals, also localized, which are capable of bringing information on electron correlation. The decomposition technique resorts to concepts that are commonly used in the analysis of the density like electron pair, connectivity and shell structure. By starting from an accurate electron density, the procedure allows the construction of a correlated wave function that is further optimized within a step of VMC computation. The functional form used in this context is taken from the J-LGVBn approach of Fracchia *et al.* [13]: it is compact, size-extensive and displays a better flexibility than that of a single determinant SJ wave function on Fermionic nodal structure. Finally, DMC is used to compute the energy. The method has been tested on some simple process namely, the fragmentation of hydrazine, the hydrogen transfer reaction between ammonia and OH radical and the formation the methane dimer.

For the reaction energy of the fragmentation of hydrazine, the previous result of Fracchia *et al.* [13] is reproduced as well as the experimental value within chemical accuracy [27]. The main achievement with respect to previous work is the great reduction of the number of variational parameters due to the information brought by the new basis set derived from KS orbitals. We pass from the 128 atomic orbitals of the full starting basis set to the new set made of only 36 localized orbitals.

For the hydrogen transfer, again the reaction energy of all best references, included Fracchia *et al.* calculations [31], is here reproduced within chemical accuracy. The two barrier heights, forward and reverse processes, show instead a slightly bigger deviation, namely 1.5 kcal/mol, but are in better agreement with high quality CCSD (T)/aug-cc-pvQZ calculations [31]. Probably, some improvement of our approach is needed for a better description of the localization of three electrons on three centers as found in the transition state of this reaction. In addition, in this case, we use only 39 localized basis functions instead of 148 atomic orbitals of the starting basis set.

Finally, for the methane dimer intermolecular complex, we have analyzed eight structures. We have been able to recover the intermolecular interaction energy within 0.1 kcal/mol of previous QMC [36] calculation and within statistical error of the literature benchmark CCSD (T)/CBS [35] data. We used 48 essentially two-center orbitals instead of the full basis set of 228 atomic orbitals. The data obtained with the J-LGVB1 wave function at the DMC level of calculation have been utilized to extrapolate a PES from standard MP2/aug-cc-pvTZ computation. The modified PES comes from a different mixing of HF and second order MP2 contributions based on a fit of DMC interaction energies. Both repulsive and attractive forces resulted as weakened in this transformation of the PES. The resulting PES has been further elaborated in order to be used through an analytical expression in the calculation of the second virial coefficient of gaseous methane. A plot is given with the dependence on the temperature. The agreement with corresponding experimental data [38–43] is much better then with the starting MP2 unmodified PES.

As a final remark, it is interesting to notice that, in the present approach, the electron density remains essentially the same in passing from KS to QMC. Of course, this is not rigorous but we can expect that, at least, both KS and QMC are able to provide a density better than HF and closer to the exact one. Under this assumption, if we look at the VMC model wave function as a partially interacting example of a link between the independent particle model of KS and the fully interacting case represented by DMC, we can argue that this point could have some relation with adiabatic connection. This point will be a matter of further study.

Acknowledgments: The authors acknowledge financial support from the University of Pisa (Fondi di Ateneo and PRA_2016_46).

Author Contributions: Claudio Amovilli conceived and supervised the work and wrote the paper. Franca Maria Floris and Andrea Grisafi performed calculations and contributed to the analysis of data and to the preparation of the manuscript.

Conflicts of Interest: The authors declare no conflict of interest.

References

1.   Fermi, E. Un metodo statistico per la determinazione di alcune proprietà dell'atomo. *Rend. Accad. Lincei* **1927**, *6*, 602–607.

2.   Thomas, L.H. The calculation of atomic fields. *Proc. Camb. Philos. Soc.* **1927**, *23*, 542–548

3.   Hohenberg, P.; Kohn, W. Inhomogeneous Electron Gas. *Phys. Rev.* **1964**, *136*, B864–B871.

4. Levy, M. Universal variational functionals of electron densities, first order density matrices and natural spin-orbitals and solution of the v-representability problem. *Proc. Natl. Acad. Sci. USA* **1979**, *76*, 6062–6065.

5. Bader, R.F.W.; MacDougall, P.J.; Lau C.D.H. Bonded and nonbonded charge concentrations and their relation to molecular geometry and reactivity. *J. Am. Chem. Soc.* **1984**, *106*, 1594–1605.

6. Becke, A.D.; Edgecombe, K.E. A simple measure of electron localization in atomic and molecular systems. *J. Chem. Phys.* **1990**, *92*, 5397–5403.

7. Kohn, W.; Sham, L.J. Self-Consistent Equations Including Exchange and Correlation Effects. *Phys. Rev.* **1965**, *140*, A1133–A1138.

8. Reynolds, P. J.; Ceperley, D.M.; Alder, B.J.; Lester, W.A., Jr. Fixed-node quantum Monte Carlo for molecules. *J. Chem. Phys.* **1982**, *77*, 5593–5603.

9. Foulkes, W.M.C.; Mitas, L.; Needs, R.J.; Rajagopal, G. Quantum Monte Carlo simulations of solids. *Rev. Mod. Phys.* **2001**, *73*, 33–83.

10. Lüchow, A. Quantum Monte Carlo methods. *WIREs Comput. Mol. Sci.* **2011**, *1*, 388–402.

11. Austin, B.M.; Zubarev, D.Y.; Lester, W.A., Jr. Quantum Monte Carlo and Related Approaches. *Chem. Rev.* **2012**, *112*, 263–288.

12. Benedek, N.A.; Snook, I.K.; Towler M.D.; Needs, R.J. Quantum Monte Carlo calculations of the dissociation energy of the water dimer. *J. Chem. Phys.* **2006**, *125*, 104302.

13. Fracchia, F.; Filippi, C.; Amovilli, C. Size-Extensive Wave Functions for Quantum Monte Carlo: A Linear Scaling Generalized Valence Bond Approach. *J. Chem. Theory Comput.* **2012**, *8*, 1943–1951.

14. Schmidt, M.W.; Baldridge, K.K.; Boatz, J.A.; Elbert, S.T.; Gordon, M.S.; Jensen, J.H.; Koseki, S.; Matsunaga, N.; Nguyen, K.A.; Su, S.; *et al.* General atomic and molecular electronic structure system. *J. Comput. Chem.* **1993**, *14*, 1347–1363.

15. Perdew, J.; Burke, K.; Ernzerhof, M. Generalized Gradient Approximation Made Simple. *Phys. Rev. Lett.* **1996**, *77*, 3865–3868.

16. Adamo, C.; Barone, V. Toward reliable density functional methods without adjustable parameters: The PBE0 model. *J. Chem. Phys.* **1999**, *110*, 6158–6170.

17. Amovilli, C.; March, N.H.; Bogar, F.; Gal, T. Use of *ab initio* methods to classify four existing energy density functionals according to their possible variational validity. *Phys. Lett. A* **2009**, *373*, 3158–3160.

18. Edmiston, C.; Ruedenberg, K. Localized Atomic and Molecular Orbitals. *Rev. Mod. Phys.* **1963**, *35*, 457–465.

19. CHAMP is a Quantum Monte Carlo Program Package. Available online: http://pages.physics.cornell.edu/cyrus/champ.html (accessed on 5 February 2016).

20. Burkatzki, M.; Filippi, C.; Dolg, M. Energy-consistent pseudopotentials for quantum Monte Carlo calculations. *J. Chem. Phys.* **2007**, *126*, 234105.

21. Dolg, M.; Filippi, C. (University of Twente, Enschede, The Netherlands). Private communication, 2012.

22. Kendall, R.; Dunning, T., Jr.; Harrison, R. Electron affinities of the first-row atoms revisited. Systematic basis sets and wave functions. *J. Chem. Phys.* **1992**, *96*, 6796–6806.

23. Casula, M. Beyond the locality approximation in the standard diffusion Monte Carlo method. *Phys. Rev. B* **2006**, *74*, 161102.

24. Filippi, C.; Umrigar, C.J. Multiconfiguration wave functions for quantum Monte Carlo calculations of first-row diatomic molecules. *J. Chem. Phys.* **1996**, *105*, 213–226.

25. Umrigar, C.J.; Toulouse J.; Filippi, C.; Sorella, S.; Hennig R.G. Alleviation of the fermion-sign problem by optimization of many-body wave functions. *Phys. Rev. Lett.* **2007**, *98*, 110201.

26. Available online: http://www.gaussian.com/ (accessed on 5 February 2016).

27. Ruscic, B.; Pinzon, R.; Morton, M.; von Laszevski, G.; Bittner, S.; Nijsure, S.; Amin, K.; Minkoff, M.; Wagner, A. Introduction to Active Thermochemical Tables: Several "Key" Enthalpies of Formation Revisited. *J. Phys. Chem. A* **2004**, *108*, 9979–9997.

28. Karton, A.; Daon, S.; Martin, J.M. W4-11: A high-confidence benchmark dataset for computational thermochemistry derived from first-principles W4 data. *Chem. Phys. Lett.* **2011**, *510*, 165–178.

29. Zhao, Y.; Lynch, B.; Truhlar, D. Multi-coefficient extrapolated density functional theory for thermochemistry and thermochemical kinetics. *Phys. Chem. Chem. Phys.* **2005**, *7*, 43–52.

30. Zhao, Y.; Truhlar, D.G. Hybrid Meta Density Functional Theory Methods for Thermochemistry, Thermochemical Kinetics, and Noncovalent Interactions: The MPW1B95 and MPWB1K Models and Comparative Assessments for Hydrogen Bonding and van der Waals Interactions. *J. Phys. Chem. A* **2004**, *108*, 6908–6918.

31. Fracchia, F.; Filippi, C.; Amovilli, C. Barrier Heights in Quantum Monte Carlo with Linear-Scaling Generalized-Valence-Bond Wave Functions. *J. Chem. Theory Comput.* **2013**, *9*, 3453–3462.

32. Minnesota Database Collection. Available online: http://t1.chem.umn.edu/misc/database_group/database_therm_bh (accessed on 5 February 2016).

33. Lynch, B.; Truhlar, D. What Are the Best Affordable Multi-Coefficient Strategies for Calculating Transition State Geometries and Barrier Heights? *J. Phys. Chem. A* **2002**, *106*, 842–846.

34. Boys, S.F.; Bernardi, F. The calculation of small molecular interactions by the differences of separate total energies. Some procedures with reduced errors. *Mol. Phys.* **1970**, *19*, 553–566.

35. Hellmann, R.; Bich, E.; Vogel, E. *Ab initio* intermolecular potential energy surface and second pressure virial coefficients of methane. *J. Chem. Phys.* **2008**, *128*, 214303.

36. Dubecký, M.; Derian, R.; Jurečka, P.; Mitas, L.; Hobza, P.; Otyepka, M. Quantum Monte Carlo for Noncovalent Interactions: Analysis of Protocols and Simplified Scheme Attaining Benchmark Accuracy. *Phys. Chem. Chem. Phys.* **2014**, *16*, 20915–20923.

37. Chai, J.D.; Head-Gordon, M. Long-range corrected hybrid density functionals with damped atom-atom dispersion corrections. *Phys. Chem. Chem. Phys.* **2008**, *10*, 6615–6620.

38. Kerl, K. Interferometric Determination of Mean Polarizabilities and Second Density Virial Coefficients of Methane Between 128 K and 890 K. *Int. J. Phys. Chem. Ber. Bunsen-Ges.* **1991**, *95*, 36–42.

39. Trusler, J.P.M. The Speed of Sound in $(0.8CH_4 + 0.2C_2H_6)$ (G) at Temperatures between 200 K and 375 K and Amount-of-Substance Densities up to 5 Mol/dm^3. *J. Chem. Therm.* **1994**, *26*, 751–763.

40. Ramazanova, A.E. Volumetric Properties and Virial Coefficients of (Water + Methane). *J. Chem. Therm.* **1993**, *25*, 249–259.

41. Renner, C.A. Excess Second Virial Coefficients for Binary Mixtures of Carbon Dioxide with Methane, Ethane and Propane. *J. Chem. Eng. Data* **1990**, *35*, 314–317.

42. Katayama, T. The Interaction Second Virial Coefficients for Seven Binary Systems Containing Carbon Dioxide, Methane, Ethylene, Ethane and Propylene at 25 °C. *J. Chem. Eng. Jpn.* **1981**, *14*, 71–72.

43. Katayama, T. Interaction Second Virial Coefficients for Six Binary Systems Containing Carbon Dioxide, Methane, Ethylene and Propylene at 125 °C. *J. Chem. Eng. Jpn.* **1982**, *15*, 85–90.

11

A Test of Various Partial Atomic Charge Models for Computations on Diheteroaryl Ketones and Thioketones

Piotr Matczak

Academic Editor: Karlheinz Schwarz

Department of Theoretical and Structural Chemistry, Faculty of Chemistry, University of Łódź, Pomorska 163/165, Lodz 90-236, Poland; p.a.matczak@gmail.com

Abstract: The effective use of partial atomic charge models is essential for such purposes in molecular computations as a simplified representation of global charge distribution in a molecule and predicting its conformational behavior. In this work, ten of the most popular models of partial atomic charge are taken into consideration, and these models operate on the molecular wave functions/electron densities of five diheteroaryl ketones and their thiocarbonyl analogs. The ten models are tested in order to assess their usefulness in achieving the aforementioned purposes for the compounds in title. Therefore, the following criteria are used in the test: (1) how accurately these models reproduce the molecular dipole moments of the conformers of the investigated compounds; (2) whether these models are able to correctly determine the preferred conformer as well as the ordering of higher-energy conformers for each compound. The results of the test indicate that the Merz-Kollman-Singh (MKS) and Hu-Lu-Yang (HLY) models approximate the magnitude of the molecular dipole moments with the greatest accuracy. The natural partial atomic charges perform best in determining the conformational behavior of the investigated compounds. These findings may constitute important support for the effective computations of electrostatic effects occurring within and between the molecules of the compounds in question as well as similar compounds.

Keywords: computational chemistry; partial atomic charge; diheteroaryl ketone; diheteroaryl thioketone

---

1. Introduction

Partial atomic charges are useful descriptors for interpreting the results of quantum chemical calculations in a chemically intuitive fashion. It comes down to the description of the electron charge distribution within molecules through assigning a partial charge to each atom of the molecules. Because partial atomic charges are not physical observables and there is no strict quantum mechanical definition of them, many different models have been proposed to extract partial atomic charges from the molecular charge distribution. In principle, the models of partial atomic charges may be classified into three groups [1]. The first one covers models based on partitioning the molecular wave function into atomic contributions in terms of basis functions used to construct this wave function. The Mulliken population analysis [2] and the natural population analysis (NPA) [3,4] are typical examples of such models. The Mulliken population analysis is probably the best known of all models of partial atomic charge. Due to its simplicity, this model is computationally very attractive. However, its results tend to vary with the basis set employed and they are unrealistic in some cases [5]. These drawbacks partially arise from the fact that the Mulliken population analysis utilizes a nonorthogonal basis set. This problem is overcome by the NPA in which orthonormal natural atomic functions are constructed. The distributed multipole analysis of Gaussian wave functions (GDMA) [6] is also ranked among the models of the first group. In this analysis, the distribution of the molecular electron density is represented by multipoles located on the individual atoms of a molecule. The partitioning of the molecular electron density between the atoms is carried out in the basis-function space because the multipoles are obtained by using the products of Gaussian basis functions. The second group of partial atomic charge models comprises models that partition the molecular electron density into atomic domains in the physical space. These atomic domains are defined by means of Bader's atoms-in-molecules (AIM) topological analysis of the molecular electron density [7] or using the so-called "promolecular" density proposed originally by Hirshfeld [8]. To be more specific, the AIM division of a molecule into atoms is based on the zero-flux surfaces of the molecular electron density, and then this density is integrated over the resulting atomic domains to obtain their partial charges. In the Hirshfeld model the partial charge of each atom is calculated by assuming that the electron density at each point is shared between the surrounding atoms in direct proportion to their free-atom electron densities at the corresponding distances from the nuclei. The original partial atomic charges obtained from the Hirshfeld population analysis can be improved through parametrization to reproduce accurately a particular molecular property. For instance, the recently developed charge model 5 (CM5) utilizes a set of parameters derived by fitting to reference values of gas-phase dipole moments [9]. As for the models belonging to the third group, their partial atomic charges are based on the reproduction of the molecular electrostatic potential. Various schemes that fit partial atomic charges to the molecular electrostatic potential are reported, e.g., the Merz-Kollman-Singh (MKS) scheme [10,11], charges from electrostatic potentials (CHELP) [12], charges from electrostatic potentials using a grid (CHELPG) [13] and the Hu-Lu-Yang (HLY) scheme [14]. The MKS, CHELP and CHELPG schemes differ in the selection of points surrounding a molecule. Such points are used for the calculation of the molecular electrostatic potential in the fitting procedure. The MKS scheme employs points located at four shells at a distance of 1.4, 1.6, 1.8 and 2.0 times the van der Waals radii of the atoms constituting a molecule. The CHELP scheme samples the molecular electrostatic potential at points at a distance of 2.5, 3.5, 4.5, 5.5 and 6.5 Å from the van der Waals surface. In the CHELPG scheme the points are selected from a regularly spaced grid, between 0 and 2.8 Å from the van der Waals surface. The HLY scheme introduces the so-called object function in the entire molecular volume space instead of the points around the molecule. The application of the object function improves the numerical stability of fitting results.

Partial atomic charges find application in the molecular modeling of several chemically relevant areas, such as explaining structural and reactivity differences between various molecules and their conformers [15–17], investigating charge transfers within a single molecule and between several molecules [18–20], and predicting pK_a variations in series of molecules [21,22]. Since the definition of partial atomic charges is not strict, various models of partial atomic charges can, however, differ significantly in the reliability of their predictions. Therefore, an evaluation of the performance of a partial atomic charge model for a given problem is necessary before using it for making reliable predictions [23–28].

In this work, various models of partial atomic charge are tested to establish their efficiency for computations on diheteroaryl ketones and thioketones. A series of five diheteroaryl ketones and their thiocarbonyl analogs is considered. These ketones and thioketones are formed by the disubstitution of formaldehyde and thioformaldehyde with a five-membered heterocyclic group. The series includes di(furan-2-yl)methanone (**1a**), di(thiophen-2-yl)methanone (**2a**), di(selenophen-2-yl)methanone (**3a**), di(1H-pyrrol-2-yl)methanone (**4a**), di(1-methylpyrrol-2-yl)methanone (**5a**) and their thiocarbonyl analogs (**1b–5b**). The structural skeletal formulas of **1a–5a** and **1b–5b** are shown in Figure 1. The thioketones **1b–5b** have recently been synthesized by the O/S exchange in the corresponding ketones by treatment with Lawesson's reagent [29]. In the first stage of the present work, various models of partial atomic charge are tested in terms of their ability to reproduce the molecular dipole moments of **1a–5a** and **1b–5b**. Next, the efficiency of the models for predicting the conformational behavior of

1a–5a and 1b–5b is studied. The prediction of the conformational behavior will be restricted here to the determination of a preferred conformer and the sequence of higher-energy conformers.

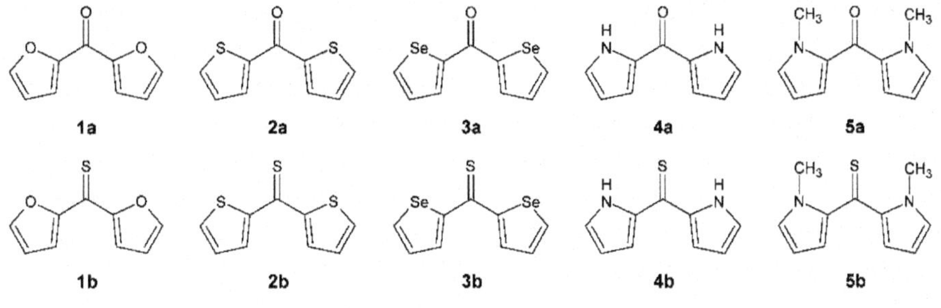

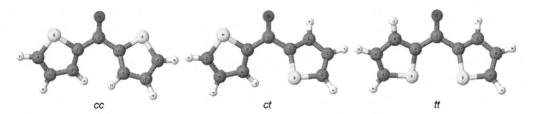

Figure 1. The structural skeletal formulas of 1a–5a and 1b–5b.

2. Computational Details

The molecular structures of **1a–5a** and **1b–5b** are taken from our previous works [30–32] in which Becke's three-parameter hybrid exchange functional combined with the correlation functional of Lee, Yang and Parr (B3LYP) [33–35] and the def2-QZVPP basis set [36] were used to optimize the geometries of the isolated molecules of **1a–5a** and **1b–5b**. It was also established there that for each of the compounds its three conformations could be formed by the rotation of heteroaryl substituents about the single C-C bonds linking these substituents with the C atom of carbonyl/thiocarbonyl group. The resulting conformers of **1a–5a** and **1b–5b** are denoted by the prefixes *cc*, *ct* and *tt*, indicating the spatial arrangement of ring heteroatoms with respect to the O/S atom of carbonyl/thiocarbonyl group (see Figure 2).

Figure 2. Three conformations of the investigated diheteroaryl ketones and thioketones. The B3LYP/def2-QZVPP-optimized conformers of **2a** are shown as an example.

For the *cc*-, *ct*- and *tt*-conformers of **1a–5a** and **1b–5b**, their molecular wave functions/electron densities are calculated at three levels of theory, that is, HF/def2-QZVPP [36–38], B3LYP/def2-QZVPP [33–36] and MP2/def2-QZVPP [36,39]. These molecular wave functions/electron densities are the starting point for deriving partial atomic charges from various models belonging to the three groups mentioned in the introduction. The partial atomic charges on all atoms of each conformer are determined by means of ten models, namely Mulliken, NPA, GDMA, AIM, Hirshfeld, CM5, MKS, CHELP, CHELPG and HLY. Then, the magnitude of the dipole moment μ of the conformer is approximated by the following formula:

$$\mu = \sqrt{\sum_{Q=x,y,z}\left(\sum_{k=1}^{N} q_k Q_k\right)^2} \tag{1}$$

where the index k runs over all atoms of the conformer having N atoms, Q denotes the Cartesian coordinates of the corresponding atom and q is the partial charge of the atom. In order to assess the accuracy of the dipole moments calculated using Equation (1), their values need to be compared with the corresponding reference results, preferably obtained from experimental measurements. However, such reference results are not available for individual gas-phase conformers of **1a–5a** and **1b–5b**. Therefore, the dipole moments calculated by the ten models of partial atomic charge are compared with the corresponding dipole moments obtained from the regular quantum chemical calculations involving the full molecular electron density (to be strict, these dipole moments are calculated as an expectation value of the appropriate quantum operator, which is well defined for the dipole moment).

The calculated partial atomic charges are also used for a rough estimation of the magnitude of electrostatic effects occurring in the conformers of **1a–5a** and **1b–5b**. On this basis, the conformational behavior of these compounds can be predicted. Interaction energies in the pairs of partial atomic charges ($E_C(i,j)$) are calculated using classical Coulomb's law. These interaction energies are summed up over all pairs of partial atomic charges within each conformer ($\Sigma_{i>j} E_C(i,j)$) to roughly estimate the energy E_{elst} associated with electrostatic effects occurring in the conformer. The conformers of each compound can be ordered with respect to their E_{elst} values. In the resulting sequence, the lower (that is, the more negative) the value of E_{elst} is obtained for a conformer, the more stable the conformer is. Such a procedure taking only E_{elst} into consideration assumes that the electrostatic effects play an important role in governing the conformational behavior of investigated compounds. These effects, indeed, contribute significantly to the ordering of conformers for diheteroaryl ketones and thioketones [30,32].

The GDMA 2.2.09 [6] and AIMAll 14.06.21 [40] programs have been used to calculate partial atomic charges derived from the GDMA and AIM models, respectively. All the remaining calculations have been carried out with the Gaussian 09 D.01 program [41]. In this program, the fitting of MKS, CHELP, CHELPG and HLY partial atomic charges to reproduce the molecular electrostatic potential has involved no additional constraint of reproducing the molecular dipole moment.

3. Results and Discussion

Since the molecular dipole moment is a primary quantity providing an essential insight into the distribution of electron charge within a molecule, a reasonable test for any model of partial atomic charge is to inspect the performance of the model in predicting such a quantity. Therefore, we start testing ten models of partial atomic charge by establishing their ability to reproduce the magnitude of the dipole moments for the conformers of **1a–5a** and **1b–5b**. Figure 3 shows the mean signed error (MSE) and root mean square error (RMSE) in the μ values approximated by the partial atomic charges derived from each model with respect to the reference results obtained from the full-density calculations. Additionally, the values of MSE and RMSE are determined for three levels of theory. When comparing here the approximated values of μ with the corresponding reference values, both the former and the latter are obtained from the molecular wave functions/electron densities generated at the same level of theory. The approximated and reference μ values used for the calculations of the MSE and RMSE presented in Figure 3 can be found in Tables S1–S6 in Supplementary Materials. The MSE provides information about systematic errors occurring in the approximated values of μ, whereas the RMSE allows us to rank the accuracy of individual models for reproducing the reference values of μ.

It is evident from what the lower plot in Figure 3 shows that the μ values obtained from the MKS and HLY partial atomic charges reproduce best the μ values calculated from the full density. Among the models that are not based on electrostatic potential fitting, the CM5 model offers the highest accuracy of the approximated μ values. The μ values approximated by the AIM model lead to the largest RMSE values. The accuracy of four models that are based on the molecular electrostatic potential is not very differentiated: the RMSE values of these models fall in the range from 0.03 D (for the HLY model) to 0.48 D (for the CHELP model). As indicated by the values of the MSE in the upper plot in Figure 3, the AIM and GDMA models overestimate the magnitude of μ significantly, whereas the Mulliken, Hirshfeld, CM5 and CHELP models tend to underestimate the values of μ. The differences in the MSE and RMSE values obtained from various levels of theory are usually relatively small, and thus all the above-mentioned findings are common to the HF, B3LYP and MP2 levels.

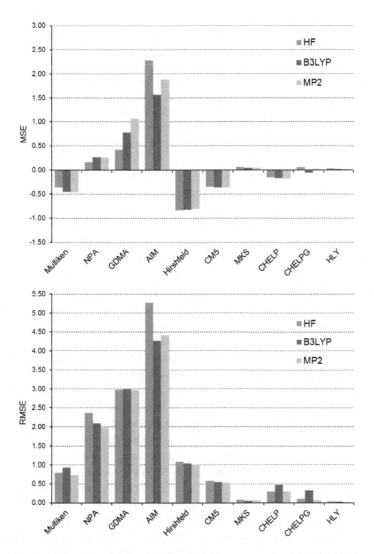

Figure 3. MSE and RMSE (in Debyes) in the μ values approximated by 10 models of partial atomic charge for 30 conformers of **1a–5a** and **1b–5b**. The errors are calculated relative to the reference results obtained from the full density at the HF/def2-QZVPP, B3LYP/def2-QZVPP and MP2/def2-QZVPP levels of theory.

Our findings should now be collated with previous observations on the performance of various models of partial atomic charge. It is known that the NPA partial atomic charges overestimate the dipole moments of polypeptides [42] and in the present work this observation is validated for smaller molecular systems (see the positive values of the MSE for the NPA model in Figure 3). The overestimation of the μ values predicted by the NPA model seems to be associated with the fact that this model generally overestimates the amplitude of the electrostatic potential, as it was reported for a large set of 500 simple organic molecules [43]. In another work taking a large set of simple molecules into account [9], it was found that the molecular dipole moment is usually underestimated when it is approximated by the Hirshfeld model. It is valid in our case, as evidenced by the negative MSE values of the Hirshfeld model in Figure 3. Both the MSE and RMSE values in Figure 3 indicate that the CM5 model outperforms the Hirshfeld one, which is also in accord with previous reports [9,44]. Furthermore, the CM5 model turns out to be slightly more accurate than the Mulliken one, and this observation is shared by the results of dipole moment calculations using the MG3S basis set [9]. It should, however, be stressed here that the CM5 model is essentially independent of a basis set [9], while the basis set dependence is the well-known weakness of the Mulliken model [1,4]. The poor performance of the AIM model results from its excessive partial atomic charges. The severe overestimation of dipole moment magnitude is typical of this model and it is observed even for the water molecule [45]. As noted in the previous paragraph, the MKS and HLY models provide excellent results for the μ values of the conformers of **1a–5a** and **1b–5b**. The CHELP and CHELPG models demonstrate larger RMSE values but both are still fairly successful in reproducing the μ values from the full density. This seems to be in line with what was previously reported for the MKS and CHELPG models [46]. The former turned out to be superior to the latter for the representation of dipole moments in ionic liquids. One of the reasons for the good performance of the MKS, CHELP, CHELPG and HLY models in reproducing μ for the conformers of **1a–5a** and **1b–5b** is that the molecular shape of these conformers is not very complex (the heteroaryl substituents are planar although they are most often not coplanar with one another) and almost all their atoms are near their molecular van der Waals surfaces. This practically eliminates the occurrence of the so-called "buried atoms" for which the electrostatic potential fitting is inaccurate, and thus, the resulting partial atomic charges are poorly determined [47].

Aside from the statistical comparison of the approximated μ values with the reference results from the full densities computed at the HF/def2-QZVPP, B3LYP/def2-QZVPP or MP2/def2-QZVPP level of theory, another comparison of the calculated μ values is meaningful. Such a comparison utilizes only a single set of reference μ values, irrespective of the level of theory which produces the molecular wave functions/electron densities for the models of partial atomic charge. This comparison allows us to directly examine whether the level of theory affects the performance of the ten models in predicting the values of μ. Because the range of the quantum chemical methods used in this work includes both the simplest *ab initio* method (that is, HF) and two more advanced methods (that is, B3LYP and MP2), the effect of electron correlation on the performance of the models can be studied. The B3LYP/def2-QZVPP level of theory is selected to provide the reference full-density values of μ for the conformers of **1a–5a** and **1b–5b**. Of three levels considered in this work, the μ values obtained from the B3LYP/def2-QZVPP full density turned out to be closest to experiment for a test set of simple molecules being the building blocks of **1a–5a** and **1b–5b** (see section S2 in Supplementary Materials). On this basis, the μ values calculated using the B3LYP/def2-QZVPP full density [32] are also assumed to be the most realistic for the conformers of **1a–5a** and **1b–5b**. These values are now used as the only reference results for the calculations of the MSE and RMSE in the μ values approximated by the ten models that, in turn, operate on the HF/def2-QZVPP, B3LYP/def2-QZVPP and MP2/def2-QZVPP wave functions/electron densities. The calculated MSE and RMSE values are presented graphically in Figure 4. For the B3LYP method, its results shown in this figure are obviously identical to those depicted in Figure 3.

Results shown in Figure 4 support our previous findings that such electrostatic potential-based models as MKS, CHELP, CHELPG and HLY are able to predict the values of μ with great accuracy. Out of these four models, it is hard to select a single model that performs best at all three levels of theory. For the molecular wave functions calculated by HF/def2-QZVPP, the CHELP model leads to the lowest RMSE value. For the molecular wave functions computed at the B3LYP/def2-QZVPP and MP2/def2-QZVPP levels, the most accurate values of μ are predicted by the HLY and MKS models, respectively. The positive values of the MSE yielded by the MKS, CHELP, CHELPG and HLY models operating on the HF/def2-QZVPP wave functions illustrate the systematic overestimation of the approximated μ values. This is in line with the previous finding made for the MKS model [47], and now it is additionally extended to the CHELP, CHELPG and HLY models. All four models consistently change their behavior while employing the MP2/def2-QZVPP wave functions (MSE < 0). Differences in the three RMSE values of each model are usually relatively small and in such cases they do not exceed 0.5 D. This indicates that, in general, the effect of the quantum chemical method applied for obtaining the molecular wave functions/electron densities is rather minor. However, at least one exception to this general conclusion can be seen in Figure 4. The AIM model combined with the HF/def2-QZVPP electron densities performs particularly badly when compared with its RMSE values obtained from both B3LYP/def2-QZVPP and MP2/def2-QZVPP electron densities. From this perspective, the AIM model seems to be particularly sensitive to the inclusion of electron correlation effects into the molecular electron density. On the other hand, it should be stressed that the performance of the AIM model still remains poor for the B3LYP/def2-QZVPP and MP2/def2-QZVPP electron densities.

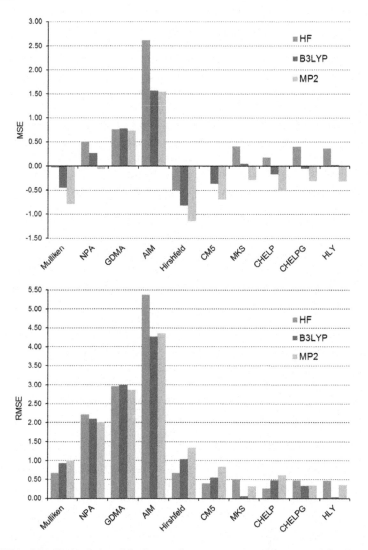

Figure 4. MSE and RMSE (in Debyes) in the μ values approximated by 10 models of partial atomic charge for 30 conformers of **1a–5a** and **1b–5b**. The errors are calculated relative to the reference results obtained from the full density at the B3LYP/def2-QZVPP level of theory.

A brief search of the literature reveals several previous mentions of the impact of electron correlation on partial atomic charges and resulting μ values. It was reported that this impact is small [48] or even minimal [46]. Our results are in agreement with these findings. The usual effect of electron correlation on the distribution of molecular electron density is to deplete electron density from the centers of bonds and increase it in shells around the atomic nuclei and at periphery of molecules [49]. However, the influence of such a depletion on molecular dipole moments is often smaller than might be expected because the charge reorganization happens around each atom and can result in only a small net change in polarization of whole molecules [48]. In the case of the AIM model, a significant insensitivity of its many parameters (also those obtained through the integration of electron density) to the addition of electron correlation and the change in basis set was observed [50,51]. On the other hand, it was detected for the water molecule that, within the framework of the AIM model, the electron density produced by the HF method leads to a slightly enhanced dipole moment compared to that obtained from the MP2 electron density [45]. This observation is in agreement with our results that, indeed, show an increase in the RMSE values for the AIM model while going from the correlation-corrected electron densities to the HF/def2-QZVPP densities.

The next stage of the present work is to establish the usability of various partial atomic charge models to predict qualitatively the conformational behavior of **1a–5a** and **1b–5b**. The E_{elst} energy calculated using the partial atomic charges determined for each conformer is considered here to be a simple measure of electrostatic effects stabilizing the conformer. It is convenient to express the E_{elst} values obtained for the conformers of each compound with respect to the E_{elst} energy of the conformer that is most favorable (in other words, with respect to the conformer possessing the lowest E_{elst} energy). The resulting relative electrostatic energy ΔE_{elst} is equal to zero for the preferred conformer while it is positive for less stable conformers. A part of the ΔE_{elst} values characterizing the cc-, ct-, and tt-conformers of **1a–5a** and **1b–5b** is given in Tables 1 and 2. The tabulated values have been calculated using selected models that have operated on the molecular wave functions/electron densities computed at the B3LYP/def2-QZVPP level of theory (a complete set of results obtained from all ten models of partial atomic charge, as well as at the HF/def2-QZVPP, B3LYP/def2-QZVPP and MP2/def2-QZVPP levels of theory can be found in Tables S8–S13 in Supplementary Materials). Additionally, the relative electron energies ΔE and full-density dipole moments μ obtained from the previous regular calculations at the B3LYP/def2-QZVPP level [30,32] are also presented in Tables 1 and 2. The values of ΔE allow us to establish the reference orderings of conformers for **1a–5a** and **1b–5b**.

Table 1. Relative electron energies (ΔE in kcal/mol), dipole moments obtained from the full density (μ in Debyes) and relative electrostatic energies (ΔE_{elst} in kcal/mol) for **1a–5a** in their three conformations. All the results are calculated at the B3LYP/def2-QZVPP level of theory.

Conformer	ΔE [a]	μ [b]	ΔE_{elst}					
			Mulliken	NPA	AIM	Hirshfeld	MKS	HLY
cc-**1a**	2.14	4.73	13.78	8.80	35.42	1.81	0.07	0.00
ct-**1a**	0.00	3.91	4.13	0.00	0.95	1.10	0.47	19.65
tt-**1a**	0.34	2.91	0.00	0.67	0.00	0.00	0.00	25.15
cc-**2a**	0.00	4.03	0.93	0.00	0.00	0.00	0.00	0.00
ct-**2a**	0.77	3.37	0.30	5.71	5.29	0.68	44.47	64.19
tt-**2a**	1.85	2.69	0.00	10.99	10.58	1.47	50.28	69.59
cc-**3a**	0.00	3.65	0.00	0.00	0.00	0.00	0.00	0.00
ct-**3a**	1.41	3.21	1.01	7.60	10.11	0.15	53.46	68.89
tt-**3a**	2.93	2.81	1.42	16.44	22.96	0.05	69.25	87.14
cc-**4a**	0.00	0.41	0.00	0.00	5.38	0.00	0.00	0.00
ct-**4a**	3.82	3.31	10.99	7.79	0.00	1.75	6.79	1.51
tt-**4a**	8.99	5.31	9.77	11.96	8.28	3.34	26.92	25.70
cc-**5a**	0.00	0.13	0.00	0.00	3.35	0.00	0.00	0.00
ct-**5a**	5.37	3.55	8.00	1.81	3.30	0.50	36.19	44.15
tt-**5a**	9.63	5.29	28.21	5.54	0.00	1.36	99.21	106.26

[a] Values taken from [30]; [b] Values taken from [32].

The tabulated values of ΔE_{elst} show that the energy of electrostatic interactions between partial atomic charges is able to give us some indication of the preferred conformations for the investigated compounds, especially for those whose preferred conformation is characterized by either the largest or the smallest values of μ. The most energetically stable conformers of **1a** and **1b** possess molecular dipole moments whose values lie in the middle between the values obtained for the other two conformers. In such case the E_{elst} energy usually turns out to be insufficient to identify the preferred conformation. Although the preference of the *ct*-conformation can be inferred from ΔE_{elst} calculated using the NPA and Mulliken partial atomic charges, none of the two sets of partial atomic charges leads to *ct*-conformation preference simultaneously for **1a** and **1b**. Nevertheless, the NPA model is recognized to be most successful in predicting the preferred conformers of **1a–5a** and **1b–5b** in terms of E_{elst}. The Mulliken, AIM and Hirshfeld models lead to a slightly greater number of incorrect indications of preferred conformers than the NPA model does. Furthermore, this model always performs best, irrespective of the level of theory used to generate the molecular wave functions. The electrostatic potential-based models are generally less accurate in identifying the preferred conformers of **1a–5a** and **1b–5b** than the models belonging to the two remaining classes. Of the electrostatic potential-based models, only MKS and HLY are able to correctly indicate the preferred conformers for more than half of the investigated compounds.

Table 2. Relative electron energies (ΔE in kcal/mol), dipole moments obtained from the full density (μ in Debyes) and relative electrostatic energies (ΔE_{elst} in kcal/mol) for **1b–5b** in their three conformations. All the results are calculated at the B3LYP/def2-QZVPP level of theory.

Conformer	ΔE [a]	μ [b]	ΔE_{elst}					
			Mulliken	NPA	AIM	Hirshfeld	MKS	HLY
cc-**1b**	1.46	4.69	7.79	0.00	0.00	0.80	51.02	42.63
ct-**1b**	0.00	4.09	0.00	1.35	2.22	0.62	10.35	11.94
tt-**1b**	0.31	3.35	0.75	10.90	36.07	0.00	0.00	0.00
cc-**2b**	0.00	4.13	0.00	0.00	0.00	0.00	0.00	0.00
ct-**2b**	0.99	3.62	1.02	2.84	2.09	0.48	37.25	49.47
tt-**2b**	2.22	3.08	1.23	6.27	4.48	1.15	35.82	51.96
cc-**3b**	0.00	3.80	0.00	0.00	0.00	0.25	0.00	0.00
ct-**3b**	1.44	3.46	2.09	3.29	1.51	0.27	56.32	57.83
tt-**3b**	3.00	3.17	3.05	8.54	5.66	0.00	65.31	67.72
cc-**4b**	0.00	1.54	0.64	0.00	0.00	0.00	27.94	31.98
ct-**4b**	3.92	3.96	5.86	1.59	11.12	1.22	37.82	41.82
tt-**4b**	9.41	5.66	0.00	0.01	38.50	1.95	0.00	0.00
cc-**5b**	0.00	1.23	0.00	0.00	0.00	0.00	180.49	180.68
ct-**5b**	3.05	4.44	10.21	2.66	0.01	0.91	117.01	113.67
tt-**5b**	5.04	5.62	17.64	2.61	7.42	1.60	0.00	0.00

[a] Values taken from [30]; [b] Values taken from [32].

Aside from the application of E_{elst} to the identification of the most stable conformation, this quantity allows us to order conformers relative to their E_{elst} values and the resulting orderings of conformers for **1a–5a** and **1b–5b** can be compared with the orderings based on ΔE. The evident relationship between μ and ΔE for **2a–5a** and their thiocarbonyl counterparts suggests that electrostatic effects are responsible to a certain extent for the ordering of individual conformers relative to their energetic stability. We focus here only on the successful reproduction of conformer orderings and not on the quantitative correlation between individual non-zero ΔE_{elst} and ΔE values. The values of ΔE_{elst} should not be compared directly with ΔE because the former are merely a crude approximation of intramolecular electrostatic effects. The electrostatic effects are undoubtedly important but not the sole factor affecting the stability of the investigated conformers. Therefore, the values of ΔE_{elst} are usually far from the corresponding ΔE values. The values of ΔE_{elst} obviously inherit the deficiencies of the applied model of partial atomic charge. The ΔE_{elst} values calculated using the AIM partial atomic charges are usually large for **1a–3a** and **1b–3b**, whereas the Hirshfeld partial atomic charges lead to very small ΔE_{elst} values for the majority of the investigated compounds. This is due to the fact that AIM partial atomic charges generally tend to adopt large absolute values [23], while the Hirshfeld model assigns partial atomic charges that are very small in magnitude [52].

Turning our attention to the predicted conformer orderings, we can see that none of the considered models of partial atomic charge provides the correct orderings of conformers for all ten compounds. Among the ten models, the NPA one appears to be most suitable for illustrating tendencies in electrostatic effects (in terms of E_{elst}) in the investigated compounds, although some inconsistencies with the orderings predicted by ΔE are found. The inconsistencies in the conformer orderings yielded by the NPA model occur mostly for diheteroaryl thioketones. The AIM and Hirshfeld models give less satisfactory results than those of the NPA model. On the other hand, they reproduce the reference orderings of conformers for a greater number of the investigated compounds than the HLY model does. Of the electrostatic potential-based models, HLY produces the conformer orderings that fit best to the corresponding reference orderings indicated by ΔE. All the aforementioned findings are common to the three levels of theory used to generate the wave functions/electron densities of the conformers. This is additionally supported by the results presented in Table 3. This table shows the percentage similarity of the conformer sequences deduced from ΔE_{elst} to the reference conformer orderings determined in terms of ΔE. The percentage similarity has been obtained through comparing the conformer orderings of all investigated compounds.

Table 3. Percentage similarity of the conformer sequences predicted by ΔE_{elst} to the reference sequences determined using ΔE. The values of ΔE_{elst} are calculated by 10 partial atomic charge models operating on the wave functions/electron densities calculated at three levels of theory.

Model	Level of Theory		
	HF	B3LYP	MP2
Mulliken	50	70	50
NPA	83	73	83
GDMA	57	53	57
AIM	67	70	80
Hirshfeld	73	70	70
CM5	37	43	47
MKS	60	60	50
CHELP	23	33	20
CHELPG	57	43	53
HLY	60	67	63

4. Conclusions

In this work, ten of the most popular models of partial atomic charge have been considered, and these models have operated on the molecular wave functions/electron densities of the conformers of **1a–5a** and **1b–5b**. These wave functions/electron densities have been calculated at three different levels of theory. The ten models were tested in order to assess their usefulness in performing effective computations on diheteroaryl ketones and thioketones. More specifically, our test assesses the models' abilities (1) to approximate the magnitude of μ for the conformers of **1a–5a** and **1b–5b**, and (2) to correctly determine the conformers' orderings through the estimation of the electrostatic interaction between partial atomic charges within the conformers.

The results of the test indicate that the simplified representation of the magnitude of μ by partial atomic charges is most effective when the MKS and HLY models are used to produce the partial atomic charges within the conformers of **1a–5a** and **1b–5b**. These models are able to reproduce very accurately the reference μ values obtained from the full density, and they perform well for the molecular wave functions calculated at all three levels of theory. Among the models that are not based directly on the molecular electrostatic potential, the CM5 model offers a reasonable accuracy in approximating the values of μ. From the subsequent results of our test it can be concluded that the most successful estimation of the intramolecular electrostatic effects governing the conformational behavior of **1a–5a** and **1b–5b** is provided by the partial atomic charges derived from the NPA model. Besides the designation of the most successful model for the determination of the conformational behavior, this part of the test also shows that the simple approach utilizing the calculation of E_{elst} by means of NPA partial atomic charges is a surprisingly effective yet still qualitative tool to anticipate the energetic orderings of the conformers of **1a–5a** and **1b–5b**. It also implies an important role of intramolecular electrostatic effects in determining the conformational behavior of the investigated compounds.

The above-mentioned results of our test may be essential for establishing the effective approximations of molecular dipole moments and intramolecular electrostatic effects for future computations on the molecules of not only the compounds in question but also similar compounds. Furthermore, these results may have implications for the tuning of force fields used in the classical molecular dynamics simulations of diheteroaryl ketones and thioketones. The accurate reproduction of molecular dipole moments by partial atomic charges is an important factor contributing to the reliable determination of intermolecular interactions in such simulations.

Acknowledgments: This work was partially supported by PL-Grid Infrastructure.

Conflicts of Interest: The author declares no conflict of interest.

References

1. Jensen, F. *Introduction to Computational Chemistry*, 2nd ed.; John Wiley & Sons, Inc.: Chichester, UK, 2007.
2. Mulliken, R.S. Electronic population analysis on LCAO-MO molecular wave functions. *J. Chem. Phys.* **1955**, *23*, 1833–1840. [CrossRef]
3. Reed, A.E.; Curtiss, L.A.; Weinhold, F. Intermolecular interactions from a natural bond orbital, donor-acceptor viewpoint. *Chem. Rev.* **1988**, *88*, 899–926. [CrossRef]
4. Reed, A.E.; Weinstock, R.B.; Weinhold, F. Natural population analysis. *J. Chem. Phys.* **1985**, *83*, 735–746. [CrossRef]
5. Thompson, J.D.; Xidos, J.D.; Sonbuchner, T.M.; Cramer, C.J.; Truhlar, D.G. More reliable partial atomic charges when using diffuse basis sets. *PhysChemComm* **2002**, *5*, 117–134. [CrossRef]
6. Stone, A.J. Distributed multipole analysis: Stability for large basis sets. *J. Chem. Theory Comput.* **2005**, *1*, 1128–1132. [CrossRef] [PubMed]
7. Bader, R.F.W. *Atoms in Molecules: A Quantum Theory*; Clarendon: Oxford, UK, 1990.
8. Hirshfeld, F.L. Bonded-atom fragments for describing molecular charge densities. *Theor. Chem. Acta* **1977**, *44*, 129–138. [CrossRef]
9. Marenich, A.V.; Jerome, S.V.; Cramer, C.J.; Truhlar, D.G. Charge model 5: An extension of Hirshfeld population analysis for the accurate description of molecular interactions in gaseous and condensed phases. *J. Chem. Theory Comput.* **2012**, *8*, 527–541. [CrossRef] [PubMed]
10. Singh, U.C.; Kollman, P.A. An approach to computing electrostatic charges for molecules. *J. Comput. Chem.* **1984**, *5*, 129–145. [CrossRef]
11. Besler, B.H.; Merz, K.M., Jr.; Kollman, P.A. Atomic charges derived from semiempirical methods. *J. Comput. Chem.* **1990**, *11*, 431–439. [CrossRef]
12. Chirlian, L.E.; Francl, M.M. Atomic charges derived from electrostatic potentials—A detailed study. *J. Comput. Chem.* **1987**, *8*, 894–905. [CrossRef]
13. Breneman, C.M.; Wiberg, K.B. Determining atom-centered monopoles from molecular electrostatic potentials—The need for high sampling density in formamide conformational analysis. *J. Comput. Chem.* **1990**, *11*, 361–373. [CrossRef]
14. Hu, H.; Lu, Z.; Yang, W. Fitting molecular electrostatic potentials from quantum mechanical calculations. *J. Chem. Theory Comput.* **2007**, *3*, 1004–1013. [CrossRef] [PubMed]
15. Rostkowski, M.; Paneth, P. Charge localization in monothiophosphate monoanions. *Pol. J. Chem.* **2007**, *81*, 711–720.
16. Balasubramanian, G.; Schulte, J.; Müller-Plathe, F.; Böhm, M.C. Structural and thermochemical properties of a photoresponsive spiropyran and merocyanine pair: Basis set and solvent dependence in density functional predictions. *Chem. Phys. Lett.* **2012**, *554*, 60–66. [CrossRef]

17. Cvijetic, I.N.; Vitorovic-Todorovic, M.D.; Juranic, I.O.; Nakarada, D.J.; Milosavljevic, M.D.; Drakulic, B.J. Reactivity of (*E*)-4-aryl-4-oxo-2-butenoic acid phenylamides with piperidine and benzylamine: Kinetic and theoretical study. *Monatsh. Chem.* **2014**, *145*, 1297–1306. [CrossRef]

18. Domagała, M.; Matczak, P.; Palusiak, M. Halogen bond, hydrogen bond and N···C interaction—On interrelation among these three noncovalent interactions. *Comput. Theor. Chem.* **2012**, *998*, 26–33. [CrossRef]

19. Domagała, M.; Palusiak, M. The influence of substituent effect on noncovalent interactions in ternary complexes stabilized by hydrogen-bonding and halogen-bonding. *Comput. Theor. Chem.* **2014**, *1027*, 173–178. [CrossRef]

20. Guidara, S.; Feki, H.; Abid, Y. Structural, vibrational, NLO, MEP, NBO analysis and DFT calculation of bis 2,5-dimethylanilinium sulfate. *J. Mol. Struct.* **2015**, *1080*, 176–187. [CrossRef]

21. Varekova, R.S.; Geidl, S.; Ionescu, C.-M.; Skrehota, O.; Bouchal, T.; Sehnal, D.; Abagyan, R.; Koca, J. Predicting pK_a values from EEM atomic charges. *J. Cheminform.* **2013**, *5*, 18. [CrossRef] [PubMed]

22. Ugur, I.; Marion, A.; Parant, S.P.; Jensen, J.H.; Monard, G. Rationalization of the pK_a values of alcohols and thiols using atomic charge descriptors and its application to the prediction of amino acid pK_a's. *J. Chem. Inf. Model.* **2014**, *54*, 2200–2213. [CrossRef] [PubMed]

23. Gross, K.C.; Seybold, P.G.; Hadad, C.M. Comparison of different atomic charge schemes for predicting pK_a variations in substituted anilines and phenols. *Int. J. Quantum Chem.* **2002**, *90*, 445–458. [CrossRef]

24. Choi, Y.; Kim, H.; Cho, K.W.; Paik, S.R.; Kim, H.-W.; Jeong, K.; Jung, S. Systematic probing of an atomic charge set of sialic acid disaccharides for the rational molecular modeling of avian influenza virus based on molecular dynamics simulations. *Carbohydr. Res.* **2009**, *344*, 541–544. [CrossRef] [PubMed]

25. Jacquemin, D.; le Bahers, T.; Adamo, C.; Ciofini, I. What is the "best" atomic charge model to describe through-space charge-transfer excitations? *Phys. Chem. Chem. Phys.* **2012**, *14*, 5383–5388. [CrossRef] [PubMed]

26. Jambeck, J.P.M.; Mocci, F.; Lyubartsev, A.P.; Laaksonen, A. Partial atomic charges and their impact on the free energy of solvation. *J. Comput. Chem.* **2013**, *34*, 187–197. [CrossRef] [PubMed]

27. Wang, B.; Li, S.L.; Truhlar, D.G. Modeling the partial atomic charges in inorganometallic molecules and solids and charge redistribution in lithium-ion cathodes. *J. Chem. Theory Comput.* **2014**, *10*, 5640–5650. [CrossRef] [PubMed]

28. Hamad, S.; Balestra, S.R.G.; Bueno-Perez, R.; Calero, S.; Ruiz-Salvador, A.R. Atomic charges for modeling metal–organic frameworks: Why and how. *J. Solid State Chem.* **2015**, *223*, 144–151. [CrossRef]

29. Mlostoń, G.; Urbaniak, K.; Gębicki, K.; Grzelak, P.; Heimgartner, H. Hetaryl thioketones: Synthesis and selected reactions. *Heteroat. Chem.* **2014**, *25*, 548–555. [CrossRef]

30. Matczak, P.; Domagała, M.; Domagała, S. Conformers of diheteroaryl ketones and thioketones: A quantum chemical study of their properties and fundamental intramolecular energetic effects. *Struct. Chem.* **2015**. [CrossRef]

31. Matczak, P. Intramolecular C–H···H–C contacts in diheteroaryl ketones and thioketones: A theoretical analysis. *Bull. Chem. Soc. Jpn.* **2015**. [CrossRef]

32. Matczak, P.; Domagała, M. Charge distribution in conformers of diheteroaryl ketones and thioketones. Submitted.

33. Becke, A.D. Density-functional thermochemistry. III. The role of exact exchange. *J. Chem. Phys.* **1993**, *98*, 5648–5642. [CrossRef]

34. Vosko, S.H.; Wilk, L.; Nusair, M. Accurate spin-dependent electron liquid correlation energies for local spin density calculations: A critical analysis. *Can. J. Phys.* **1980**, *58*, 1200–1211. [CrossRef]

35. Lee, C.; Yang, W.; Parr, R.G. Development of the Colle-Salvetti correlation-energy formula into a functional of the electron density. *Phys. Rev. B* **1988**, *37*, 785–789. [CrossRef]

36. Weigend, F.; Ahlrichs, R. Balanced basis sets of split valence, triple zeta valence and quadruple zeta valence quality for H to Rn: Design and assessment of accuracy. *Phys. Chem. Chem. Phys.* **2005**, *7*, 3297–3305. [CrossRef] [PubMed]

37. Hartree, D.R. The wave mechanics of an atom with a non-Coulomb central field. Part I: Theory and methods. *Proc. Camb. Philos. Soc.* **1928**, *24*, 89–110. [CrossRef]

38. Fock, V. Näherungsmethode zur lösung des quantenmechanischen mehrkörperproblems. *Z. Phys.* **1930**, *61*, 126–148. (In German) [CrossRef]

39. Møller, C.; Plesset, M.S. Note on an approximation treatment for many-electron systems. *Phys. Rev.* **1934**, *46*, 618–622. [CrossRef]

40. Keith, T.A. *AIMAll (Version 14.06.21)*; TK Gristmill Software: Overland Park, KS, USA, 2014.

41. Frisch, M.J.; Trucks, G.W.; Schlegel, H.B.; Scuseria, G.E.; Robb, M.A.; Cheeseman, J.R.; Scalmani, G.; Barone, V.; Mennucci, B.; Petersson, G.A.; *et al. Gaussian 09 D.01*; Gaussian, Inc.: Wallingford, CT, USA, 2013.

42. Verstraelen, T.; Pauwels, E.; de Proft, F.; van Speybroeck, V.; Geerlings, P.; Waroquier, M. Assessment of atomic charge models for gas-phase computations on polypeptides. *J. Chem. Theory Comput.* **2012**, *8*, 661–676. [CrossRef] [PubMed]

43. Verstraelen, T.; van Speybroeck, V.; Waroquier, M. The electronegativity equalization method and the split charge equilibration applied to organic systems: Parametrization, validation, and comparison. *J. Chem. Phys.* **2009**, *131*, 044127. [CrossRef] [PubMed]

44. Seidler, T.; Champagne, B. Which charge definition for describing the crystal polarizing field and the $\chi^{(1)}$ and $\chi^{(2)}$ of organic crystals? *Phys. Chem. Chem. Phys.* **2015**, *17*, 19546–19556. [CrossRef] [PubMed]

45. Martin, F.; Zipse, H. Charge distribution in the water molecule—A comparison of methods. *J. Comput. Chem.* **2005**, *26*, 97–105. [CrossRef] [PubMed]

46. Rigby, J.; Izgorodina, E.I. Assessment of atomic partial charge schemes for polarisation and charge transfer effects in ionic liquids. *Phys. Chem. Chem. Phys.* **2013**, *15*, 1632–1646. [CrossRef] [PubMed]

47. Bayly, C.I.; Cieplak, P.; Cornell, W.D.; Kollman, P.A. A well-behaved electrostatic potential based method using charge restraints for deriving atomic charges: The RESP model. *J. Phys. Chem.* **1993**, *97*, 10269–10280. [CrossRef]

48. Wiberg, K.B.; Hadad, C.M.; LePage, T.J.; Breneman, C.M.; Frisch, M.J. Analysis of the effect of electron correlation on charge density distributions. *J. Phys. Chem.* **1992**, *96*, 671–679. [CrossRef]

49. Stephens, M.E.; Becker, P.J. Virial partitioning analysis of electron correlation and nuclear motion in diatomic molecules. *Mol. Phys.* **1983**, *49*, 65–89. [CrossRef]

50. Jabłoński, M.; Palusiak, M. Basis set and method dependence in atoms in molecules calculations. *J. Phys. Chem. A* **2010**, *114*, 2240–2244. [CrossRef] [PubMed]

51. Jabłoński, M.; Palusiak, M. Basis set and method dependence in quantum theory of atoms in molecules calculations for covalent bonds. *J. Phys. Chem. A* **2010**, *114*, 12498–12505. [CrossRef] [PubMed]

52. Davidson, E.R.; Chakravorty, S. A test of the Hirshfeld definition of atomic charges and moments. *Theor. Chim. Acta* **1992**, *83*, 319–330. [CrossRef]

12

Direct Numerical Simulation of Turbulent Channel Flow on High-Performance GPU Computing System

Giancarlo Alfonsi *, **Stefania A. Ciliberti** [†,‡], **Marco Mancini** [†,‡] **and Leonardo Primavera** [‡]

Fluid Dynamics Laboratory, Università della Calabria, Via P. Bucci 42b, 87036 Rende (Cosenza), Italy; stefania.ciliberti@cmcc.it (S.A.C.); marco.mancini@cmcc.it (M.M.); lprimavera@fis.unical.it (L.P.)
* Correspondence: giancarlo.alfonsi@unical.it
† Current address: Euro-Mediterranean Centre on Climate Change, Via A. Imperatore 16, 73100 Lecce, Italy.
‡ These authors contributed equally to the work.

Academic Editors: Markus Kraft and Ali Cemal Benim

Abstract: The flow of a viscous fluid in a plane channel is simulated numerically following the DNS approach, and using a computational code for the numerical integration of the Navier-Stokes equations implemented on a hybrid CPU/GPU computing architecture (for the meaning of symbols and acronyms used, one can refer to the Nomenclature). Three turbulent-flow databases, each representing the turbulent statistically-steady state of the flow at three different values of the Reynolds number, are built up, and a number of statistical moments of the fluctuating velocity field are computed. For turbulent-flow-structure investigation, the vortex-detection technique of the imaginary part of the complex eigenvalue pair in the velocity-gradient tensor is applied to the fluctuating-velocity fields. As a result, and among other types, hairpin vortical structures are unveiled. The processes of evolution that characterize the hairpin vortices in the near-wall region of the turbulent channel are investigated, in particular at one of the three Reynolds numbers tested, with specific attention given to the relationship that exists between the dynamics of the vortical structures and the occurrence of ejection and sweep quadrant events. Interestingly, it is found that the latter events play a preminent role in the way in which the morphological evolution of a hairpin vortex develops over time, as related in particular to the establishment of symmetric and persistent hairpins. The present results have been obtained from a database that incorporates genuine DNS solutions of the Navier-Stokes equations, without superposition of any synthetic structures in the form of initial and/or boundary conditions for the simulations.

Keywords: Navier-Stokes equations; DNS; turbulent channel flow; swirling-strength criterion for vortex detection; hairpin vortices; quadrant events

1. Introduction

The flow of a viscous fluid in a channel has been investigated numerically by several authors in the recent past, becoming a reference case for the study of wall turbulence with DNS.

Accurate DNS calculations of the turbulent channel flow have been carried out by Kim et al. [1], Lyons et al. [2], Antonia et al. [3], Kasagi et al. [4], Rutledge and Sleicher [5], Moser et al. [6], Abe et al. [7], Iwamoto et al. [8], Del Alamo and Jiménez [9], Del Alamo et al. [10], Tanahashi et al. [11], Iwamoto et al. [12], Hoyas and Jiménez [13], Hu et al. [14], Alfonsi and Primavera [15], Lozano-Durán et al. [16], Lozano-Durán and Jiménez [17], Vreman and Kuerten [18,19], Bernardini et al. [20], and Lee and Moser [21], at different values of the Reynolds number (see also at Table 1).

The aim of these simulations is mainly that of calculating a given number of time steps of the statistically-steady turbulent flow in the channel, to build up DNS databases, and extracting from the latter useful information for a better comprehension of the wall-turbulence phenomena.

Overall, in the above-mentioned works, the Navier-Stokes equations system is mainly solved within a fractional-step-method framework, in conjunction with Runge-Kutta algorithms for time marching. In particular, in the milestone work of Kim et al. [1], and in Lyons et al. [2], Antonia et al. [3], Kasagi et al. [4], Rutledge and Sleicher [5], Moser et al. [6], Iwamoto et al. [8], Del Alamo and Jiménez [9], Del Alamo et al. [10], Iwamoto et al. [12], Hu et al. [14], Lozano-Durán et al. [16], Lozano-Durán and Jiménez [17], Vreman and Kuerten [18,19], and Lee and Moser [21], the unsteady three-dimensional Navier-Stokes equations are integrated in space by using either the fully spectral Fourier-Chebychev numerical technique originally introduced by Kim and Moin [22], minor variants of the latter, or fully spectral techniques introduced by other authors. In Abe et al. [7] and Bernardini et al. [20], the flow governing equations is integrated by means of a finite-difference algorithm in which a grid-stretching law is inserted orthogonally to the walls. In Tanahashi et al. [11] and Hoyas and Jiménez [13], mixed spectral-high-order finite difference numerical schemes are used. In Alfonsi and Primavera [15], the Navier-Stokes equations in conservative form are integrated by means of the mixed Fourier-finite difference method originally introduced by Alfonsi et al. [23], where a grid-stretching law of hyperbolic-tangent type is inserted along y (the direction orthogonal to the solid walls).

Table 1. Outline of turbulent-channel-flow DNSs.

Author(s)	Year	Numerical Technique
Kim et al. [1]	1987	Spectral
Lyons et al. [2]	1991	Spectral
Antonia et al. [3]	1992	Spectral
Kasagi et al. [4]	1992	Spectral
Rutledge and Sleicher [5]	1993	Spectral
Moser et al. [6]	1999	Spectral
Abe et al. [7]	2001	Finite Difference
Iwamoto et al. [8]	2002	Spectral
Del Alamo and Jiménez [9]	2003	Spectral
Del Alamo et al. [10]	2004	Spectral
Tanahashi et al. [11]	2004	Spectral-Finite Difference
Iwamoto et al. [12]	2005	Spectral
Hoyas and Jiménez [13]	2006	Spectral-Finite Difference
Hu et al. [14]	2006	Spectral
Alfonsi and Primavera [15]	2007	Spectral-Finite Difference
Lozano-Durán et al. [16]	2012	Spectral
Lozano-Durán and Jiménez [17]	2014	Spectral
Vreman and Kuerten [18]	2014	Spectral
Vreman and Kuerten [19]	2014	Spectral
Bernardini et al. [20]	2014	Finite Difference
Lee and Moser [21]	2015	Spectral

As for velocity boundary conditions, periodic conditions are generally imposed along the streamwise (x) and spanwise (z) directions, in conjunction with no-slip (and impermeability) conditions at the walls, while Neumann conditions are enforced for the pressure. In Table 1, an outline of the above-mentioned works is reported.

In the aforementioned channel-flow simulations, interesting results have been obtained, as related in particular to the evolution of the fluctuating-velocity statistical moments with the Reynolds number (see also Alfonsi [24], Marusic et al. [25], Smits et al. [26], Kim [27], Jiménez [28]).

Though, there are several aspects of the channel-flow case that can be further investigated, in particular related to the processes of development of the wall-turbulence flow structures (see also Alfonsi and Primavera [29]).

In the present work, three DNS channel-flow database have been calculated, respectively, at friction-velocity Reynolds numbers $Re_\tau = 200, 400$ and 600 (one can see at the Nomenclature for the meaning of symbols and acronyms used). Statistical moments of the fluctuating-velocity field have been computed and compared with results obtained by other authors, obtaining a rather good agreement with the latter. The vortex-detection technique of the imaginary part of the complex eigenvalue pair of the velocity-gradient tensor (the λ_{ci} or swirling-strength criterion) as introduced by Zhou et al. [30] has been applied to the computed fluctuating-velocity fields. As a result, and among other shapes, hairpin-like vortical structures are unveiled. The processes of evolution that characterize the hairpin vortices are investigated giving particular attention to the relationship that exists between vortex dynamics and the occurrence of Q2 and/or Q4 quadrant events. Interestingly, it is found that the physical condition for the development of a complete and stable hairpin is twofold, namely:

(i) the development of ejections distributed on spheric-like isosurfaces behind an initial Ω-shaped vortex filament;

(ii) the subsequent development of sweeps distributed on elongated isosurfaces adjacent to the external sides of hairpins' heads and necks.

The present work is organized as follows. Section 2 contains an outline of the numerical technique used for the solution of the Navier-Stokes equations in the plane-channel-flow computing domain, in Section 3 a concise presentation is given of the vortex-detection method used for flow-structure extraction, and in Section 4, the numerical simulations are described. In Section 5, the results are presented and compared with data obtained by other authors, mainly in terms of turbulence statistics, while in Section 6, the results of the simulations are presented in terms of vortical structures and quadrant events. Concluding remarks are given at the end.

2. Numerical Techniques

The three-dimensional time-dependent Navier-Stokes equations for incompressible fluids are considered in non-dimensional, conservative form (Einstein summation convention applies to repeated indices, $i, j = 1, 2, 3$):

$$\frac{\partial u_i}{\partial t} + \frac{\partial}{\partial x_j}\left(u_i u_j\right) = -\frac{\partial p}{\partial x_i} + \frac{1}{Re_\tau}\frac{\partial^2 u_i}{\partial x_j \partial x_j} \tag{1}$$

$$\frac{\partial u_i}{\partial x_i} = 0 \tag{2}$$

Variables and operators are nondimensionalized by the channel half-height (h) for lengths, the wall-shear velocity (u_τ) for velocities, the group (ρu_τ^2) for pressure, and (h/u_τ) for time, being $Re_\tau = u_\tau h/\nu$ the friction-velocity Reynolds number (ρ is fluid density, ν is fluid kinematic viscosity. Note that, for simplicity, the symbols of both dependent and independent variables have not been altered in switching from the dimensional to the dimensionless formalism). The computing domain (Figure 1) is considered homogeneous along the x (streamwise) and z (spanwise) directions, so that Equations (1) and (2) are Fourier-transformed accordingly:

$$\frac{\partial \hat{u}}{\partial t} + ik_x\left(\hat{u^2}\right) + \frac{\partial\left(\hat{uv}\right)}{\partial y} + ik_z\left(\hat{uw}\right) + ik_x\hat{p} = \frac{1}{Re_\tau}\left(\frac{\partial^2 \hat{u}}{\partial y^2} - k^2\hat{u}\right) \tag{3a}$$

$$\frac{\partial \hat{v}}{\partial t} + ik_x\left(\hat{vu}\right) + \frac{\partial\left(\hat{v^2}\right)}{\partial y} + ik_z\left(\hat{vw}\right) + \frac{\partial\hat{p}}{\partial y} = \frac{1}{Re_\tau}\left(\frac{\partial^2 \hat{v}}{\partial y^2} - k^2\hat{v}\right) \tag{3b}$$

$$\frac{\partial \hat{w}}{\partial t} + ik_x\left(\hat{wu}\right) + \frac{\partial\left(\hat{wv}\right)}{\partial y} + ik_z\left(\hat{w^2}\right) + ik_z\hat{p} = \frac{1}{Re_\tau}\left(\frac{\partial^2 \hat{w}}{\partial y^2} - k^2\hat{w}\right) \tag{3c}$$

$$ik_x\hat{u} + \frac{\partial \hat{v}}{\partial y} + ik_z\hat{w} = 0 \tag{4}$$

where the superscript (ˆ) indicates variables in Fourier space, and $k^2 = k_x^2 + k_z^2$. The nonlinear terms in the momentum Equations (3a–c) are evaluated pseudospectrally by anti-transforming the velocities in physical space to perform the products (FFTs are used). Here, in order to avoid errors in transforming the results back to Fourier space, the discrete Fourier transforms are applied on "$3n/2$" points along each homogeneous direction.

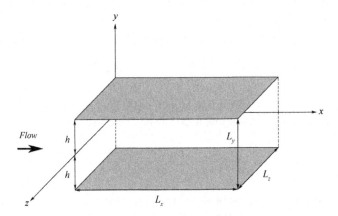

Figure 1. Computing-domain scheme.

Due to the presence of the steepest variable-gradients near the walls, and in order to obtain a suitable spatial resolution in the calculations, a grid-stretching law of hyperbolic tangent type is used for the grid points along y (the direction orthogonal to the walls):

$$y_{str} = PPy + (1 - PP)\left(1 - \frac{tanh\left[QQ\left(1 - y\right)\right]}{tanh\left[QQ\right]}\right) \tag{5}$$

where y indicates the uniform grid and PP, QQ are two parameters characterising the distribution. The partial derivatives along y are calculated according to grid-point distribution Equation (5) using second-order centered finite-difference expressions. For time advancement, the third-order Runge-Kutta procedure originally introduced by Le and Moin [31] is implemented. For each Fourier mode one has:

$$\frac{\hat{u}_i^{(l)} - \hat{u}_i^{(l-1)}}{\Delta t} = \alpha_l D\left(\hat{u}_i^{(l-2)}\right) + \beta_l D\left(\hat{u}_i^{(l-1)}\right) - \gamma_l C\left(\hat{u}_i^{(l-1)}\right) - \zeta_l C\left(\hat{u}_i^{(l-2)}\right) - (\alpha_l + \beta_l)\frac{\partial \hat{p}^{(l)}}{\partial x_i} \tag{6}$$

where $l = 1,2,3$ denote the Runge-Kutta sub-steps, and where:

$$C\left(\hat{u}_i\right) = \frac{\partial}{\partial x_j}\left(u_i u_j\right) = ik_x\left(\widehat{u_i u}\right) + \frac{\partial\left(\widehat{u_i v}\right)}{\partial y} + ik_z\left(\widehat{u_i w}\right) \tag{7}$$

$$D\left(\hat{u}_i\right) = \frac{1}{Re_\tau}\frac{\partial^2 u_i}{\partial x_j \partial x_j} = \frac{1}{Re_\tau}\left(\frac{\partial^2 \hat{u}_i}{\partial y^2} - k^2 \hat{u}_i\right) \tag{8}$$

are the advective- and diffusive terms, respectively. Both terms are treated explicitly and, in Equation (6), $\alpha_l, \beta_l, \gamma_l, \zeta_l$ assume constant values, so that the time advancement results are third-order accurate in the convective part, and second-order accurate in the diffusive:

$$\alpha_1 = \frac{4}{15}, \alpha_2 = \frac{1}{15}, \alpha_3 = \frac{1}{6}; \beta_1 = \frac{4}{15}, \beta_2 = \frac{1}{15}, \beta_3 = \frac{1}{6};$$

$$\gamma_1 = \frac{8}{15}, \gamma_2 = \frac{5}{12}, \gamma_3 = \frac{3}{4} \tag{9a}$$

$$\zeta_1 = 0, \zeta_2 = -\frac{17}{60}, \zeta_3 = -\frac{5}{12}; \sum_{l=1}^{3} (\alpha_l + \beta_l) = \sum_{l=1}^{3} (\gamma_l + \zeta_l) = 1 \tag{9b}$$

Time marching is coupled with the fractional-step method. In Equation (6), the velocity and pressure fields are decoupled, so that two distinct expressions are generated. At each Runge-Kutta sub-step (l) and for each Fourier mode ($\hat{\ }$), an intermediate velocity field is introduced (superscript *):

$$\frac{\hat{u}_i^{*(l)} - \hat{u}_i^{(l-1)}}{\Delta t} = \alpha_l D \left(\hat{u}_i^{(l-2)} \right) + \beta_l D \left(\hat{u}_i^{(l-1)} \right) - \gamma_l C \left(\hat{u}_i^{(l-1)} \right) - \zeta_l C \left(\hat{u}_i^{(l-2)} \right) \tag{10}$$

$$\frac{\hat{u}_i^{(l)} - \hat{u}_i^{*(l)}}{\Delta t} = - (\alpha_l + \beta_l) \frac{\partial \hat{p}^{(l)}}{\partial x_i} \tag{11}$$

where, by applying the divergence operator to Equation (11) (and so enforcing mass conservation) one obtains a Poisson equation for the pressure, to be solved at each sub-step (l):

$$\nabla^2 \hat{p}^{(l)} = \frac{1}{\Delta t (\alpha_l + \beta_l)} \left(\frac{\partial \hat{u}^{*(l)}}{\partial x} + \frac{\partial \hat{v}^{*(l)}}{\partial y} + \frac{\partial \hat{w}^{*(l)}}{\partial z} \right) \tag{12}$$

The final values of the velocity are obtained from Equation (11). No-slip boundary conditions at the walls, and cyclic conditions in the streamwise and spanwise directions, have been applied to the velocity (for further details on the numerical algorithm one can refer to Passoni et al. [32–34]).

3. Flow-Structure Extraction

Among the different techniques used for the extraction of the coherent structures of turbulence (see Wallace [35], Alfonsi [36], Alfonsi and Primavera [37,38], among others), the swirling-strength criterion as devised by Zhou et al. [30] has been used. The latter is concisely summarized here.

By considering the system of the governing equations, an arbitrary point O can be chosen in the field, and a Taylor-series expansion of each velocity component can be performed in terms of space coordinates with the origin at O, so that the first-order pointwise linear approximation at that point becomes:

$$u_i = A_i + A_{ij} x_j \tag{13}$$

($A_{ij} = \partial u_i / \partial x_j$ is the velocity-gradient tensor). If O is located at a critical point, the zero-order terms in Equation (13) are zero. From the characteristic equation of A_{ij} one has:

$$\lambda^3 + P\lambda^2 + Q\lambda + R = 0 \tag{14}$$

where:

$$P = -tr (A_{ij}); \ Q = \frac{1}{2} \left\{ [tr (A_{ij})]^2 - tr \left(A_{ij}^2 \right) \right\}; \ R = -det (A_{ij}) \tag{15}$$

are the scalar invariants of the velocity-gradient tensor (tr is trace, det is determinant). In the case of incompressible flow, $P = 0$, and:

$$\lambda^3 + Q\lambda + R = 0 \tag{16}$$

$$Q = -\frac{1}{2} tr \left(A_{ij}^2 \right) \tag{17}$$

where the discriminant of the characteristic equation of A_{ij} becomes:

$$Dsc = \frac{R^2}{4} + \frac{Q^3}{27} \tag{18}$$

When $Dsc > 0$, the velocity-gradient tensor has one real eigenvalue ($\lambda_1 = \lambda_r$), and a pair of complex-conjugate eigenvalues ($\lambda_2, \lambda_3 = \lambda_{cr} \pm i\lambda_{ci}$). Zhou et al. [30] adopted the criterion of identifying vortices by visualizing isosurfaces of prescribed values of the imaginary part of the complex-eigenvalue pair of the velocity-gradient tensor. The swirling strength (λ_{ci}) represents a measure of the local swirling rate inside a vortical structure, so that isosurfaces of the imaginary part of the complex eigenvalue pair of the velocity-gradient tensor can be used to visualize vortices (the strength of stretching or compression is given by λ_r). The method is frame independent. It automatically eliminates regions having no local spiralling motion (due to the fact that the eigenvalues are complex only in regions of local circular or spiralling streamlines), and has proven to give rather satisfactory results in several different cases (see [39], among others). As concerns the choice of the threshold value of the swirling strength chosen for structure representation ($\lambda_{ci}|_{th}$), one can refer to Alfonsi and Primavera [40].

4. Numerical Simulations

Direct numerical simulations have been executed in the plane-channel domain (Figure 1) with dimensions, grid points, resolutions and Reynolds numbers as reported in Table 2.

Table 2. Characteristic parameters of the numerical simulations.

Quantities	$Re_\tau = 200$	$Re_\tau = 400$	$Re_\tau = 600$
L_x	$4\pi h$	$4\pi h$	$4\pi h$
L_y	$2h$	$2h$	$2h$
L_z	$2\pi h$	$2\pi h$	$2\pi h$
L_x^+	2513	5026	7540
L_y^+	400	800	1200
L_z^+	1256	2513	3770
N_x	256	343	512
N_y	181	321	451
N_z	256	343	512
N_{tot}	11.9×10^6	37.8×10^6	118.2×10^6
Δx^+	9.82	14.65	14.73
Δy_{wall}^+	0.25	0.28	0.30
Δy_{center}^+	3.87	4.36	4.66
Δz^+	4.91	7.33	7.36
η^+	1.89	2.19	2.42
$\Delta x^+/\eta^+$	5.20	6.69	6.09
$\Delta y_{wall}^+/\eta^+$	0.13	0.13	0.12
$\Delta y_{center}^+/\eta^+$	2.05	1.99	1.93
$\Delta z^+/\eta^+$	2.6	3.35	3.04
Δt^+	0.02	0.04	0.06
Δt	$1 \times 10^{-4} h/u_\tau$	$1 \times 10^{-4} h/u_\tau$	$1 \times 10^{-4} h/u_\tau$
t_{DB}^{tot}	$50 \cdot h/u_\tau$	$50 \cdot h/u_\tau$	$50 \cdot h/u_\tau$
$t_{DB}^+|_{saved}$	$500 \cdot \Delta t^+$	$500 \cdot \Delta t^+$	$500 \cdot \Delta t^+$
τ_η^+	3.56	4.79	5.87
$\Delta t^+/\tau_\eta^+$	0.006	0.008	0.010

As concerns the calculation of the Kolmogorov microscales, they have been evaluated by estimating the average rate of dissipation of turbulent kinetic energy per unit mass (ε).

This method was first introduced by Bakewell and Lumley [41], where in the case of the plane channel, one has:

$$\varepsilon \cong \frac{2L_x L_z \tau_w u_b}{2\rho h L_x L_z} = u_\tau^2 u_b \qquad (19)$$

The calculations have been executed on a specially-assembled hybrid multicore/manycore computing architecture. The system includes:

(i) 2 Intel Xeon 5660 exa-core CPU processors (12 cores) at 2.8 GHz, with 48 GB GDDR3 RAM;

(ii) 3 Nvidia C-1060 (Tesla) 240-core GPU boards (720 computing cores) at 1.3 GHz, each with 4 GB GDDR3 RAM at 102 GB/s (12 GB available);

(iii) 1 Nvidia GTS-450 (GeForce) 192-core GPU board at 1804 MHz, with 1 GB GDDR5 RAM at 57.7 GB/s (mainly used for visualization);

(iv) storage system including 5 Hard Drives at 7200 rpm, for a total supply of 5 TB.

Each GPU Nvidia C-1060 board handles a multiprocessor unit, the latter organized in 30 processors. Each processor includes eight floating-point units, 16 kB shared memory, and 4 GB of GDDR3 memory at 102 GB/s bandwidth. The process of implementation of the numerical algorithm (Section 2) on the above computing architecture is described in detail in Alfonsi *et al.* [42]. The possibility of running the computational code on different partitions of the hybrid computing machine has enabled the execution of the numerical simulations in remarkably limited runtimes (Table 3). According to a procedural viewpoint, the initial transient of the flow in the channel has been first simulated, the turbulent statistically-steady state has been reached, and thereafter (for each value of the Reynolds numbers tested) 500,000 time steps of the statistical steady state have been gathered, with temporal resolution $\Delta t = 1 \times 10^{-4} h/u_\tau$. The flow fields have been saved every given Δt interval, finally giving a $500 \cdot \Delta t^+$ database for each of the Reynolds numbers tested. The adequacy of length and span of the computing domain has been tested by verifying that the velocity fluctuations at streamwise and spanwise separations on half the domain dimensions were uncorrelated. The adequacy of the grid resolution has been also tested, through the analysis of the one-dimensional energy spectra. It has been verified that the energy densities associated to the high wavenumbers are up to nine orders of magnitude lower than those corresponding to the low wavenumbers (for more details on these issues one can refer to Ciliberti [43]).

Table 3. Runtime of the calculations with different computing-platform configurations (seconds per Δt).

CPU/GPU Cores	$Re_\tau = 200$	$Re_\tau = 400$	$Re_\tau = 600$
1 CPU/240 GPU Cores	0.37	1.71	-
3 CPU/720 GPU Cores	-	-	3.32

5. Turbulence Statistics

In Table 4 and Figures 2–6 results are presented in terms of turbulence statistics. Figure 2 reports the values of the Reynolds shear stress $(-\overline{u'v'})$ in wall coordinates, in a comparison with the data.

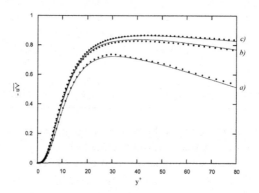

Figure 2. Reynolds shear stress (wall coordinates); $-\overline{u'v'}$: (●●●) present work, (—) data from Moser *et al.* [6]; **(a)** present work at $Re_\tau = 200$, data from Moser *et al.* [6] at $Re_\tau = 180$; **(b)** present work at $Re_\tau = 400$, data from Moser *et al.* [6] at $Re_\tau = 395$; **(c)** present work at $Re_\tau = 600$, data from Moser *et al.* [6] at $Re_\tau = 590$.

Table 4. Characteristic computed quantities of the numerical simulations.

Quantities	$Re_\tau = 200$	$Re_\tau = 400$	$Re_\tau = 600$
u_τ (nominal)	200	400	600
u_τ (present work)	200.23	399.94	600.55
u_b (nominal, after Dean [44])	3390.71	7254.35	11,343.22
u_b (present work)	3197.67	6966.95	11,106.17
u_c (nominal, after Dean [44])	3918.71	8310.35	12,927.22
u_c (present work)	3706.26	7978.80	12,701.63
u_b/u_τ (nominal, after Dean [44])	16.95	18.14	18.91
u_b/u_τ (present work)	16.97	17.42	18.49
u_c/u_τ (nominal, after Dean [44])	19.59	20.78	21.55
u_c/u_τ (present work)	18.51	19.95	21.15
u_c/u_b (nominal, after Dean [44])	1.16	1.15	1.14
u_c/u_b (present work)	1.16	1.14	1.14
C_{fb} (nominal, after Dean [44])	8.04×10^{-3}	6.65×10^{-3}	5.95×10^{-3}
C_{fb} (present work)	7.86×10^{-3}	6.86×10^{-3}	6.58×10^{-3}
$-\overline{u'v'}\big|_{peak}$ (present work)	0.739	0.828	0.866
$-\overline{u'v'}\big|_{peak}$ (from Moser _et al._ [6])	0.723	0.837	0.864
$y^+\big|_{peak}^{-\overline{u'v'}}$ (present work)	30.238	40.170	43.938
$y^+\big|_{peak}^{-\overline{u'v'}}$ (from Moser _et al._ [6])	30.019	41.882	44.698
$u'_{rms}\big|_{peak}$ (present work)	2.680	2.720	2.751
$u'_{rms}\big|_{peak}$ (from Moser _et al._ [6])	2.660	2.740	2.770
$y^+\big|_{peak}^{u'_{rms}}$ (present work)	14.909	14.199	13.444
$y^+\big|_{peak}^{u'_{rms}}$ (from Moser _et al._ [6])	15.281	14.209	13.268
$S_{u'}\big|_{peak}$ (present work)	1.003	1.096	1.141
$S_{u'}\big|_{peak}$ (from Moser _et al._ [6])	0.922	1.013	1.066
$y^+\big|_{peak}^{S_{u'}}$ (present work)	1.315	1.423	1.504
$y^+\big|_{peak}^{S_{u'}}$ (from Moser _et al._ [6])	1.339	1.446	1.591
$F_{v'}\big|_{peak}$ (present work)	26.679 at $y^+ = 0.249$	19.424 at $y^+ = 0.280$	20.882 at $y^+ = 0.298$
$F_{v'}\big|$ (from Moser _et al._ [6])	26.712 at $y^+ = 0.249$	34.757 at $y^+ = 0.280$	37.653 at $y^+ = 0.298$

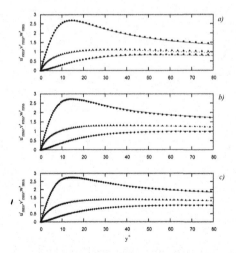

Figure 3. _Rms_ values of the velocity fluctuations (wall coordinates); u'_{rms}: (●●●) present work, (—) data from Moser _et al._ [6]; v'_{rms}: (♦♦♦) present work, (— —) data from Moser _et al._ [6]; w'_{rms}: (▲▲▲) present work, (– –) data from Moser _et al._ [6]: (**a**) present work at $Re_\tau = 200$, data from Moser _et al._ [6] at $Re_\tau = 180$; (**b**) present work at $Re_\tau = 400$, data from Moser _et al._ [6] at $Re_\tau = 395$; (**c**) present work at $Re_\tau = 600$, data from Moser _et al._ [6] at $Re_\tau = 590$.

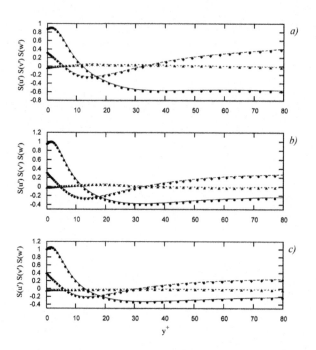

Figure 4. Skewness factors of the velocity fluctuations (wall coordinates); $S_{u'}$: (●●●) present work, (—) data from Moser *et al.* [6]; $S_{v'}$: (◆◆◆) present work, (— —) data from Moser *et al.* [6]; $S_{w'}$: (▲▲▲) present work, (– –) data from Moser *et al.* [6]: **(a)** present work at $Re_\tau = 200$, data from Moser *et al.* [6] at $Re_\tau = 180$; **(b)** present work at $Re_\tau = 400$, data from Moser *et al.* [6] at $Re_\tau = 395$; **(c)** present work at $Re_\tau = 600$, data from Moser *et al.* [6] at $Re_\tau = 590$.

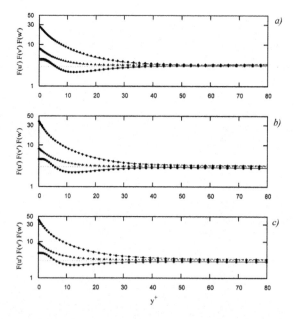

Figure 5. Flatness factors of the velocity fluctuations (wall coordinates); $F_{u'}$: (●●●) present work, (—) data from Moser *et al.* [6]; $F_{v'}$: (◆◆◆) present work, (— —) data from Moser *et al.* [6]; $F_{w'}$: (▲▲▲) present work, (– –) data from Moser *et al.* [6]: **(a)** present work at $Re_\tau = 200$, data from Moser *et al.* [6] at $Re_\tau = 180$; **(b)** present work at $Re_\tau = 400$, data from Moser *et al.* [6] at $Re_\tau = 395$; **(c)** present work at $Re_\tau = 600$, data from Moser *et al.* [6] at $Re_\tau = 590$.

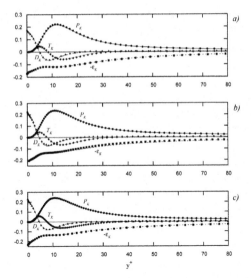

Figure 6. Terms of the turbulent kinetic-energy transport equation; P_K: (●●●) present work, (—) data from Moser *et al.* [6]; T_K: (◆◆◆) present work, (····) data from Moser *et al.* [6]; D_K: (▲▲▲) present work, (— —) data from Moser *et al.* [6]; ε_K: (■■■) present work, (– –) data from Moser *et al.* [6]: **(a)** present work at $Re_\tau = 200$, data from Moser *et al.* [6] at $Re_\tau = 180$; **(b)** present work at $Re_\tau = 400$, data from Moser *et al.* [6] at $Re_\tau = 395$; **(c)** present work at $Re_\tau = 600$, data from Moser *et al.* [6] at $Re_\tau = 590$.

Figure 3 reports the *rms* values of the velocity fluctuations ($u'_{rms}, v'_{rms}, w'_{rms}$) in a comparison with those of Moser *et al.* [6]. In a similar manner, Figure 4 reports the skewness factors of the velocity fluctuations ($S_{u'}, S_{v'}, S_{w'}$), and Figure 5 the flatness factors ($F_{u'}, F_{v'}, F_{w'}$). In Figure 6, the values of the production terms (P_K), the transport terms (T_K), the diffusion terms (D_K), and the dissipation terms (ε_K) of the turbulent-kinetic-energy transport equation ($K = \overline{u'_i u'_i}/2$), as calculated in the present work, are reported, again in a comparison with Moser *et al.* [6].

As concerns mean-flow quantities, in Table 4 the values of a number of quantities [$u_\tau, u_b, u_c,$ (u_b/u_τ), (u_c/u_τ), (u_c/u_b), C_{fb}] as calculated in the present work are reported in a comparison with the experimental data of Dean [44]. As for mean-velocity distribution, the linear distribution ($u^+ = y^+$) is satisfactorily followed in the viscous sublayer ($y^+ < 5$), while at larger distances from the wall ($y^+ > 30$), the logarithmic distribution ($u^+ = \frac{1}{\kappa} ln y^+ + C$) is also satisfactorily followed, with $\kappa = 0.4$ and $C = 5.5$ (not shown).

As concerns fluctuating velocity components (Table 4), the peak values of the Reynolds shear stress ($-\overline{u'v'}\big|_{peak}$), those of the *rms*-fluctuating streamwise velocities ($u'_{rms}\big|_{peak}$), and the fluctuating streamwise velocities skewness factors ($S_{u'}\big|_{peak}$) [and their positions ($y^+\big|_{peak}^{-\overline{u'v'}}$, $y^+\big|_{peak}^{u'_{rms}}$, $y^+\big|_{peak}^{S_{u'}}$)], exhibit a good agreement with the values of Moser *et al.* [6]. Moreover, it has been found that the peak values of the *rms*-fluctuating streamwise velocities and their positions satisfactorily follow the expressions devised by Mochizuki and Nieuwstadt [45] as a function of Re_τ, as deduced from the analysis of a large number of experimental works (see also Alfonsi [46]):

$$u'_{rms}\big|_{peak} = -0.0000024 Re_\tau + 2.70 \tag{20}$$

$$y^+\big|_{peak}^{u'_{rms}} = 0.00020 Re_\tau + 14.6 \tag{21}$$

The values of the skewness factors of the streamwise fluctuations ($S_{u'}$, Figure 4) are rather close to zero at the position of *rms*-fluctuating-streamwise-velocities peak values ($y^+\big|_{peak}^{u'_{rms}}$) and, except for these latter positions, are significantly different from the Gaussian values. The values of the flatness factors of the wall-normal fluctuations ($F_{v'}$, Figure 5) also significantly differ from the Gaussian ones, and assume remarkably-high values approaching the walls, so unveiling the highly-intermittent character of the normal-velocity fluctuations near the walls. In particular (Table 4), approaching the walls, the flatness factor $F_{v'}$ assumes values that result in an excellent agreement with the data of Moser et al. [6] (see also at Xu et al. [47] and Alfonsi [48]).

By looking at the budgets of the mean turbulent kinetic-energy (K, Figure 6), it can be noted that, at $y^+ > 30$, the homogeneous character of the flow is reasonably confirmed, while, moving toward the wall, the turbulent-transport rate becomes relevant. The turbulent-transport term is a consuming term approaching the wall, and a producing term near the wall. Close to the wall, the dissipation rate balances the viscous-diffusion and pressure-diffusion rates, and, at the wall, the dissipation rate is nonzero, while being almost equal to the viscous-diffusion rate.

Overall, the comparison of the results of present work with data obtained by other authors, both numerically and experimentally, is rather satisfactory.

6. Flow Structures

After the application of the λ_{ci} vortex-detection technique (Section 3), the flow field in the channel appears to be highly populated by turbulent structures adjacent to both the upper and the lower wall of the computing domain, with a wide range of inclination angles. The majority of them has no definite shape. Side views of the phenomenon (at $Re_\tau = 200$ and $Re_\tau = 600$) are given in Figure 7 at a generic instant. It can be noticed how the turbulent structures are noticeably smaller in size and more numerous in the case of $Re_\tau = 600$ with respect to $Re_\tau = 200$, as expected. In particular, Figure 7 shows that several structures also exist outside the buffer layer, protruding toward the center of the channel. Figure 8 shows a general view of vortical structures at $Re_\tau = 600$ on both walls of the computing domain. Here, the external surfaces of the structures are colored with the values of the local streamwise velocity (reddish indicates high values, greenish indicates low values). It can be noted, as expected, how the streamwise velocities increase towards the center of the computing domain, with respect to the more peripheral zones. Figure 9 shows a general view of vortical structures in conjunction with isosurfaces of Q2 and Q4 quadrant events (ejection and sweeps) at $Re_\tau = 400$, on the lower wall of the computing domain, at a generic instant. It can be noticed how flow structures and quadrant events are more densely located in streamwise-elongated zones of the domain, the latter being separated from the adjacent by low-speed streaks (arrows, see also Kline et al. [49]).

Through Figures 10–13 the process of evolution in time is shown with a single hairpin-like vortical structure. At $t^+ = 450$ (Figure 10), the onset is represented by the process of formation of a single, isolated, two-leg, symmetric and stable hairpin. It can be noted how an ejecting surface is pushing the perspective hairpin upwards (actually a Ω-shaped vortex filament) while, mainly on its left side (the flow goes from left to right), a sweeping surface starts to develop. Moreover, Figure 10b shows that the head of the structure is subjected to stretching, while the neck and legs are subjected to compression.

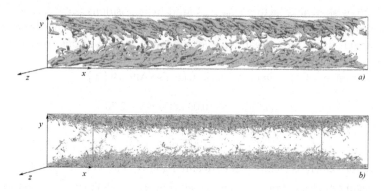

Figure 7. Side view of vortical structures in the computing domain: (a) $Re_\tau = 200$; (b) $Re_\tau = 600$.

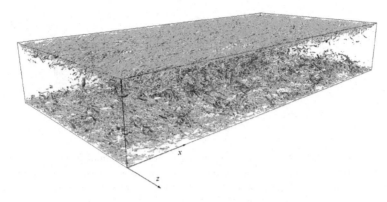

Figure 8. General view of vortical structures on both walls of computing domain at $Re_\tau = 600$ (vortical structures are colored with values of local streamwise velocity, reddish indicates high values, greenish indicates low values).

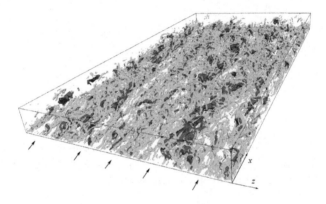

Figure 9. General view of vortical structures and $Q2 / Q4$ quadrant events on lower wall of computing domain at $Re_\tau = 400$ (vortical structures are shown in cyan, isosurfaces of ejections are shown in red, isosurfaces of sweeps are shown in yellow).

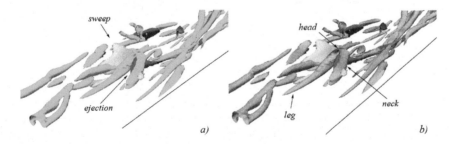

Figure 10. $\lambda_{ci}-$ isosurface representation of vortical structures in conjunction with quadrant events at $t^+ = 450$ (isosurfaces of ejections are shown in red, isosurfaces of sweeps are shown in yellow): (a) vortical structures are shown in cyan; (b) vortical structures are colored with the values of λ_r (reddish indicates stretching, bluish indicates compression).

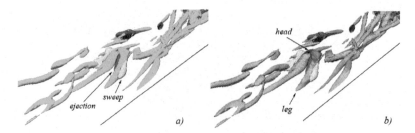

Figure 11. $\lambda_{ci}-$ isosurface representation of vortical structures in conjunction with quadrant events at $t^+ = 451$ (isosurfaces of ejections are shown in red, isosurfaces of sweeps are shown in yellow): (**a**) vortical structures are shown in cyan; (**b**) vortical structures are colored with the values of λ_r (reddish indicates stretching, bluish indicates compression).

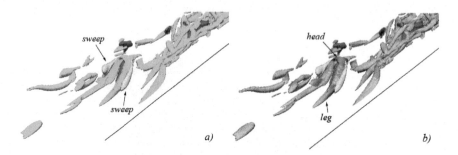

Figure 12. $\lambda_{ci}-$ isosurface representation of vortical structures in conjunction with quadrant events at $t^+ = 452$ (isosurfaces of ejections are shown in red, isosurfaces of sweeps are shown in yellow): (**a**) vortical structures are shown in cyan; (**b**) vortical structures are colored with the values of λ_r (reddish indicates stretching, bluish indicates compression).

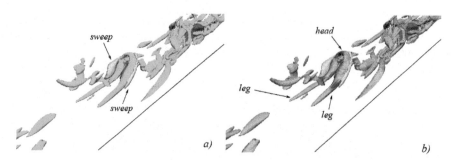

Figure 13. $\lambda_{ci}-$ isosurface representation of vortical structures in conjunction with quadrant events at $t^+ = 453$ (isosurfaces of ejections are shown in red, isosurfaces of sweeps are shown in yellow): (**a**) vortical structures are shown in cyan; (**b**) vortical structures are colored with the values of λ_r (reddish indicates stretching, bluish indicates compression).

The process continues through instants $t^+ = 451$ and $t^+ = 452$ (Figures 11 and 12) during which the ejecting surface keeps pushing the head of the structure upwards, and the sweeping surface, adjacent to the right side of the structure, further grows, so that both the right and the left portions of the structure neck become adjacent, externally to the sweeping isosurface, and internally to the ejecting isosurface. The head of the structure (Figures 11b and 12b) continues to be stretched under the action of the ejecting surface, while neck and legs are subjected to compression, due to the action of the sweeping surfaces.

At instant $t^+ = 453$ (Figure 13) the ejecting surface starts to extinguish, while the sweeping surface now exerts its characteristic stabilizing action onto the entire external structure of the now fully-formed hairpin vortex (head, neck and legs). From Figure 13b it can be also noted that the head of the vortical structure is subjected to a less intense stretching, due to the gradual process of extinction of the previously upward-pushing underlying ejecting isosurface, while the legs of the structure are subjected to compression when subjected to the action of the overlying sweeping surfaces.

Figures 14–17 show the evolution in time of a more complex aggregate of vortical structures in a different portion of the computing domain.

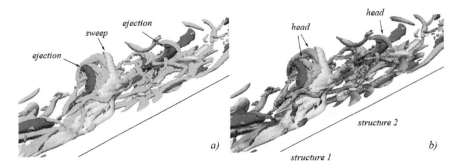

Figure 14. $\lambda_{ci}-$ isosurface representation of vortical structures in conjunction with quadrant events at $t^+ = 220$ (isosurfaces of ejections are shown in red, isosurfaces of sweeps are shown in yellow): **(a)** vortical structures are shown in cyan; **(b)** vortical structures are colored with the values of λ_r (reddish indicates stretching, bluish indicates compression).

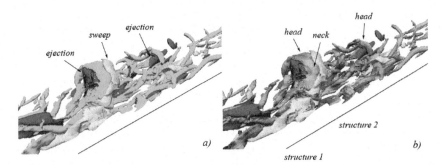

Figure 15. $\lambda_{ci}-$ isosurface representation of vortical structures in conjunction with quadrant events at $t^+ = 221$ (isosurfaces of ejections are shown in red, isosurfaces of sweeps are shown in yellow): **(a)** vortical structures are shown in cyan; **(b)** vortical structures are colored with the values of λ_r (reddish indicates stretching, bluish indicates compression).

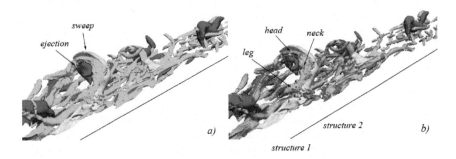

Figure 16. $\lambda_{ci}-$ isosurface representation of vortical structures in conjunction with quadrant events at $t^+ = 222$ (isosurfaces of ejections are shown in red, isosurfaces of sweeps are shown in yellow): **(a)** vortical structures are shown in cyan; **(b)** vortical structures are colored with the values of λ_r (reddish indicates stretching, bluish indicates compression).

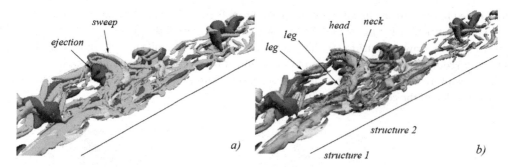

Figure 17. $\lambda_{ci}-$ isosurface representation of vortical structures in conjunction with quadrant events at $t^+ = 223$ (isosurfaces of ejections are shown in red, isosurfaces of sweeps are shown in yellow): (a) vortical structures are shown in cyan; (b) vortical structures are colored with the values of λ_r (reddish indicates stretching, bluish indicates compression).

At $t^+ = 220$ (Figure 14) two main primary Ω-shaped vortex filaments are visible at the center of the field (arrows). Right below the head of each filament, the internal space of the structure is occupied by an ejecting isosurface, again showing that, in this initial phase, ejections represent the main mechanism according to which the heads of the structures are raised upwards. Correspondingly (Figure 14b), the process of progressive stretching of the vortex head (actually still a double head) also starts.

In Figure 15, the flow field at $t^+ = 221$ is shown. The heads of both structures 1 and 2 continue to raise (being subjected to stretching, Figure 15b) due to the upward-pushing action of the ejections. The sweeping surface mainly maintains its position adjacent to the right side of hairpin 1, causing the compression of the contiguous vortical-structure neck (Figure 15b). Note again that the ejecting isosurface below hairpin 1 is almost equally developed in the streamwise, spanwise and normal-to-the-wall directions (a spheric-like surface), so guaranteeing that the pushing action of the ejecting surface against the internal part of the vortical structure is exerted almost uniformly. It can be also noticed that the presence of sweeping isosurfaces adjacent to hairpin 2 is not so evident as in the case of hairpin 1, and this is the reason why vortex 2 will be destroyed much sooner with respect to vortex 1 (not shown). At $t^+ = 222$ (Figure 16), the vortical structures continue their development. The heads of hairpins 1 and 2 continue to raise under the residual influence of the ejection events (the underlying ejecting isosurfaces are now reduced) while a well-defined sweeping isosurface assumes its definite position, adjacent to the external side of head, neck and legs of hairpin 1. The action of compression (Figure 16b) exerted by the sweeping vortex-overlying surface, in particular onto the neck of hairpin 1, becomes more intense. At $t^+ = 223$ (Figure 17), the process of evolution of the vortical structures continues in a similar manner, with respect to the previous instants. The action of the ejection events is decreasing, while the sweeping isosurface acts towards the maintenance of the stability of hairpin 1. Also, in this case, the result is hairpin 1 becoming a two-leg, symmetric, and stable vortical structure.

7. Concluding Remarks

The Direct Numerical Simulation (DNS) of the turbulent flow of incompressible fluid in a plane channel has been executed at three values of the friction-velocity Reynolds number, using a hybrid CPU/GPU computing architecture, and an analysis has been performed of the characteristics of the vortical structures in the wall region of the turbulent channel flow. Turbulent flow structures have been extracted from the simulated flow fields using the λ_{ci} or swirling strength criterion, as devised by Zhou *et al.* [24].

The joint analysis of hairpin vortices and ejection/sweep quadrant events has led to the following conclusions:

(i) the physical condition for the development and subsequent morphological evolution of a stable hairpin-like vortical structure is the occurrence of ejections distributed onto an isosurface almost equally developed along the streamwise, spanwise and normal-to-the-wall directions (a spheric-like isosurface) behind an initially connected Ω-shaped vortex filament, lying near the wall. These ejections actually constitute the physical mechanism according to which the head of the hairpin is raised upward;

(ii) the physical condition for the development of a complete and persistent hairpin is the subsequent occurrence of sweeps, as distributed on elongated isosurfaces adjacent to the external sides of the neck and legs of the hairpin.

The sweeps actually constitute the physical mechanism according to which:

(ii/a) the legs of the hairpin are stably kept near the wall;

(ii/b) the right portion (leg and neck) of the hairpin is characterized by local clockwise particle rotation, the left portion (leg and neck) by counter clockwise local particle rotation.

Author Contributions: All the authors contributed equally to this paper.

Conflicts of Interest: The authors declare no conflict of interest.

Nomenclature

Roman symbols (upper case)

$A_{ij} = \partial u_i / \partial x_j$	velocity-gradient tensor
$C_{fb} = 2\tau_w / \rho u_b^2$	bulk-velocity friction coefficient
Dsc	discriminant of characteristic equation
D_K	viscous-diffusion term of turbulent kinetic-energy transport equation
$F_{u'}, F_{v'}, F_{w'}$	flatness factors of velocity fluctuations
$F_{v'}\vert_{peak}$	peak value of $F_{v'}$
$K = \overline{u'_i u'_i}/2$	mean turbulent kinetic energy
L_x, L_y, L_z	domain dimensions along x,y,z (h units)
L_x^+, L_y^+, L_z^+	domain dimensions along x,y,z (wall units)
N_x, N_y, N_z	number of grid points along x,y,z
N_{tot}	total number of grid points
P_K	production term of turbulent kinetic-energy transport equation
P, Q, R	scalar invariants of velocity-gradient tensor
PP, QQ	parameters in the grid-stretching law
$Q2$	second-quadrant event (ejection)
$Q4$	fourth-quadrant event (sweep)
$Re_\tau = u_\tau h / \nu$	friction-velocity Reynolds number
$S_{u'}, S_{v'}, S_{w'}$	skewness factors of velocity fluctuations
$S_{u'}\vert_{peak}$	peak value of $S_{u'}$
T_K	transport term of turbulent kinetic-energy transport equation

Roman symbols (lower case)

h	channel half-height
k	wavenumber
p	pressure
t	time coordinate
t^+	time coordinate (wall units)
t_{DB}^{tot}	total database calculated time
$t_{DB}^+\vert_{saved}$	actually saved database calculated time (wall units)

$t^+_{DB}\big|_{saved}$ actually saved database calculated time (wall units)

$u_i\,(u, v, w)$ velocity components along x,y,z

$u'_i\,(u', v', w')$ fluctuating-velocity components along x,y,z

$u'_{rms}, v'_{rms}, w'_{rms}$ rms velocity fluctuations

$u'_{rms}\big|_{peak}$ peak value of u'_{rms}

$-\overline{u'v'}$ Reynolds shear stress

$-\,\overline{u'v'}\big|_{peak}$ peak value of $-\overline{u'v'}$

u_b bulk velocity

u_c centerline velocity

u_τ friction velocity

$x_i(x, y, z)$ Cartesian coordinates

$x^+_i\,(x^+, y^+, z^+)$ Cartesian coordinates (wall units)

$y^+\big|^{u'_{rms}}_{peak}$ y-position of $u'_{rms}\big|_{peak}$ (wall units)

$y^+\big|^{-\overline{u'v'}}_{peak}$ y-position of $-\,\overline{u'v'}\big|_{peak}$ (wall units)

$y^+\big|^{S_{u'}}_{peak}$ y-position of $S_{u'}\big|_{peak}$ (wall units)

$y^+\big|^{F_{v'}}_{peak}$ y-position of $F_{v'}\big|_{peak}$ (wall units)

Greek symbols (upper case)

Δt^+ time resolution of calculations (wall units)

$\Delta x^+, \Delta z^+$ space resolution of calculations along x,z (wall units)

Δy^+_{wall} space resolution of calculations along y at channel wall (wall units)

Δy^+_{center} space resolution of calculations along y at channel center (wall units)

Greek symbols (lower case)

ε average rate of dissipation of turbulent kinetic energy per unit mass

ε_K dissipation term of mean turbulent kinetic-energy transport equation

η^+ Kolmogorov space microscale (wall units)

λ eigenvalue

λ_r real eigenvalue

λ_{cr} real part of complex eigenvalue

λ_{ci} imaginary part of complex eigenvalue

$(\lambda_{ci})_{th}$ threshold value of swirling strength

ν fluid kinematic viscosity

ρ fluid density

τ_w mean shear stress at wall

τ^+_η Kolmogorov time microscale (wall units)

Acronyms

CPU   Central Processing Unit

DNS   Direct Numerical Simulation (of turbulence)

GPU   Graphic Processing Unit

References

1.   Kim, J.; Moin, P.; Moser, R. Turbulence statistics in fully developed channel flow at low Reynolds number. *J. Fluid Mech.* **1987**, *177*, 133–166. [CrossRef]

2.   Lyons, S.L.; Hanratty, T.J.; McLaughlin, J.B. Large-scale computer simulation of fully developed turbulent channel flow with heath transfer. *Int. J. Num. Meth. Fluids* **1991**, *13*, 999–1028. [CrossRef]

3. Antonia, R.A.; Teitel, M.; Kim, J.; Browne, L.W.B. Low-Reynolds-number effects in a fully developed turbulent channel flow. *J. Fluid Mech.* **1992**, *236*, 579–605. [CrossRef]

4. Kasagi, N.; Tomita, Y.; Kuroda, A. Direct numerical simulation of passive scalar field in a turbulent channel flow. *ASME J. Heat Transf.* **1992**, *114*, 598–606. [CrossRef]

5. Rutledge, J.; Sleicher, C.A. Direct simulation of turbulent flow and heat transfer in a channel. Part I: Smooth walls. *Int. J. Num. Meth. Fluids* **1993**, *16*, 1051–1078. [CrossRef]

6. Moser, R.D.; Kim, J.; Mansour, N.N. Direct numerical simulation of turbulent channel flow up to $Re_\tau = 590$. *Phys. Fluids* **1999**, *11*, 943–945. [CrossRef]

7. Abe, H.; Kawamura, H.; Matsuo, Y. Direct numerical simulation of a fully developed turbulent channel flow with respect to the Reynolds number dependence. *ASME J. Fluids Eng.* **2001**, *123*, 382–393. [CrossRef]

8. Iwamoto, K.; Suzuki, Y.; Kasagi, N. Reynolds number effect on wall turbulence: Toward effective feedback control. *Int. J. Heat Fluid Flow* **2002**, *23*, 678–689. [CrossRef]

9. Del Alamo, J.C.; Jiménez, J. Spectra of the very large anisotropic scales in turbulent channels. *Phys. Fluids* **2003**, *15*, L41–L44. [CrossRef]

10. Del Alamo, J.C.; Jiménez, J.; Zandonade, P.; Moser, R.D. Scaling of the energy spectra of turbulent channels. *J. Fluid Mech.* **2004**, *500*, 135–144. [CrossRef]

11. Tanahashi, M.; Kang, S.J.; Miyamoto, T.; Shiokawa, S.; Miyauchi, T. Scaling law of the fine-scale eddies in turbulent channel flows up to $Re_\tau = 800$. *Int. J. Heat Fluid Flow* **2004**, *25*, 331–340. [CrossRef]

12. Iwamoto, K.; Kasagi, N.; Suzuki, Y. Direct numerical simulation of turbulent channel flow at $Re_\tau = 2320$. Available online: http://www.nmri.go.jp/turbulence/PDF/symposium/FY2004/Iwamoto.pdf (accessed on 17 February 2016).

13. Hoyas, S.; Jiménez, J. Scaling of the velocity fluctuations in turbulent channels up to $Re_\tau = 2003$. *Phys. Fluids* **2006**, *18*, 011702. [CrossRef]

14. Hu, Z.W.; Morfey, C.L.; Sandham, N.D. Wall pressure and shear stress spectra from direct simulations of channel flow. *AIAA J.* **2006**, *44*, 1541–1549. [CrossRef]

15. Alfonsi, G.; Primavera, L. Direct numerical simulation of turbulent channel flow with mixed spectral-finite difference technique. *J. Flow Visual. Image Proc.* **2007**, *14*, 225–243.

16. Lozano-Durán, A.; Flores, O.; Jiménez, J. The three-dimensional structure of momentum transfer in turbulent channels. *J. Fluid Mech.* **2012**, *694*, 100–130. [CrossRef]

17. Lozano-Durán, A.; Jiménez, J. Effect of the computational domain on direct simulations of turbulent channels up to $Re_\tau = 4200$. *Phys. Fluids* **2014**, *26*, 011702. [CrossRef]

18. Vreman, A.W.; Kuerten, J.G.M. Comparison of direct numerical simulation databases of turbulent channel flow at $Re_\tau = 180$. *Phys. Fluids* **2014**, *26*, 015102. [CrossRef]

19. Vreman, A.W.; Kuerten, J.G.M. Statistics of spatial derivatives of velocity and pressure in turbulent channel flow. *Phys. Fluids* **2014**, *26*, 085103. [CrossRef]

20. Bernardini, M.; Pirozzoli, S.; Orlandi, P. Velocity statistics in turbulent channel flow up to $Re_\tau = 4000$. *J. Fluid Mech.* **2014**, *742*, 171–191. [CrossRef]

21. Lee, M.; Moser, R.D. Direct numerical simulation of turbulent channel flow up to $Re_\tau = 5200$. *J. Fluid Mech.* **2015**, *774*, 395–415. [CrossRef]

22. Kim, J.; Moin, P. Application of a fractional-step method to incompressible Navier-Stokes equations. *J. Comput. Phys.* **1985**, *59*, 308–323. [CrossRef]

23. Alfonsi, G.; Passoni, G.; Pancaldo, L.; Zampaglione, D. A spectral-finite difference solution of the Navier-Stokes equations in three dimensions. *Int. J. Numer. Meth. Fluids* **1998**, *28*, 129–142. [CrossRef]

24. Alfonsi, G. On direct numerical simulation of turbulent flows. *Appl. Mech. Rev.* **2011**, *64*, 020802. [CrossRef]

25. Marusic, I.; McKeon, B.J.; Monkewitz, P.A.; Nagib, H.M.; Smits, A.J.; Sreenivasan, K.R. Wall-bounded turbulent flows at high Reynolds numbers: Recent advances and key issues. *Phys. Fluids* **2010**, *22*, 065103. [CrossRef]

26. Smits, A.J.; McKeon, B.J.; Marusic, I. High-Reynolds number wall turbulence. *Annu. Rev. Fluid Mech.* **2011**, *43*, 353–375. [CrossRef]

27. Kim, J. Progress in pipe and channel flow turbulence, 1961–2011. *J. Turbul.* **2012**, *13*. [CrossRef]

28. Jiménez, J. Cascades in wall-bounded turbulence. *Annu. Rev. Fluid Mech.* **2012**, *44*, 27–45. [CrossRef]

29. Alfonsi, G.; Primavera, L. Temporal evolution of vortical structures in the wall region of turbulent channel flow. *Flow Turbul. Combust.* **2009**, *83*, 61–79. [CrossRef]

30. Zhou, J.; Adrian, R.J.; Balachandar, S.; Kendall, T.M. Mechanisms for generating coherent packets of hairpin vortices in channel flow. *J. Fluid Mech.* **1999**, *387*, 353–396. [CrossRef]

31. Le, H.; Moin, P. An improvement of fractional step methods for the incompressible Navier-Stokes equations. *J. Comput. Phys.* **1991**, *92*, 369–379. [CrossRef]

32. Passoni, G.; Alfonsi, G.; Tula, G.; Cardu, U. A wavenumber parallel computational code for the numerical integration of the Navier-Stokes equations. *Parall. Comput.* **1999**, *25*, 593–611. [CrossRef]

33. Passoni, G.; Cremonesi, P.; Alfonsi, G. Analysis and implementation of a parallelization strategy on a Navier-Stokes solver for shear flow simulations. *Parall. Comput.* **2001**, *27*, 1665–1685. [CrossRef]

34. Passoni, G.; Alfonsi, G.; Galbiati, M. Analysis of hybrid algorithms for the Navier-Stokes equations with respect to hydrodynamic stability theory. *Int. J. Numer. Meth. Fluids* **2002**, *38*, 1069–1089. [CrossRef]

35. Wallace, J.M. Twenty years of experimental and direct numerical simulation access to the velocity gradient tensor: What have we learned about turbulence? *Phys. Fluids* **2009**, *21*, 021301. [CrossRef]

36. Alfonsi, G. Coherent structures of turbulence: Methods of eduction and results. *Appl. Mech. Rev.* **2006**, *59*, 307–323. [CrossRef]

37. Alfonsi, G.; Primavera, L. The structure of turbulent boundary layers in the wall region of plane channel flow. *Proc. R. Soc. A* **2007**, *463*, 593–612. [CrossRef]

38. Alfonsi, G.; Primavera, L. On identification of vortical structures in turbulent shear flow. *J. Flow Visual. Image Proc.* **2008**, *15*, 201–216.

39. Alfonsi, G. Numerical simulations of wave-induced flow fields around large-diameter surface-piercing vertical circular cylinder. *Computation* **2015**, *3*, 386–426. [CrossRef]

40. Alfonsi, G.; Primavera, L. Determination of the threshold value of the quantity chosen for vortex representation in turbulent flow. *J. Flow Visual. Image Proc.* **2009**, *16*, 41–49.

41. Bakewell, H.P.; Lumley, J.L. Viscous sublayer and adjacent wall region in turbulent pipe flow. *Phys. Fluids* **1967**, *10*, 1880–1889. [CrossRef]

42. Alfonsi, G.; Ciliberti, S.A.; Mancini, M.; Primavera, L. GPGPU implementation of mixed spectral-finite difference computational code for the numerical integration of the three-dimensional time-dependent incompressible Navier-Stokes equations. *Comput. Fluids* **2014**, *102*, 237–249. [CrossRef]

43. Ciliberti, S.A. Coherent Structures of Turbulence in Wall-Bounded Turbulent Flows. Ph.D. Thesis, Università della Calabria, Rende, Italy, 2011.

44. Dean, R.B. Reynolds number dependence of skin friction and other bulk flow variables in two-dimensional rectangular duct flow. *ASME J. Fluids Eng.* **1978**, *100*, 215–223. [CrossRef]

45. Mochizuki, S.; Nieuwstadt, F.T.M. Reynolds-number-dependence of the maximum of the streamwise velocity fluctuations in wall turbulence. *Exp. Fluids* **1996**, *21*, 218–226. [CrossRef]

46. Alfonsi, G. Analysis of streamwise velocity fluctuations in turbulent pipe flow with the use of an ultrasonic Doppler flowmeter. *Flow Turbul. Combust.* **2001**, *67*, 137–142. [CrossRef]

47. Xu, C.; Zhang, Z.; den Toonder, J.M.J.; Nieuwstadt, F.T.M. Origin of high kurtosis level in the viscous sublayer. Direct numerical simulation and experiment. *Phys. Fluids* **1996**, *8*, 1938–1944. [CrossRef]

48. Alfonsi, G. Evaluation of radial velocity fluctuations in turbulent pipe flow by means of an ultrasonic Doppler velocimeter. *J. Flow Visual. Image Proc.* **2003**, *10*, 155–161. [CrossRef]

49. Kline, S.; Reynolds, W.C.; Schraub, F.A.; Rundstadler, P.W. The structure of turbulent boundary layers. *J. Fluid Mech.* **1967**, *30*, 741–773. [CrossRef]

13

Enhancing Computational Precision for Lattice Boltzmann Schemes in Porous Media Flows

Farrel Gray [1] and Edo Boek [1,2,*]

[1]   Qatar Carbonates and Carbon Storage Research Centre (QCCSRC), Department of Chemical Engineering, South Kensington Campus, Imperial College London, London SW7 2AZ, UK; farrel.gray09@imperial.ac.uk

[2]   Department of Chemistry, University of Cambridge, Lensfield Road, Cambridge CB2 1EW, UK

*   Correspondence: esb30@cam.ac.uk

Academic Editors: Qinjun Kang and Li Chen

Abstract: We reassess a method for increasing the computational accuracy of lattice Boltzmann schemes by a simple transformation of the distribution function originally proposed by Skordos which was found to give a marginal increase in accuracy in the original paper. We restate the method and give further important implementation considerations which were missed in the original work and show that this method can in fact enhance the precision of velocity field calculations by orders of magnitude and does not lose accuracy when velocities are small, unlike the usual LB approach. The analysis is framed within the multiple-relaxation-time method for porous media flows, however the approach extends directly to other lattice Boltzmann schemes. First, we compute the flow between parallel plates and compare the error from the analytical profile for the traditional approach and the transformed scheme using single (4-byte) and double (8-byte) precision. Then we compute the flow inside a complex-structured porous medium and show that the traditional approach using single precision leads to large, systematic errors compared to double precision, whereas the transformed approach avoids this issue whilst maintaining all the computational efficiency benefits of using single precision.

Keywords: lattice Boltzmann; porous media; precision

---

1. Introduction

The lattice Boltzmann (LB) method solves a discrete, meso-scale form of the Boltzmann equation [1], which can be shown to reduce to the incompressible Navier-Stokes equation in the low Mach number limit. Because of its computational efficiency and simplicity, the LB approach is now widely-used in many fields of computational fluid dynamics such as thermal and multiphase flows [2] and reactive transport [3], while rapidly developing in applications such as turbulent flows [4].

In a 1993 paper, Skordos presented an approach to increase the computational precision of lattice Boltzmann schemes in which the distribution functions were transformed by negating the equilibrium zero-velocity distribution function [5]. In principle, this should have maintained more significant bits during the calculation, leading to higher accuracy which no longer depended on the local velocity. Curiously though, when compared with the standard method of calculation involving the unmodified distribution functions, the approach was shown only to provide a very minor benefit to the accuracy of the calculation, which was still strongly dependent on the velocity (see Figure 4 in [5]).

In this work, we revisit the idea and show that application of the method with an important extra consideration can indeed lead to orders of magnitude increase in the accuracy of LB calculations while incurring no extra computational cost. The velocity-dependence of the accuracy, which is observed with the standard approach, is also removed. In the first section, we describe the method and highlight important considerations in the implementation that were missed in Skordos' original paper which probably account for the underwhelming result. Then we demonstrate in a simple capillary how the accuracy of the solution is greatly improved, and unfavourable velocity-dependence of the accuracy is removed. Finally, the method is applied to the calculation of single-phase flow in a complex porous medium and shown to be critical to obtaining the correct flow-field if single precision is to be used. Many researchers have incorporated this method into their codes in recent years, including the open-source codes Palabos [6] and OpenLB [7]. Dellar, for example, also used Skordos' approach [8] but, to the best of our knowledge, the full potential of this method has not been shown or quantified in the literature. This paper is intended to serve as a concise manual which will help LB practitioners fully exploit this simple but highly effective method.

The performance of optimised implementations of the LB model are known to be bound by memory bandwidth on CPUs and graphics processing units (GPUs). Using the single precision (float) datatype rather than double precision can provide up to twice the throughput between the main memory and the cache, offering a comparable performance enhancement. Cache occupancy is also doubled, resulting in fewer cache-misses. Single-precision arithmetic itself is faster than double precision in GPUs, and can be on CPUs if compiled using optimal hardware instructions. The performance benefits of using single precision rather than double precision are greatly advantageous in multi-component or reactive flow simulations which may take days to run, as well as the reduced memory requirement, which is often a limiting factor on modern GPUs.

Here, we apply LB to single-phase flow calculations in a porous medium, such as is used for permeability and transport calculations in petro-physical analysis, as a practical example. Pore structures in certain carbonate rocks can be extremely heterogeneous [9] and as such lead to wide flow-velocity distributions. When simulating flow in these cases, it is important not to have velocity-dependence in the accuracy of the calculation as low velocity regions are found to play an important role in transport properties [10,11].

We use an LB model which is particularly suited to porous media flows in this work. Although the Bhatnagar-Gross-Krook (BGK) approximation of the collision operator in conjunction with the halfway bounce-back scheme for treating solid-fluid boundaries is most commonly found in the literature, this model suffers from deficiencies such as viscosity-dependent slip at the walls [12] and low numerical stability. As such, it is difficult to obtain the true flow properties of a porous medium with this method. Instead, the multiple-relaxation-time (MRT) model offers much greater flexibility by transforming the distribution function into a set of moments, each of which may be relaxed with an individual rate [13,14]. By tuning the unphysical relaxation parameters, viscosity-independence can be achieved with the bounce-back boundary conditions [15]. Although boundary interpolation schemes demonstrate slightly more consistent behaviour [16,17], we have found that the standard bounce-back method gives accurate results for flow in complex porous media [18] and remain with this approach here for its computational efficiency. The fluid is driven by a body-force term, for which a precise treatment is needed to eliminate error terms in velocity gradients [19] and is incorporated into the MRT framework [20,21].

2. Method

The multiple-relaxation-time (MRT) calculation proceeds through the following steps.

Firstly, the macroscopic node variables density ρ and velocity u are obtained from the distribution function $f(x, t)$

$$\rho = \sum_i f_i \qquad \rho u = \sum_i e_i f_i + \frac{\rho g}{2} \tag{1}$$

The definition for velocity is according to the forcing scheme of Guo [21] where g is a body-force, and e_i is the ith of the 19 velocity vectors at each node (Figure 1) which are defined as

$$e = c \begin{bmatrix} 0 & 1 & -1 & 0 & 0 & 0 & 0 & 1 & -1 & 1 & -1 & 0 & 0 & 0 & 0 & 1 & -1 & 1 & -1 \\ 0 & 0 & 0 & 1 & -1 & 0 & 0 & 1 & 1 & -1 & -1 & 1 & -1 & 1 & -1 & 0 & 0 & 0 & 0 \\ 0 & 0 & 0 & 0 & 0 & 1 & -1 & 0 & 0 & 0 & 0 & 1 & 1 & -1 & -1 & 1 & 1 & -1 & -1 \end{bmatrix}^T \quad (2)$$

where $c = dx/dt$ is the lattice speed. The lattice spacing dx and time-step dt are both unity.

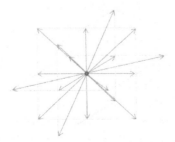

Figure 1. The 19 velocity components of the D3Q19 scheme.

The equilibrium distribution $f^{Eq}(\rho, u)$ and forcing term F are then computed from the density and velocity of the node where the components are [21]

$$f_i^{Eq}(\rho, v) = \rho w_i \left[1 + 3e_i \cdot u + \frac{9}{2}(e_i \cdot u)^2 - \frac{3}{2}u^2 \right] \quad (3)$$

$$F_i = 3w_i \left[e_i \cdot g + ug : (3e_i e_i - I) \right] \quad (4)$$

Here w_i is the weight coefficient for the corresponding velocity vector, given by $w_0 = 1/3$, $w_{1-7} = 1/18$, $w_{8-18} = 1/36$ and I is the identity matrix.

The post-collision distribution function $f'(x, t)$ is computed using the MRT operator

$$f'(x, t) = f(x, t) + M^{-1} \left[SM \left(f^{Eq} - f \right) + \left(I - \frac{1}{2}S \right) MF \right] \quad (5)$$

where M is the orthogonal matrix which transforms the distribution function into moment space and M^{-1} is its inverse. S is the diagonal matrix of relaxation rates for each moment. Full details of the MRT model can be found in [13]. Finally, the post-collisional distribution is streamed to the neighbouring nodes

$$f_i(x + e_i dt, t + dt) = f_i'(x, t) \quad (6)$$

To illustrate how accuracy is lost when computing the algorithm numerically, we consider an expansion of the summations involved in computing the macroscopic velocity at the node

$$\rho u = \begin{pmatrix} f_1 - f_2 + f_7 - f_8 + f_9 - f_{10} + f_{15} - f_{16} + f_{17} - f_{18} \\ f_3 - f_4 + f_7 + f_8 - f_9 - f_{10} + f_{11} - f_{12} + f_{13} - f_{14} \\ f_5 - f_6 + f_{11} + f_{12} - f_{13} - f_{14} + f_{15} + f_{16} - f_{17} - f_{18} \end{pmatrix} + \frac{\rho g}{2} \quad (7)$$

Each component of the velocity is a summation of differences (subtractions). Physically this is the difference between vectors of opposing direction (Figure 1). If the node velocity is very small (and hence the distribution is quite symmetric), these differences can become smaller than the ability of the floating point data type to resolve, and the calculation becomes unstable.

Floating point types are stored as two parts: a mantissa (1.2666665) and exponent (−1) in the example

$$1.2666665 \times 10^{-1} \quad (8)$$

The mantissa in single precision (4-byte float) types is accurate to around 7 decimal places (in base 10), and the exponent ranges from -38 to $+38$. Therefore a difference can only be resolved to an accuracy of 10^{-7} the largest value in the negation. For a node with a small velocity, and distribution close to the zero-velocity (equilibrium) distribution $f^0(\rho_0 = 1, u_0 = 0)$, defined in D3Q19 by

$$f^0 = \rho_0 w_i = \begin{cases} 3.3333333 \times 10^{-1} & i = 0 \\ 5.5555556 \times 10^{-2} & i = 1 \text{ to } 6 \\ 2.7777778 \times 10^{-2} & i = 7 \text{ to } 18 \end{cases} \tag{9}$$

only velocities larger than $O(10^{-2}) \cdot 10^{-7} = 10^{-9}$ can be resolved at all, and the calculation is verifiably unstable when velocities are less than 10^{-7} since only a few decimal places accuracy is maintained.

When computing the flow in complex geometries, often with minimal connectivity, the magnitude of the velocity vectors can become smaller than this. A double precision implementation can handle this easily, but comes with the drawback of requiring considerably more compute time and memory than float precision. The small velocity can, in some cases, be counteracted by choosing a larger body-force. However if this is too large, it can exceed the model stability limits and the calculation will fail. Non-Darcy effects may also begin to appear in faster flow paths if the Reynolds number becomes too high [22]. In these cases, slow flows are desirable for accurate permeability calculation. Ideally, it should not become an art to choose an appropriate body-force for a given simulation domain; often the connectivity in a simulation is not known beforehand.

The calculation variables can be transformed so that greater accuracy is obtained. Instead of storing the distribution function $f(x, t)$, we define a perturbation df from the zero-velocity distribution in the following way, as was suggested by Skordos [5]

$$f(x,t) = f^0 + df(x,t) \tag{10}$$

so that the distribution function at the node is decomposed into a reference distribution, chosen as the zero-velocity equilibrium distribution $f^0(\rho_0, u_0)$ with $\rho_0 = 1$ and $u_0 = 0$, and a perturbation df. The appropriateness of this transformation rests on the lattice Boltzmann algorithm being memory-bandwidth-limited. This means that it would be preferable to compute the full distribution function locally by adding together f^0_{dbl} and df_{flt} using double precision arithmetic (and where the subscripts dbl and flt express the variable's data type), storing df as a single-precision (float) data type in the main memory. However, even this is unnecessary if we transform the macroscopic quantities

$$\rho = \sum_i f^0 + \sum_i df_i = 1 + \sum_i df_i \tag{11}$$

$$\rho u - \frac{\rho g}{2} = \sum_i e_i df_i \tag{12}$$

Although we are still computing differences in the expression for velocity, the zero-velocity expression for the distribution df is 0, so these differences are not bound by the order of magnitude of the calculation values, and are computed to full 7 d.p. accuracy. Note that the expression for the local density is still bound by the order 10^0.

The difference $f^{Eq} - f$ which arises in the collision term should be considered as well to maximise the accuracy of the calculation. Writing this in terms of the deviation distribution df, and using the subscripts dbl and flt to indicate the precision (double and single respectively) to which the variables might be stored or calculated, we obtain

$$\left(f^{Eq} - f\right)_{flt} = f^{Eq}_{dbl} - \left(f^0_{dbl} + df_{flt}\right)_{dbl} \tag{13}$$

The difference could be computed to double precision and converted back to single precision afterwards. This is because the node distribution and equilibrium distribution will be of order 10^{-1}, but the difference often considerably smaller.

Finally though, the need for double precision can be avoided completely if we first compute the equilibrium distribution as a perturbation from the zero equilibrium $df^{Eq} = f^{Eq}(\rho, u) - f^0(\rho_0, u_0)$ such that

$$df_i^{Eq} = \rho w_i \left[3e_i \cdot u + \frac{9}{2}(e_i \cdot u)^2 - \frac{3}{2}u^2 \right] + (\rho - \rho_0) w_i \tag{14}$$

The density difference $\rho - \rho_0$ will be small relative to the density values of order 10^0. However, this calculation can be made more accurate if we identify the following

$$\rho - \rho_0 = \sum_i df_i \tag{15}$$

We must explicitly compute this density difference from the right hand side summation and not via the densities themselves, otherwise precision is lost. This substitution is particularly important in the low velocity limit and was not mentioned in Skordos' original paper which only considered how the now comparable magnitudes of each term in (our) Equation (14) increases accuracy under addition, rather than the precision of each individual term [5]. Using the transformed quantities, the evolution of the LB equation is given as

$$df'(x, t) = df(x, t) + M^{-1} \left[SM \left(df^{Eq} - df \right) + \left(I - \frac{1}{2}S \right) MF \right] \tag{16}$$

$$df_i(x + e_i dt, t + dt) = df_i'(x, t) \tag{17}$$

In the single-relaxation-time (BGK) scheme, the collision part would similarly be written with a relaxation time τ

$$df'(x, t) = df(x, t) + \frac{1}{\tau} \left(df^{Eq} - df \right) + \left(1 - \frac{1}{2\tau} \right) F \tag{18}$$

3. Results

The two methods of calculating the collision term are compared by computing the velocity distribution $U(x)$ between two infinite parallel plates of separation L (Figure 2), for which the analytical solution is well known, using a viscosity μ and body-force component g in a direction parallel to the plates:

$$U(x) = \frac{g}{2\mu} x (L - x) \tag{19}$$

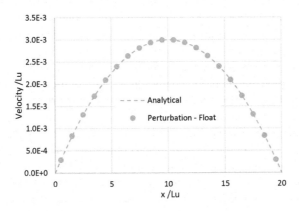

Figure 2. Poiseuille flow between two plates separated by 20 lattice units (Lu).

The method in which the complete distribution function is used, Equation (5) is referred to as the distribution method, and the scheme evolving the perturbation from the zero distribution, Equation (16) is referred to as the perturbation method. The deviation from the analytical solution for each method is computed as the relative error

$$\varepsilon(x) = \frac{|u(x) - U(x)|}{U(x)} \tag{20}$$

where $u(x)$ is the computed velocity component in the body-force direction as a function of position x between the plates.

For assuredly good convergence, computations are run for 10^6 time-steps. The error is shown in Figure 3 for the distribution and perturbation methods using respectively float (single-precision) data types and double (precision) data types. The body force used was $g = 10^{-6}$ in dimensionless lattice units (Lu) and the viscosity $\mu = \frac{1}{6}$ For this system, the perturbation methods are consistently 2 to 3 orders of magnitude more accurate than the distribution method of the same data type, though the perturbation method with float precision cannot match the accuracy of the double-precision distribution method in this calculation.

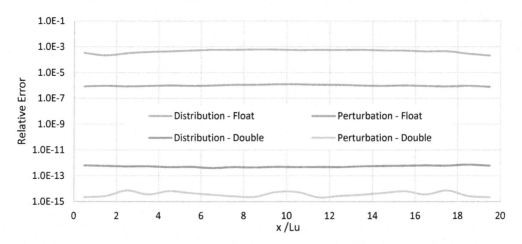

Figure 3. The relative error of the flow between plates for different calculation schemes and precisions for a body-force of 10^{-6}.

To illustrate how the accuracy of the perturbation scheme is freed from dependence on the magnitude of the velocities, the relative error averaged across the flow profile is plotted in Figure 4 for different average flow velocities. These were obtained by systematically reducing the body-force. It is clear that as the distribution methods lose accuracy for lower lattice velocities, the perturbation methods maintain a consistent relative error. We also note that the accuracy of the distribution methods converge to those of the perturbation schemes as the magnitude of the velocities approaches that of the zero equilibrium distribution Equation (9). Finally, the accuracy of the perturbation method with float precision can exceed that of the distribution method with double precision at grid velocities below around 10^{-11}.

To demonstrate the practical advantages of the enhanced accuracy afforded by the perturbation scheme at low velocities, we compute the flow in a 3D pore space image of a Portland carbonate rock sample (Figures 5 and 6) obtained from micro-CT imaging [10]. The sample is 400^3 lattice units in size, but reflected about the $x = 0$ plane to give continuous loop boundary conditions so that a body-force may be used [10]. The structure of the pore-space is highly heterogeneous and of low permeability. The body-force used was again $g_x = 10^{-6}$ and the viscosity $\mu = \frac{1}{6}$.

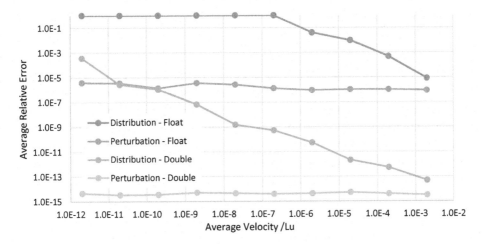

Figure 4. The average relative error of the flow profile between plates for different calculation schemes against mean flow velocity.

Figure 5. A sample of Portland carbonate of porosity 9.0%.

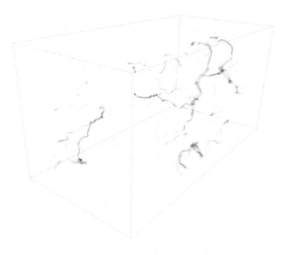

Figure 6. The velocity distribution computed in the pore space image of the Portland carbonate sample.

The average velocity throughout the medium is given over the simulation time for the different schemes in Figure 7. Most strikingly, the distribution method using floating point precision exhibits a large, systematic deviation from the double precision calculation of almost 50% and as such would give an overestimate of the permeability by the same amount. The perturbation method with float precision on the other hand matches the double-precision distribution calculation closely, yet requires considerably less memory and computing time to perform. Run on a Tesla K20 GPU, the float precision calculations required 27.8 s per 1000 time-steps and the double precision calculation required 48.3 s. In our sparse grid implementation, the array indices of each fluid node's 18 neighbours are also read in from the memory. Since these are stored as 4-byte integers in both float and double implementations, the speed up of 1.74x is in line with a memory-bandwidth-limited model.

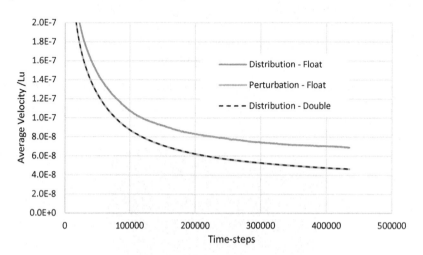

Figure 7. The average velocity throughout the Portland carbonate sample over the simulation. Points are sampled every 1000 time-steps.

4. Conclusions

We have shown how the simple transformation of the LB distribution function proposed by Skordos [5], does indeed lead to a considerable increase in computational precision when correctly implemented. Furthermore, the accuracy of this approach is no longer dependent on the magnitude of the velocity at the grid node. With application to flows in complex porous media, the modified scheme was shown to accurately compute the velocity field inside a heterogeneous pore-space when the average velocity became small. This means that it is no longer imperative to revert to using double precision arithmetic to achieve numerical stability and accuracy in simulations involving small grid velocities. Since the perturbation method incurs no extra computational burden, the computational efficiency is dramatically improved for these applications.

Acknowledgments: We gratefully acknowledge funding from the Qatar Carbonates and Carbon Storage Research Centre (QCCSRC), provided jointly by Qatar Petroleum, Shell, and Qatar Science and Technology Park. We would also like to thank three anonymous reviewers for their helpful comments and suggestions.

Author Contributions: Farrel Gray conceived and carried out the study, and prepared the text and images for the paper. Edo Boek gave critical review and made minor revisions to the text.

Conflicts of Interest: The authors declare no conflict of interest.

References

1.   He, X.; Luo, L.-S. Theory of the lattice Boltzmann method: From the Boltzmann equation to the lattice Boltzmann equation. *Phys. Rev. E* **1997**, *56*, 6811. [CrossRef]

2. Sukop, M.C.; Thorne, D.T., Jr. *Lattice Boltzmann Modeling: An Introduction for Geoscientists and Engineers*; Springer Publishing Company: Berlin, Germany, 2007.

3. Kang, Q.; Lichtner, P.C.; Viswanathan, H.S.; Abdel-Fattah, A.I. Pore Scale Modeling of Reactive Transport Involved in Geologic CO_2 Sequestration. *Transp. Porous Media* **2009**, *82*, 197–213. [CrossRef]

4. Bösch, F.; Chikatamarla, S.S.; Karlin, I.V. Entropic Multi-Relaxation Models for Turbulent Flows. *Phys. Rev. E* **2015**, *92*, 043309. [CrossRef] [PubMed]

5. Skordos, P. Initial and boundary conditions for the lattice Boltzmann method. *Phys. Rev. E* **1993**, *48*, 4823. [CrossRef]

6. FlowKit Ltd. *Palabos CFD*; FlowKit Ltd.: Lausanne, Switzerland, 2011.

7. Krause, M.J. OpenLB. 2014. Available online: http://optilb.com/openlb/ (accessed on 14 February 2016).

8. Dellar, P.J. Incompressible limits of lattice Boltzmann equations using multiple relaxation times. *J. Comput. Phys.* **2003**, *190*, 351–370. [CrossRef]

9. Crawshaw, J.P.; Boek, E.S. Multi-scale imaging and simulation of structure, flow and reactive transport for CO_2 storage and EOR in carbonate reservoirs. *Rev. Mineral. Geochem.* **2013**, *77*, 431–458. [CrossRef]

10. Yang, J.; Crawshaw, J.; Boek, E.S. Quantitative determination of molecular propagator distributions for solute transport in homogeneous and heterogeneous porous media using lattice Boltzmann simulations. *Water Resour. Res.* **2013**, *49*, 8531–8538. [CrossRef]

11. Blunt, M.J.; Bijeljic, B.; Dong, H.; Gharbi, O.; Iglauer, S.; Mostaghimi, P.; Paluszny, A.; Pentland, C. Pore-scale imaging and modelling. *Adv. Water Resour.* **2013**, *51*, 197–216. [CrossRef]

12. He, X.; Zou, Q.; Luo, L.; Dembo, M. Analytic solutions of simple flows and analysis of nonslip boundary conditions for the lattice Boltzmann BGK model. *J. Stat. Phys.* **1997**, *87*, 115–136. [CrossRef]

13. D'Humières, D. Multiple-relaxation-time lattice Boltzmann models in three dimensions. *Philos. Trans. A Math. Phys. Eng. Sci.* **2002**, *360*, 437–451. [CrossRef] [PubMed]

14. Lallemand, P.; Luo, L.-S. Theory of the lattice Boltzmann method: Dispersion, dissipation, isotropy, Galilean invariance, and stability. *Phys. Rev. E* **2000**, *61*, 6546. [CrossRef]

15. Pan, C.; Luo, L.-S.; Miller, C.T. An evaluation of lattice Boltzmann schemes for porous medium flow simulation. *Comput. Fluids* **2006**, *35*, 898–909. [CrossRef]

16. Ginzburg, I.; d'Humières, D. Multireflection boundary conditions for lattice Boltzmann models. *Phys. Rev. E* **2003**, *68*, 066614. [CrossRef] [PubMed]

17. Bouzidi, M.H.; Firdaouss, M.; Lallemand, P. Momentum transfer of a Boltzmann-lattice fluid with boundaries. *Phys. Fluids* **2001**, *13*, 3452–3459. [CrossRef]

18. Shah, S.; Gray, F.; Crawshaw, J.P.; Boek, E.S. Micro-computed tomography pore-scale study of flow in porous media: Effect of voxel resolution. *Adv. Water Resour.* **2015**. in press. [CrossRef]

19. Guo, Z.; Zheng, C.; Shi, B. Discrete lattice effects on the forcing term in the lattice Boltzmann method. *Phys. Rev. E* **2002**, *65*, 046308. [CrossRef] [PubMed]

20. Kuzmin, A.; Guo, Z.; Mohamad, A. Simultaneous incorporation of mass and force terms in the multi-relaxation-time framework for lattice Boltzmann schemes. *Philos. Trans. A Math. Phys. Eng. Sci.* **2011**, *369*, 2219–2227. [CrossRef] [PubMed]

21. Guo, Z.; Zheng, C. Analysis of lattice Boltzmann equation for microscale gas flows: Relaxation times, boundary conditions and the Knudsen layer. *Int. J. Comput. Fluid Dyn.* **2008**, *22*, 465–473. [CrossRef]

22. Jones, B.; Feng, Y. Effect of image scaling and segmentation in digital rock characterisation. *Comput. Part. Mech.* **2015**. [CrossRef]

14

Applications of Computational Modelling and Simulation of Porous Medium in Tissue Engineering

Carrie L. German and Sundararajan V. Madihally *

School of Chemical Engineering, Oklahoma State University, 212 Cordell North Stillwater, OK 74078, USA; carrilg@okstate.edu
* Correspondence: sundar.madihally@okstate.edu

Academic Editors: Qinjun Kang and Li Chen

Abstract: In tissue engineering, porous biodegradable scaffolds are used as templates for regenerating required tissues. With the advances in computational tools, many modeling approaches have been considered. For example, fluid flow through porous medium can be modeled using the Brinkman equation where permeability of the porous medium has to be defined. In this review, we summarize various models recently reported for defining permeability and non-invasive pressure drop monitoring as a tool to validate dynamic changes in permeability. We also summarize some models used for scaffold degradation and integrating mass transport in the simulation.

Keywords: simulation; mathematical modelling; tissue engineering

1. Introduction

Tissue engineering refers to the *in vitro* regeneration or growth of a tissue or an organ for the purpose of biomedical studies in areas such as toxicology, tissue/organ repair, and medical device development. The technology is based on using biodegradable porous scaffolds to guide and support the in-growth of cells during tissue regeneration either at the site of grafting or *in vitro* [1]. The scaffold transiently degrades leaving only the necessary healthy tissue. Currently, the primary goal of tissue engineering is to address the massive discrepancy between organ/tissue transplant needs and availability. Another goal is to use engineered tissue to develop safe and effective medication, treatments, and medical devices without threat to life [2]. *In vitro* cell culture can help achieve these goals, although the growth of cells outside of the body can be difficult due to cell sensitivity. For this reason, cell culture environments closely mimic body conditions such as temperature, pH, and shear stress, as well as mechanical stimuli in some cases. Advancements in tissue engineering have led to the development of numerous techniques and housing environments in cell culture including bioreactors that aim to meet such requirements [3]. However, due to the complex nature of cell systems, gaps exist in the knowledge of the interactions occurring within.

Tissue regeneration is a dynamic process where cell numbers are expected to increase. These cells also need to secrete matrix elements native to that tissue and matrix components need to assemble in the scaffold while the scaffold material degrades. These processes reduce the pore size available for fluid flow to reach a permeability matching that of the healthy tissues. Purely experimentally driven studies to determine parameter change and stimuli effects are costly in time and money, and do not provide a complete understanding of dynamic process [4]. Computational modelling and simulation for optimization of *in vitro* tissue growth environments decreases experimental costs and allows easy variable manipulation to determine effect. Modeling is currently limited to activities that are capable of predicting or characterizing all of the processes that occur within a given cell culture system, but the success lies in the combination of well validated models into one simulation to tell the entire story of molecular metabolism, mass transport, scaffold decomposition, and many other phenomena on multiple levels. The combination of multiple models in simulation is necessary to build a complete understanding of what occurs throughout the tissue engineering process and what is needed to produce healthy, fully functional tissue [5].

The field of tissue engineering will find great success due to understanding gained from modeling and simulation compilations. This review will focus on the mathematical models currently available for describing mass transport in static and dynamic cell culture environments, as well as discuss methods for describing fluid flow effects on scaffolds.

2. Cell Culture

Numerous *in vitro* cell culturing techniques, such as growth on tissue culture plastic, cell suspension, cell aggregates, and bioreactors, have been investigated in an attempt to mimic body tissue. Each technique has advantages and faces varying challenges. Two-dimensional (2D) cell culture involves the growth of cells on pre-treated, flat, polystyrene plastic surfaces (Figure 1a). Cells attach to the stiff, plastic surface and spread until surface area runs out. Cells in 2D environments are submerged in nutrient-rich media, typically changed every 48 h, to promote cell vitality and proliferation.

Two-dimensional cell culturing techniques have had success in maintaining cell proliferation, and are easy to set up and maintain; however, 2D cultures are poor approximations of tissue *in vivo*. Two-dimensional cell cultures lack necessary architectural structure and face significant exposure limitations [6]. Three-dimensional (3D) cell culture can provide necessary architectural structure, generally via a biocompatible, biodegradable scaffold. The scaffold is a porous medium that supports cell organization and motility and allows nutrient transport inside the 3D structure, creating an environment that more closely mimics tissue formations *in vivo* [7–9]. In addition, 3D culture allows for higher cell density seeding over a given surface area, allowing for increased sensitivity and stronger signal strength during system analysis. Three-dimensional cultures are generally preferred to 2D cultures in tissue engineering, and for that purpose, the remainder of this review will focus on simulation of 3D cultures only.

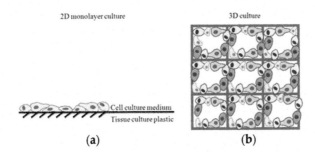

2D monolayer culture   3D culture

Cell culture medium
Tissue culture plastic

(a)   (b)

Figure 1. Structural comparison of (a) Two-dimensional cell culture and (b) Three-dimensional cell culture.

2.1. Cell Culture under Static Conditions

Static cell culture systems are easy to maintain, but require regular media replenishment to maintain adequate nutrient supply. Mass transport of molecules, such as nutrients, can be modelled mathematically. The distribution of components in static condition is driven by diffusion as described by Fick's first law. Hence, theoretical models used in simulation apply some form of Fick's law to characterize mass transport in a system [10],

$$N_{i,\,diffusive} = \nabla \cdot (D_i \nabla C_i) \tag{1}$$

where $N_{i,\,diffusive}$ represents the diffusive mass flux through the system, D_i represents the effective diffusivity of the component, ∇ represents the gradient operator used when evaluating a function in more than one dimension and ∇C_i represents the gradient of concentration. The conservation of mass is given as,

$$\frac{\partial C_i}{\partial t} + \nabla \cdot N_i = 0 \tag{2}$$

where t represents time. Substitution of Equation (1) into Equation (2) yields:

$$\frac{\partial C_i}{\partial t} = \nabla \cdot (D_i \nabla C_i) \tag{3}$$

Assumptions for simplification of a system are commonly made in simulation, especially in the beginning stages. For example, the assumption of a constant diffusion coefficient gives Equation (3) as:

$$\frac{\partial C_i}{\partial t} = D_i \nabla^2 C_i \tag{4}$$

And for a steady state assumption, Equation (3) becomes:

$$0 = \nabla \cdot (D_i \nabla C_i) \tag{5}$$

As most of the systems considered in tissue engineering evaluate consumption of nutrients or formation of signature products, a reactive term, R_i, is added to Equation (3) giving [11]:

$$\frac{\partial C_i}{\partial t} = \nabla \cdot (D_i \nabla C_i) + R_i \tag{6}$$

The sign convention of the reaction term depends upon whether the molecule is being consumed (negative) or produced (positive). Unlike convection where nutrient transport can be estimated by the flow rate and concentration gradient, diffusion transport mainly requires evaluating the diffusivity of the nutrient molecule. The major factors affecting diffusion include porosity and morphology, scaffold biodegradation, swelling due to biodegradation, and shrinkage due to deposition of new biopolymers and cells. Standard approach to defining D_i [12] in the literature of flow through porous medium is

$$D_i = D_\infty \left(\frac{\varepsilon_p}{\tau}\right) \tag{7}$$

where τ is the tortuosity of the porous medium, ε_p is the porosity of the scaffold, and D_∞ is the free diffusivity of the component in water. Since determining τ of the porous medium is difficult, some use that of cells. Alternatively, Mackie-Meares relationship can be used to determine the effective diffusivity. An example of Mackie-Meares relationship [13] is

$$D_i = D_\infty \left(\frac{\varepsilon_p}{2 - \varepsilon_p}\right)^2 \tag{8}$$

Since there are many techniques to determine the porosity of the porous medium particularly in tissue engineering scaffolds, those porosity values can be directly utilized to determine effective diffusivity.

2.2. Cell Culture Involving Fluid Flow

Many 3D cell culture environments encounter challenges due to nonhomogeneous molecular distribution, particularly those on the interior of 3D cultures [14]. Further, many body parts are exposed to stresses either due to the weight they carry (such as bone), function they perform (such as bladder and cartilage) or due to the flow of fluid (lung and blood vessels). These parts regenerate if mechanical stimulus is applied. In an effort to address distribution issues and applications of mechanical stimulus, some have investigated convection driven cell culture environments. In the case of bioreactors, convection can be introduced by a flow of fresh, nutrient-rich media into the environment as seen in parallel-flow and flow-through bioreactors. Convection can be introduced into a system via agitation or stirring, as seen in spinner flasks and rotating wall vessel bioreactors. Bioreactors of different flow configurations and sizes have been with an even wider array of nutrient distributing and mechanical simulating techniques [15].

Appropriate characterization of transport phenomena in cell culture simulation is vital to obtaining results that could be utilized for optimizing tissue regeneration. Mathematical modelling of fluid behavior, due to the addition of convection, increases the complexity and number of equations required to describe fluid behavior. Characterization of fluid behavior in a system where convection is present requires the addition of a momentum equation. Fluid momentum in non-porous regions is characterized by the Navier-Stokes equation written as:

$$-\nabla P + \nabla \cdot \left(\mu \left(\nabla u + (\nabla u)^T \right) - \frac{2}{3} \mu \left(\nabla \cdot u \right) I \right) + F = \rho \left(\frac{\partial u}{\partial t} + u \cdot \nabla u \right) \tag{9}$$

where P represents fluid pressure, μ represents the fluid kinematic viscosity, ∇u represents the gradient of fluid velocity, ρ represents fluid mass density, I represents the identity matrix, and F represents the sum of the external forces (like gravity) applied to the fluid. The Navier-Stokes equation is used for Newtonian fluids, such as growth medium used in cell culture. Assumptions, such as steady state operation and negligible external forces, are often applied to simulation, eliminating the $\frac{\partial u}{\partial t}$ and F terms respectively from Equation (10). In addition to these two assumptions, consideration of the fluid as incompressible with a constant density and viscosity would yield Equation (8) as:

$$-\nabla P + \mu \left(\nabla \left(\nabla u + (\nabla u)^T \right) \right) = \rho \left(u \cdot \nabla u \right) \tag{10}$$

Use of the conservation of momentum equation must also include the use of the conservation of mass equation, or continuity equation, when solving. The continuity equation is given as:

$$\frac{\partial \rho}{\partial t} + \nabla \cdot (\rho u) = 0 \tag{11}$$

And if considered at steady state and constant density:

$$\rho \nabla \cdot u = 0 \tag{12}$$

Velocity selection does not affect equation selection for characterization of non-porous regions, but has a direct impact on the equation for characterizing the effect of fluid flow through porous scaffolds. In order to determine the applicable fluid flow equations, the Reynolds number within the pores (and/or Forchheimer number) is calculated. Based on the local Reynolds number, one can determine whether Darcy, Brinkman or Forchheimer equations are most appropriate. The Darcy equation is based on experimental observations of the one-dimensional flow of water at low velocities through a porous medium made of sand particles, and is written as:

$$-\frac{dP}{dX} = \frac{\mu * v}{\kappa} \tag{13}$$

where X is the direction of fluid flow, v represents the superficial velocity, and κ represents the porous structure permeability. Many derivations for Darcy's law are used but one must be cautious, as this assumption is only valid when the local Reynolds number is below one [16]. When the local Reynolds number is in the order of 100 or greater, the Forchheimer equation is used to incorporate the turbulent flow conditions. Forchheimer added a quadratic velocity term to the Darcy equation to account for microscopic inertial effects. The Forchheimer equation for one-dimensional flow is written as:

$$-\frac{dP}{dX} = \frac{\mu * v}{\kappa} + \beta \rho v^2 \tag{14}$$

where β is the non-Darcy coefficient. Taking into account local shearing effects between the fluid and porous walls, and the gradient pressure forces involved in transport of fluids from non-porous regions into porous regions, second order derivatives of the velocity are added to the Darcy equation, yielding the Brinkman equation:

$$-\frac{dP}{dX} = \frac{\mu * v}{\kappa} - \mu \left(\frac{\partial^2 v}{\partial Y^2} + \frac{\partial^2 v}{\partial Z^2} \right) \tag{15}$$

where X, Y, and Z represent directions that are mutually perpendicular. The Brinkman equation is useful when the local Reynolds numbers are in the range of one and 100. Brinkman equation can be viewed as an equation consisting of two terms (i) Darcy's equation and (ii) a viscous term, similar to Navier-Stokes equation, which provides molecular transport due to convection.

$$N_{i, \, convective} = \nabla \cdot \left(\vec{u} C_i \right) \tag{16}$$

where $N_{i, \, convective}$ represents the convective mass flux, $\vec{u}$ represents the average velocity of the fluid, and again, C_i represents the species concentration. Combining Equations (1) and (16) gives an expression for the transport of solutes within the fluid to give the advective-diffusive equation:

$$N_{i, diffusive- \, convective} = \nabla \cdot (D_i \nabla C_i) + \nabla \cdot \left(\vec{u} C_i \right) \tag{17}$$

Cell metabolism equations are not affected by the inclusion of convection for molecular transport. However, local concentrations of molecules are dictated by the advective-diffusive equation. Hence the rate of reactions are altered, which further leads to altered concentration profiles.

3. Modeling Porous Medium Properties

3.1. Incorporating Permeability

Properties of the porous scaffolds used in tissue engineering, such as biocompatible material, porosity, and tensile strength, play an important role in characterizing mass transport. The Darcy, Forchheimer, and Brinkman equations, which characterize fluid flow through porous scaffolds, require an important porous structure parameter, the permeability, κ. Sensitivity of model predictions are directly dependent on the accurate κ values, which depend on the geometric parameters of the pores in the scaffold [17]. In order to predict flow properties with high fidelity, determining the permeability using physical characteristics of the porous scaffold such as porosity and pore shape is an approach. Kozeny proposed a relationship in 1927 given as:

$$\kappa = \frac{K_c \varepsilon_p^3}{S^2} \tag{18}$$

where S represents the specific surface area, the ratio of total interstitial surface area to the bulk volume of the porous scaffold and K_C represents the Kozeny constant, a dimensionless parameter that depends on the pore geometry. In human physiology, permeability of various tissues is defined using this Kozeny definition [18]. The above expression of κ does not depend on fluid viscosity and density, which helps in extrapolating the simulation results to different fluids and flow conditions. There are a number of approaches available for calculating permeability, based on fiber orientation and size or pore area and number, depending on method and materials used for porous scaffold development. When scaffolds are formed through the process of electrospinning, fibers are randomly oriented (Figure 2a).

In order to calculate the permeability in randomly packed fibers, there have been many correlations. One popular equation that seem to agree with the electrospun scaffolds is:

$$\kappa = \frac{3r^2}{20\,(1-\varepsilon_p)}\,\left(-\ln\left(1-\varepsilon_p\right)-0.931\right) \tag{19}$$

where r is the radius of the fibers. Since these scaffolds are very thin relative to their surface area, one could assume negligible porosity across the thickness. Then, porosity can be estimated using digital micrographs collected from scanning electron microscopy. Image analysis is performed to calculate the ratio of the open pore area to the total area of the image analyzed, which is considered as the porosity of the scaffold [19]. If the fiber sizes are large, another correlation is developed using Lattice-Boltzmann method. In that case, the permeability is calculated using:

$$\kappa = \frac{5.55 * r^2}{\left(e^{10.1\varepsilon_p}-1\right)} \tag{20}$$

Other methods do not use fibers to create scaffolds, but rather create pores within a solid medium. For example, freeze drying of water-based polymer solutions such as collagen, chitosan, and alginate produce pores mimicking water crystals. Permeability for such scaffolds are calculated [20], assuming pores to be cylindrical (Figure 2b), and calculated using the equation,

$$\kappa = \frac{\pi}{128}\,n_A d^4 \tag{21}$$

where d is the pore diameter and n_A represents the number of pores per unit area. However, some porous medium preparation techniques using leaching salt from organic solvent-based polymeric blocks such as polycaprolactone and poly lactic-co-glycolic acid (Figure 2c). One could assume the pores to be rectangular and then calculate the permeability using the expression:

$$\kappa = \frac{1}{12}\,n_A L W^3 \tag{22}$$

where L is the pore length, and W is the pore width. Utilizing permeability equations based on pore geometric characteristics such as pore size, shape, and n_A is advantageous because experimental data can be used from scaffold analyses, typically reported in tissue engineering literature.

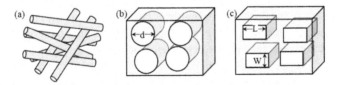

Figure 2. Schematic of different pore configurations in porous scaffolds used in tissue engineering. These are in the flow direction. (a) Fibrous scaffolds formed by electrospinning; (b) Scaffolds with nearly circular pores when formed using freeze-drying; (c) Scaffolds with rectangular pores when formed using salt-leaching technique.

Scaffold permeability depends on a combination of factors including pore size, porosity, pore geometry, and pore distribution [21]. Alterations in any of these parameters affects permeability, and changes in scaffold permeability directly affects the structural integrity of the scaffold [22]. Increased pore size decreases solid material volume and, as a result, the strength of the material. Scaffold strength is of particular importance during the initial cell seeding, as the extracellular matrix (ECM) that provides stability *in vivo* is not yet formed. In order to mimic the ECM and promote appropriate cellular behavior, scaffold strength should match *in vivo* tissue strength [23]. Permeability also influences diffusion of nutrients into and waste out of the porous medium. The transport of nutrients necessary for cell survival into the scaffold, and waste metabolites which can be toxic to cells, is controlled by permeability [21]. Thus, selection of appropriate scaffold permeability for achieving desired effects is critical.

The majority of scaffolds are designed with homogeneous porosity and pore distribution due to manufacturing and design limitations [24]. Homogenous scaffolds or scaffolds of constant porosity are a common assumption employed in tissue engineering simulations. Many reports confirm that this to be a good assumption and useful in calculating scaffold permeability [25,26]. However, many issues arise when considering uniform scaffold permeability. For example, natural tissue is not structurally homogeneous. Additionally, homogeneously porous scaffolds cannot address all of the mechanical and biological tissue requirements. Hence, heterogeneous scaffold development is currently of particular interest to researchers. Scaffolds with separate regions of porosity and scaffolds with porosity gradients have been investigated [27]. In some cases, a multi-scale simulation approach is advantageous in accounting for environmental heterogeneity. Multi-scale approaches allow simultaneous investigation of the interaction and dependence of various factors on the micro (cellular) and macro (entire scaffold) scale [28].

3.2. Incorporating Scaffold Degradation

Characterization of scaffold degradation over time is important to producing and maintaining high-integrity, engineered tissue for *in vivo* use. If scaffolds degrade too quickly, the necessary structural architecture for promoting appropriate cell proliferation and functionality is lost, resulting in cell death. Computational modelling and simulation can provide a better understanding of the mechanism driving structural degradation. Some mathematical models consider scaffold degradation by chemical reactions and erosion due to fluid flow. Many studies have investigated the effects of environment (*i.e.*, fluid velocity), porosity, and scaffold material on degradation rates by surface and bulk erosion, as well as by chemical reactions [29,30]. For example [31], polymer degradation by hydrolysis is modeled using the following coupled equations,

$$\frac{dC_m}{dt} = k_1 C_e + k_2 C_e C_m^\beta + \nabla \cdot (D_i \nabla C_m) \tag{23}$$

and

$$\frac{dC_e}{dt} = -(k_1 C_e + k_2 C_e C_m^\tau) \tag{24}$$

where C_e is the mole concentration of ester bonds of polymer chains, C_m is the mole concentration of monomers, k_1 is the rate constant of the reaction which is independent of any catalyst, k_2 is the rate constant of a reaction catalyzed by the previously formed products, and γ is the disassociation power of the acid end group. These reactions are then related to the MW of the polymer present in the scaffold, which can be measured and then the model can be validated. The rate of scaffold degradation by hydrolysis is not restricted to the combination of Equations (23) and (24), but can also be characterized by an exponential decay or first order equation. Other research has considered enzymatic degradation according to Michaelis Menten kinetics in addition to degradation by hydrolysis [32]. Scaffold degradation can take on many forms and is highly dependent upon scaffold composition and component concentrations.

3.3. Incorporating Scaffold Deformation

Most porous scaffolds used in soft tissue regeneration *i.e.*, except in bone regeneration, have low mechanical strength and are very elastic. In addition, porosity of the scaffolds affects their mechanical characteristics. Further, cells respond to stresses in the substrates [33]. Hence, velocity selection in flow-through systems can directly impact cell vitality and scaffold structural stability. In order to understand how fluid flow deforms the porous scaffold, novel computational tools offer a moving mesh that can be used to predict deformation. The simulation needs generalized mechanical property of the scaffolds such as elastic modulus and Poisson ratio in drained conditions [20]. Initial simulation with Navier-Stokes equation without moving mesh is used to create boundary condition such as the initial total load (F_T) applied by the fluid on the scaffold. This is calculated using,

$$F_T = -n \cdot (-PI + \tau) \tag{25}$$

where n represents the normal vector. In addition to the stress due to the elastic nature of the scaffold, there is a hydrodynamic stress from fluid pore pressure, which is incorporated by coupling the strain using the relationship,

$$\sigma + \alpha_B P_f = C\varepsilon \tag{26}$$

where σ represents the Cauchy stress tensor, ε-represents the strain tensor, C represents the elasticity matrix, α_B represents the Biot-Willis coefficient, and P_f is the fluid pore pressure. Equation (26) reduces to Hooks Law of linear elasticity when α_B is zero. Poroelasticity models in earth sciences for understanding soil consolidation use similar models in conjunction with Darcy's equation. However, these models have to use Brinkman or Forchheimer equations based on the flow regimes, as described above. Assuming the material to behave isotropically, and porosity to remain constant, elasticity matrix is obtained using the values of elastic modulus, E, and the shear modulus, G. In the linear region, shear modulus and elastic modulus can be coupled using the equation.

$$E = 2(1+v)G \tag{27}$$

where v represents the Poisson's ratio of the porous scaffold. Some have used quasistatic approximations and solved the equations analytically [34]. Similar models have been attempted in cartilage and other tissues [35]. In order to use these simulations, mechanical characteristics in particular elastic modulus and Poisson's ratio have to be analyzed in wet conditions similar to the condition where scaffolds are used. Currently, some of these properties are not available for many scaffolds and hence, they need to be determined. Nevertheless, adding these simulations help understand the local stresses experienced by cells. These can be then analyzed with the biological response of cells, and further optimization of the flow can be performed to improve the quality of the regenerated tissues.

4. Validation Techniques

One of the primary requirements for successful mathematical modelling and computational simulation is validation of the experimental results. Well-validated, mathematical characterizations of phenomena occurring within a tissue culture environment would help close knowledge gaps in tissue engineering. The computational approach summarized above utilizes scaffold properties routinely measured and reported in literature and pressure drop can be predicted by using an appropriate flow through porous medium equation. Further, pressure drop profiles for various flow regions can be simulated using a range of permeability encompassing scaffold permeability to healthy tissue.

In order to utilize these profiles, experimental validation can be performed at various flow rates using scaffolds alone. A simple flow-scheme for such purposes is shown in Figure 3. Placing a pressure transducer at the inlet of the bioreactor and another at the outlet will provide pressure drop across the scaffold. The pressure transducers would be connected to a computer to record pressure values for both the transducers. In addition, performing experiments without the scaffold could be used to account for pressure drop occurring without the scaffold. These experiments can help validate the simulations.

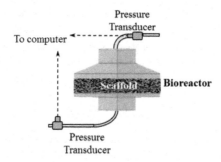

Figure 3. Flow-scheme to determine the pressure drop across the porous scaffold.

The advantage of this approach is that pressure drop can be continuously monitored non-invasively, even when biological experiments are performed in sterile environment. The method allows for simulation validation without harming or contaminating the cell cultures. This is unlike many of the destructive assays performed for understanding the quality of the regenerated tissues. Permeability is expected to change during the course of tissue regeneration as cells will proliferate, synthesize extracellular matrix elements that are deposited in the porous scaffolds. Hence, the pressure drop increases as the permeability decreases.

In order to understand the implications of dynamic changes in permeability, simulations with decreasing pore sizes can be utilized. Matching with the simulated pressure drop to flow rate correlation can be utilized to understand the changes in permeability, quality of the regenerated tissue, and adjusting the flow rate in order to ensure nutrient distribution. There are a few commercialized products available to measure the permeability of the porous scaffolds by Darcy's Law that is used to monitor bone growth. The primary caveat is that pressure drop is a significant function of the flow pattern. Hence, for each bioreactor configuration, few profiles have to be generated. Nevertheless, these advances of monitoring pressure drop in real time would be invaluable to the tissue regeneration process.

5. Conclusion

Computational simulation of flow through porous medium is gaining significant attention in tissue engineering. As we validate developed correlations between pressure drop and scaffold pore architecture for wide variety of porous media used in tissue engineering, they can be utilized as a standard quality assessment method for regenerated tissues. Furthermore, simulation and modeling can guide preparation of better scaffolds and bioreactors for regenerating high quality tissues. These can be used in transplantation, drug screening, or understanding of disease progression. Modelling and simulation will allow ideas to be tested without waste of materials. The growth of an entire organ requires the inclusion of multiple cell types, as well as a vascular system. Addressing the physical and mechanical requirements of multiple cell types in a single environment is extremely difficult and too complex for current application. Perhaps, modeling will help develop individualize medicine. This is the future of tissue engineering.

Acknowledgments: Financial support provided by the Oklahoma Center for Advancement of Science and Technology (HR15-142) and the Edward Joullian Endowment. Financial support also provided by Jerry and Nona Wilhm. There are no conflict of interests to disclose.

Author Contributions: Carrie L. German worked on the paper. Sundararajan V. Madihally helped with the concept and editing.

Conflicts of Interest: The authors declare no conflict of interest.

References

1. Place, E.S.; Evans, N.D.; Stevens, M.M. Complexity in biomaterials for tissue engineering. *Nat. Mater.* **2009**, *8*, 457–470. [CrossRef] [PubMed]
2. Astashkina, A.; Mann, B.; Grainger, D.W. A critical evaluation of *in vitro* cell culture models for high-throughput drug screening and toxicity. *Pharmacol. Ther.* **2012**, *134*, 82–106. [CrossRef] [PubMed]
3. Ravi, M.; Paramesh, V.; Kaviya, S.R.; Anuradha, E.; Solomon, F.D. 3D cell culture systems: Advantages and applications. *J. Cell. Physiol.* **2015**, *230*, 16–26. [CrossRef] [PubMed]
4. Haycock, J. 3D cell culture: A review of current approaches and techniques. In *3D Cell Culture*; Haycock, J.W., Ed.; Humana Press: New York, NY, USA, 2011; pp. 1–15.
5. Sander, E.A.; Stylianopoulos, T.; Tranquillo, R.T.; Barocas, V.H. Image-based multiscale modeling predicts tissue-level and network-level fiber reorganization in stretched cell-compacted collagen gels. *Proc. Natl. Acad. Sci. USA* **2009**, *106*, 17675–17680. [CrossRef] [PubMed]
6. ElectrospinningCompany. Why 3d Cell Culture? Availabe online: http://www.electrospinning.co.uk/why-3d-cell-culture/ (accessed on 1 February 2016).
7. Pal, A.; Kleer, C.G. Three dimensional cultures: A tool to study normal acinar architecture *vs.* Malignant transformation of breast cells. *J. Vis. Exp.* **2014**, *86*. [CrossRef] [PubMed]
8. Edmondson, R.; Broglie, J.J.; Adcock, A.F.; Yang, L. Three-dimensional cell culture systems and their applications in drug discovery and cell-based biosensors. *Assay Drug Dev. Technol.* **2014**, *12*, 207–218. [CrossRef] [PubMed]
9. Shamir, E.R.; Ewald, A.J. Three-dimensional organotypic culture: Experimental models of mammalian biology and disease. *Nat. Rev. Mol. Cell Biol.* **2014**, *15*, 647–664. [CrossRef] [PubMed]
10. Granot, Y.; Rubinsky, B. Mass transfer model for drug delivery in tissue cells with reversible electroporation. *Int. J. Heat Mass Transf.* **2008**, *51*, 5610–5616. [CrossRef] [PubMed]
11. Patrachari, A.R.; Podichetty, J.T.; Madihally, S.V. Application of computational fluid dynamics in tissue engineering. *J. Biosci. Bioeng.* **2012**, *114*, 123–132. [CrossRef] [PubMed]
12. Curcio, E.; Macchiarini, P.; De Bartolo, L. Oxygen mass transfer in a human tissue-engineered trachea. *Biomaterials* **2010**, *31*, 5131–5136. [CrossRef] [PubMed]
13. Podichetty, J.T.; Dhane, D.V.; Madihally, S.V. Dynamics of diffusivity and pressure drop in flow-through and parallel-flow bioreactors during tissue regeneration. *Biotechnol. Prog.* **2012**, *28*, 1045–1054. [CrossRef] [PubMed]
14. Vunjak-Novakovic, G.; Martin, I.; Obradovic, B.; Treppo, S.; Grodzinsky, A.J.; Langer, R.; Freed, L.E. Bioreactor cultivation conditions modulate the composition and mechanical properties of tissue-engineered cartilage. *J. Orthop. Res.* **1999**, *17*, 130–138. [CrossRef] [PubMed]
15. Martin, I.; Wendt, D.; Heberer, M. The role of bioreactors in tissue engineering. *Trends Biotechnol.* **2004**, *22*, 80–86. [CrossRef] [PubMed]
16. Zeng, Z.W.; Grigg, R. A criterion for non-darcy flow in porous media. *Transp. Porous Media* **2006**, *63*, 57–69. [CrossRef]
17. Pennella, F.; Cerino, G.; Massai, D.; Gallo, D.; Falvo D'Urso Labate, G.; Schiavi, A.; Deriu, M.A.; Audenino, A.; Morbiducci, U. A survey of methods for the evaluation of tissue engineering scaffold permeability. *Ann. Biomed. Eng.* **2013**, *41*, 2027–2041. [CrossRef] [PubMed]
18. Swartz, M.A.; Fleury, M.E. Interstitial flow and its effects in soft tissues. *Annu. Rev. Biomed. Eng.* **2007**, *9*, 229–256. [CrossRef] [PubMed]
19. Podichetty, J.T.; Bhaskar, P.R.; Khalf, A.; Madihally, S.V. Modeling pressure drop using generalized scaffold characteristics in an axial-flow bioreactor for soft tissue regeneration. *Ann. Biomed. Eng.* **2014**, *42*, 1319–1330. [CrossRef] [PubMed]
20. Podichetty, J.T.; Madihally, S.V. Modeling of porous scaffold deformation induced by medium perfusion. *J. Biomed. Mater. Res. Part B Appl. Biomater.* **2014**, *102*, 737–748. [CrossRef] [PubMed]
21. O'Brien, F.J.; Harley, B.A.; Waller, M.A.; Yannas, I.V.; Gibson, L.J.; Prendergast, P.J. The effect of pore size on permeability and cell attachment in collagen scaffolds for tissue engineering. *Technol. Health Care* **2007**, *15*, 3–17. [PubMed]
22. Loh, Q.L.; Choong, C. Three-dimensional scaffolds for tissue engineering applications: Role of porosity and pore size. *Tissue Eng. Part B Rev.* **2013**, *19*, 485–502. [CrossRef] [PubMed]

23. Leong, K.F.; Chua, C.K.; Sudarmadji, N.; Yeong, W.Y. Engineering functionally graded tissue engineering scaffolds. *J. Mech. Behav. Biomed. Mater.* **2008**, *1*, 140–152. [CrossRef] [PubMed]

24. Sogutlu, S.; Koc, B. Stochastic modeling of tissue engineering scaffolds with varying porosity levels. *Computer-Aided Des. Appl.* **2007**, *4*, 661–670. [CrossRef]

25. Hollister, S.J.; Lin, C.Y. Computational design of tissue engineering scaffolds. *Comput. Methods Appl. Mech. Eng.* **2007**, *196*, 2991–2998. [CrossRef]

26. Sanz-Herrera, J.A.; Garcia-Aznar, J.M.; Doblare, M. A mathematical approach to bone tissue engineering. *Philos. Trans. R. Soc. A Math Phys. Eng. Sci.* **2009**, *367*, 2055–2078. [CrossRef] [PubMed]

27. Khoda, A.K.; Ozbolat, I.T.; Koc, B. Engineered tissue scaffolds with variational porous architecture. *J. Biomech. Eng.* **2011**, *133*, 011001. [CrossRef] [PubMed]

28. Zhao, F.; Vaughan, T.; McNamara, L. Multiscale fluid-structure interaction modelling to determine the mechanical stimulation of bone cells in a tissue engineered scaffold. *Biomech. Modeling Mechanobiol.* **2015**, *14*, 231–243. [CrossRef] [PubMed]

29. Chen, Y.; Zhou, S.; Li, Q. Mathematical modeling of degradation for bulk-erosive polymers: Applications in tissue engineering scaffolds and drug delivery systems. *Acta Biomater.* **2011**, *7*, 1140–1149. [CrossRef] [PubMed]

30. Shirazi, R.N.; Ronan, W.; Rochev, Y.; McHugh, P. Modelling the degradation and elastic properties of poly(lactic-co-glycolic acid) films and regular open-cell tissue engineering scaffolds. *J. Mech. Behav. Biomed. Mate.* **2016**, *54*, 48–59. [CrossRef] [PubMed]

31. Wang, Y.; Pan, J.; Han, X.; Sinka, C.; Ding, L. A phenomenological model for the degradation of biodegradable polymers. *Biomaterials* **2008**, *29*, 3393–3401. [CrossRef] [PubMed]

32. Dhote, V.; Vernerey, F.J. Mathematical model of the role of degradation on matrix development in hydrogel scaffold. *Biomech. Modeling Mechanobiol.* **2014**, *13*, 167–183. [CrossRef] [PubMed]

33. Lawrence, B.J.; Madihally, S.V. Cell colonization in degradable 3d porous matrices. *Cell Adh. Migr.* **2008**, *2*, 9–16. [CrossRef] [PubMed]

34. Naili, S.; Oddou, C.; Geiger, D. A method for the determination of mechanical parameters in a porous elastically deformable medium : Applications to biological soft tissues. *Int. J. Solids Struct.* **1998**, *35*, 4963–4979. [CrossRef]

35. Chung, C.-Y.; Mansour, J.M. Using regression models to determine the poroelastic properties of cartilage. *J. Biomech.* **2013**, *46*, 1921–1927. [CrossRef] [PubMed]

15

On the v-Representabilty Problem in Density Functional Theory: Application to Non-Interacting Systems

Markus Däne [*,†] and **Antonios Gonis** [†]

Lawrence Livermore National Laboratory, P.O. Box 808, L-372, Livermore, CA 94551, USA; gonis1@llnl.gov
* Correspondence: daene1@llnl.gov
† These authors contributed equally to this work.

Academic Editors: Karlheinz Schwarz and Agnes Nagy

Abstract: Based on a computational procedure for determining the functional derivative with respect to the density of any antisymmetric N-particle wave function for a non-interacting system that leads to the density, we devise a test as to whether or not a wave function known to lead to a given density corresponds to a solution of a Schrödinger equation for some potential. We examine explicitly the case of non-interacting systems described by Slater determinants. Numerical examples for the cases of a one-dimensional square-well potential with infinite walls and the harmonic oscillator potential illustrate the formalism.

Keywords: density functional theory; v-representability; constrained search

1. Introduction

The Hohenberg–Kohn theorems [1] form the foundation of density functional theory (DFT), on which most ab initio electronic structure methods currently are based. The first theorem proves that the ground state of a many-electron system, described by an external potential, is uniquely determined by the ground state density (within an arbitrary constant). Therefore, the ground state density is the independent variable of DFT. In practice, it is still challenging to find the many-body wave function for the ground state of a potential. That task has been simplified by Kohn and Sham [2], who introduced a non-interacting system (Kohn–Sham system) with the same density as the interacting system that minimized the kinetic energy only. The existence of such a system is only assumed, but essential to the Kohn–Sham formulation of DFT.

In most of today's applications of DFT, only one direction of the Hohenberg–Kohn theorem is used, to find the ground state density for a given system described by an external potential. For the other direction, the inverse problem, it is a priori not clear if even a potential exists that leads to a given density through the solution of the Schrödinger equation, whether for the interacting or non-interacting system, the problem of v-representability. We refer to the literature [3–11] for discussions on the issue of v-representability. Specific examples of v-representable densities as well as non-v-representable densities have been identified.

An alternative formulation of the problem can be developed based on the N-representability property [3–6] of any density normalized to an integral number of particles, namely that a density can always be obtained from a wave function for a state of N-particles that, for fermions, is antisymmetric with respect to interchange of individual particle coordinates (and spins for electrons). The v-representability problem can be stated as follows: given a density corresponding to a minimizing wave function, as obtained through the constrained search [3], determine whether or not the wave function is derived as the solution of the Schrödinger equation for a system of N electrons, either interacting, or non-interacting. A more general question is concerned with whether or not a wave function that leads to a given density is either interacting or non-interacting v-representable. A formal procedure that addresses this problem for general interacting systems has been published elsewhere [12]. In the following, a density defined with the following properties: it is everywhere non-negative, is normalized to the number of particles, and leads to a finite value of the kinetic energy.

In this work, we focus on the v-representability for non-interacting systems, even though all procedures presented here can be applied for the interacting system in the same way [12]. In previous work [13–15], we have derived closed expressions for the functional derivative of terms that only depend indirectly on the density, with respect to it. Using that formalism, we now show analytically that differentiating the non-interacting kinetic energy for a v-representable wave function leads to the negative potential (Kohn–Sham potential), up to a constant. This does not hold for arbitrary wave functions leading to the density. We obtain different wave functions leading to the same density by using a procedure by Cioslowski [16,17], who also showed that each of these wave functions is differentiable with respect to the density. This provides a test establishing whether a given wave function (non-interacting), leading to a density, is non-interacting v-representable. We illustrate these procedures on the one-dimensional particle in a box problem as well as the harmonic oscillator.

2. Results

2.1. Background

The Hamiltonian describing an interacting system of N electrons in an external potential takes the usual form,

$$\hat{H}^N = \hat{V} + \hat{T}^N + \hat{U}^N \tag{1}$$

with the operators $\hat{V}$, $\hat{T}^N$ and $\hat{U}^N$ corresponding, respectively, to the external field, the kinetic energy and the inter-particle interaction (Coulomb repulsion for electrons). The ground-state energy of the system is given by the expectation value:

$$E_g = \left\langle \Psi_g^N \middle| \hat{H}^N \middle| \Psi_g^N \right\rangle, \quad \left\langle \Psi_g^N \middle| \Psi_g^N \right\rangle = 1 \tag{2}$$

where $\left| \Psi_g^N \right\rangle$ denotes the many-particle ground state of $\hat{H}^N$. We use the notation, $\left| \Psi^N \right\rangle \to n(\mathbf{r})$, and say $\left| \Psi^N \right\rangle$ leads to the density $n(\mathbf{r})$, to denote the property:

$$n(\mathbf{r}) = N \int \left| \Psi^N(\mathbf{r}, \mathbf{r}_2, \ldots, \mathbf{r}_N) \right|^2 d\mathbf{r}_2 \ldots d\mathbf{r}_N \tag{3}$$

where $n(\mathbf{r})$ denotes the single-particle density function normalized to the total number of particles, N. We now write Equation (2) in the form,

$$E_g = \int v(\mathbf{r}) \, n_g(\mathbf{r}) \, d\mathbf{r} + \left\langle \Psi_g^N \middle| \hat{T} + \hat{U} \middle| \Psi_g^N \right\rangle = \underset{n(\mathbf{r})}{\text{Min}} \left[\int v(\mathbf{r}) \, n(\mathbf{r}) \, d\mathbf{r} + F[n] \right] = \underset{n(\mathbf{r})}{\text{Min}} \, E[n] \tag{4}$$

in terms of the constrained search functional [3,18],

$$F[n] = \underset{|\Psi\rangle \to n(\mathbf{r})}{\text{Min}} \left\langle \Psi \middle| \hat{T}^N + \hat{U}^N \middle| \Psi \right\rangle \tag{5}$$

Given a density, $n(\mathbf{r})$, the constrained search examines all antisymmetric N-particle wave functions that lead to the density and delivers the state (in the absence of degeneracy) that produces the minimum value of $\left\langle \Psi^N \middle| \hat{T}^N + \hat{U}^N \middle| \Psi^N \right\rangle$.

As in the initial formulation of DFT by Kohn and Sham [2], we postulate the existence of a fictitious non-interacting N-particle system described by the Hamiltonian,

$$\hat{H}_s^N = \hat{V}_s + \hat{T}^N \tag{6}$$

under the action of an external potential, $\hat{V}_s$, whose ground-state density is identical to the density of the interacting system described by $\hat{H}^N$. In analogy with Equation (5), we define the constrained search functional [3],

$$T_s[n] = \underset{|\Phi^N\rangle \to n(\mathbf{r})}{\text{Min}} \; \left\langle \Phi^N \middle| \hat{T}^N \middle| \Phi^N \right\rangle = \left\langle \Phi_{GS}^N \middle| T^N \middle| \Phi_{GS}^N \right\rangle$$

$$= \int \Phi^{N*}(\mathbf{r}_{(N)}) \left| \sum_j \left[-\frac{1}{2}\nabla_{\mathbf{r}_j}^2 \right] \right| \Phi^N(\mathbf{r}_{(N)}) \, d\mathbf{r}_{(N)} \tag{7}$$

implying a search over all Slater determinants leading to a given density and returning that determinant that minimizes the expectation value of the kinetic energy for a system of N particles.

Now, assume that the density is non-interacting v-representable for some potential, $v_s(\mathbf{r})$, so that from the second theorem of Hohenberg and Kohn [1], it follows that:

$$\frac{\delta T_s[n]}{\delta n(\mathbf{r})} = -v_s(\mathbf{r}) \tag{8}$$

defined within an arbitrary constant. The potential, $v_s(\mathbf{r})$, is such that the orbitals entering the construction of $\Phi^N(\mathbf{r}_{(N)})$ arise through the solutions of a single-particle Schrödinger equation

$$\left[-\frac{1}{2}\nabla_\mathbf{r}^2 + v_s(\mathbf{r}) \right] \phi_j(\mathbf{r}) = \epsilon_j \phi_j(\mathbf{r}) \tag{9}$$

with eigenenergies ϵ_j. Clearly, the orbitals minimize the expectation value of the kinetic energy, and, as such, form the Slater determinant identified by the constrained search in establishing $T_s[n]$. For the case of Slater determinants, Equation (7) reduces to the direct sum:

$$T_s[n] = \sum_j \int \phi_j^*(\mathbf{r}) \left[-\frac{1}{2}\nabla_\mathbf{r}^2 \right] \phi_j(\mathbf{r}) \, d\mathbf{r} \tag{10}$$

2.2. Functional Differentiation

The process of performing the functional differentiation of expectation values with respect to the density, however, is not immediately evident: The dependence of a given wave function on the density is implicit, rather than explicitly displayed in terms of the density (or analytic functions of it). This difficulty is resolved through the use of the *equidensity orbitals* [19–21] that are written as explicit functionals of the density and, as shown in [21], form an orthonormal and complete basis in three-dimensional space. This property has been exploited in previous work [13–15] to allow the functional differentiation of the Coulomb energy associated with a Slater determinant with respect to the density in order to determine the Coulomb potential including the contribution of the exchange term. A complete discussion is given in [14]. Here, we apply that formalism to derivatives of the non-interacting kinetic energy with respect to the density.

We can obtain the functional derivative of $T_s[n]$ by differentiating the wave functions under the integral signs in Equation (7), and determine the potential-like quantity,

$$-v_s(\mathbf{r}) = \frac{\delta T_s[n]}{\delta n(\mathbf{r})} = \left\langle \frac{\delta \Phi^N}{\delta n(\mathbf{r})} \middle| \middle| \hat{T}^N \middle| \Phi^N \right\rangle + \left\langle \Phi^N \middle| \hat{T}^N \middle| \middle| \frac{\delta \Phi^N}{\delta n(\mathbf{r})} \right\rangle \tag{11}$$

where the double bars prohibit the operators from acting on the quantity beyond them. The reason for this is that functional derivatives of wave functions with respect to the density are generally not elements of the Hilbert space. Because of this feature, the operators in the last two equations act on the wave functions, either to their left or their right. It is seen that the combination of the constrained search and functional differentiation allows in principle the determination of all Slater determinants associated with given density that may correspond to a potential.

For the case of a Slater determinant, the last expression takes the form,

$$\frac{\delta T_s[n]}{\delta n(\mathbf{r})} = \sum_j \int \frac{\delta \phi^*(\mathbf{r}')}{\delta n(\mathbf{r})}\left[-\frac{1}{2}\nabla_{\mathbf{r}'}^2\right]\phi_j(\mathbf{r}')\,d\mathbf{r}' + \sum_j \int \frac{\delta \phi(\mathbf{r}')}{\delta n(\mathbf{r})}\left[-\frac{1}{2}\nabla_{\mathbf{r}'}^2\right]\phi_j^*(\mathbf{r}')\,d\mathbf{r}' = -v_s(\mathbf{r}) \qquad (12)$$

where the del operator acts on arguments to its right, and the last line gives the functional derivative as a function of the coordinates that may or may not correspond to a potential. In this expression, the quantity, $T_s[n]$, denotes the expectation value of the non-interacting kinetic energy operator, $\hat{T}^N$, with respect to any wave function that leads to a density.

In previous work [13–15], we derived a closed-form expression of the functional derivative of an orbital $f(\mathbf{r})$ with respect to the density, $\frac{\delta f(\mathbf{r})}{\delta n(\mathbf{r}')}$, in terms of ordinary (spatial) derivatives. In the one-dimensional case, excluding terms that would lead to a constant shift in the potential (constants and expressions solely depending on x but not x'), the derivative reads

$$\frac{\delta f(x)}{\delta n(x')} = \frac{f(x)}{2n(x)}\delta(x - x') + \frac{\Theta(x - x')}{n(x)}\left[f'(x) - \frac{f(x)\,n'(x)}{2\,n(x)}\right] \qquad (13)$$

Primes on functions denote spatial derivatives with respect to x, and Θ is the Heaviside step function. Expressions for the three-dimensional case can be found in references [14,15] for both the cases of cartesian and spherical coordinates, respectively.

In Appendix A, we derive an expression for the differentiation of the expression for the kinetic energy (one-dimensional for simplicity) using Equations (12) and (13) (see Equation (A4)). If all orbitals contributing to the kinetic energy originate from the same potential through the Schrödinger or Kohn–Sham equations, we show analytically that the differentiation leads to the negative potential (within an arbitrary constant). The three-dimensional case follows analogously.

2.3. Illustration of the Formalism

The calculations quoted here illustrate the formalism developed above for cases where the potential is given and the wave functions are known analytically. The goal is to reproduce the potential from the functional derivative of the kinetic energy with respect to the density.

For simplicity, we discuss one-dimensional systems in the non-interacting case where the wave function can be represented as a Slater determinant. Analogous procedures will apply in higher dimensions and the interacting framework.

For our first example, we consider N non-interacting particles in a box of length L bounded by potential walls of infinite height. The wave functions of the particles confined in the box are determined through the single-particle Schrödinger equation,

$$\left[-\frac{1}{2}\frac{d^2}{dx^2} + v(x)\right]\phi_n(x) = \epsilon_n\,\phi_n(x) \qquad (14)$$

and vanish at the edges of the box. The ϵ_n denote the eigenvalues. When $v(x) = 0$ (or a constant), the normalized single-particle wave functions are given by the expressions,

$$\phi_n(x) = \sqrt{\frac{2}{L}}\sin\left(\frac{n\pi x}{L}\right) = A_n\sin(k_n x) \qquad 0 \le x \le L \qquad (15)$$

with quantum numbers $n = 1, 2, 3, \ldots$. The energies take the form,

$$\epsilon_n = \frac{\hbar^2}{2m} \left(\frac{n\pi}{L} \right)^2 = \frac{\hbar^2}{2m} k_n^2 \tag{16}$$

with the ground state density for a system of N Fermions given by $n(x) = \sum_{n=1}^{N} |\phi_n(x)|^2$. Figure 1 illustrates the six lowest in energy eigenstates ($L = 1$) (left panel) and their moduli squared (corresponding to single-particle densities) on the right.

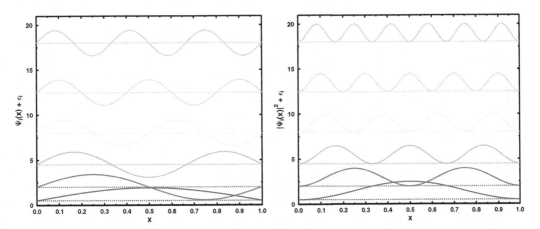

Figure 1. The six lowest in energy wave functions (**left**) and the corresponding single particle densities (**right**) for the particle-in-a-box model ($L = 1$). For illustrative purposes, all curves are shifted by the corresponding energies (see Equation (16)) in atomic units $\hbar = m = 1$.

The second example discussed here is the one-dimensional harmonic oscillator. The potential is given by

$$V(x) = \frac{1}{2} k x^2 = \frac{1}{2} m \omega x^2 \qquad \omega = \sqrt{\frac{k}{m}} \tag{17}$$

We make the usual transformation $y = \sqrt{\alpha} x$ and $\alpha = \frac{m\omega}{\hbar}$. The normalized solutions of the Schrödinger equation with the potential (17) read as

$$\Psi_n(y) = \left(\frac{\alpha}{\pi} \right)^{\frac{1}{4}} \frac{1}{\sqrt{2^n \, n!}} H_n(y) \, e^{-\frac{y^2}{2}} \tag{18}$$

where the $H_n(y)$ are Hermite polynomials, which are solutions of the differential equations $H_n''(y) - 2y H_n'(y) + 2ny = 0$, and n are integer quantum numbers ≥ 0. The corresponding energies are given by

$$E_n = \left(n + \frac{1}{2} \right) \hbar \omega, \qquad n = 0, 1, 2, \ldots \tag{19}$$

In the following discussion, we set $m = \omega = \hbar = 1$, which corresponds to $\alpha = 1$ and $V(x) = \frac{1}{2} x^2$. The six lowest in energy single particle wave functions and their corresponding moduli squared are shown in Figure 2.

For both examples, we use Equation (A4) to compute the potential. Since the wave functions are given analytically, the potentials can be calculated analytically. We use *Mathematica*® [22] to accomplish that task. We tested cases up to $N = 6$, and obtained every time the corresponding potential up to a constant. That is not surprising because we have shown in Appendix A that the formalism to calculate those functional derivatives leads to the potential. Equation (A9) also obtains a constant that does not have a physical meaning. Applying l'Hopital's rule twice at the right boundary for the particles in a box example we obtain the constant:

$$c = \frac{\sum_{n=1}^{N} \epsilon_n n^2}{\sum_{n=1}^{N} n^2} = \frac{\pi^2}{2L^2} \frac{\hbar^2}{m} \frac{\sum_{n=1}^{N} n^4}{\sum_{n=1}^{N} n^2} \tag{20}$$

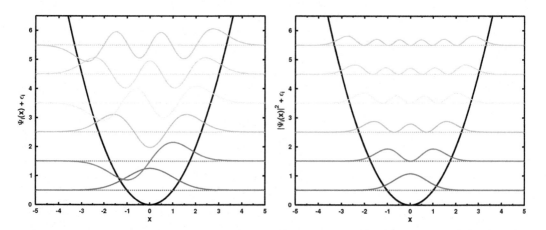

Figure 2. The six lowest in energy wave functions (**left**) and the corresponding single particle densities (**right**) for the Harmonic oscillator. All curves are shifted by the corresponding energies (see Equation (19)). The quadratic potential is shown in black.

Due to the exponential decay of the wave function and the density in the harmonic oscillator example, only the highest in energy of the occupied orbitals contributes to the constant. We find the constant to be equal to the eigenvalue of the highest occupied orbital.

So far, those tests have been performed occupying the lowest N orbitals. We find that any other combination, mimicking a non-ground state, e.g., by occupying orbitals $1, 2, 3, 4, 5$ and 7, also leads to the same potential. The constants for the particles in the box example contains then the sum over occupied orbitals instead a sum from 1 to N, for the harmonic oscillator the constant is still determined by the highest occupied orbital.

The finding that the formalism yields the potential from the kinetic energy is not obvious because the condition $\frac{\delta T_s[n]}{\delta n(\mathbf{r})} = -v_s(\mathbf{r})$ implies the condition of the ground state. On the other hand, those states correspond to a local extremum so that the expression still holds.

Obtaining the potential by a functional differentiation for these examples may sound trivial, but it demonstrates the power of the procedure and the ability to calculate the functional derivative analytically. On the other hand, the procedure can be applied to cases where the the single particle orbitals are given numerically.

So far, we have shown the formalism determines the potential exact (up to a constant) from wave functions by functional differentiation of the kinetic energy, where it is known that all orbitals originate from the same potential, the condition for v-representability. The next step is to determine if a given set of orbitals, forming the density, is v-representable. That can be accomplished by calculating the potential $v_s(\mathbf{r})$ as shown above, and then checking if each of the orbitals fulfills the Kohn–Sham equation by comparing the right and left-hand sides of the expression:

$$-\frac{1}{2}\nabla^2_{\mathbf{r}}\phi_j(\mathbf{r}) + v_s(\mathbf{r})\phi_j(\mathbf{r}) = \alpha_j\phi_j((\mathbf{r})) \tag{21}$$

The determinant is v-representable when the equality holds, (for some α_j), for all orbitals forming the determinant. It is convinient for the comparison to normalize the left and right-hand side separately in order to be independent of the α_j.

Now, we apply this procedure to the case when the density is given. Generally, the task would be to find the wave function that minimizes the kinetic energy through the procedure of the constrained search [3]. Cioslowski [16,17] has established the formal procedure for generating the complete set of antisymmetric wave functions that lead to a given density. For a Slater determinant, the procedure is outlined in Appendix B. Based on his procedure, for each density, we construct a number of different Slater determinants that leads to it. For each Slater determinant, we differentiate the expectation value of kinetic energy with respect to the the density, obtaining $v_s(\mathbf{r})$. Finally, we apply Equation (21) for every orbital of the determinant. The results of the test for the case of the particle in the box and harmonic oscillator are shown in Figures 3 and 4, respectively, for a three particle system.

In the figures, the top rows exhibit the density, the second shows the set of three mutually orthonormal orbitals, leading to the density. The third row contains v_s, obtained using Equation (A4), for each set of orbitals and the remaining rows compare each of the orbitals with the normalized output corresponding to Equation (21), where, in some, the output is multiplied by -1.

In both examples, the target density (top row) is obtained using the three lowest in energy orbitals (see Equations (15) and (18); $L = 1$) for panels A,B and C, the density in panel D is constructed by using orbitals 2, 3 and 4. We applied Cioslowski's procedure [16] for a single Slater determinant using auxiliary functions ϕ given in Tables 1 and 2 to obtain new Slater determinants leading to the given density. Those new orbitals are shown in the second row. If the exact orbitals are used, Cioslowski's procedure returns the same orbitals (column A); otherwise, different orbitals are obtained. We note that the auxiliary functions ϕ do not need to be orthogonal or normalized, as long as they are linearly independent. The new orbitals, although mutually orthonormal, can have quite strange forms, as seen in the second row. They do not even have to obey the symmetry of the problem, nor have a specific number of nodes.

Table 1. Initial test functions used in Cioslowski's procedure [16] for the square well example corresponding to Figure 3. The functions in the first row are the exact orbitals (see Equation (15)).

Column	Test Orbital 1	Test Orbital 2	Test Orbital 3
A	$\sqrt{2}\sin(\pi x)$	$\sqrt{2}\sin(2\pi x)$	$\sqrt{2}\sin(3\pi x)$
B	1	$\cos(2\pi x)$	$\cos(4\pi x)$
C	1	x	x^2
D	$\frac{1}{4}+x$	$\left(\frac{1}{2}+x\right)^2$	$\left(\frac{3}{4}+x\right)^3$

Table 2. Initial test functions used in Cioslowski's procedure [16] for the harmonic oscillator example corresponding to Figure 4. The functions in the first row are the exact orbitals (see Equation (18)).

Column	Test Orbital 1	Test Orbital 2	Test Orbital 3
A	$\frac{1}{\sqrt[4]{\pi}}e^{-\frac{1}{2}x^2}$	$\frac{\sqrt{2}}{\sqrt[4]{\pi}}e^{-\frac{1}{2}x^2}x$	$\frac{1}{\sqrt{2}\sqrt[4]{\pi}}e^{-\frac{1}{2}x^2}\left(2x^2-1\right)$
B	1	x	x^2
C	1	$\frac{x}{6}$	$\frac{x^2}{18}-1$
D	1	$\cos\left(\frac{\pi x}{6}\right)$	$\cos\left(\frac{\pi x}{3}\right)$

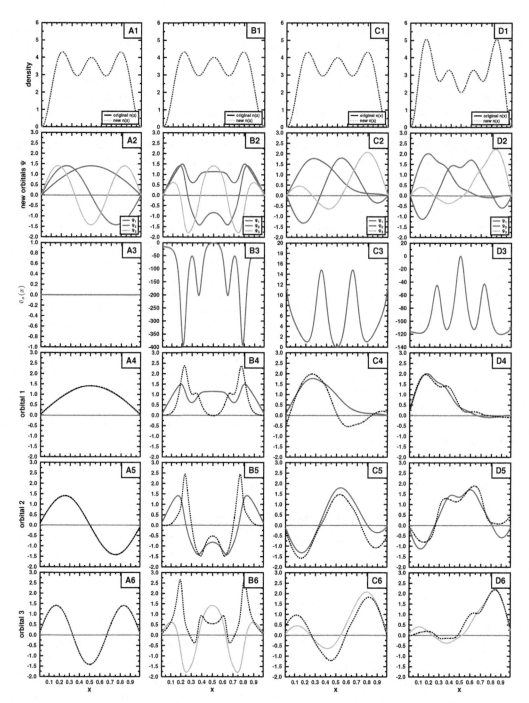

Figure 3. Results for the square well example, as described in the text. The given density is shown in the top row, where the new orbitals obtained though Cioslowski's procedure [16] using initial functions from Table 1. The potential, obtained using functional differentiation of the expression of the kinetic energy, is plotted in the third row. The three rows at the bottom show the results of the test (see Equation (21)), where the dashed line corresponds to the left-hand side of the equation, and the solid line to the right-hand side, equal to the new orbital, both normalized. Some of the dashed functions are multiplied by -1 for better comparison, corresponding to a negative α in Equation (21).

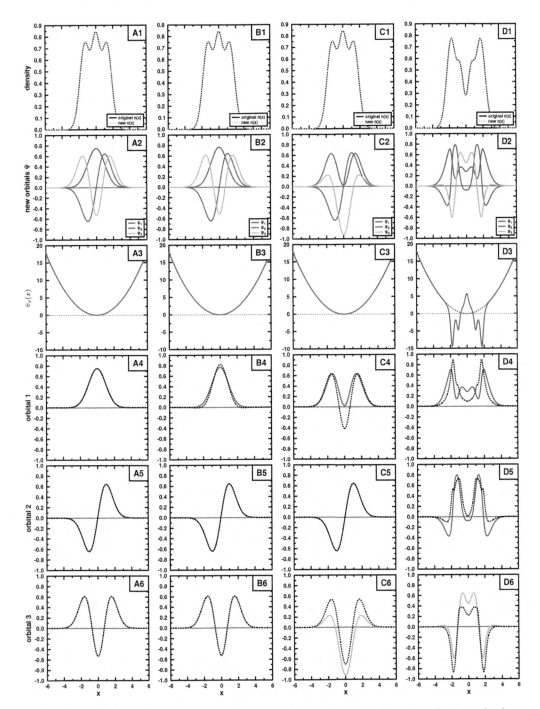

Figure 4. Results analogous to those of Figure 3, but for the harmonic oscillator example. New orbitals were obtained through Cioslowski's procedure [16] using initial functions from Table 2. The dashed line in subfigure D3 shows $\frac{1}{2}x^2$ for comparison.

Examining these cases, where different sets of orbitals form the same density (columns B and C), we see that the left- and right-hand side of Equation (21) are not the same (see bottom three rows), even though we know the density to be v-representable. This suggests that most of the sets generated by Cioslowski's procedure [16] may not correspond to a potential, yet all lead to the same density by construction. This behavior is expected from the first theorem of Hohenberg and Kohn: if v-representable, the ground state density determines uniquely the potential and hence the corresponding ground state wave function.

We also applied the procedure to a different density to mimic an exited state (panel D). As seen in panels D4, D5 and D6, the set of obtained wave functions fail to satisfy Equation (21) and hence are not v-representable. The choice of the exact orbitals passes the test of v-representability, as already pointed out above.

In order to quantify the deviation of the left- and right-hand side of Equation (21), the L^2 norm of the difference is shown in Tables 3 and 4. L^2 norms smaller than the machine epsilon are marked as 0.

Table 3. L^2 norm of the difference of left and right hand side of Equation (21) for the square well example, corresponding to rows 4–6 in Figure 1.

	A	B	C	D
orbital 1	0	0.5134	0.2508	0.0148
orbital 2	0	0.7795	0.1833	0.1158
orbital 3	0	1.9006	0.1694	0.0428

Table 4. L^2 norm of the difference of left and right hand side of Equation (21) for the harmonic oscillator example, corresponding to rows 4–6 in Figure 2.

	A	B	C	D
orbital 1	0	0.01390	0.23676	0.33567
orbital 2	0	0	0	0.34787
orbital 3	0	0.00057	0.43090	0.23184

3. Conclusions

For a non-interacting system, we have shown how v-representability of a given wave function can be determined. This is accomplished by functional differentiation of the kinetic energy with respect to the density, and checking whether that derivative is a potential leading to the wave function. We have shown analytically (in one dimension), that, in the case of v-representability, the previously derived expressions for the functional derivative of orbitals lead to the correct result, the negative of the potential, when applied to terms depending on the diagonal part of the single-particle density matrix like the expression for the kinetic energy.

Acknowledgments: Comments by Malcolm Stocks and Don Nicholson are gratefully acknowledged. This work was supported by the Critical Materials Institute, an Energy Innovation Hub funded by the U.S. Department of Energy and performed under the auspices of the U.S. Department of Energy by Lawrence Livermore National Laboratory under Contract DE-AC52-07NA27344.

Author Contributions: M.D. derived the analytic proof given in Appendix A, all numerical examples, and also contributed to writing the paper; A.G. contributed to deriving the formalism and writing the paper.

Conflicts of Interest: The authors declare no conflict of interest.

Appendix A. Functional Differentiation of the Kinetic Energy (Non-Interacting)

The non-interacting kinetic energy and its derivative with respect to the density reads (in units $\hbar = m = 1$)

$$T_s = \sum_i \int f_i^*(\mathbf{r}) \left[-\frac{\nabla^2}{2} \right] f_i(\mathbf{r}) \, d\mathbf{r}, \tag{A1}$$

$$\frac{\delta T_s}{\delta n(\mathbf{r}')} = \sum_i \int \frac{f_i^*(\mathbf{r})}{\delta n(\mathbf{r}')} \left[-\frac{\nabla^2}{2} f_i(\mathbf{r}) \right] d\mathbf{r} + \sum_i \int \frac{f_i(\mathbf{r})}{\delta n(\mathbf{r}')} \left[-\frac{\nabla^2}{2} f_i^*(\mathbf{r}) \right] d\mathbf{r}, \tag{A2}$$

where f_i are solutions of the Kohn–Sham equation, and the sum runs over the lowest in energy states. The last expression can be obtained through twice integrating by parts.

For simplicity, we continue in one dimension. The functional derivative of an orbital with respect to the density reads then, using Equation (13):

$$
\begin{aligned}
\frac{\delta T_s}{\delta n(x')} &= \sum_i \int \frac{f_i^*(x)}{2n(x)}\left[-\frac{1}{2}f_i''(x)\right]\delta(x-x')\,dx + \sum_i \int \frac{f_i(x)}{2n(x)}\left[-\frac{1}{2}f_i^{*''}(x)\right]\delta(x-x')\,dx \\
&+ \sum_i \int_{x'}^{\infty}\frac{1}{n(x)}\left[f_i'^*(x)-f_i^*(x)\frac{n'(x)}{2n(x)}\right]\left[-\frac{1}{2}f_i''(x)\right]dx \\
&+ \sum_i \int_{x'}^{\infty}\frac{1}{n(x)}\left[f_i'(x)-f_i(x)\frac{n'(x)}{2n(x)}\right]\left[-\frac{1}{2}f_i^{*''}(x)\right]dx
\end{aligned}
\tag{A3}
$$

$$
\begin{aligned}
&= \sum_i \frac{f_i^*(x')}{2n(x')}\left[-\frac{1}{2}f_i''(x')\right]+\sum_i \frac{f_i(x')}{2n(x')}\left[-\frac{1}{2}f_i^{*''}(x')\right] \\
&+ \sum_i \int_{x'}^{\infty}\left[\frac{f_i'^*(x)}{n(x)}\left[-\frac{1}{2}f_i''(x)\right]+\frac{f_i'(x)}{n(x)}\left[-\frac{1}{2}f_i^{*''}(x)\right]\right]dx \\
&- \sum_i \int_{x'}^{\infty}\left[\frac{f_i^*(x)}{n(x)}\frac{n'(x)}{2n(x)}\left[-\frac{1}{2}f_i''(x)\right]+\frac{f_i(x)}{n(x)}\frac{n'(x)}{2n(x)}\left[-\frac{1}{2}f_i^{*''}(x)\right]\right]dx
\end{aligned}
\tag{A4}
$$

If the f_i correspond to the same potential V and are solutions of a Schrödinger (or Kohn–Sham) equation:

$$
\left[-\frac{1}{2}f_i''(x)\right]=[\epsilon_i-V(x)]f_i(x)
\tag{A5}
$$

then the expression simplifies to:

$$
\begin{aligned}
\frac{\delta T_s}{\delta n(x')} &= \sum_i \epsilon_i \frac{f_i^*(x')f_i(x')+f_i(x')f_i^*(x')}{2n(x')} - \underbrace{\left[\sum_i \frac{f_i^*(x')f_i(x')}{2n(x')}+\sum_i \frac{f_i(x')f_i^*(x')}{2n(x')}\right]}_{=1}V(x') \\
&+ \int_{x'}^{\infty}\left[\frac{\sum_i \epsilon_i\left(f_i'^*(x)f_i(x)+f_i'(x)f_i^*(x)\right)}{n(x)}\right]dx \\
&- \underbrace{\int_{x'}^{\infty}\left[\frac{\sum_i\left(f_i'^*(x)f_i(x)+f_i'(x)f_i^*(x)\right)}{n(x)}V(x)\right]dx}_{=\frac{n'(x)}{n(x)}V(x)} \\
&- \int_{x'}^{\infty}\frac{n'(x)}{2n(x)n(x)}\sum_i \epsilon_i\left[f_i^*(x)f_i(x)+f_i(x)f_i^*(x)\right]dx \\
&+ \underbrace{\int_{x'}^{\infty}\frac{n'(x)}{2n(x)n(x)}V(x)\sum_i\left[f_i^*(x)f_i(x)+f_i(x)f_i^*(x)\right]dx}_{=\frac{n'(x)}{n(x)}V(x)}
\end{aligned}
\tag{A6}
$$

$$
\frac{\delta T_s}{\delta n(x')} = -V(x')+\frac{\sum_i \epsilon_i f_i^*(x')f_i(x')}{n(x')}+\int_{x'}^{\infty}\left[\frac{\sum_i \epsilon_i f_i^*(x)f_i(x)}{n(x)}\right]'dx,
\tag{A7}
$$

$$
= -V(x')+\underbrace{\frac{\sum_i \epsilon_i f_i^*(x)f_i(x)}{n(x)}\bigg|_{x=\infty}}_{=const},
\tag{A8}
$$

$$
\frac{\delta T_s}{\delta n(x')} = -V(x')+c
\tag{A9}
$$

For a finite system, the $x = \infty$ in Equation (A8) signifies the right boundary. To derive Equation (A8), integration by parts is used: $\int_a^b f'[x]\,\mathrm{d}x = f[x]|_{x=b} - f[x]|_{x=a}$.

Appendix B. Cioslowski's Procedure

For a single Slater determinant, we briefly describe how orthogonal orbitals, $\psi(x)$, can be obtained, leading to a given density $n(x) = \sum_{i=1}^{N} |\psi_i|^2$, using Cioslowski's precedure [16]. From a set of linearly independent auxiliary functions $\phi(x)$, the $\psi_i(x)$ are given by the expression:

$$\psi_i(x) = \sqrt{f(x)} \sum_{i=1}^{N} s_{ij}\phi_j(x) \tag{B1}$$

The matrix $\underline{s}$ is given by

$$\underline{s} = \underline{S}^{-1/2} \tag{B2}$$

with

$$S_{ij} = \int f(x)\,\phi_i(x)\,\phi_j(x)\,\mathrm{d}x \tag{B3}$$

and

$$f(x) = n(r)\left[\sum_{ij}\phi_i(x)\left(\underline{S}^{-1}\right)_{ij}\phi_j(x)\right]^{-1} \tag{B4}$$

The matrix $\underline{S}$ exists and has to be obtained self-consistently. That can be accomplished by iterating the equations above, e.g., using an identity matrix as a starting point.

References

1. Hohenberg, P.; Kohn, W. Inhomogeneous electron gas. *Phys. Rev.* **1964**, *136*, B864–B871.
2. Kohn, W.; Sham, L.J. Self-consistent equations including exchange and correlation effects. *Phys. Rev.* **1965**, *140*, A1133–A1138.
3. Levy, M. Universal variational functionals of electron densities, first-order density matrices, and natural spin-orbitals and solution of the v-representability problem. *Proc. Natl. Acad. Sci. USA* **1979**, *76*, 6062–6065.
4. Levy, M. Electron densities in search of Hamiltonians. *Phys. Rev. A* **1982**, *26*, 1200–1208.
5. Shimony, A.; Feshbach, H. (Eds.) Density functionals for coulomb systems. In *Physics as Natural Philosophy: Essays in Honor of Laszlo Tisza on His 75th Birthday*; MIT Press: Cambridge, MA, USA, 1982; pp. 111–149.
6. Dreizler, R.; Providencia, J. (Eds.) *Density Functional Methods in Physics*; Nato ASI Series B123; Plenum Press: Berlin/Heidelberg, Germany, 1985.
7. Kohn, W. v-representability and density functional theory. *Phys. Rev. Lett.* **1983**, *51*, 1596–1598.
8. Englisch, H.; Englisch, R. Hohenberg–Kohn theorem and non-v-representable densities. *Phys. A Stat. Mech. Appl.* **1983**, *121*, 253–268.
9. Chen, J.; Stott, M.J. v-representability for noninteracting systems. *Phys. Rev. A* **1993**, *47*, 153–160.
10. Parr, R.G.; Yang, C.Y. *Density Functional Theory of Atoms and Molecules*; Oxford University Press: Oxford, UK, 1989.
11. Dreitzler, R.M.; Gross, E.K.U. *Density Functional Theory*; Springer Verlag: Berlin, Germany; New York, NY, USA, 1990.
12. Gonis, A.; Zhang, X.G.; Däne, M.; Stocks, G.; Nicholson, D. Reformulation of density functional theory for N-representable densities and the resolution of the v-representability problem. *J. Phys. Chem. Solids* **2016**, *89*, 23–31.
13. Gonis, A.; Däne, M.; Nicholson, D.; Stocks, G. Computationally simple, analytic, closed form solution of the Coulomb self-interaction problem in Kohn–Sham density functional theory. *Solid State Commun.* **2012**, *152*, 771–774.
14. Däne, M.; Gonis, A.; Nicholson, D.; Stocks, G. On a solution of the self-interaction problem in Kohn–Sham density functional theory. *J. Phys. Chem. Solids* **2014**, *75*, 1160–1178.

15. Däne, M.; Gonis, A.; Nicholson, D.; Stocks, G. Solving the self-interaction problem in Kohn–Sham density functional theory: Application to atoms. *J. Phys. Chem. Solids* **2015**, *79*, 55–65.

16. Cioslowski, J. Density functionals for the energy of electronic systems: Explicit variational construction. *Phys. Rev. Lett.* **1988**, *60*, 2141–2143.

17. Cioslowski, J. Density driven self-consistent field method. II. Construction of all one-particle wavefunctions that are orthonormal and sum up to a given density. *Int. J. Quantum Chem.* **1989**, *36*, 255–262.

18. Lieb, E.H. Density functionals for coulomb systems. In *Physics as Natural Philosophy, Essays in Honor of Laszlo Tisza*; Shimony, A., Feshbach, H., Eds.; MIT Press: Cambridge, MA, USA, 1982.

19. Macke, W. Zur wellenmechanischen Behandlung von Vielkörperproblemen. *Ann. Phys.* **1955**, *452*, 1–9. (In German)

20. Harriman, J.E. Orthonormal orbitals for the representation of an arbitrary density. *Phys. Rev. A* **1981**, *24*, 680–682.

21. Zumbach, G.; Maschke, K. New approach to the calculation of density functionals. *Phys. Rev. A* **1983**, *28*, 544–554.

22. *Mathematica*, Version 10.4; Wolfram Research, Inc.: Champaign, IL, USA, 2016.

Permissions

The contributors of this book come from diverse backgrounds, making this book a truly international effort. This book will bring forth new frontiers with its revolutionizing research information and detailed analysis of the nascent developments around the world.

We would like to thank all the contributing authors for lending their expertise to make the book truly unique. They have played a crucial role in the development of this book. Without their invaluable contributions this book wouldn't have been possible. They have made vital efforts to compile up to date information on the varied aspects of this subject to make this book a valuable addition to the collection of many professionals and students.

This book was conceptualized with the vision of imparting up-to-date information and advanced data in this field. To ensure the same, a matchless editorial board was set up. Every individual on the board went through rigorous rounds of assessment to prove their worth. After which they invested a large part of their time researching and compiling the most relevant data for our readers.

The editorial board has been involved in producing this book since its inception. They have spent rigorous hours researching and exploring the diverse topics which have resulted in the successful publishing of this book. They have passed on their knowledge of decades through this book. To expedite this challenging task, the publisher supported the team at every step. A small team of assistant editors was also appointed to further simplify the editing procedure and attain best results for the readers.

Apart from the editorial board, the designing team has also invested a significant amount of their time in understanding the subject and creating the most relevant covers. They scrutinized every image to scout for the most suitable representation of the subject and create an appropriate cover for the book.

The publishing team has been an ardent support to the editorial, designing and production team. Their endless efforts to recruit the best for this project, has resulted in the accomplishment of this book. They are a veteran in the field of academics and their pool of knowledge is as vast as their experience in printing. Their expertise and guidance has proved useful at every step. Their uncompromising quality standards have made this book an exceptional effort. Their encouragement from time to time has been an inspiration for everyone.

The publisher and the editorial board hope that this book will prove to be a valuable piece of knowledge for researchers, students, practitioners and scholars across the globe.

List of Contributors

Malgorzata Peszynska and Francis Patricia Medina
Department of Mathematics, Oregon State University, Corvallis, OR 97331, USA

Wei-Li Hong
College of Earth, Ocean, and Atmospheric Sciences, Oregon State University, Corvallis, OR 97331, USA
CAGE (Centre for Arctic Gas Hydrate, Environment and Climate), Department of Geology, UiT The Arctic University of Norway, Tromso, Norway

Marta E. Torres
College of Earth, Ocean, and Atmospheric Sciences, Oregon State University, Corvallis, OR 97331, USA

Dominique Derome
Laboratory of Multiscale Studies in Building Physics, EMPA (Swiss Federal Laboratories for Materials Science and Technology), Dübendorf 8600, Switzerland

Soyoun Son and Jan Carmeliet
Laboratory of Multiscale Studies in Building Physics, EMPA (Swiss Federal Laboratories for Materials Science and Technology), Dübendorf 8600, Switzerland
Chair of Building Physics, ETH Zürich (Swiss Federal Institute of Technology in Zürich), Zürich 8093, Switzerland

Li Chen
Earth and Environment Sciences Division (EES-16), Los Alamos National Laboratory, Los Alamos, NM 87545, USA
Key Laboratory of Thermo-Fluid Science and Engineering of MOE, School of Energy and Power Engineering, Xi'an Jiaotong University, Xi'an 710049, China

Qinjun Kang
Earth and Environment Sciences Division (EES-16), Los Alamos National Laboratory, Los Alamos, NM 87545, USA

Costantino Masciopinto   and Domenico Palmiotta
Consiglio Nazionale delle Ricerche, Istituto di Ricerca Sulle Acque, Reparto di Chimica e Tecnologia delle Acque, 5 via Francesco De Blasio, 70132 Bari, Italy

Zhiqiang Chen, Chiyu Xie, Yu Chen and Moran Wang
Department of Engineering Mechanics and CNMM, Tsinghua University, Beijing 100084, China

Bartolomeo Civalleri and Roberto Dovesi
Department of Chemistry and Center for Nanostructured Interfaces and Surfaces, University of Torino, Via P. Giuria 7, Torino I-10125, Italy

Pascal Pernot
Centre National de la Recherche Scientifique (CNRS), UMR8000, Laboratoire de Chimie Physique, Orsay F-91405, France
Université Paris-Sud, UMR8000, Laboratoire de Chimie Physique, Orsay F-91405, France

Davide Presti
Department of Chemical and Geological Sciences, University of Modena and Reggio-Emilia Via Campi 103, Modena I-41125, Italy

Andreas Savin
Centre National de la Recherche Scientifique (CNRS), UMR7616, Laboratoire de Chimie Théorique, Paris F-75005, France
Université Paris 06 (UPMC), UMR7616, Laboratoire de Chimie Théorique, F-75005 Paris, France

Chiara Vassena and Alessandro Comunian
Università degli Studi di Milano, Dipartimento di Scienze della Terra "A. Desio", via Cicognara 7, I-20129 Milano, Italy

Laura Cattaneo
Università degli Studi di Milano, Dipartimento di Scienze della Terra "A. Desio", via Cicognara 7, I-20129 Milano, Italy
CNR-IDPA (Consiglio Nazionale delle Ricerche, Istituto per la Dinamica dei Processi Ambientali), via Mario Bianco 9, I-20131 Milano, Italy

Giovanna de Filippis
Università degli Studi di Milano, Dipartimento di Scienze della Terra "A. Desio", via Cicognara 7, I-20129 Milano, Italy

Mauro Giudici
Università degli Studi di Milano, Dipartimento di Scienze della Terra "A. Desio", via Cicognara 7, I-20129 Milano, Italy
CNR-IDPA (Consiglio Nazionale delle Ricerche, Istituto per la Dinamica dei Processi Ambientali), via Mario Bianco 9, I-20131 Milano, Italy
CINFAI, Consorzio Interuniversitario Nazionale per la Fisica delle Atmosfere e delle Idrosfere, Piazza Niccolò Mauruzi 17, I-62029 Tolentino (MC), Italy

Giuliano Malloci , Giovanni Serra, Andrea Bosin and Attilio Vittorio Vargiu
Dipartimento di Fisica, Università di Cagliari, Cittadella Universitaria, I-09042 Monserrato (CA), Italy

M. W. C. Dharma-wardana
National Research Council of Canada, 1200, Montreal Rd, Ottawa, ON K1A 0R6, Canada
Département de Physique, Université de Montreal, Montreal, QC H3C 3J7, Canada

Claus Vogl
Institute of Animal Breedings and Genetics, Veterinärmedizinische Universität Wien, Veterinärplatz 1, A-1210 Vienna, Austria

Juraj Bergman
Institut für Populationsgenetik, Veterinärmedizinische Universität Wien, Veterinärplatz 1, A-1210 Vienna, Austria
Vienna Graduate School of Population Genetics, Veterinärmedizinische Universität Wien, Veterinärplatz 1, A-1210 Vienna, Austria

Claudio Amovilli , Franca Maria Floris and Andrea Grisafi
Dipartimento di Chimica e Chimica Industriale, University of Pisa, Via Giuseppe Moruzzi 13, Pisa 56124, Italy

Piotr Matczak
Department of Theoretical and Structural Chemistry, Faculty of Chemistry, University of Łódź, Pomorska 163/165, Lodz 90-236, Poland

Giancarlo Alfonsi
Fluid Dynamics Laboratory, Università della Calabria, Via P. Bucci 42b, 87036 Rende (Cosenza), Italy

Stefania A. Ciliberti , Marco Mancini and Leonardo Primavera
Current address: Euro-Mediterranean Centre on Climate Change, Via A. Imperatore 16, 73100 Lecce, Italy

Farrel Gray
Qatar Carbonates and Carbon Storage Research Centre (QCCSRC), Department of Chemical Engineering, South Kensington Campus, Imperial College London, London SW7 2AZ, UK

Edo Boek
Qatar Carbonates and Carbon Storage Research Centre (QCCSRC), Department of Chemical Engineering, South Kensington Campus, Imperial College London, London SW7 2AZ, UK
Department of Chemistry, University of Cambridge, Lensfield Road, Cambridge CB2 1EW, UK

Carrie L. German and Sundararajan V. Madihally
School of Chemical Engineering, Oklahoma State University, 212 Cordell North Stillwater, OK 74078, USA

Markus Däne and Antonios Gonis
Lawrence Livermore National Laboratory, P.O. Box 808, L-372, Livermore, CA 94551, USA

Index

CPSIA information can be obtained
at www.ICGtesting.com
Printed in the USA
BVOW07*2335010218
506942BV00004BA/235/P